Investigations in the
Economics of Aging

**A National Bureau of
Economic Research
Conference Report**

Investigations in the Economics of Aging

Edited by **David A. Wise**

The University of Chicago Press

Chicago and London

DAVID A. WISE is the John F. Stambaugh Professor of Political
Economy at the Kennedy School of Government at Harvard
University. He is the area director of Health and Retirement Programs
and director of the Program on the Economics of Aging at the
National Bureau of Economic Research.

The University of Chicago Press, Chicago 60637
The University of Chicago Press, Ltd., London
© 2012 by the National Bureau of Economic Research
All rights reserved. Published 2012.
Printed in the United States of America

21 20 19 18 17 16 15 14 13 12   1 2 3 4 5
ISBN-13: 978-0-226-90313-2 (cloth)
ISBN-13: 978-0-226-90316-3 (e-book)
ISBN-10: 0-226-90313-3 (cloth)
ISBN-10: 0-226-90316-8 (e-book)

Library of Congress Cataloging-in-Publication Data

Investigations in the economics of aging / edited by David A. Wise.
        p. cm.—(A National Bureau of Economic Research conference
report) Papers presented at a conference held in Carefree, Arizona, in
May 2011.
    Includes bibliographical references and index.
    ISBN-13: 978-0-226-90313-2 (cloth : alkaline paper)
    ISBN-10: 0-226-90313-3 (cloth : alkaline paper)
    ISBN-13: 978-0-226-90316-3 (e-book)
    ISBN-10: 0-226-90316-8 (e-book) 1. Aging—Economic aspects—
United States—Congresses. 2. Retirees—Economic conditions—
21st century—Congresses. 3. Older people—Medical care—United
States—Costs—Congresses. 4. Older people—Health and hygiene—
United States—Congresses. I. Wise, David A., editor. II. Series:
National Bureau of Economic Research conference report.
HQ1064.U5I634 2012
305.260973—dc23
                                                        2011041362

Relation of the Directors to the
Work and Publications of the
National Bureau of Economic Research

1. The object of the NBER is to ascertain and present to the economics profession, and to the public more generally, important economic facts and their interpretation in a scientific manner without policy recommendations. The Board of Directors is charged with the responsibility of ensuring that the work of the NBER is carried on in strict conformity with this object.

2. The President shall establish an internal review process to ensure that book manuscripts proposed for publication DO NOT contain policy recommendations. This shall apply both to the proceedings of conferences and to manuscripts by a single author or by one or more co-authors but shall not apply to authors of comments at NBER conferences who are not NBER affiliates.

3. No book manuscript reporting research shall be published by the NBER until the President has sent to each member of the Board a notice that a manuscript is recommended for publication and that in the President's opinion it is suitable for publication in accordance with the above principles of the NBER. Such notification will include a table of contents and an abstract or summary of the manuscript's content, a list of contributors if applicable, and a response form for use by Directors who desire a copy of the manuscript for review. Each manuscript shall contain a summary drawing attention to the nature and treatment of the problem studied and the main conclusions reached.

4. No volume shall be published until forty-five days have elapsed from the above notification of intention to publish it. During this period a copy shall be sent to any Director requesting it, and if any Director objects to publication on the grounds that the manuscript contains policy recommendations, the objection will be presented to the author(s) or editor(s). In case of dispute, all members of the Board shall be notified, and the President shall appoint an ad hoc committee of the Board to decide the matter; thirty days additional shall be granted for this purpose.

5. The President shall present annually to the Board a report describing the internal manuscript review process, any objections made by Directors before publication or by anyone after publication, any disputes about such matters, and how they were handled.

6. Publications of the NBER issued for informational purposes concerning the work of the Bureau, or issued to inform the public of the activities at the Bureau, including but not limited to the NBER Digest and Reporter, shall be consistent with the object stated in paragraph 1. They shall contain a specific disclaimer noting that they have not passed through the review procedures required in this resolution. The Executive Committee of the Board is charged with the review of all such publications from time to time.

7. NBER working papers and manuscripts distributed on the Bureau's web site are not deemed to be publications for the purpose of this resolution, but they shall be consistent with the object stated in paragraph 1. Working papers shall contain a specific disclaimer noting that they have not passed through the review procedures required in this resolution. The NBER's web site shall contain a similar disclaimer. The President shall establish an internal review process to ensure that the working papers and the web site do not contain policy recommendations, and shall report annually to the Board on this process and any concerns raised in connection with it.

8. Unless otherwise determined by the Board or exempted by the terms of paragraphs 6 and 7, a copy of this resolution shall be printed in each NBER publication as described in paragraph 2 above.

Contents

Preface ix

Introduction 1
David A. Wise and Richard Woodbury

I. FINANCING RETIREMENT

1. **Were They Prepared for Retirement?**
   Financial Status at Advanced Ages in
   the HRS and AHEAD Cohorts 21
   James M. Poterba, Steven F. Venti, and
   David A. Wise
   Comment: David Laibson

2. **Economic Preparation for Retirement** 77
   Michael D. Hurd and Susann Rohwedder
   Comment: Robert J. Willis

3. **How Well Are Social Security Recipients**
   Protected from Inflation? 119
   Gopi Shah Goda, John B. Shoven, and
   Sita Nataraj Slavov
   Comment: Michael D. Hurd

4. **The Availability and Utilization of**
   401(k) Loans 145
   John Beshears, James J. Choi,
   David Laibson, and Brigitte C. Madrian
   Comment: Gopi Shah Goda

II. HEALTH AND HEALTH CARE

5. Dimensions of Health in the Elderly Population   179
David M. Cutler and Mary Beth Landrum
Comment: David R. Weir

6. The Value of Progress against Cancer
in the Elderly   203
Jay Bhattacharya, Alan M. Garber,
Matthew Miller, and Daniella Perlroth
Comment: Amitabh Chandra

7. Self-Reported Disability and Reference Groups   237
Arthur van Soest, Tatiana Andreyeva,
Arie Kapteyn, and James P. Smith
Comment: David M. Cutler

8. "Healthy, Wealthy, and Wise?" Revisited:
An Analysis of the Causal Pathways from
Socioeconomic Status to Health   267
Till Stowasser, Florian Heiss,
Daniel McFadden, and Joachim Winter
Comment: Robert J. Willis

9. Childhood Health and Differences in
Late-Life Health Outcomes between
England and the United States   321
James Banks, Zoë Oldfield, and
James P. Smith
Comment: Amitabh Chandra

10. The Financial Crisis and the
Well-Being of America   343
Angus Deaton
Comment: Daniel McFadden

Contributors   377
Author Index   381
Subject Index   385

Preface

This volume consists of papers presented at a conference held in Carefree, Arizona, in May 2011. Most of the research was conducted as part of the Program on the Economics of Aging at the National Bureau of Economic Research. The majority of the work was sponsored by the US Department of Health and Human Services, through the National Institute on Aging grants P01-AG005842 and P30-AG012810 to the National Bureau of Economic Research. Any other funding sources are noted in the individual chapters.

Any opinions expressed in this volume are those of the respective authors and do not necessarily reflect the views of the National Bureau of Economic Research or the sponsoring organizations.

Introduction

David A. Wise and Richard Woodbury

One of the most persistent findings from research in the economics of aging is the depth of the relationship between health and financial circumstances—two core dimensions of individual well-being as people age. In continuing research, a major focus is on understanding these dimensions of well-being, the strong correlations and causal connections between them, and how they are changing over time.

For both demographic and economic reasons, it is a particularly important time to be studying the economics of aging. We are in the midst of a substantial evolution in how people live in later life. The aging of the baby boom generation into older ages is one factor. Another major change of the last two decades has been the growth in retirement saving programs, particularly 401(k) plans, and a parallel decline in traditional defined-benefit pension programs. Reforms to Social Security, Medicare, and Medicaid are also being implemented, as necessitated by changing population demographics and mounting fiscal pressures. Health and health care are evolving as well, with continuing advances in medicine, better disease management, improvement in health and functional ability, and increased longevity. An aging workforce, strained macroeconomic conditions, and fiscal imbalances in government are additional dimensions of the changing times.

The characteristics, causal influences, and dynamic interrelationship be-

David A. Wise is the John F. Stambaugh Professor of Political Economy at the Kennedy School of Government at Harvard University. He is the area director of Health and Retirement Programs and director of the Program on the Economics of Aging at the National Bureau of Economic Research. Richard Woodbury is a senior administrator with the Economics of Aging Program at the National Bureau of Economic Research.

For acknowledgments, sources of research support, and disclosure of the authors' material financial relationships, if any, please see http://www.nber.org/chapters/c12428.ack.

tween evolving health and evolving financial well-being are a core substantive focus of current research in the economics of aging field. Are people adequately prepared for the financial needs of later life? How do people's finances and financial well-being evolve over the course of later life? Do people have the right mix of annuitized payment streams and nonannuitized savings at older ages? What are the dimensions of health and functional ability that are most important to well-being at older ages? How do these dimensions of health evolve over the course of later life? How is health and work capacity changing over time? What factors contribute to health and economic well-being as people age? And how do these multiple health and financial aspects of well-being interrelate? These are core questions of ongoing research, each of which is addressed in some way in the studies in this volume.

This is the fourteenth in a series of NBER volumes synthesizing complementary analyses of economics of aging research. The goal is to bring together studies that are at the forefront of research in the field. The volumes are not intended to cover the entire area of economics of aging research, but rather to highlight cutting edge research projects that together contribute to a more comprehensive understanding of health and economic well-being as people age. The chapters encompass advances in research methodology, data resources, current trends, and changing policies in health, work, financial well-being, and retirement. Many of the studies are components of longer-term research themes of the NBER program on aging, and an attempt is made to place these new studies in the context of our larger agenda. Through fourteen volumes, the large majority of this research has been funded by the National Institute on Aging, which has made a long-term commitment to advancing the economics of aging field.

The previous volumes in this NBER series are *The Economics of Aging, Issues in the Economics of Aging, Topics in the Economics of Aging, Studies in the Economics of Aging, Advances in the Economics of Aging, Inquiries in the Economics of Aging, Frontiers in the Economics of Aging, Themes in the Economics of Aging, Perspectives on the Economics of Aging, Analyses in the Economics of Aging, Developments in the Economics of Aging, Research Findings in the Economics of Aging,* and *Explorations in the Economics of Aging.* This volume continues the series with a collection of investigations in the economics of aging.

The volume is divided into two sections: the first weighted more heavily toward people's changing financial circumstances as they age, and the second weighted more heavily toward people's changing health and health care. Even in the first section, however, the emerging importance of out-of-pocket health care costs, or the risk of such costs, is emphasized as a growing need for financial resources at older ages. Indeed, the interactions between health and financial resources, and between health care costs and resource adequacy, are the general topic of the first several chapters in the volume. The studies raise new questions about what constitutes resource adequacy later in life, when out-of-pocket health care expenses are an increasing component of household budgets, on an ongoing basis, as well as an increased risk of much larger expenditure shocks (or reduced income) from adverse health events and health decline.

Chapter 1 analyzes people's finances in the years leading up to their death, focusing on the variations in financial circumstances and well-being across the population. Chapter 2 looks at the extent to which large out-of-pocket costs increase the risk of financial hardship at older ages. Chapter 3 documents how health care cost growth has limited the inflation-protection in the Social Security program, so that the buying power of Social Security income for other needs is in fact reduced over the post-retirement years. Chapter 4 extends a long-term research agenda on the factors influencing saving and asset accumulation during people's working years, focusing more narrowly on how loan provisions affect 401(k) balances.

Together, these studies add substantial new pieces to our understanding of financial circumstances in later life, as well as new perspective on how health and out-of-pocket costs for health care influence financial well-being and resource adequacy. As noted, health and health care costs turn out to be major influences on both the level of financial resources in later life, on the one hand, and the need for financial resource expenditures, on the other. The results raise new questions about the appropriate income-replacement rate necessary to maintain standards of living, the distinct roles of annuitized versus nonannuitized financial holdings, the appropriate formulas for inflation-adjustment for older households, and the role of insurance for health declines—all of which are integrally related to resource adequacy.

The next three studies in the volume focus more intensively on health status, health trends, and health measurement. Chapter 5 more clearly defines the major dimensions of health and functional ability, and how health is changing over time along these various dimensions. Chapter 6 focuses more narrowly on progress in cancer treatment and cancer outcomes as a more targeted case study of evolving health, as well as the complications in disentangling improved prevention, diagnosis, and treatment, and their respective effect on health outcomes. Chapter 7 is a methodological study on health measurement, improving our ability to interpret self-reported disability measures through the use of reference groups. All three studies add to our understanding of health and health trends, complementing the focus on financial well-being in the first four chapters.

The last three chapters in the volume consider in greater depth the relationship between health and economic circumstances. Chapter 8 analyzes the causal pathways from socioeconomic circumstances to health, establishing a deeper understanding of the relationship, and how results may change with the data, sample size, and time span being studied. Chapter 9 looks at the lifelong impact of childhood health on later-life health outcomes. Finally, chapter 10 explores measures of subjective well-being, which may encompass aspects of health, finances, and psychological well-being, and how these measures of subjective well-being may be affected by financial and macroeconomic conditions. The particular value of these last three chapters is their explicit recognition of how different aspects of well-being interrelate, including the financial aspects of well-being emphasized in the early chapters, the health aspects of well-being emphasized in the middle chapters of the volume, and still broader measures of subjective well-being introduced in the final chapter.

The remainder of this introduction provides an overview of the studies contained in the volume, relying to a significant extent on the authors' own language to summarize their work. Also important are the comments on each chapter provided by discussants. These comments add a depth of perspective on each research topic. In some cases, the discussant comments put the primary study into a larger context. In some cases, they are critical commentary. And in some cases, they are expansions of either the theoretical underpinnings or empirical findings that are reported in the primary studies. The result is a richer treatment of each topic addressed. Because the volume focuses on studies that are at the forefront of economics of aging research, they are by their nature more exploratory or innovative. The discussant comments provide a certain grounding or breadth of perspective that is particularly valuable in assessing these more exploratory and innovative research directions.

I.1   Part I: Financing Retirement

The composition of financial support at older ages and the demands on financial resources later in life are two key aspects of the changing retirement landscape in the United States. As noted, the trends to date suggest that private saving, particularly through 401(k) plans, will be far more important and widespread in its implications than employer-provided pensions achieved at their peak. The implications of this saving will play out over time, as new retirees will have spent an increasing portion of their careers contributing and accumulating assets in private retirement accounts. While financial market declines have had an impact, the most recent generation of new retirees is the first to have significant numbers of people with more substantial 401(k) accumulations. This has inspired a redirection of research in the field from the accumulation phase in these retirement savings accounts, while people are working, to how the accumulated assets are used in later life.

On the expense side, out-of-pocket health care costs are a significant and growing demand on financial resources in later life. This burden may be particularly acute for individuals in poorer health, who not only face higher costs, but who (on average) have less financial resources to support them. Thus the first several chapters deal with interactions between health and financial resources, and between health care costs and resource adequacy.

In chapter 1, James Poterba, Steven Venti, and I analyze people's finances in the years leading up to their death. We ask, were they prepared for retirement? The study's methodology relies on panel data to analyze the evolution of each household's financial assets over this later life period. The sample consists of households who were age seventy and older in 1993. Each household is followed until they die, or until the most recent survey period in 2008. Separate analyses are conducted for households in each of three family pathway groups: (1) one-person households; (2) households that begin in 1993 as two-person households, but with a deceased spouse over the study period; and (3) two-person households in which both spouses are living when last observed. Much of the analysis is restricted to people who are known to have died.

Several results stand out. First, median total wealth was relatively high in the year last observed for each of the three family pathway groups. Second, wealth in the last year before death is greatest for persons who were in two-person households the longest period of time. For example, the average assets in the last year observed were $141,606 for persons in one-person households in 1993 whose last year observed before death was 2006, $252,849 for persons in two-person households in 1993 whose spouse was deceased when last observed in 2006, and $691,588 for persons in two-person households in 1993 whose spouse was alive when last observed in 2006. Third, for total wealth and for each of the asset subcategories there is a strong correspondence between the level of assets in 1993 and the number of years a person survives after 1993. Persons who lived longer had higher initial assets. Fourth, for each family pathway group, there is a very strong relationship between health status and wealth in the last year observed. Thus there is a strong association between health and wealth even among persons who would die within the next two years. And fifth, despite the appearance of substantial assets at the median, a substantial fraction of people die with income less than $10,000, with no financial assets, and with zero housing wealth.

A rather large fraction of the original single-person households have low income judged by the income poverty thresholds. We find that 12.1 percent are below the poverty threshold and have no financial assets, and that 23 percent are below twice the income poverty line and have no financial assets. To put the results in context, we first compare the total income in the last year observed to total income in 1993, the first year the Asset and Health Data Among the Oldest Old (AHEAD) data were collected. Total income in the last year observed was about 4 percent higher, on average, than total income in 1993. We also compare total median income in the last year observed to median earnings (in 2008 dollars) of the same persons when they were between ages fifty-seven and sixty-two. While the difference is hard to evaluate because the two measures are not clearly comparable, overall median income in the last year observed was approximately 50 percent lower than median earnings of the same persons at ages fifty-seven to sixty-two.

There are also important differences across the pathways. Consider, for example, the proportion of persons with annuity income less than $20,000 (approximately twice the poverty level for single persons over age sixty-five) and financial assets less than $10,000: 52 percent of persons in the single-household pathway fall below these thresholds, but only 36.4 percent of those in the two- to one-person pathway, and only 26.3 percent of those in the two-person pathway fall below these thresholds. Similarly, consider the proportion of persons with annuity income in the $10,000 to $20,000 interval and financial assets less than $10,000 who have zero housing wealth: of those in the single-family pathway 63.3 percent have zero housing wealth, and 53.0 percent of those in the two- to one-person pathway, and only 25.9 percent of those in the two-person pathway have zero housing wealth. A perhaps striking similarity across the pathways is that given income and housing wealth, the health status of the persons in the three pathways is very close. The median health percentile of persons with annuity income in the $10,000 to $20,000 interval and financial assets less than $10,000 is 28.2 for persons in the single-household pathway, 23.9 percent for those in the two- to one-person pathway, and 28.2 for persons in the two-person pathway.

The results raise several issues. First, a noticeable fraction of persons die with virtually no financial assets—46.1 percent with less than $10,000. Based on a replacement rate comparison, many of these may be deemed to have been well-prepared for retirement, in the sense that their income in their final years was not substantially lower than their income in their late fifties or early sixties. Yet with such low asset levels, they would have little capacity to pay for unanticipated needs such as health or other shocks or to pay for entertainment, travel, or other activities. This raises a question of whether the replacement ratio is a sufficient statistic for the "adequacy" of retirement preparation. In addition, this group relies almost entirely on Social Security benefits for support in retirement. These people balance on only one leg of the oft touted three-legged stool that is said to provide retirement support—Social Security, pension benefits, and personal saving. If the one leg is judged inadequate it raises the question of how to strengthen the other legs which in turn may, for example, increase interest in the spread of 401(k)-like plans to low-wage workers in firms with high turnover.

In discussing the results from chapter 1, David Laibson compares actual savings behavior and accumulations in 401(k) plans with the asset accumulations that might be necessary to assure resource adequacy in retirement. He does this by applying a rough conversion formula between asset amounts, on the one hand, and their annuitized income equivalent, on the other. Compared with his ideal vision for savings-based retirement planning, he raises concerns about resource adequacy resulting from many factors, including pre-retirement withdrawals, individuals without access to plans, low employer match rates, high management fees and risks of low returns, nonparticipation among those who are eligible, starting to save too late, the continuing decline of defined-benefit pension arrangements, reductions in housing equity at older ages, increased credit card debt, and rising out-of-pocket costs for medical care.

Chapters 2 and 3 focus on health care costs as a growing demand on financial resources at older ages. A key issue is the risk of being inadequately prepared. For example, a person may seem to have been well-prepared for retirement if they turn out to have lived an average life span, earned an average return on their investments, and had average out-of-pocket medical spending needs. But what if their experience turns out to be different than the average? Specifically, what if they live longer than average, or earn less than average on their investments, or have larger than average medical care needs? In that case, the same household in retrospect may have been unprepared. Risk and uncertainty raise diverse questions about the magnitude of retirement assets needed, the annuitization of assets, insurance, and the distribution of financial preparedness across the population of retirees.

In chapter 2, Michael Hurd and Susann Rohwedder look at the risk of out-of-pocket spending for health care on economic preparation for retirement. It follows up on their earlier work that focuses on longevity risk. In their prior research, which excludes medical spending risk from their models, Hurd and Rohwedder find that a substantial majority of those just past the usual retirement age are adequately prepared for retirement, in that they will be able to finance a path of consumption that begins at their current level of consumption and then follows an age-pattern similar to that of current retirees. However, almost half of singles without a high school education will be likely to be forced to reduce consumption, and a substantial number of married college graduates will also have to reduce consumption. The model used for this work did not account for health care spending risk.

The goal of the study in chapter 2 is to explicitly account for the risk of large out-of-pocket spending on health care. Variation in out-of-pocket spending for health care changes quite sharply the percentage of single persons adequately prepared for retirement. When there are no shocks, 57 percent are adequately prepared. With serially correlated health shocks, just 44 percent are adequately prepared—even though average out-of-pocket spending on health care does not change (by design). The difference for single women specifically is even larger: 58 percent with no shocks versus 39 percent with. For single women without a high school degree, the percent adequately prepared drops from 33 percent to just 15 percent.

The effects on married people are not nearly as large because many couples have wealth substantially in excess of what is required to deal with most health care spending shocks. In this sample, the percentage of those adequately prepared declined from 80 percent with no health care spending shocks, to 73 percent with shocks.

Averaging both single and married households, the percentage adequately prepared is 72 percent when out-of-pocket spending does not have a stochastic component. But when out-of-pocket spending is stochastic (with the distribution recorded in the 2008 wave of the HRS survey) and when spending is serially correlated (as estimated from 2004 and 2005 Medicare Current Beneficiary Surveys), the percentage of those who are financially prepared for retirement declines by 9 percentage points to about 63 percent.

In his discussion of chapter 2, Robert Willis notes the sequencing of asset use based on post-retirement needs. Annuitized resources, such as Social Security and traditional pension benefits, are used as the initial or baseline resource, followed by financial asset savings and housing equity as the longest protected asset. Willis also raises questions about the availability of annuity and other insurance products that may better protect against later life risks, as well as the roles of bequest motives and "excess wealth" that is not consumed before death.

In chapter 3, Gopi Shah Goda, John Shoven, and Sita Slavov ask, how well are Social Security recipients protected from inflation, after accounting for increased Medicare premium and other out-of-pocket health care costs?

Social Security is widely believed to protect its recipients from a number of risks, including uncertainty regarding length of life and inflation, due to the inflation-indexed life annuity form of the benefit. The inflation protection comes from the fact that Social Security benefits are indexed to the Consumer Price Index for Urban Wage Earners and Clerical Workers (CPI-W). The CPI-W is based on the spending patterns of a broad group of workers, representing approximately 32 percent of the US population. However, the CPI-W may not accurately reflect the experience of retirees for two reasons. First, retirees generally have higher medical expenses than workers, and medical costs, in recent years, have tended to rise faster than the prices of other goods. Second, even if medical costs did not rise faster than the prices of other goods, individual retirees would still, on average, need to devote a larger share of income to medical spending as they age. This means that individual retirees would still see a decline in the real income they have available for nonmedical spending. Chapter 3 explores both of these factors, the extent to which they undermine the inflation protection in Social Security, and what alternative methods of indexing benefits might be considered.

The study accounts for two major components of medical costs. First, most Social Security recipients are also participants in Medicare Part B. These premiums are automatically deducted from Social Security retirement benefits and have increased approximately 1,600 percent between 1975 and 2011, while the Social Security cost-of-living adjustments have accumulated to just over 300 percent over this period. Second, retirees often have substantial out-of-pocket medical expenses, including Medicare deductibles and copayments, and payments for services with limited Medicare coverage, such as nursing home care.

The authors find that, after subtracting both of these components of health spending from Social Security benefits, available income net of medical expenses for a Social Security participant with average out-of-pocket medical spending has, in fact, been increasing more slowly than a price index of nonmedical goods and services. For example, the average man born in 1918 has seen his monthly Social Security benefit, net of medical expenses, rise from $528 at the end of 1983 (when he was sixty-five) to $867 at the end of 2007 (when he was eighty-nine). However, if his net-of-medical-expenses benefit had kept pace with inflation in the prices of nonmedical goods over that time period, he would have had $1,086 per month in 2007 after medical expenses. That is, his net-of-medical-spending benefit has declined by around 20 percent, relative to the nonmedical goods price index. Similarly, the average woman born in 1918 has seen her net-of-medical-expenses benefit decline by around 27 percent, relative to the nonmedical goods price index.

An alternative inflation index is the Consumer Price Index for the Elderly (CPI-E), an experimental measure that targets the cost of living for people aged sixty-two and older. If Social Security benefits had been indexed to the CPI-E instead of the CPI-W, men born in 1918 would have $961 net of medical expenses, falling only 11.5 percent short of the $1,086 needed to hold nonmedical expenditures constant in real terms; similarly, women born in 1918 would fall only 18.1 percent short. The reason indexing to the CPI-E does not fully compensate retirees for inflation is that, even if medical costs remained constant over time for the elderly, they tend to spend more on out-of-pocket medical expenses as they age, crowding out nonmedical spending. Thus, each cohort's Social Security benefit net of average out-of-pocket medical spending would tend to decline in real terms even if the price of medical care rose at the same rate as the prices of other goods, or alternatively, even if the average retiree's real net Social Security benefit remained constant.

Both the authors and Michael Hurd's discussion of the study highlight limitations in both the CPI-W and CPI-E measures of inflation. For example, the failure to account properly for technological progress can be quite serious when it comes to health care. Higher medical costs likely reflect the consumption of better quality medical care, and retirees may be better off even if they are left with less to spend on other nonmedical goods. The study's authors, therefore, emphasize that they cannot draw any conclusions about changes in the utility of Social Security recipients from this analysis. All they show is that Social Security benefits may not be fully inflation-indexed in the sense that recipients with average out of pockct medical spending cannot, from one year to the next, purchase the same bundle of nonmedical goods with their Social Security benefits.

Chapter 4 looks narrowly at one aspect of 401(k) plans that has not been studied extensively in past research: the availability and use of 401(k) loans. These loans may decrease accumulation in 401(k) plans if their repayment displaces new contributions to the plans. They may increase asset accumulations, however, if they enable people to make larger contributions to the plans, knowing that they can still access their savings if necessary before retirement. In chapter 4, John Beshears, James Choi, David Laibson, and Brigitte Madrian provide an introductory overview of how 401(k) loans work, and how often they are used. This chapter is the first step in a research agenda on how the availability of 401(k) loans affects retirement wealth accumulation.

About 90 percent of 401(k) participants are in plans that offer a loan option. Within those plans, about one in five eligible participants has a loan outstanding at a given point in time. Loan utilization rates follow hump-shaped patterns with respect to age, tenure, compensation, and plan balances, reaching peaks for participants in their forties, those with ten to twenty years of tenure, those earning $40,000 to $60,000 per year, and those with $20,000 to $30,000 in plan balances. Conditional on having a loan, the loan balance to 401(k) balance ratio is declining in age, tenure, compensation, and 401(k) plan balance.

Despite the prevalence of 401(k) loans, they constitute only 2.5 percent of total plan assets among plans with a loan option. For some individuals, however, 401(k) loans can be an important source of credit. Our empirical analysis finds that 401(k) loan utilization is correlated with the types of loan rules adopted by firms. Loans are more likely to be used in plans that charge low interest rates, and conditional on taking a loan, loan sizes are larger when multiple loans are allowed to be outstanding simultaneously, the maximum loan duration allowed is long, and the loan interest rate is high.

In her discussion of the study, Gopi Shah Goda suggests numerous directions for further research, most notably on the initial question of whether the loan provisions increase or decrease asset accumulation in the plans. She also asks what factors determine whether a plan adopts a loan policy, what factors determine whether an individual takes out a loan and, importantly, whether 401(k) plan participants have other borrowing (such as credit card debt) that could be attained less expensively through 401(k) loans.

I.2   Part II: Health and Health Care

The relationships between financial circumstances and health are emphasized throughout this volume. Part II is more heavily weighted toward studies of health. Understanding changes in the health of the elderly is a central policy issue. A healthier elderly population is able to work to later ages, spends less on medical care each year, and requires less informal care from family and friends.

By many metrics, the health of the elderly has improved over time. For example, the share of elderly people with basic physical impairments has declined markedly over the past two decades. By other metrics, however, the health of the elderly is worsening. Problems with more advanced functional measures such as stooping and walking moderate distances have increased over time, and obesity among the elderly has soared along with weight in the nonelderly population.

Researchers have attempted to combine these different measures of disability into one summary measure, but these summaries are generally ad hoc and difficult to interpret. The most common single measures of disability ask whether the person has impairments in Activities of Daily Living (ADLs, such as bathing or dressing) or Instrumental Activities of Daily Living (IADLs, such as doing light housework or managing money). In the Medicare Current Beneficiary Survey, which is analyzed in chapter 5, the share of the elderly population that is disabled by this definition has declined from 49 percent in 1992 to 43 percent in 2007. However, this summary measure exhibits somewhat different trends in different surveys and for different measures of health, and ignores some aspects of functional impairment (e.g., can the person walk a reasonable distance?), cognitive problems such as memory loss, and sensory impairments such as difficulty seeing and hearing.

In chapter 5, David Cutler and Mary Beth Landrum aim to more carefully decompose the elderly population's dimensions of health and how health is changing over time along these various dimensions. In the first part of the chapter, they consider how to optimally combine different measures of health into a smaller number of summary measures. Of course, the best way to summarize multiple measures of health depends on the question being asked. The optimal measure to predict medical spending may be somewhat different than the optimal measure to predict health transitions, for example. Cutler and Landrum estimate factor models for nineteen indicators of health. These measures include specific ADL impairments, IADL impairments, functional impairments, cognitive limitations, and sensory impairments.

The study shows that these nineteen dimensions can be compressed into three broad summary measures. The dominant factor is impairment in very basic physical and social tasks such as dressing, eating, transferring in and out of bed, preparing meals, doing light housework, and managing money. This encompasses many of the ADLs and IADLs, but not all. The second factor loads heavily on functional limitations and includes measures such as walking moderate distances, stooping, and reaching. The third dimension is sensory impairments—trouble seeing and hearing.

After determining these factors, the authors analyze the evolution of these health dimensions over time, and as people age over the course of later life. Analyzing historical patterns, they show that the set of physical and social limitations and sensory impairments have declined rapidly over time. Functional ability was flat or increasing, after declining early in the time period. They offer several potential explanations for this latter result.

The authors also investigate the evolution of health states with age, comparing the early years in the sample (1991–1996), middle years (1997–2001), and later years (2002–2007). The study shows that health deteriorates less rapidly with age in the later years of the sample than in earlier years. The authors do not attempt to explain this observation, but they do note significant variation across the population that is masked by population averages. Even as health deteriorates overall as people age, health improves for a significant minority of people. The authors also describe the next step in their research agenda, emphasizing the development of a richer model of changes in health over time. For example, to what extent is the improvement in health a result of fewer new conditions developing, existing problems being cared for better, or changes in the social and environmental circumstances that the elderly face?

In his discussion of chapter 5, David Weir emphasizes the importance of age standardization to the effective interpretation of the results. He notes that the study is more about the disability aspects of health than about chronic illness and disease. Because issues of disability are dramatically more prevalent in the older old population, such as people in their eighties and older, one needs to differentiate between the sixty-five-plus population generally, and this older old group. This is particularly important in interpreting long-term population trends, as the baby boom generation moves into their sixties now, their seventies soon, and their eighties further in the future.

Chapter 6, by Alan Garber, Jay Bhattacharya, Matt Miller, and Daniella Perlroth, focuses more narrowly on the value of advances in cancer treatment in the elderly. Cancer remains one of the most common causes of death in the elderly, but the number of cancer deaths in the United States began falling in the early 2000s. This trend of improved overall survival, including for the most common types of cancers—breast, prostate, lung, and colorectal cancers—continued at least through the end of the last decade, when the latest national statistics were available.

Improvements in health outcomes from cancer and other diagnoses have come at a time of unsustainable growth in health expenditures. This has led to research that more carefully evaluates the relationship between rising costs, on the one hand, and health outcomes, on the other. The goal of the research in chapter 6 is to match changes in survival for cancer matched with changes in spending for those conditions. The study begins by evaluating the relative contribution of changes in diagnosis and treatment to changes in survival after a diagnosis of breast, prostate, lung, or colorectal cancer, separately for men and women. Understanding the relative effectiveness of early diagnosis and treatment advances for these cancers is important in deciding where increasingly limited anticancer resources should be allocated. The analysis is applied over two study periods: 1988 to 1994 and 2000 to 2004.

The study finds that changes in treatment during these periods may have improved outcomes for some but not all cancers evaluated, and even under favorable assumptions would only be considered cost-effective for a subset of cancers. The years of analysis most corresponding to the recent treatment era did show generally cost-effective medical advances for cancer treatment, with the possible exception of men with lung cancer. The findings suggest that advances in treatment did not lead to improved survival for women during the former period, but did for men in the former, and for both men and women in the latter period. Costs increased for all periods of analysis. The incremental cost-effectiveness of medical progress for cancer varied by treatment era and cohort. In the recent treatment era, the authors find a consistent positive effect on survival as compared with previously, and lower incremental cost-effective ratios for recent cancer advances.

Chapter 7 focuses on the measurement and interpretation of self-reported disability as a more specific measure of health. The problem in interpreting self-reported health is that it may be influenced or biased by people's frame of reference or by social norms. Most people do not live in social isolation. Instead, they interact repeatedly with family, friends, and neighbors. As a consequence of those pervasive interactions, they allow themselves to be transformed in many ways, a transformation of which they may often be unaware.

One type of transformation involves the formation of social norms about what normal or acceptable behavior might be. These social norms then fix the scales that they may be using in responding to questions about their own behaviors and current situations. If they had different neighbors and friends, their self-descriptions about their lives may well be quite different. While this may be true within a country where there exists a shared history and culture, it is especially likely to be the case when cross-national comparisons are made, such as between the Netherlands and the United States.

In chapter 7, "Self-Reported Disability and Reference Groups," Arthur van Soest, Tatiana Andreyeva, Arie Kapteyn, and James P. Smith test the importance of social interactions in people's self-reported work disability. The research uses data from a household survey representative of the Dutch population. As part of the survey, respondents are asked to evaluate work disability of hypothetical people with some work-related health problem, described in vignettes. They are also asked how many people among their friends and acquaintances receive DI benefits. Combining the vignette responses with self-reports on the number of people receiving disability insurance benefits (DI) among one's friends and acquaintances, the authors estimate a model describing the influence of DI prevalence in one's reference group on the subjective scale used to report work disability.

The main feature of the model is the notion that response scales for reporting no, mild, or severe work disability can be affected by a "peer group effect"; that is, by the number of people in the reference group receiving disability benefits. The study finds that DI benefit receipt in one's reference group has a significant effect on response scales in the expected direction.

The effects are sufficiently strong to explain a good deal of the higher rates of self-reported work disability in the Netherlands compared to the United States, as the Dutch population appears to have much more lenient thresholds about what constitutes a work disability.

These findings are suggestive of how policy programs affect social norms. If a policy makes receipt of DI benefits more attractive or easier (e.g., by loosening eligibility requirements) thus increasing the number of DI recipients, this changes social norms. Individuals are now more likely to label a given health condition as work limiting and the prevalence of self-reported work will rise.

David Cutler's discussion of chapter 7 focuses more intently on the theoretical foundations of why reference groups matter. He emphasizes three hypotheses for why people who have more disabled peers are more likely to describe themselves as disabled. The first is that it lowers the threshold for reporting someone as disabled. The second is that people sort themselves into groups with similar characteristics as themselves. The third is that having more disabled peers makes you feel worse yourself, so that your perception of your own disability changes. While the study emphasizes the importance of the first explanation, Cutler makes the case for follow-up work that more comprehensively differentiates between these hypotheses.

The last three chapters consider in greater depth the relationship between health and economic circumstances, the causal pathways from socioeconomic circumstances to health, the lifelong impact of childhood health on later-life health outcomes, and how well-being is affected by financial and macroeconomic conditions.

Throughout the expansive literature in the economics of aging, there is little dispute that the socioeconomic status (SES) of individuals is positively correlated with their health status. The size of the body of literature documenting that wealthy and well-educated people generally enjoy better health and longer life is impressive. The robustness of this association is underscored by the fact that the so-called health-wealth gradient has been detected in different times, countries, populations, age structures, and for both men and women. Moreover, the results are largely insensitive to the choice of SES measures (such as wealth, income, education, occupation, or social class) and health outcomes.

While the existence of the gradient may be uncontroversial, the same cannot be said about its explanation. Medical researchers, economists, and other social scientists have developed a large number of competing theories that can broadly be categorized as follows: there may be causal effects from SES to health, causal effects that work in the opposite direction, and unobserved common factors that influence both variables in the same direction without a causal link between the two. A full explanation of the gradient likely encompasses aspects of all three categories of causation, though the relative weighting of explanations remains controversial.

Chapter 8 revisits a 2004 study by Peter Adams, Michael Hurd, Daniel McFadden, Angela Merrill, and Tiago Ribeiro, originally entitled "Healthy, Wealthy, and Wise? Tests for Direct Causal Paths between Health and Socioeconomic Status." Using an innovative research methodology and drawing on the first three waves of the AHEAD survey, that study found that in an elderly US population, causal channels that operate from wealth to health are an exception rather than the rule. Considering these strong results, as well as the methodological novelty of the approach used, it is not surprising that their work has subsequently been the subject of vivid debate within the literature, focused in particular on the validity of the study's identification strategy in general.

The new research, "Healthy, Wealthy and Wise?, Revisited, an Analysis of the Causal Pathways from Socioeconomic Status to Health," by Till Stowasser, Florian Heiss, Daniel McFadden, and Joachim Winter, reviews the methodological challenges involved in testing the causal relationships between socioeconomic status and health. It also repeats the earlier analysis using the full range of Health and Retirement Study (HRS) and AHEAD data that have become available since the original study was completed. This enriches the original study along multiple dimensions. First, the same individuals can be tracked for a longer period of time. Second, the analysis can be extended to new cohorts of respondents, and the working sample can be widened by including younger individuals aged fifty and older. Third, because of the wider age range, there is variation in health insurance status that is not available in a Medicare-eligible population. To understand which of these data changes contribute to any deviating conclusions, the study does not apply the whole bundle of modifications at once. Instead, the model is estimated multiple times, by applying it to several different data samples, which are gradually augmented along these dimensions.

The new analysis shows that causal inference critically depends on which time periods are used for estimation. Taken together, the estimations with more extended HRS data alter quite significantly the previous study's conclusions about SES causation. Using the information of many (ideally all) waves at once has the greatest effect on results, with many health conditions moving to the column of illnesses for which SES causality may well play a role. Adding younger individuals to the sample has a very similar effect, reducing the number of medical conditions for which the existence of causal links can be statistically rejected even further. This represents a stark contrast to the original findings, where the rejection of structural causality was the most frequent outcome. Given that the greatest changes are triggered by the addition of panel waves, the driving force behind this reversal in results is most likely an increase in test power as sample sizes soar.

Robert Willis's discussion of chapter 8 emphasizes the important bridge the chapter provides between the original analysis, the large amount of commentary and critique that resulted, the updated application of the methods, and future work on causal pathways. He emphasizes the complexity of identifying causation, and distinguishing between correlation and causation, particularly when the pathways between health and financial well-being have such multifaceted theoretical underpinnings.

Chapter 9 looks at the sources of later-life health differences between England and the United States. Based on self-reported prevalence of seven important illnesses (diabetes, heart attack, hypertension, heart disease, cancer, diseases of the lung, and stroke), Americans were much less healthy than their English counterparts. These differences were large at all socioeconomic status levels, for both self-reported measures and biological markets, among both men and women, and largely independent of conventional risk factors such as smoking, obesity, and drinking. Much of the US-English difference in later life adult health remains unexplained.

Considerable evidence has emerged that variation in health outcomes at middle and older ages may be traced in part to health and other conditions during childhood. In chapter 9, "Childhood Health and Differences in Late-Life Health Outcomes between England and the United States," James Banks, Zoë Oldfield, and James P. Smith analyze how much of the large differences in illness at middle and older ages in America compared to England can be explained by differences that originated when these people were children and adolescents.

The results suggest that differences in prevalence of childhood diseases between England and the United States and a higher rate of transmission into poorer adult health in the United States do appear to contribute to higher rates of adult illness in the United States compared to England. Based on comparable retrospective questionnaires placed in the HRS survey in the US and the English Longitudinal Study of Aging (ELSA) survey in England, the origins of poorer adult health among older Americans compared to the English traces back right into the childhood years. The transmission rates of childhood illness into poor health in later life also appear to be higher in America compared to England.

A larger question raised by the results is why conditions in America appear to make people of all ages sicker than the English. In his discussion of chapter 9, Amitabh Chandra focuses on this question. He raises a number of possible explanations, ranging from differences in health behaviors, neighborhood or environment effects, differences in health insurance or health care, genetics, stress, socioeconomic circumstances, or socioeconomic disparities. He speculates that the United States may do comparatively worse at preventive health care, but comparatively better at treatment once a health problem arises.

Chapter 10 is the most exploratory in the volume, analyzing daily measures of self-reported well-being, and how they respond to financial and macroeconomic circumstances. Since January 2008, the Gallup Organization has been collecting daily data on 1,000 Americans each day, with a range of self-reported well-being questions. These data provide an opportunity to examine how large changes in the macroeconomic environment affected the emotional and evaluative lives of the population, as well as of subgroups within it. The period covered by these data is characterized by very substantial volatility in financial markets, unemployment, income, and macroeconomic performance.

The financial crisis that began in the summer of 2008 saw a rise in the unemployment rate from 4.8 percent in April 2008 to 10.6 percent at its peak in January 2010, and a 4.4 percent drop in employee compensation over five months in 2009 and 2010. There were also large stimulus-associated tax credits and rebates, 4.7 percent of personal disposable income in May 2008 and 1.7 percent in May 2009, as well as a collapse and subsequent recovery of the stock market—the S&P 500 Index on March 6, 2009 had fallen to 40 percent of its all-time high of October 2007, and then more than doubled again by the end of 2010. Through the fall in the market and the fall in the prices of housing and other assets, 60 percent of households saw their wealth decline between 2007 and 2009, and 25 percent lost more than half of their wealth. These declines were widespread, affecting large shares of households across all age, income, and education groups.

These large fluctuations provide an unparalleled opportunity to examine how these events affected the standards of living, the emotional experiences, and life evaluations of those who lived through it. In chapter 10, "The Financial Crisis and the Well-Being of America," Angus Deaton analyzes the impact of these economic events using data from the Gallup Healthways Well-Being Index (GHWBI), which contains about a million observations on self-reported well-being, as well as on demographics, income, occupation, employment status, and numerous health measures. These data allow daily tracking, not only of national averages, but of the outcomes of different groups.

Deaton finds that the well-being measures in the survey tracked the stock market to a significant degree. For example, in the fall of 2008 (around the time of the collapse of Lehman Brothers), and lasting into the spring of 2009 (at the bottom of the stock market), Americans reported sharp declines in their life evaluation, sharp increases in worry and stress, and declines in positive affect. By the end of 2010, in spite of continuing high unemployment, these measures had largely recovered, though worry remained higher and life evaluation lower than in January 2008.

The subjective well-being (SWB) measures do a much better job of monitoring short-run levels of anxiety as the crisis unfolded than they do of reflecting the evolution of the economy over a year or two. Even large macroeconomic shocks to income and unemployment can be expected to produce only small and difficult to detect effects on SWB measures.

Subjective well-being, particularly evaluation of life as a whole, is very sensitive to question order effects. For example, asking political questions before the life evaluation question reduces reported life evaluation by an amount that dwarfs the effects of even the worst of the crisis; these order effects persist deep into the interview, and condition the reporting of hedonic experience and of satisfaction with standard of living. Because these order effects are so large and persistent, methods for controlling these effects need to be developed and tested if national measures are to be comparable over space and time.

In his discussion of chapter 10, Daniel McFadden raises the concept of "cognitive bubbles" that may be particularly relevant to measures of subjective well-being. He suggests that news reports affect the salience of economic conditions (and other aspects of well-being), making people feel them more emotionally; and that social networks amplify and compound their impact on subjective well-being in the population more generally. A substantial aim of our continuing research effort at the NBER involves further analysis of subjective well-being, as another dimension of well-being that relates and to some degree incorporates both health and financial circumstances.

I

Financing Retirement

1

Were They Prepared for Retirement?
Financial Status at Advanced Ages in the HRS and AHEAD Cohorts

James M. Poterba, Steven F. Venti, and David A. Wise

Many analysts have considered whether households approaching retirement age have accumulated enough assets to be well prepared for retirement. Various methods have been used to evaluate retirement preparedness, and the range of studies that apply these methods have yielded a diverse set of conclusions. Some studies are based on comparisons between observed saving or consumption and the predictions of the life cycle model. Others measure the ability of households to replace pre-retirement levels of income or consumption, or compare post-retirement income to poverty thresholds. Many recent studies have been based on the Health and Retirement Study (HRS), with emphasis on the original HRS cohort that was between the ages of fifty-one and sixty-one in 1992. Other studies use the Survey of Consumer Finances or the Social Security Administration's (SSA) Employee Beneficiary Survey. A partial list of recent studies of retirement preparedness would include Bernheim (1992); Mitchell and Moore (1998); Engen, Gale, and Uccello (1999); Haveman et al. (2005); Scholz, Seshadri, and Khitatrakun (2006); Munnell, Webb, and Golub-Sass (2007); Love, Smith, and McNair (2008); Hurd and Rohwedder (2008); VanDerhei and Copeland (2010).

James M. Poterba is the Mitsui Professor of Economics at the Massachusetts Institute of Technology and president of the National Bureau of Economic Research. Steven F. Venti is the DeWalt Ankeny Professor of Economic Policy and professor of economics at Dartmouth College and a research associate of the National Bureau of Economic Research. David A. Wise is the John F. Stambaugh Professor of Political Economy at the Kennedy School of Government at Harvard University. He is the area director of Health and Retirement Programs and director of the Program on the Economics of Aging at the National Bureau of Economic Research.

Poterba is a trustee of the College Retirement Equity Fund and the TIAA-CREF mutual funds, which provide retirement saving products. This research has been supported by the National Institute of Aging through grant P01-AG005842. For acknowledgments, sources of research support, and disclosure of the authors' material financial relationships, if any, please see http://www.nber.org/chapters/c12429.ack.

In this chapter, we shift from studying household finances at the start of the retirement period, an ex ante measure of retirement preparation, to studying the asset holdings of households in their last years of life. We focus on nonannuitized assets and income. Virtually all households have a Social Security annuity, and many have a defined-benefit (DB) pension annuity as well. We examine nonannuitized assets held at the end of life, in addition to income, because they can provide an ex post indicator of whether households were well-prepared for retirement. If there are substantial numbers of very old households with very low asset levels, relative to the number of households with low asset levels at the start of retirement, then many households exhausted their retirement resources. If most households still hold substantial assets at very advanced ages, or in the last few years before their death, the pattern is more difficult to interpret. It is difficult to determine whether such households had what they would have considered "sufficient" resources for retirement, and did not need to reduce their consumption outlays in late life, or if they conserved the (insufficient) resources they had throughout the retirement period.

We study the level of assets that households hold in the last survey wave preceding their death. In parts of the analysis we make use of all of the cohorts that are now part of the Health and Retirement Study. We give special attention, however, to the older Asset and Health Dynamics Among the Oldest Old (AHEAD) cohort. We calculate the level of wealth at death and offer several metrics for determining the proportion of households that may be thought of as having "insufficient assets" for their retirement. In addition to summarizing the level of assets, we also study how assets at the end of life depend on family status pathways prior to death. We are particularly interested in the strong relationship between health and assets near the end of life. We also give special attention to the relationship between assets and longevity after the 1993 first wave of the AHEAD cohort. We find a strong relationship between health status and wealth at death.

Our chapter is divided into six sections. In the first, we show detailed balance sheets in 2008 for households by five-year age intervals—sixty-five to sixty-nine, seventy to seventy-four, seventy-five to seventy-nine, eighty to eighty-four, and eighty-five and older, respectively. These balance sheets are based on households in all HRS cohorts—HRS, AHEAD, Children of Depression (CODA), War Baby (WB) and Early Baby Boomer (EBB). We find that the change in assets with age, as well as the level of assets, differs greatly between single households and married couples.

We explore this pattern further by considering the evolution of assets of the AHEAD as well as the HRS cohorts, distinguishing two-person households, one-person households, and households that transition from two- to one-person households. We emphasize the distinction between the evolution of assets between survey waves for persons who are alive in adjacent waves, and the evolution of assets with age that can be attributed to "mortality selection effects" and the progressive selection over time of households with greater financial assets and lower mortality risk. We are also careful to distinguish between death and attrition as separate reasons why persons do not remain in the sample through 2008. The selection effects we calculate are due to death and not due to sample attrition.

In the second section, we present greater detail on the evolution of wealth for AHEAD households. We distinguish three family status pathways based on family status in 1993 (the first year observed) and family status when last observed: (1) original one-person households in 1993 who were also single at death; (2) original two-person households in 1993 in which one spouse is deceased in the last year observed; and (3) original two-person households in 1993 in which both spouses remain alive in the last year observed. A fourth group—those who were single in 1993 and who later remarried—is not analyzed because of its small sample size. Within each of these groups we show the evolution of wealth by the last year observed (LYO), which is the last wave prior to death for those who die, or 2008, the most recent survey wave available, for those who are still alive in that year. We highlight the strong relationship between wealth in 1993 and subsequent longevity. We consider several components of wealth—total wealth, financial assets including personal retirement accounts, housing wealth, and annuity wealth, including both Social Security benefits and defined-benefit pension benefits. We also report information on an indicator variable for whether the household owns a home.

In the third and fourth sections, we present results for the single-person family pathway group. We focus attention on this group because it is the largest of the three pathway groups and because it is the group most likely to have low wealth prior to death. In section three, we present estimates of the relationship between wealth and age, and between wealth and health, with separate estimates of the health and age effects for each LYO. The health measure we use is similar to the index developed in Poterba, Venti, and Wise (2010a, 2010b). Using the regression estimates we predict assets by health and age interval and by LYO. In section four, we show the distribution of assets by asset category within each health quintile and age interval. We also suggest metrics to help to put the results in context.

In the fifth section, we present data for all family pathway groups combined and we compare results across all three family pathways. The last section summarizes and concludes.

1.1   Balance Sheets and Evolution of Nonannuity Wealth by Family Status

Table 1.1 summarizes information in the HRS on household balance sheets for three age groups and for five aggregated asset categories—financial assets (balances in taxable financial assets as well as balances in IRA plans, Keogh plans, 401(k) and similar plans), equity in the primary home,

Table 1.1   Balance sheets for households in 2008, by age and marital status

	Single-person households			Two-person households		
Asset category	Percent of households with asset	Median holding	Mean holding	Percent of households with asset	Median holding	Mean holding
Aged 65 to 69 in 2008						
Financial assets	84.2	12,500	130,156	92.6	111,600	354,455
Home equity	65.9	52,000	107,483	91.1	150,000	232,300
Other nonannuity assets	18.8	0	96,357	38.8	0	171,441
PV of Social Security and DB pension benefits	90.5	268,766	315,165	92.3	571,575	617,767
Net worth	99.1	414,435	649,161	99.6	1,015,317	1,375,963
Aged 75 to 79 in 2008						
Financial assets	86.4	13,000	128,522	93.9	112,500	331,901
Home equity	65.7	60,000	123,144	88.9	151,000	228,371
Other nonannuity assets	15.2	0	47,447	31.7	0	198,979
PV of Social Security and DB pension benefits	99.0	200,303	243,304	99.9	460,509	525,772
Net worth	99.4	336,058	542,416	100.0	858,331	1,285,024
Aged 85 or older in 2008						
Financial assets	88.6	22,000	152,958	91.8	125,000	332,631
Home equity	54.1	35,000	101,728	84.8	125,000	210,917
Other nonannuity assets	13.3	0	45,294	28.2	0	155,145
PV of Social Security and DB pension benefits	99.0	82,855	108,582	99.7	224,317	284,348
Net worth	99.7	214,371	408,562	100.0	674,965	983,042

other nonannuity assets (the net value of other real estate, equity in second homes and business assets less nonhousing debt), the expected present discounted value of Social Security and defined-benefit pension benefits, and net worth (total wealth). These balance sheets are based on households in all HRS cohorts—HRS, AHEAD, Children of Depression (CODA), War Baby (WB), and Early Baby Boomer (EBB). The data on 401(k) balances in these tables are incomplete because respondents in the two oldest cohorts, CODA and AHEAD, were not asked for their 401(k) balances. However, these cohorts were unlikely to have substantial accumulations because they left the labor force before or shortly after 401(k) accounts became available in 1982. Members of the CODA cohort were age sixty-eight to seventy-four when first surveyed in 1998 and members of the AHEAD cohort were age seventy and older when first surveyed in 1993. Appendix tables 1A.1 through 1A.5 show detailed balance sheets in 2008 for households by five-year age intervals—sixty-five to sixty-nine, seventy to seventy-four, seventy-five to seventy-nine, eighty to eighty-four, and eighty-five and older, respectively.

Separate panels are shown for all households as well as for one-person and two-person households. Data are shown for both means and medians.

Several features of the summary data in table 1.1 warrant comment. First, whether measured by medians or means, the net worth of older households, even those aged eighty-five and older, seems rather large. The net worth of two-person households is more than twice as large as the net worth of one-person households. Median (mean) total net worth for households aged sixty-five to sixty-nine is $414,435 ($649,161) for singles and $1,015,317 ($1,375,963) for couples in 2008. Net worth is lower at older ages, in large part because of the decline in expected present value of benefits from Social Security and defined-benefit pensions. Wealth from these sources is lower for older households than for younger households because expected payments from these sources are weighted by survival probabilities.

We do not focus on cross-age comparisons in the balance sheets. The pattern of levels across ages depends on at least two competing effects: assets are lower for older households because of "cohort effects" (older generations had lower lifetime earnings, on average, than younger generations), and assets are higher for older households because of "mortality effects" (on average, within each cohort, poorer households die at younger ages). We give special attention to mortality effects in the subsequent analysis.

The largest components of nonannuity net worth are housing wealth and financial assets (including personal retirement accounts). Of single-person households, 66 percent of those aged sixty-five to sixty-nine own homes and this rate remains about the same for nearly twenty years; for the group aged eighty-five and older, the rate drops to 54 percent. About 91 percent of married couples aged sixty-five to sixty-nine own homes. Thereafter the rate drops gradually to about 89 percent for ages seventy-five to seventy-nine and 85 percent for those aged eighty-five and older.

Table 1.2 shows selected percentiles of the distribution of assets. It demonstrates that a large proportion of households have very few, or no, liquid financial assets. This is especially true for single-person households. The twenty-fifth percentile of financial assets for singles is less than $1,300 for all age groups. Many single-person households also have no home equity. The twenty-fifth percentile is zero for all age groups. In addition, a large fraction of both single- and two-person households have no other nonannuity assets. The seventy-fifth percentile is zero for single-households at all ages and the fiftieth percentile is zero for two-person households at all ages.

Recall that the balance sheets pertain to the wealth of those who survive to each age. In contrast, Figures 1.1 and 1.2 show the evolution of assets by family status—two-person households, one-person households, and households that transition from two- to one-person households during the interval between survey waves—for HRS and AHEAD households, respectively. The figures exclude persons in households that transitioned from one-person

Table 1.2   Selected percentiles of the distribution for households in 2008, by age and marital status

Asset category	Percentile	Single-person households			Two-person households		
		Age 65 to 69	Age 75 to 79	Age 85 or older	Age 65 to 69	Age 75 to 79	Age 85 or older
Financial assets	10	0	0	0	300	450	750
	25	300	500	1,300	13,500	11,000	27,000
	50	12,500	13,000	22,000	111,600	112,500	125,000
	75	110,721	110,000	133,500	442,000	355,715	402,000
	90	380,000	408,000	430,000	878,000	839,000	927,200
Home equity	10	0	0	0	7,000	0	0
	25	0	0	0	63,000	75,000	46,000
	50	52,000	60,000	35,000	150,000	151,000	125,000
	75	150,000	175,000	140,000	290,000	275,000	240,000
	90	300,000	345,000	300,000	450,000	475,000	438,000
Other nonannuity assets	10	-7,000	-5,000	0	-7,000	-3,700	0
	25	-1,000	0	0	-100	0	0
	50	0	0	0	0	0	0
	75	0	0	0	80,000	42,000	20,000
	90	80,000	60,000	80,000	450,000	400,000	500,000
PV of Social Security and DB pension benefits	10	37,796	97,040	38,288	128,811	257,448	118,705
	25	173,114	141,069	56,932	353,873	344,486	160,940
	50	268,766	200,303	82,855	571,575	460,509	224,317
	75	410,707	276,711	124,659	789,737	620,279	350,825
	90	610,166	410,850	196,096	1,155,331	840,320	478,903
Net worth	10	157,921	123,191	56,266	346,946	388,174	223,847
	25	237,154	193,157	93,411	609,949	566,980	350,801
	50	414,435	336,058	214,371	1,015,317	858,331	674,965
	75	778,662	662,494	470,768	1,660,631	1,443,753	1,177,966
	90	1,291,336	1,155,530	1,051,622	2,582,332	2,279,724	1,821,628

to two-person because the sample sizes for this group were too small to give reliable results. Wealth includes all assets reported in table 1.1 except Social Security wealth, defined-benefit pension wealth, and 401(k) balances. For the HRS cohort, 401(k) balances are not included because of missing data in some of the early years, as discussed in Venti (2011). Balances in 401(k) accounts were not collected in the AHEAD.

Figure 1.1 shows the wave-to-wave change in median nonannuity wealth in the three family status groups for HRS households. All values are converted to 2008 dollars using the Consumer Price Index (CPI). For example, the median wealth of persons who remained in two-person households between 1992 and 1994 (labeled as "2 to 2") increased from about $184,000 to $213,000. For those who remained in two-person households between 1994 and 1996, median wealth increased from about $223,000 to $231,000. In all intervals, wealth increased for persons in continuing two-person households.

It is important to distinguish between the within-interval changes in wealth shown by the line segments in the figure and the effect of differential mortality indicated by the vertical height of the "gaps" between segments. To illustrate this point, note that persons in two-person households present in both the 1996 and 1998 waves had $243,706 in wealth in 1998, but that persons in two-person households present in both the 1998 and 2000 waves had $254,419 in 1998. This difference is circled in the figure. The difference between $243,706 and $254,419 is the "selection" effect—two-person households that dissolved because of death of a spouse, divorce, or separation

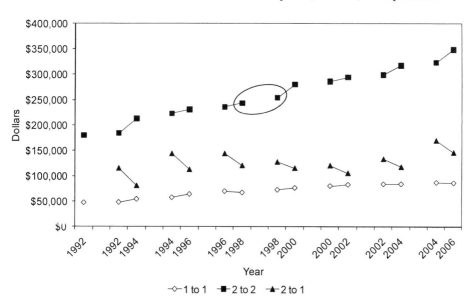

Fig. 1.1   Median nonannuity wealth of persons in the HRS, by family status

between 1998 and 2000 had lower wealth in 1998 than those who continued as two-person households through the 1998 to 2000 period.

To understand the evolution of wealth with age, as distinct from the selection effect, it is important to focus on the wave-to-wave changes (segment slopes). For two-person households in the HRS who were between the ages of fifty-one and sixty-one in 1992, the wave-to-wave changes are positive in all intervals. The increase in wealth for persons in continuing two-person households can be seen by tracking the assets in the first year of each interval. Some component of this increase is due to the progressive selection of households with greater wealth. For one-person households wealth increased in all but two wave-to-wave intervals. The mortality selection effects are not so apparent for single-person households, in part because a large fraction of one-person households had relatively low wealth, with median levels between $50,000 and $100,000 over the 1992 to 2008 period.

Figure 1.1 also shows that the nonannuity wealth of persons in two-person households that dissolve between waves declines substantially. This is observed in each of the intervals. The assets of persons in two- to one-person households were also much lower at the beginning of an interval than the assets of persons in continuing two-person households. After dissolution, however, the wealth of the surviving single persons was still larger than the wealth of continuing one-person households.

Figure 1.2 shows the evolution of nonannuity wealth for persons in AHEAD households. The data for 1993 are omitted from the figure because, as Rohwedder, Haider, and Hurd (2006) explain, financial assets were underreported in AHEAD in that year. For the AHEAD households, the mortality selection effects are extremely important (circles in the figure). Persons who continued in two-person households from one interval to the next typically held much greater wealth balances than those who did not. For AHEAD households, the within-interval change in wealth for persons in continuing two-person households was negative in all but the first interval, 1995 to 1998. The wealth of continuing one-person households declined in each period. For AHEAD households the decline in the wealth for persons in two-person households that dissolved during an interval is similar in magnitude to the decline for persons in continuing two-person households. For these households dissolution was primarily the consequence of mortality, whereas for HRS households dissolution was more often the consequence of divorce or separation. As with the HRS cohort, the level of wealth of persons in two-person households that dissolved during an interval was much lower than the level of wealth of persons in continuing two-person households. Among persons in households that dissolved in an interval the wealth of the surviving spouse remained much higher than the wealth of continuing one-person households.

In short, the figures show the within-interval change in the wealth of households that survive over the interval, but they also make clear that

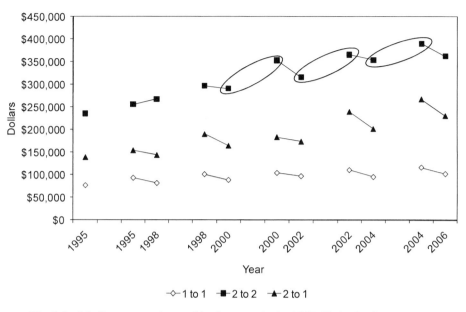

Fig. 1.2   Median nonannuity wealth of persons in the AHEAD, by family status

some of the change from interval to interval is due to the progressive selection of households with greater wealth. This effect plays a key role in the subsequent analysis.

1.2   The Evolution of Wealth for AHEAD Households

The remainder of the chapter focuses on AHEAD households. The goal is to describe the evolution of wealth by family pathway group and by asset category from 1993 to 2008 and to consider the wealth of persons in the last year observed (LYO). All persons last observed in years before 2008 are known to be deceased—persons who leave the sample but are not known to be deceased are excluded from the analysis. Persons whose last year observed is 2008 are not deceased. Most waves are spaced two years apart, with the exception of a three-year gap between the 1995 and 1998 waves. Thus for persons who have an LYO before 2008, the last observation may be up to two years before the actual date of death (or three years if the LYO is 1995.)

We begin by dividing the AHEAD respondents into three groups defined by family status when first observed in 1993 and family status in the LYO. These groups, which we call "family pathway groups," are: (1) original one-person households in 1993, (2) persons in two-person households in 1993 with a deceased spouse in the last year observed before death, and (3) persons in two-person households in 1993 with the spouse alive when last observed. For shorthand we sometimes refer to the groups as one-person, two-person

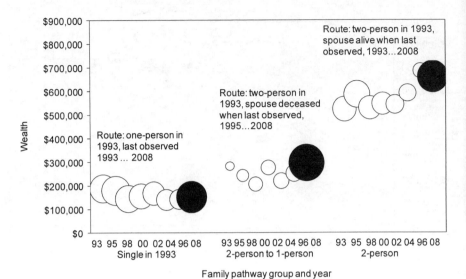

Fig. 1.3   Total wealth in year last observed by route to death and percentage of observations (circle size)

to one-person, and two-person, respectively. A fourth group of persons, in a one-person household in 1993 and in a two-person household when last observed, is excluded because this group is too small for meaningful analysis. Also, all persons who joined the AHEAD sample after 1993 are excluded. Some persons in one-person households in 1993 may have been in two-person households prior to 1993. Figure 1.3 is a graphical description of the total wealth (including the present values of Social Security and DB pension benefits) and the relative size of each of these groups in each LYO. For each family progression group, the location of each circle indicates the level of median wealth (shown on the vertical axis) and the associated LYO (shown on the horizontal axis). The size of each circle indicates the percent of the total sample in each LYO group accounted for by the particular subgroup.

In each family progression group, the wealth and the percent of persons last observed in 2008 (not deceased) is represented by the black circles. The other circles indicate wealth in the last wave prior to death. One-person households in 1993 died with the least wealth, between $142,000 and $188,000 at the median. Those in two-person households in 1993 with a spouse alive when they died had the greatest wealth in the wave prior to death, between $585,000 and $685,000. Those in two-person households in 1993 whose spouse was deceased when last observed had median wealth in the wave prior to death between $206,000 and $286,000.

A general feature of the data is the strong and consistent relationship between wealth in 1993 and survival, the year a person is last observed in the data. Among persons first observed in 1993, those who will die the earliest begin with the lowest assets in 1993. The relationship holds for all

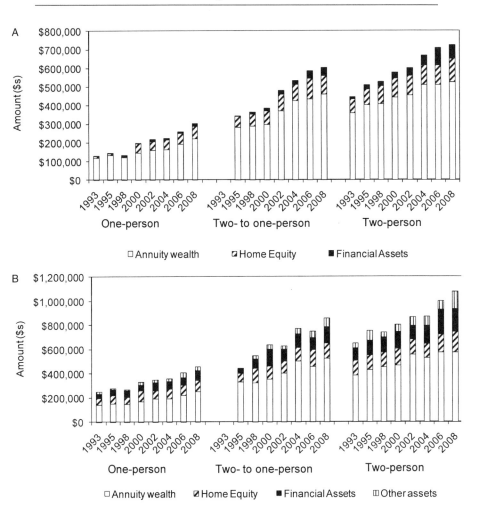

Fig. 1.4   *A*, Median annuity wealth, home equity, and financial assets in 1993 by family route and last year observed; *B*, Mean annuity wealth, home equity, financial assets, and other wealth in 1993 by family route and last year observed

asset categories. Figure 1.4, panel A, shows the relationship for three of the four asset categories shown in table 1.1—annuity wealth, home equity, and financial assets—for each of the family progression groups. The figure shows medians for each asset category in 1993. The fourth category in table 1.1, other nonannuity assets, is not shown because the median is zero in all years for all groups. Because medians are used in the figure, the stacked vertical height of the bars in the figure is not equal to median total wealth. Panel B of figure 1.4 shows means for all four categories. In the subsequent discussion we often show medians and not means.

For each of the groups, Social Security and defined-benefit pension wealth is by far the largest wealth holding. The relationship between wealth when first observed and subsequent mortality is striking. For example, the rising profiles within each group shows that annuity wealth in 1993 is higher for persons who die prior to the 2000 wave (whose LYO is 1998) than for persons who die prior to the 1998 wave (whose LYO is 1995). Similarly, persons who die prior to the 2002 wave have higher annuity wealth in 1993 than persons who die prior to the 2000 wave, and so forth. Similar patterns are evident for the home equity and financial assets. The wealth-mortality gradient that has been widely observed by others is strongly evident in these data. Examples of previous studies that have found strong positive correlation between wealth and longevity include Smith (1999, 2004, 2005); Adams et al. (2003); Wu (2003); Michaud and van Soest (2008); Case and Deaton (2005); Attanasio and Emmerson (2003); and Hurd, McFadden, and Merrill (2001).

We do not address the direction of causality between health and wealth or between wealth and mortality, although here and elsewhere in the chapter we often implicitly assume that health is given and subsequent outcomes follow. This assumption is consistent with the findings of Smith (1999, 2004, 2005); Adams et al. (2003); Wu (2003); Michaud and van Soest (2008); and Case and Deaton (2005). The general consensus is that causation from health to wealth is the dominant pathway, at least in the United States, but there is no universal agreement.

Figure 1.4 shows that persons "closer" to death in 1993 have lower assets in 1993 than those who will live longer. We can see the same pattern over time by showing how assets evolve over time for groups of persons identified by the last year observed in the sample. Again, an LYO of 2006 or earlier indicates that the person died in the two-year interval following the LYO. An LYO of 2008 indicates that the person is still alive in 2008, the last year of our sample. The next series of figures show the evolution of assets for several wealth subcategories—total wealth, financial assets (including IRA and Keogh accounts), home equity, Social Security wealth, and defined-benefit pension wealth. We also show the percentage of households who own their homes and the evolution of total income. There is one figure for each wealth category, with data for each of three family pathway groups. For each figure the evolution of median wealth is shown by LYO.

Figure 1.5 shows median total wealth for the three family pathway groups. Total wealth in 1993 is lowest for the first family pathway group (one-person households) and highest for the third pathway group (two-person households with a spouse alive when last observed). In each of the groups, total wealth in 1993 is very strongly related to the LYO. Those who live longer have higher wealth. In addition, total wealth typically declines as persons get "closer" to death for each of the groups, largely because of the mechanical decline in annuity wealth. But the decline is much slower for the persons in two-person families who have a spouse alive when last observed, a group that also has much greater wealth in 1993.

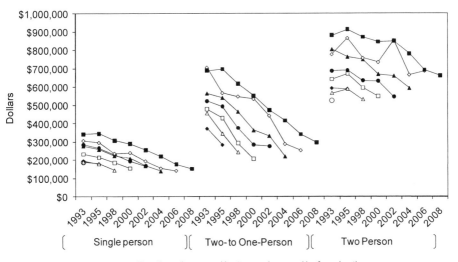

Fig. 1.5   Median total wealth by family pathway and by last year observed before death

Figure 1.6 shows the evolution of financial assets (including IRA and Keogh accounts) for the three pathway groups. The vertical line between 1993 and 1995 is a reminder that some financial assets were underreported in 1993, although we present the data because IRA and Keogh assets are not underreported. Again, the financial assets of the first group decline quite systematically after 1995 and the financial assets of the second group typically decline as well, at least after 1998. The decline is in part induced by the minimum distribution requirement for 401(k) and non-Roth IRA accounts. Nonetheless, there is much less decline in the financial assets of the third pathway group.

Figure 1.7 shows the evolution of home equity. For one-person households the data show a very sharp decline in median home equity beginning two or three years before death. Indeed, for each LYO, median home equity in the wave prior to death was zero for all but those whose LYO was 1993. For original two-person households with the spouse deceased at the LYO, a sharp decline near the end of life is also apparent, although the median at death is zero only for those whose LYO was 2002 or 2004. For original two-person households with the spouse alive at the LYO, there is a decline in home equity in the year or two before death, but it is more modest than that for the previous two groups. Home equity declines relatively little in prior years for this group. The results are consistent with the findings of Venti and Wise (2002, 2004) who emphasize that home equity tends to be husbanded until a precipitating shock such as entry to a nursing home or death of a spouse.

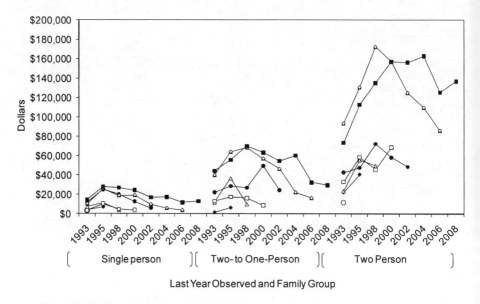

Fig. 1.6   Median financial wealth by family progression group and last year observed

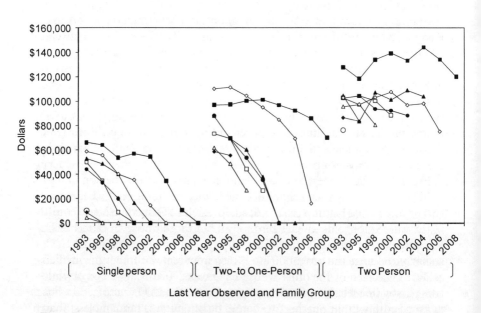

Fig. 1.7   Median housing wealth by family progression group and last year observed

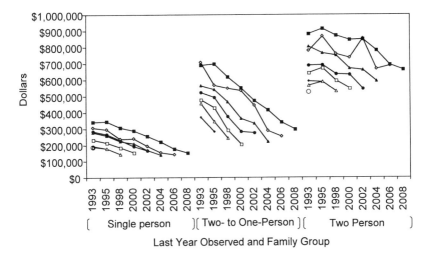

Fig. 1.8   Home ownership rate by family progression group and last year observed

Figure 1.8 shows the evolution of home ownership rates. The decline in ownership seems more consistent over time than the decline in housing wealth for all family pathway groups. Housing wealth typically declined sharply near the end of life. The decline in ownership between 1993 and the year last observed was greatest for the one-person and the two- to one-person family groups. For the one-person group the decline ranged from –3.4 percent for persons whose LYO was 1995 to –39.9 percent for persons whose LYO was 2006. For the two- to one-person group, the decline ranged from –0.1 percent for persons whose LYO was 1995 to –31.6 percent for persons whose LYO was 2006. For the two-person group, however, the decline was less than 3 percent through 2000 and then ranged from –6.9 percent for persons whose LYO was 2002 to –11.5 percent for persons whose LYO was 2006.

The evolution of Social Security wealth is shown in figure 1.9. The pattern of decline for each group is a mechanical feature of the way annuity wealth is calculated: benefits in each future year are weighted by the probability of survival. As an individual ages, the present value of remaining benefits declines because the probability of surviving for any number of years declines. Like each of the other wealth categories, the Social Security wealth data show that wealth in 1993 is very strongly related to year of death. The data also show that one-person households have substantially less Social Security wealth in 1993 than persons in the second pathway whose spouse had died before the LYO, who in turn have less wealth than the third pathway group—persons in two-person households whose spouse is alive when last observed. These data are consistent with the large literature cited earlier showing the strong relationship between measures of SES such as life-

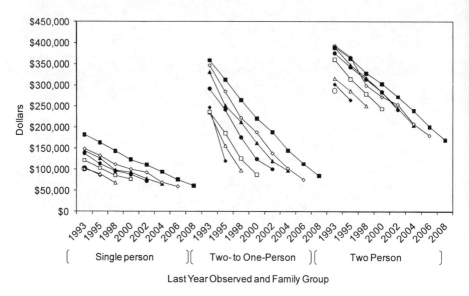

Fig. 1.9   Median Social Security wealth by family progression group and last year observed

time earnings (the primary determinant of Social Security benefits) and mortality.

Figure 1.10 shows the evolution of defined-benefit pension wealth. Single persons in the first pathway group essentially have no DB pension wealth. The median is zero for all one-person households except for those who survive to 2008. But persons who were in two-person households in 1993 with the spouse deceased by the LYO do have substantial median DB wealth in 1993, and persons in two-person households in 1993 with the spouse alive in the LYO had even more DB wealth. Most of the persons in the second group had zero or close to zero DB wealth at death, but persons in the third group still had noticeable DB wealth at death. Part of the explanation for the very low level of DB wealth among persons in the two-person to one-person group apparently lies with the waiver of survivorship benefits. The Employee Retirement Income Security Act (ERISA, 1974) requires employers to offer joint and survivor annuities as the default option, and the Retirement Equity Act (1984) requires written consent to waive survivor benefits. Nonetheless, Johnson, Uccello, and Goldwyn (2005) report that in 2000, 28 percent of men and 69 percent of women covered by DB plans had waived survivor benefits. Even if survivor benefits are not waived, the surviving spouse's benefit is often less than 100 percent of the deceased's benefit. The implications of the husband's death for the finances of widows is discussed further in Hurd and Wise (1989); Weir and Willis (2000); and Sevak, Weir, and Willis (2003).

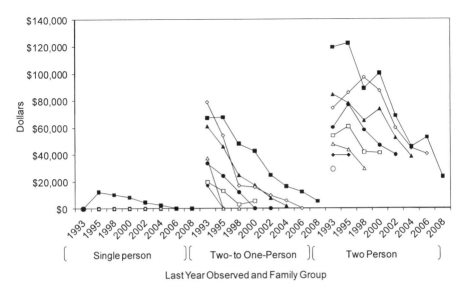

Fig. 1.10   Median DB wealth by family progression group and last year observed

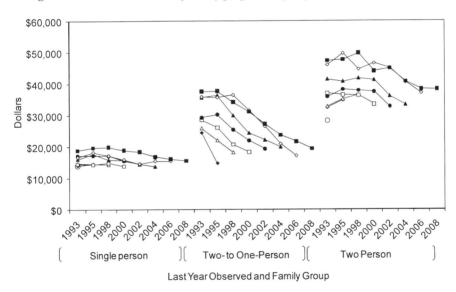

Fig. 1.11   Median total income by family progression group and last year observed

Finally, Figure 1.11 shows the evolution of total household income for persons in each of the three pathway groups. We will discuss the level and path of total income in more detail in the next section, but we include the pathway figure here because it is in the same format as the figures for asset categories. The figure shows little decline for the one-person group, a mod-

Table 1.3   Percent change in total income from 1993 to year last observed by family pathway group and by YLO

	Year last observed						
Family pathway group	1995 (%)	1998 (%)	2000 (%)	2002 (%)	2004 (%)	2006 (%)	2008 (%)
One-person	4.4	5.7	0.5	−2.3	−10.8	−14.5	−17.6
Two- to one-person	0.4	−8.9	−17.1	−27.4	−36.9	−42.4	−48.5
Two-person	0.6	5.0	−7.2	−5.3	−14.0	−19.1	−19.2

est decline for the two-person group, and a substantial decline for the two- to one-person group. The percent decline between 1993 and the year last observed is shown in table 1.3. As might be expected, the decline is especially large for persons in the two- to one-person family pathway group. For persons last observed in 2008 the decline is −48.5 percent.

1.3   The Effect of Health and Age: The Single-Person Pathway

In the previous section we emphasized the strong relationship between wealth in 1993 and the time until death. In this section we emphasize the relationship between wealth and health, given the year last observed, and we draw attention to the strong relationship between health and wealth just prior to death.

We begin by using a simple median regression framework to describe how the level of assets in the last year observed depends on age and health. For each person we construct an index of health based on the first principal component of responses to twenty-seven health-related questions contained in AHEAD. These questions asked about functional limitations, the presence of health conditions, and other indicators of overall health. The list of questions used to construct the index and a discussion of the properties of the index are reported in Poterba, Venti, and Wise (2010a). There are two differences between our approach in the current chapter and that in our past work. First, the earlier paper constructed an index for each wave using information from the contemporaneous and all preceding waves. The index used here only uses contemporaneous wave information. Many of the questions are of the form "have you ever experienced" a health condition, so there is little extra information obtained by using prior wave information. Second, the principal component estimates varied little from wave to wave, so in the present analysis we have pooled the waves.

In the median regression estimates following, we use percentiles of the index where the first percentile is the poorest health and the one hundredth percentile corresponds to the best health. The index used pertains to health in the last year observed. We present estimates of the effect of health and age on wealth in the LYO, with separate estimates of the health and age effects for each LYO.

Table 1.4 shows median regression estimates for the single-person pathway group. The age and health effects are statistically significant for all LYOs. The estimated effect of a 10 percentile increase in health and the effect of an additional year of age are graphed in figure 1.12. The effect of health on wealth in the last year observed is substantial. The estimated effect of an increase of 10 percentile points in health ranges from $7,530 in 1993 to $28,004 in 2006. Thus, persons who have better health when last observed prior to death have much more wealth. Recall that these estimated effects are conditional on LYO, which is also related to health. For persons last observed in 2008, the estimated health effect is $17,340. The effect of an additional year of age on wealth ranges from –$10,596 in 1993 to –$5,570

Table 1.4	Median regression estimates of the effect of health and age on wealth in the last year observed for single-person households		
Variable	Coefficient	Std. error	t-stat
Last year observed			
1995	–157,361	132,956	–1.18
1998	–147,607	142,618	–1.03
2000	–361,097	163,023	–2.22
2002	–342,259	172,101	–1.99
2004	–301,661	202,467	–1.49
2006	–463,905	232,967	–1.99
2008	39,185	188,511	0.21
Effect of health in each year			
1993	753	324	2.32
1995	1,109	310	3.58
1998	1,730	371	4.67
2000	1,412	355	3.98
2002	1,738	425	4.09
2004	1,390	436	3.19
2006	2,800	508	5.51
2008	1,734	267	6.49
Effect of age in each year			
1993	–10,596	1,096	–9.66
1995	–8,811	1,120	–7.87
1998	–9,236	1,252	–7.38
2000	–6,652	1,528	–4.35
2002	–6,737	1,636	–4.12
2004	–7,275	1,986	–3.66
2006	–5,570	2,377	–2.34
2008	–11,125	1,810	–6.14
Constant	1,046,502	91,989	11.38

Note: $N = 3,003$ and pseudo $R^2 = 0.0562$.

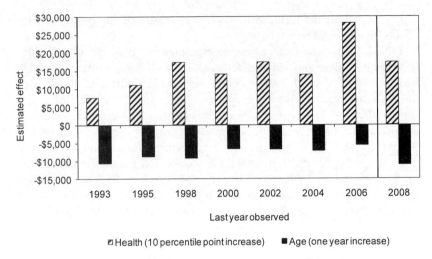

Fig. 1.12   Estimated effect of health and age on total wealth for original single-person households, by last year observed

in 2006. The age effect is –$11,125 for those who are last observed in 2008. Those who are last observed in 2008 have substantially more wealth than those who die before 2008.

To get an idea of how much wealth in the LYO varies by health and age, we use the estimated effects from the median regression to predict total wealth for selected health percentiles and for selected ages. Table 1.5 shows predicted total wealth for every other LYO between 1993 and 2006. The estimates show the very large effects of health, as well as age, on wealth in the LYO. The pattern is quite similar in each of the LYO panels.

These results suggest that persons who die at older ages and in poorer health are likely to die with less wealth than persons who die young and in good health. We are particularly interested in the proportion of people that die with little wealth. Without trying to define what "little" is, we begin by calculating selected percentiles of total wealth and selected categories of wealth in the last year observed by health quintile and by age interval. Unlike the previous table, these percentiles are based on actual data rather than predictions from the median regression.

Table 1.6 shows the percentiles combining all LYOs between 1993 and 2006 (the LYOs associated with death) for original single-person households. One cell in the lower left is blank because it contains fewer than ten observations. The small cell size reflects the fact that the young and healthy are least likely to die. The shaded cells help to identify cell entries with less that $100,000 of wealth. There are twenty-five such cells. All are for persons older than age eighty and twenty-one of the twenty-five are for persons eighty-five and older. Seventeen of the twenty-five are for persons in the

Table 1.5   **Predicted wealth by last year observed, health, and age for original single-person households**

Health percentile	Age				
	70	75	80	85	90
		Last year observed: 1993			
10	312,294	259,313	206,331	153,349	100,368
30	327,362	274,380	221,399	168,417	115,436
50	342,429	289,448	236,466	183,485	130,503
70	357,497	304,515	251,534	198,552	145,571
90	372,565	319,583	266,602	213,620	160,638
		Last year observed: 1998			
10	269,706	223,528	177,350	131,172	84,994
30	304,316	258,138	211,960	165,781	119,603
50	338,926	292,747	246,569	200,391	154,213
70	373,535	327,357	281,179	235,001	188,823
90	408,145	361,967	315,789	269,611	223,433
		Last year observed: 2002			
10	250,069	216,387	182,704	149,021	115,339
30	284,837	251,154	217,472	183,789	150,106
50	319,605	285,922	252,239	218,557	184,874
70	354,372	320,690	287,007	253,324	219,642
90	389,140	355,457	321,775	288,092	254,409
		Last year observed: 2006			
10	220,711	192,861	165,012	137,163	109,314
30	276,718	248,868	221,019	193,170	165,321
50	332,725	304,876	277,026	249,177	221,328
70	388,732	360,883	333,033	305,184	277,335
90	444,739	416,890	389,041	361,191	333,342

bottom three health quintiles and twelve of twenty-five are for persons in the bottom two quintiles. Only eight are for persons in the top two health quintiles. Thus, dying with "little" wealth is clearly concentrated among older persons who are also less healthy.

Table 1.7 shows the distribution of annuity wealth in the last year observed before death by health quintile and age interval. Levels less than $50,000 are highlighted. The decline in annuity wealth by age is largely mechanical and is reflected in the concentration of low annuity wealth among persons who are aged ninety or older. But the differences across health quintiles indicate the large differences in percentiles by health status. For example, over all age intervals, the twenty-fifth percentiles range from $49,795 for persons in the lowest health quintile to $119,704 for persons in the top quintile.

Table 1.8 shows the distribution of nonannuity wealth by health quintile and by age interval. A large fraction of single-person households have essentially no nonannuity wealth, particularly those in the bottom two health quintiles. In these health groups, the twenty-fifth percentile is zero or close

Table 1.6   Selected percentiles of the distribution of total wealth by age interval and health quintile for original single-person households, based on actual data

Health quintile	Percentile	Age interval					
		70–74	75–79	80–84	85–89	90+	All
1st	10	146,504	113,251	76,147	45,965	30,435	41,245
	25	226,187	140,603	105,001	64,086	43,329	68,885
	50	289,289	190,574	169,315	111,297	74,131	141,767
	75	400,516	325,225	263,544	225,118	215,388	271,178
	90	611,455	634,392	412,432	468,717	491,710	489,875
2nd	10	151,751	122,305	83,788	50,762	22,337	42,682
	25	198,163	178,408	126,530	84,101	41,995	84,109
	50	259,629	268,122	194,964	148,420	97,552	169,308
	75	430,948	422,380	295,601	282,716	205,091	295,601
	90	529,604	957,304	441,308	467,657	400,654	484,527
3rd	10	151,813	170,324	83,137	53,708	33,517	59,240
	25	173,241	205,106	115,090	80,575	66,561	103,906
	50	265,021	298,352	232,848	135,976	130,760	194,578
	75	376,713	499,910	512,820	284,931	364,276	394,142
	90	441,416	897,024	847,482	545,362	770,434	763,727
4th	10	151,281	104,359	82,397	73,714	33,549	62,765
	25	310,036	177,720	121,934	89,622	56,037	113,915
	50	393,199	308,350	238,307	196,087	117,708	211,847
	75	501,495	461,537	425,897	334,731	241,294	398,834
	90	659,133	690,508	560,694	615,394	718,681	618,513
5th	10		113,930	181,567	51,116	30,700	86,427
	25		137,305	228,253	101,239	82,943	137,305
	50		419,738	331,494	154,716	178,331	297,729
	75		589,394	643,717	297,729	307,344	592,381
	90		1,728,930	1,035,252	876,750	580,655	1,122,089
All	10	151,281	116,460	80,674	50,234	28,603	44,509
	25	198,785	159,336	117,758	75,127	44,509	81,537
	50	293,117	250,722	189,450	133,062	90,477	166,904
	75	442,282	428,277	320,667	264,543	230,651	311,081
	90	610,956	735,176	532,784	508,185	520,890	580,655

to zero for all age intervals. Even for the higher health quintiles the tenth percentile is zero averaged over all age intervals.

Perhaps a better way to judge whether persons have "low" resources at death is to look at resources immediately available for day-to-day expenses. Table 1.9 shows the distribution of total income in the last year observed before death by health quintile and age interval.

Total income includes benefits from Social Security and defined-benefit pension plans, government transfer income, and dividends, interest payments, rent received, and other income from assets. Again, the relationship between health and income is quite pronounced. Even controlling for age

Table 1.7   **Selected percentiles of the distribution of annuity wealth by age interval and health quintile for original single-person households, based on actual data**

Health quintile	Percentile	Age interval 70–74	75–79	80–84	85–89	90+	All
1st	10	146,504	84,462	67,373	39,226	19,763	32,939
	25	182,397	119,670	87,452	53,120	33,127	49,795
	50	216,478	156,883	122,644	75,127	46,334	84,024
	75	282,159	200,956	172,217	104,866	65,745	140,074
	90	377,282	261,551	222,440	157,881	95,294	210,203
2nd	10	148,035	119,461	68,332	39,576	16,836	32,194
	25	162,059	133,168	95,812	55,257	31,063	49,626
	50	220,464	204,342	139,005	87,861	43,734	90,542
	75	287,001	303,756	181,787	115,311	63,601	152,832
	90	447,557	390,558	243,032	165,576	86,446	232,899
3rd	10	119,705	126,846	53,078	48,710	25,754	35,450
	25	148,999	160,141	81,537	64,803	35,450	62,783
	50	173,241	202,302	120,631	87,226	51,376	103,906
	75	287,228	267,148	183,379	112,799	90,138	175,249
	90	338,406	374,556	255,310	175,742	150,621	261,526
4th	10	149,020	78,089	54,787	47,065	26,932	42,615
	25	198,785	137,287	102,542	59,469	38,403	62,909
	50	264,892	193,126	126,194	83,256	53,681	108,879
	75	388,554	224,004	189,339	113,048	74,544	177,660
	90	422,514	262,745	297,670	149,315	131,100	262,745
5th	10		94,456	64,562	35,307	25,417	37,543
	25		115,549	104,903	58,256	30,690	86,713
	50		182,547	129,124	89,660	52,569	119,704
	75		223,477	192,981	128,086	93,537	197,206
	90		416,116	363,229	192,280	139,621	307,168
All	10	137,815	100,415	64,540	39,576	20,482	33,407
	25	171,467	132,378	90,512	55,968	33,348	53,120
	50	219,310	176,458	126,979	81,725	46,697	92,262
	75	284,306	231,936	178,023	110,868	67,334	154,082
	90	408,161	345,033	243,032	164,827	101,357	228,345

and health, total income varies considerably within each cell. The ninetieth percentile is typically at least four times as large as the tenth percentile. Of particular interest is the association between health and total income summarized in the last column. The tenth percentile of total income is surprisingly similar across all levels of health—between $7,342 for persons in the lowest health quintile and $8,718 for persons in the top health quintile. However, health has a more depressive effect at higher percentiles. The ninetieth percentile of total income for persons in the poorest health quintile is only $32,541, but the ninetieth percentile for persons in the top health quintile is $61,494.

Table 1.8   Selected percentiles of the distribution of nonannuity wealth by age interval and health quintile for original single-person households, based on actual data

Health quintile	Percentile	Age interval					
		70–74	75–79	80–84	85–89	90+	All
1st	10	0	0	0	0	0	0
	25	51	0	184	73	115	56
	50	45,844	11,021	20,259	16,692	16,165	16,692
	75	136,583	126,857	101,098	122,901	148,621	126,579
	90	337,745	401,714	206,677	322,781	394,736	310,659
2nd	10	0	0	0	0	0	0
	25	1,391	1,669	605	3,464	0	848
	50	38,180	58,738	42,985	47,293	24,338	44,511
	75	125,188	199,710	138,035	164,180	160,536	155,743
	90	161,530	340,609	243,986	329,213	338,341	326,323
3rd	10	0	0	0	0	0	0
	25	4,405	8,811	5,564	670	6,695	3,027
	50	43,259	110,155	88,401	37,986	53,690	70,272
	75	161,530	186,494	316,551	166,327	276,853	211,569
	90	232,292	572,698	685,591	417,742	584,826	584,826
4th	10	1,028	727	1,717	506	190	506
	25	2,261	33,506	23,495	10,279	4,405	10,279
	50	88,034	113,819	63,310	96,362	70,969	87,631
	75	170,728	225,384	214,759	290,754	151,311	225,384
	90	273,867	528,644	344,849	561,945	682,263	487,412
5th	10	27,819	734	18,163	0	0	734
	25	120,514	22,792	63,504	18,242	57,579	27,819
	50	199,465	177,683	174,076	81,037	151,312	145,613
	75	393,645	308,796	506,481	192,525	235,284	365,620
	90	4,384,988	1,523,115	671,987	365,620	441,034	696,237
All	10	0	0	0	0	0	0
	25	1,391	556	693	974	462	644
	50	58,052	58,560	44,188	37,558	26,163	39,648
	75	160,657	186,494	142,440	154,188	155,789	158,007
	90	325,488	468,666	354,847	365,620	404,116	382,018

We next consider summary measures of financial resources that focus on the joint distribution of annuity income and liquid financial assets. The top panel of table 1.10 shows the selected points on the bivariate cumulative distribution of annuity income and liquid financial assets (including IRA accounts) in the LYO (again combining all LYO between 1993 and 2006). For convenience, the diagonals are shown in bold. The upper-left entry in the table shows, for example, that 12.1 percent of single-person households have less than $10,000 in annuity income and no financial assets in the last year observed. The entry below it shows that 23.9 percent of households have less than $10,000 in annuity income and less than $10,000 in financial assets.

Table 1.9   Selected percentiles of the distribution of total income by age interval and health quintile for original single-person households, based on actual data

Health quintile	Percentile	70–74	75–79	80–84	85–89	90+	All
1st	10	8,847	7,730	7,597	6,992	7,177	7,342
	25	11,684	9,648	9,251	9,214	9,422	9,480
	50	16,353	12,791	14,071	13,219	13,040	13,341
	75	23,648	19,197	20,441	19,505	19,973	19,935
	90	31,225	36,968	29,344	33,890	33,487	32,541
2nd	10	8,179	9,715	7,979	7,177	6,534	7,597
	25	10,978	11,965	11,084	9,876	9,498	10,332
	50	18,862	18,077	15,877	15,452	13,440	15,012
	75	28,758	30,250	21,808	24,665	20,390	23,931
	90	83,614	51,954	34,577	39,745	36,232	38,631
3rd	10	8,482	10,978	6,510	8,000	8,421	8,179
	25	9,075	13,810	9,898	10,555	10,662	10,662
	50	13,353	21,525	15,802	14,253	14,264	15,802
	75	21,699	29,463	28,376	23,009	24,264	26,651
	90	26,705	49,487	47,586	37,734	44,434	42,780
4th	10	10,749	7,628	8,838	8,112	7,785	8,124
	25	17,621	10,610	12,353	10,623	10,680	10,783
	50	22,432	16,904	17,809	14,840	15,814	16,887
	75	27,272	33,481	29,057	22,623	27,672	26,009
	90	33,994	72,054	35,681	40,342	54,600	47,314
5th	10	8,936	8,346	11,087	6,911	8,718	8,718
	25	13,320	12,335	13,798	10,015	11,102	12,335
	50	20,586	21,146	22,342	18,483	19,472	20,586
	75	47,216	43,383	30,410	30,518	28,329	33,283
	90	341,744	79,189	46,596	33,383	47,215	61,494
All	10	8,413	8,282	7,774	7,177	7,265	7,634
	25	11,219	10,916	10,516	9,560	9,641	10,059
	50	16,952	15,935	15,423	14,097	13,440	14,344
	75	26,009	27,255	23,123	21,849	21,018	22,806
	90	32,692	51,625	34,194	36,390	36,513	37,209

More than half of all households (57 percent) have less than $10,000 in financial assets in the last year we observe them. As a point of reference, the 2008 poverty threshold for single persons aged sixty-five and older is about $10,000. The table also shows that 52.0 percent of single-person households have annuity income less than $20,000 (about twice the poverty level) and financial assets less than $10,000. Although not shown in the table, the percentage of single-person households with annuity income less that $15,000 (about one and one-half times the poverty level) and financial assets less than $5,000 is 39.6 percent. Over all financial asset levels, 31.9 percent have annuity income less than $10,000 and 82 percent of households have less

Table 1.10   Selected characteristics of single-person households, by annuity income
                    and financial assets in the last year observed before death

Financial assets ($000s)	Annuity income ($000s)				
	<$10	<$20	<$30	<$40	All
	Percentage distribution				
Zero	**12.1**	23.0	24.2	24.7	24.9
<$10	23.9	**52.0**	55.7	56.4	57.0
<$25	26.3	58.8	**64.5**	65.7	66.5
<$50	27.9	65.5	72.8	**74.4**	75.4
All	31.9	82.0	94.1	97.7	100.0

Financial asset interval ($000s)	Annuity income interval ($000s)				
	$0–$10	$10–$20	$20–$30	$30–$40	All
	Percent of households with zero home equity				
Zero	**76.3**	69.8	74.8	63.6	73.1
$0–$10	62.9	**63.3**	57.8	53.8	61.2
$10–$25	49.8	46.8	**52.2**	53.5	50.0
$25–$50	48.6	47.2	48.3	**47.0**	47.7
All	63.7	57.7	53.9	47.6	57.1
	Mean health percentile				
Zero	**24.1**	24.8	22.4	28.3	24.5
$0–$10	23.4	**28.2**	24.3	26.2	25.6
$10–$25	28.5	33.3	**38.3**	35.6	33.5
$25–$50	26.6	25.3	26.8	**43.3**	30.2
All	25.1	28.4	29.5	33.4	28.5

than $20,000 of annuity income. Of this latter group, 23 percent also has
no financial assets.

Home equity is an illiquid asset that households tend to hold through late
life. Venti and Wise (2004) and several other studies find that households
typically sell their homes only when confronted with a precipitating shock
to family structure, like death of a spouse or entry into a nursing home. By
the time single-person AHEAD households approach the last year observed,
many have divested their housing wealth, as shown earlier in figure 1.7.

The middle panel of table 1.10 shows the proportion of single-person
households with zero housing wealth (including persons with negative home
equity) by annuity income and financial asset *intervals* that are comparable
to the cumulative levels in the first panel. For example, of persons with annuity income less than $10,000 and no financial assets, 76.3 percent have no
housing wealth. Of persons with $30,000 to $40,000 in annuity income and
$25,000 to $50,000 in financial assets, 47.0 percent have no housing equity.
Overall, 57.1 percent of persons in the single-household family pathway
have no housing equity in the last year observed before death. The bottom
panel of table 1.10 shows the mean health percentile of persons in each of

the annuity income/financial asset intervals. For example, the mean health percentile of persons with annuity income less than $10,000 and no financial assets is 24.1. For those with annuity income between $30,000 and $40,000 and financial assets between $25,000 and $50,000 the median health percentile is 43.3. Thus again the strong relationship between health and wealth is evident.

In short, we find that a large fraction of original single-person households has no housing wealth and very limited financial assets in the last year observed before death. This suggests that the sole source of wealth for many persons is the value of annuity benefits. Most persons receive Social Security benefits (either directly or as a survivor) and about half receive income from a DB pension (again, either directly or as a survivor).

1.4 Compared to What?

It is not clear how we should judge what constitutes a "low" or "sufficient" level of either assets or income. In table 1.9 we highlighted the distribution of total income by health quintile and age, showing the level of income for persons at the tenth, twenty-fifth, fiftieth, seventy-fifth, and ninetieth percentiles with wealth below given levels. At all ages and for all levels of health, total income at the tenth percentile was between $7,000 and $10,000. In table 1.10 we showed the percentage of single-person households with annuity income below levels that were chosen to approximate multiples of the poverty threshold in 2008 (about $10,000).

We will now provide some rough benchmarks to give context to these income levels just before death. First, we compare total income in the year last observed with total income in 1993 when these persons were first observed in AHEAD. The top panel of table 1.11 shows median total income by age interval and health quintile in the last year observed before death (which can be any year from 1993 to 2006). These are the same data that were shown as the fiftieth percentile in table 1.9. The lower panel shows the total income of these same households in 1993, the first year they were observed in AHEAD. All dollar amounts have been converted to 2008 dollars. On balance, income was slightly lower in the last year before death. It was 1 percent higher for the first health quintile, and then –6 percent for the second quintile, –2 percent for the third, –7 percent for the fourth, and –3 percent for the fifth health quintile. The similarity of incomes in 1993 and the last year observed should not be surprising because a large fraction of income is indexed Social Security benefits. These sample members were single in 1993 and single at the time of death and thus did not transition to survivorship benefits. On the other hand, some income is DB pension benefits, which are not fully indexed. These data do not suggest that household income declined in the years just before death. Household assets, in contrast, do show a decline.

Table 1.11   **Comparison of total income in last year observed to total income in 1993, original one-person households**

Health quintile	Age interval					
	70–74	75–79	80–84	85–89	90+	All
	Total income in last year observed					
1	16,353	12,791	14,071	13,219	13,040	13,341
2	18,862	18,077	15,877	15,452	13,440	15,012
3	13,353	21,525	15,802	14,253	14,264	15,802
4	22,432	16,904	17,809	14,840	15,814	16,887
5	20,586	21,146	22,342	18,483	19,472	20,586
All	16,952	15,935	15,423	14,097	13,440	14,344
	Total income in 1993					
1	16,917	12,406	14,221	13,269	12,864	13,269
2	18,890	21,868	17,586	15,119	14,993	15,947
3	15,031	21,513	18,027	13,690	14,285	16,153
4	22,432	20,532	17,445	16,887	17,375	18,132
5	28,159	28,488	25,296	16,564	19,472	21,146
All	17,621	17,340	16,317	14,097	13,906	14,943

Although it is informative to consider the change in income over the (at most) thirteen years of AHEAD (from 1993 to 2006 for persons who died before 2008), we would like to compare resources just before death to resources at a younger age, say prior to "retirement age." Such a comparison is not easy to make. Nonetheless, we begin by comparing total income of single persons in the last year observed before death to median earnings of these same persons when they were between ages fifty-seven and sixty-two, based on Social Security earnings records. We first index earnings to 2008 using the SSA Average Index of Monthly Earnings (AIME). We then calculate the median of earnings for ages fifty-seven to sixty-two, excluding years in which earnings were not positive. Approximately half of the original single-person households have matched SSA earnings records. The SSA only records earnings up to the SSA earnings limit, which ranged from $57,600 in 1993 to $94,200 in 2006. Thus our estimate of pre-retirement earnings may be low for some higher-earning workers. More importantly, the Social Security earnings of these original single persons in 1993 may be a very inexact indicator of household resources at the younger age. Many persons may have been married at ages fifty-seven to sixty-two, but were single when first interviewed in 1993. Single women who were previously married may have substantially greater Social Security benefits at older ages than women who never married.

Table 1.12 shows the comparison. Overall median total income in the last year observed was less than half of median earnings at ages fifty-seven to sixty-two. The percentage difference is greatest for those in the poorest

Table 1.12   **Comparison of earnings at ages fifty-seven to sixty-two and potential annuity income in last year observed, original one-person households with matched SSA earnings records**

Health quintile	Age interval					
	70–74	75–79	80–84	85–89	90+	All
Median of nonzero pre-retirement earnings for ages 57 to 62, AIME indexed						
1	21,468	31,017	29,594	27,711	28,828	28,828
2	32,321	33,539	37,551	31,978	29,465	32,172
3	31,957	42,526	31,318	28,073	28,896	31,318
4	31,029	41,584	26,969	45,607	27,318	34,202
5	51,203	35,990	24,493	38,227	47,373	35,990
All	31,957	35,029	29,981	30,602	29,078	30,651
Total median income in last year observed						
1	16,353	12,791	14,071	13,219	13,040	13,341
2	18,862	18,077	15,877	15,452	13,440	15,012
3	13,353	21,525	15,802	14,253	14,264	15,802
4	22,432	16,904	17,809	14,840	15,814	16,887
5	20,586	21,146	22,342	18,483	19,472	20,586
All	16,952	15,935	15,423	14,097	13,440	14,344

health and smallest for those in the best health. Combining all age intervals, LYO income was only 46.3 percent of "pre-retirement" earnings in the first health quintile and 57.2 percent of "pre-retirement" earnings in the fifth health quintile. If these "pre-retirement" earnings are an underestimate of actual pre-retirement earning, then these "replacement" rates are an overestimate of true replacement rates.

Overall, for the original single-person pathway, we find that a rather large fraction of these single persons have low income judged by poverty thresholds—12.1 percent below the poverty threshold and with no financial assets, 23 percent below twice the poverty line and no financial assets. And the proportion in poverty is much greater for those in poor health than for those in good health. On the other hand, the data show little difference between income just prior to death and income in 1993 when first observed in the AHEAD survey. However, total income in the last year observed is, on average, only about 50 percent of (possibly poorly measured) income in the pre-retirement years. While this difference is hard to evaluate because the two measures are not directly comparable, the implied replacement rate is likely an overestimate of the true replacement rate.

1.5   The Other Marital Pathway Groups and All Groups Combined

Table 1.13 presents median regression estimates of the effects of age and health on assets in the last year observed. Separate estimates are presented

Table 1.13   Median regression estimates of the effects of health and age on assets in last year observed, by family pathway

Variable	Original singles		Original two-person household with spouse deceased at death		Original two-person household with spouse alive at death	
	Coefficient	t-stat	Coefficient	t-stat	Coefficient	t-stat
LYO						
1995	−7,707	−0.67			94,130	2.98
1998	−14,346	−1.19	−44,452	−0.62	106,030	3.15
2000	−13,933	−1.12	−68,460	−1.01	118,320	3.32
2002	18,767	1.42	10,161	0.15	106,023	2.69
2004	4,266	0.30	−48,988	−0.73	204,739	4.87
2006	20,731	1.36	−16,651	−0.25	318,929	6.46
2008	3,788	0.31	−7,164	−0.12	275,335	8.08
Health	**1,260**	**9.53**	**2,063**	**5.01**	**2,042**	**6.02**
Age	**−9,323**	**−17.14**	**−7,203**	**−3.52**	**−20,619**	**−12.24**
Constant	933,078	20.16	808,133	4.58	2,038,368	15.06
N	3,003		1,357		2,286	
R^2	0.0545		0.0246		0.036	

for each of three marital pathway groups. The estimates control for last year observed as a marker for financial market returns that the household experienced since 1993. These estimated age and year effects are the average over all last years observed. Unlike the estimates for single-person households in table 1.4, these estimated health and age effects are not interacted with LYO but instead show the average effects over all years. The estimates are graphed for all three marital pathway groups on the left side of figure 1.13. The figure shows the effect of a 10 percentile increase in health on total wealth. The estimates range from $10,000 for single persons to $20,000 for the other two pathways. The estimated age effect varies from a decline of $7,203 per year of age for persons in original two-person households whose spouse is deceased in the last year observed to $20,619 for persons in original two-person households whose spouse is alive in the last year observed.

We next consider summary measures of financial resources that focus on the joint distribution of annuity income and liquid financial assets. We first present these results for all family pathways combined. We then compare the results across family pathways. Table 1.14 shows results for all family pathways combined. The table follows the same format as table 1.10 for persons in the single household pathway. Among all family pathways, 9.1 percent of persons have annuity income less than $10,000 (approximately the poverty rate for single persons sixty-five and older) and no liquid financial assets; 40.0 percent have annuity income less than $20,000 and financial assets less than $10,000. Overall, 50.4 percent have no housing wealth. Of those with annuity income less than $10,000 and no liquid financial assets, 67.0 percent have no housing wealth.

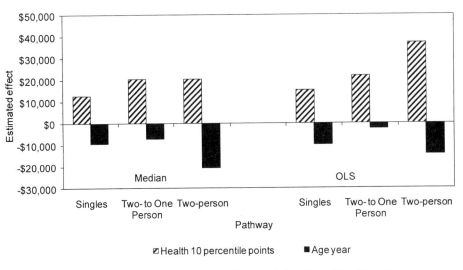

Fig. 1.13 **Estimated median and OLS estimates of the effect of health and age on assets in last year observed, by family pathway**

Table 1.14 Selected characteristics of persons in all family pathways, by annuity income and financial assets in the last year observed before death

Financial assets ($000s)	Annuity income ($000s)				
	<$10	<$20	<$30	<$40	All
	Percentage distribution				
Zero	**9.1**	17.0	18.2	18.5	18.8
<$10	19.1	**40.0**	44.5	45.2	46.1
<$25	21.7	47.3	**53.3**	54.6	55.5
<$50	23.7	54.1	62.0	**63.7**	64.9
All	31.0	76.2	92.0	96.2	100.0

Financial asset interval ($000s)	Annuity income interval ($000s)				
	$0–$10	$10–$20	$20–$30	$30–$40	All
	Percent of households with zero home equity				
Zero	**67.0**	60.7	64.9	49.7	63.2
$0–$10	51.9	**54.6**	51.5	45.0	51.7
$10–$25	42.2	36.9	**37.3**	37.2	38.5
$25–$50	30.8	39.0	37.9	**25.3**	33.2
All	48.4	46.5	40.3	31.2	50.4
	Mean health percentile				
Zero	**24.3**	26.6	23.2	33.9	25.8
$0–$10	26.5	**28.2**	30.1	30.3	28.2
$10–$25	31.3	35.4	**34.7**	36.4	34.3
$25 $50	31.1	32.7	35.0	**42.4**	35.5
All	28.0	30.9	32.2	37.2	31.7

The strong relationship between wealth and health is again observed for persons in all family pathways combined. The median health percentile ranges from 24.3 percent for persons with annuity income less than $10,000 to 42.4 percent for those with annuity income between $30,000 and $40,000 and financial assets between $25,000 and $50,000.

Tables 1.15, 1.16, and 1.17 compare results across family pathways. Table 1.15 compares the bivariate cumulative distribution of annuity income and financial assets. The easiest way to compare across pathways is to consider the diagonals in the tables for each pathway. Entries are the proportion of persons below any annuity income/financial asset level. The table shows that more single-person households have low resources than persons in the two-person to one-person pathway (persons in original two-person households whose spouse predeceased them), which in turn have lower resources than persons in the two-person pathway (persons in original two-person households whose spouse is alive at their death). For example, the proportion of persons below $30,000 in annuity income and below $25,000 in financial assets is 64.5 percent for one-person households, 52.2 percent of two- to one-person households, and 38.9 percent for two-person households.

Table 1.16 shows the proportion of households with zero housing wealth for each of the three pathways. Again, the diagonal values facilitate the comparison. For example, in the $20,000 to $30,000 annuity interval and the

Table 1.15   **Percentage distribution of persons by annuity income and financial assets in the last year observed before death, by family pathway**

Financial assets ($000s)	Annuity income ($000s)				
	<$10	<$20	<$30	<$40	All
One-person households					
Zero	**12.1**	23.0	24.2	24.7	24.9
<$10	23.9	**52.0**	55.7	56.4	57.0
<$25	26.3	58.8	**64.5**	65.7	66.5
<$50	27.9	65.5	72.8	**74.4**	75.4
All	31.9	82.0	94.1	97.7	100.0
Two-person to one-person households					
Zero	**6.2**	14.1	16.0	16.1	16.6
<$10	13.2	**36.4**	43.7	44.3	45.5
<$25	15.0	43.6	**52.2**	53.1	54.7
<$50	15.6	50.0	60.2	**61.5**	63.6
All	18.7	67.5	87.7	93.0	100.0
Two-person households					
Zero	**6.2**	10.1	11.0	11.2	11.6
<$10	14.8	**26.3**	30.1	30.8	31.7
<$25	18.1	33.4	**38.9**	40.3	41.3
<$50	21.1	40.5	48.3	**50.3**	51.6
All	34.2	71.7	90.7	95.3	100.0

Table 1.16   **Percentage of persons with zero home equity by annuity income and financial assets in the last year observed before death, by family pathway**

	Annuity income interval ($000s)				
Financial asset interval ($000s)	$0–$10	$10–$20	$20–$30	$30–$40	All
One-person households					
Zero	**76.3**	69.8	74.8	63.6	73.1
$0–$10	62.9	**63.3**	57.8	53.8	61.2
$10–$25	49.8	46.8	**52.2**	53.5	50.0
$25–$50	48.6	47.2	48.3	**47.0**	47.7
All	63.7	57.7	53.9	47.6	**57.1**
Two-person to one-person households					
Zero	**70.5**	63.5	82.1	74.5	69.6
$0–$10	60.0	**53.0**	60.6	63.0	58.0
$10–$25	65.6	28.6	**27.9**	48.2	39.4
$25–$50	44.0	33.4	49.0	**11.8**	32.7
All	61.7	50.3	50.0	41.7	**49.6**
Two-person households					
Zero	**42.0**	24.2	19.3	11.7	31.7
$0–$10	29.4	**25.9**	35.2	23.1	28.3
$10–$25	30.8	22.0	**20.0**	15.3	23.1
$25–$50	17.5	27.4	14.0	**10.5**	16.9
All	27.0	21.2	18.0	13.1	**20.4**

$10,000 to $25,000 financial asset interval 52.2 percent of one-person households have no housing wealth but only 27.9 percent of one- to two-person households, and just 20 percent of two-person households have no housing wealth. Overall, in the last year before death, 57.1 percent of single-person households have no housing wealth and 49.6 percent of persons in two to one-person households have no housing wealth. Remarkably, only 20.4 percent of persons who die with a surviving spouse have no home equity.

Table 1.17 shows the mean health percentile of persons in each of the three pathways. Unlike the very dissimilar proportions of households below annuity income/financial asset thresholds across family pathways, and the very different proportions with zero housing wealth within annuity income/financial asset intervals, the levels of health within the cells are very similar across family pathways. That is, given similar annuity income and levels of financial assets, the mean health percentile is about the same for persons in each family status pathway. For example, the overall mean health percentile in the three groups is 28.5, 32.3, and 28.5, respectively, in the one-person, two- to one-person, and the two-person pathways. For persons in the zero to $10,000 annuity income and zero housing wealth interval, the mean health percentiles are 24.1, 22.7, and 24.1, respectively.

Finally, table 1.18 compares median income in the last year observed with income in 1993. Because of small sample sizes in many cells, the table shows

Table 1.17   **Mean health percentile by annuity income and financial assets in the last year observed before death, by family pathway**

Financial asset interval ($000s)	Annuity income interval ($000s)				
	$0–$10	$10–$20	$20–$30	$30–$40	All
One-person households					
Zero	**24.1**	24.8	22.4	28.3	24.5
$0–$10	23.4	**28.2**	24.3	26.2	25.6
$10–$25	28.5	33.3	**38.3**	35.6	33.5
$25–$50	26.6	25.3	26.8	**43.3**	30.2
All	25.1	28.4	29.5	33.4	**28.5**
Two-person to one-person households					
Zero	**22.7**	28.5	30.6	46.3	29.2
$0–$10	33.7	**23.9**	36.1	28.1	28.9
$10–$25	24.9	42.0	**31.5**	29.3	32.6
$25–$50	41.2	40.7	47.9	**49.1**	45.4
All	29.1	31.0	33.2	35.0	**32.3**
Two-person households					
Zero	**24.1**	24.8	22.4	28.3	24.5
$0–$10	23.4	**28.2**	24.3	26.2	25.6
$10–$25	28.5	33.3	**38.3**	35.6	33.5
$25–$50	26.6	25.3	26.8	**43.3**	30.2
All	25.1	28.4	29.5	33.4	**28.5**

Table 1.18   **Comparison of median total income in last year observed to median income in 1993 and median earnings when age fifty-seven to sixty-two, all persons, by pathway**

	Pathway		
Comparison	One to one	Two to one	Two to two
For all persons			
Total income in 1993	14,943	31,719	34,656
Total income in last year observed	14,344	18,143	33,449
Percent change	–4.2%	–74.8%	–3.6%
For men with matched Social Security records			
Median earnings when age 57 to 62	25,604	40,855	41,584
Medial total income in last year observed	15,213	19,844	33,759
Percent change	–68.3%	–105.9%	–23.2%

data for all health quintiles and for all last years observed combined. For men with matched Social Security records the table also compares median income in 1993 with median earnings for ages fifty-seven to sixty-two. For one-person households and for two-person households total income in the last year observed was, on average, only slightly below income in 1993, for two- to one-person households the decline in income between 1993 and the last year observed was almost 75 percent.

For men with matched Social Security records, table 1.18 shows that for one- to one and for two- to one-person households total income in the last year observed much lower than income when aged fifty-seven to sixty-two— over 68 percent less for one to one households and almost 106 percent less for two to one households. The decline was only 23.2 percent for two- to two-person households.

1.6 Summary and Conclusions

We began by summarizing the balance sheets of households in the Health and Retirement Study by five-year age intervals from age sixty-five to sixty-nine through age eighty-five and older. These balance sheets show that many households have accumulated considerable wealth, ranging in 2008 from a median of $214,371 for older single-person households to a median of $1,015,317 for younger two-person households. Interpretation of these balances is confounded by cohort effects (older generations have lower lifetime earnings than younger generations) and mortality effects (persons in poorer households within a cohort die at younger ages). Thus, although these balance sheets present the point-in-time wealth of households who survive to a given age, they do not reveal the evolution of assets of the same households over time.

To analyze this evolution, we direct attention to the AHEAD households, who were aged seventy and older in 1993 when first observed and age eighty-seven and older in 2008 when last observed. We divide the AHEAD households into three family pathway groups: (1) original one-person households in 1993; (2) persons in two-person households in 1993 with a deceased spouse in the last year observed; and (3) persons in two-person households in 1993 with the spouse alive when last observed. For each of these pathways we describe the evolution of assets from 1993 to the year last observed. We describe the evolution of total wealth and several of its components—financial assets including IRA accounts, housing wealth and housing ownership, Social Security annuity wealth, and DB pension annuity wealth. We find a very strong relationship between health when last observed and the level of assets just before death. Those in poor health have much lower assets than those in good health.

Much of our analysis is restricted to persons who are known to have died. For these persons we are able to calculate wealth in the last year observed before their death. Because waves of the AHEAD are typically spaced two years apart, our last observation for each person is at most two years prior to death. Several general results stand out: (1) Median total wealth was relatively high in the year last observed for each of the three family pathway groups. (2) Wealth in the last year before death is greatest for persons who were in two-person households the longest period of time. For example, the average assets in the last year observed were $141,606 for persons in one-person households in 1993 whose last year observed before death was 2006, $252,849 for persons in two-person households in 1993 whose spouse was deceased when last observed in 2006, and $691,588 for persons in two-person households in 1993 whose spouse was alive when last observed in 2006. (3) For total wealth and for each of the asset subcategories there is a strong correspondence between the level of assets in 1993 and the number of years a person survives after 1993. Persons who lived longer had higher initial assets. (4) For each family pathway group, there is a very strong relationship between health status and wealth in the last year observed. Thus there is a strong association between health and wealth even among persons who would die within the next two years. (5) Despite the appearance of substantial assets at the median, a substantial fraction of people die with income less than $10,000, with no financial assets, and with zero housing wealth.

A rather large fraction of the original single-person households have low income, judged by the income poverty thresholds. We find that 12.1 percent are below the poverty threshold and have no financial assets, and that 23 percent are below twice the income poverty line and have no financial assets. To put the results in context we first compare the total income in the last year observed to total income in 1993, the first year the AHEAD data were collected. Total income in the last year observed was about 4 percent higher, on average, than total income in 1993. We also compare total median income in the last year observed to median earnings (in 2008 dollars) of the same persons when they were between ages fifty-seven and sixty-two. While the difference is hard to evaluate because the two measures are not clearly comparable, overall median income in the last year observed was approximately 50 percent lower than median earnings of the same persons at ages fifty-seven to sixty-two.

There are also important differences across the pathways. Consider, for example, the proportion of persons with annuity income less than $20,000 (approximately twice the poverty level for single persons over age sixty-five) and financial assets less than $10,000: 52 percent of persons in the single-household pathway fall below these thresholds, but only 36.4 percent of those in the two- to one-person pathway, and only 26.3 percent of those in the two-person pathway. Similarly, consider the proportion of persons with annuity income in the $10,000 to $20,000 interval and financial assets less than $10,000 who have zero housing wealth: 63.3 percent of those in the single-family pathway, 53.0 percent of those in the two- to one-person pathway, and only 25.9 percent of those in the two-person pathway. A perhaps striking similarity across the pathways is that given income and housing wealth, the health status of the persons in the three pathways is very close.

The median health percentile of persons with annuity income in the $10,000 to $20,000 interval and financial assets less than $10,000 is 28.2 for persons in the single-household pathway, 23.9 percent for those in the two- to one-person pathway, and 28.2 for persons in the two-person pathway. Finally, the total household income of one to one and two to two households when last observed was only slightly less than income in 1993, while income of two to one households was almost 75 percent lower when last observed than in 1993. And for men with matched Social Security records, income when last observed was over 68 percent lower than earning at ages fifty-seven to sixty-two for one to one households, 106 percent lower for two to one households, but only 23 percent less for two to two households.

The results raise several issues. First, a noticeable fraction of persons die with virtually no financial assets—46.1 percent with less than $10,000. Based on a replacement rate comparison, many of these may be deemed to have been well-prepared for retirement, in the sense that their income in their final years was not substantially lower than their income in their late fifties or early sixties. Yet with such low asset levels, they would have little capacity to pay for unanticipated needs such as health or other shocks or to pay for entertainment, travel, or other activities. This raises a question of whether the replacement ratio is a sufficient statistic for the "adequacy" of retirement preparation. In addition, this group relies almost entirely on Social Security benefits for support in retirement. These persons balance on only one leg of the oft touted three-legged stool that is said to provide retirement support— Social Security, pension benefits, and personal saving. If the one leg is judged inadequate it raises the question of how to strengthen the other legs, which in turn may, for example, increase interest in the spread of 401(k)-like plans to low-wage workers in firms with high turnover.

Appendix

Table 1A.1   Balance sheets for households aged sixty-five to sixty-nine in 2008

Asset category	Percent of households with asset	Median holding	Mean holding	Share of total wealth	Values conditional on positive holding	
					Mean	Median
All households						
Financial assets	86.7	15,000	132,484	12.6	152,805	25,000
Nonmortgage debt	36.2	0	−3,679	−0.4	10,225	5,000
Home equity (primary home)	79.8	100,000	176,188	16.8	222,546	145,000
Home equity (second home)	15.8	0	26,280	2.5	166,423	50,000
Other real estate	14.8	0	69,137	6.6	466,416	125,000
Business assets	9.7	0	45,966	4.4	473,289	200,000
Personal retirement accounts	52.2	5,000	121,137	11.5	231,910	100,000
IRAs and Keoghs	41.5	0	75,299	7.2	181,577	80,000
401(k)s and similar plans	26.1	0	45,839	4.4	175,670	80,000
Social Security	88.2	315,163	341,556	**32.6**	387,195	351,709
Defined-benefit pension	42.1	0	140,176	13.4	332,834	232,492
Nonannuity net worth	90.8	221,700	567,496	54.1	626,768	269,800
Net worth	99.4	731,121	1,049,228	100.0	1,056,245	732,866
Single-person households						
Financial assets	82.3	5,000	83,082	12.8	100,941	12,000
Nonmortgage debt	34.8	0	−3,042	−0.5	8,734	4,000
Home equity (primary home)	65.9	52,000	107,483	16.6	*165,712*	*110,000*
Home equity (second home)	9.4	0	7,969	1.2	86,894	*20,000*

Other real estate	8.7	0	73,361	11.3	845,335	150,000
Business assets	6.1	0	18,069	2.8	297,513	100,000
Personal retirement accounts	36.4	0	47,074	7.3	129,148	64,000
IRAs and Keoghs	27.9	0	32,206	5.0	115,385	52,000
401(k)s and similar plans	15.6	0	14,869	2.3	95,604	30,000
Social Security	86.6	230,060	225,842	34.8	260,890	256,051
Defined-benefit pension	38.0	0	89,323	13.8	235,059	190,032
Nonannuity net worth	84.4	100,000	333,996	51.5	398,690	150,000
Net worth	99.1	414,435	649,161	100.0	655,857	420,494
Married couples						
Financial assets	90.3	27,750	172,830	12.6	191,419	39,000
Nonmortgage debt	37.2	0	-4,232	-0.3	11,364	5,000
Home equity (primary home)	91.1	150,000	232,300	16.9	256,111	160,000
Home equity (second home)	21.1	0	41,235	3.0	195,369	70,000
Other real estate	19.8	0	65,688	4.8	331,062	120,000
Business assets	12.7	0	68,750	5.0	542,028	250,000
Personal retirement accounts	65.1	35,000	181,625	13.2	278,881	122,000
IRAs and Keoghs	52.5	5,841	110,493	8.0	210,295	100,000
401(k)s and similar plans	34.7	0	71,132	5.2	204,975	59,600
Social Security	89.6	473,933	436,059	31.7	486,901	494,485
Defined-benefit pension	45.5	0	181,708	13.2	399,557	272,490
Nonannuity net worth	96.0	357,000	758,196	55.1	790,385	385,000
Net worth	99.6	1,015,317	1,375,963	100.0	1,381,422	1,016,076

Source: Authors' tabulations using Health and Retirement Survey, Wave 9 (2008).

Table 1A.2   Balance sheets for households aged seventy to seventy-four in 2008

Asset category	Percent of households with asset	Median holding	Mean holding	Share of total wealth	Values conditional on positive holding	
					Mean	Median
		All households				
Financial assets	88.1	17,000	146,663	14.8	166,540	28,000
Nonmortgage debt	27.8	0	2,991	0.3	−10,776	−3,000
Home equity (primary home)	76.9	100,000	156,484	15.8	204,387	150,000
Home equity (second home)	13.7	0	26,975	2.7	197,037	92,000
Other real estate	14	0	44,987	4.5	321,528	120,000
Business assets	7.4	0	50,443	5.1	682,759	200,000
Personal retirement accounts	45.9	0	94,632	9.6	206,233	83,000
IRAs and Keoghs	40.6	0	77,796	7.9	191,775	88,144
401(k)s and similar plans	11.8	0	16,836	1.7	142,647	35,000
Social Security	98.1	287,912	320,915	**32.4**	327,011	292,487
Defined-benefit pension	49.1	0	152,105	15.4	309,847	189,075
Nonannuity net worth	90.6	202,500	517,194	52.2	572,153	243,200
Net worth	99.7	660,495	990,214	100.0	993,139	661,260
		Single-person households				
Financial assets	84	5,000	86,738	14.4	103,207	11,300
Nonmortgage debt	27.9	0	−1,980	−0.3	−7,100	−2,500
Home equity (primary home)	63.1	50,000	107,729	17.9	171,368	*129,000*
Home equity (second home)	7.1	0	9,669	1.6	135,861	70,000
Other real estate	8.2	0	20,458	3.4	248,626	100,000

Business assets	4.4	0	36,342	6.0	817,311	200,000
Personal retirement accounts	34	0	38,520	6.4	113,276	47,000
IRAs and Keoghs	29.6	0	35,258	5.9	118,981	56,000
401(k)s and similar plans	6.3	0	3,262	0.5	51,824	14,000
Social Security	97.4	207,740	212,967	35.4	218,590	209,732
Defined-benefit pension	42	0	91,236	15.2	217,174	132,887
Nonannuity net worth	84.7	95,300	297,478	49.4	352,107	151,200
Net worth	99.7	389,592	601,680	100.0	603,457	390,909
Married couples						
Financial assets	92.3	40,000	209,205	15.0	226,751	50,000
Nonmortgage debt	27.6	0	−4,046	−0.3	−14,649	−3,500
Home equity (primary home)	91.4	150,000	207,368	14.9	228,178	*160,000*
Home equity (second home)	20.6	0	45,037	3.2	219,136	*110,000*
Other real estate	20	0	70,586	5.1	352,821	130,000
Business assets	10.5	0	65,159	4.7	623,052	235,000
Personal retirement accounts	58.3	20,000	153,195	11.0	262,835	117,000
IRAs and Keoghs	52	9,000	122,193	8.8	235,088	116,000
401(k)s and similar plans	17.6	0	31,002	2.2	176,645	41,000
Social Security	98.9	427,936	433,578	31.1	438,510	429,213
Defined-benefit pension	56.5	55,539	215,633	15.4	381,789	254,016
Nonannuity net worth	96.7	355,700	746,505	53.5	773,307	373,000
Net worth	99.7	1,009,818	1,395,716	100.0	1,399,833	1,012,407

Source: Authors' tabulations using Health and Retirement Survey, Wave 9 (2008).

Table 1A.3   Balance sheets for households aged seventy-five to seventy-nine in 2008

Asset category	Percent of households with asset	Median holding	Mean holding	Share of total wealth	Values conditional on positive holding	
					Mean	Median
All households						
Financial assets	88.6	16000	144,536	16.8	163,087	25,000
Nonmortgage debt	23.2	0	–2,760	–0.3	–11,883	–4,300
Home equity (primary home)	75.7	100,000	168,464	19.5	223,100	150,000
Home equity (second home)	11.6	0	21,243	2.5	183,253	75,000
Other real estate	10.9	0	63,748	7.4	584,397	190,000
Business assets	6.9	0	30,479	3.5	444,372	200,000
Personal retirement accounts	41.2	0	71,579	8.3	173,870	75,000
IRAs and Keoghs	39.4	0	68,179	7.9	173,252	76,139
401(k)s and similar plans	4.3	0	3,401	0.4	79,890	30,000
Social Security	98.2	216,900	249,219	**28.9**	253,707	219,136
Defined-benefit pension	51.8	11,613	115,742	13.4	223,644	130,383
Nonannuity net worth	91.5	195,000	497,290	57.7	544,699	230,000
Net worth	99.7	565,440	862,250	100.0	865,427	566,676
Single-person households						
Financial assets	85.6	8,000	96,633	17.8	112,913	15,000
Nonmortgage Debt	24.9	0	–3,134	–0.6	–12,562	–4,000
Home equity (primary home)	65.7	60,000	123,144	22.7	187,707	130,000
Home equity (second home)	7.6	0	10,826	2.0	143,125	60,000
Other real estate	7.2	0	24,687	4.6	341,794	200,000

Business assets	3.9	0	15,067	2.8	386,937	200,000
Personal retirement accounts	28.9	0	31,888	5.9	110,192	50,000
IRAs and Keoghs	28.3	0	30,716	5.7	108,481	50,000
401(k)s and similar plans	1.6	0	1,173	0.2	72,316	14,000
Social Security	97.3	166,846	164,939	**30.4**	169,456	168,794
Defined-benefit pension	45.2	0	78,365	14.4	173,531	103,213
Nonannuity net worth	87.3	113,000	299,112	55.1	344,599	150,900
Net worth	99.4	336,058	542,416	100.0	546,110	337,517
Married couples						
Financial assets	92.6	50,000	207,856	16.2	224,353	60,000
Nonmortgage debt	21	0	-2,266	-0.2	-10,816	-5,000
Home equity (primary home)	88.9	151,000	228,371	17.8	257,672	175,000
Home equity (second home)	17	0	35,013	2.7	206,890	75,000
Other real estate	15.8	0	115,381	9.0	731,182	175,000
Business assets	10.8	0	50,852	4.0	471,801	200,000
Personal retirement accounts	57.3	14,000	124,045	9.7	216,355	92,000
IRAs and Keoghs	53.9	11,000	117,700	9.2	218,192	96,000
401(k)s and similar plans	7.7	0	6,345	0.5	81,987	30,000
Social Security	99.4	348,675	360,624	**28.1**	362,742	349,695
Defined-benefit pension	60.5	61,531	165,148	12.9	273,115	174,047
Nonannuity net worth	97.1	345,000	759,251	59.1	782,508	364,500
Net worth	100	858,331	858,331	100.0	1,285,024	858,331

Source: Authors' tabulations using Health and Retirement Survey, Wave 9 (2008).

Table 1A.4 Balance sheets for households aged eighty to eighty-four in 2008

Asset category	Percent of households with asset	Median holding	Mean holding	Share of total wealth	Values conditional on positive holding	
					Mean	Median
All households						
Financial assets	88.8	23,000	185,056	24.7	208,370	35,700
Nonmortgage debt	17.3	0	–1,179	–0.2	–6,820	–3,000
Home equity (primary home)	72.3	90,000	149,537	20.0	207,112	140,000
Home equity (second home)	9.2	0	18,553	2.5	201,880	80,000
Other real estate	9.6	0	38,186	5.1	396,044	95,000
Business assets	6.1	0	28,029	3.7	461,058	230,000
Personal retirement accounts	35.3	0	54,757	7.3	155,294	55,000
IRAs and Keoghs	35	0	52,459	7.0	149,766	55,000
401(k)s and similar plans	1.1	0	2,298	0.3	203,348	107,000
Social Security	98.1	146,095	177,651	**23.7**	181,080	147,263
Defined-benefit pension	53.7	9,872	97,520	13.0	181,722	98,386
Nonannuity net worth	92.2	180,000	472,940	63.2	512,981	207,000
Net worth	99.9	418,124	748,110	100.0	748,615	418,221
Single-person households						
Financial assets	86.7	12,000	120,453	24.8	138,870	20,000
Nonmortgage debt	16.3	0	–1,037	–0.2	–6,360	–2,000
Home equity (primary home)	65.4	70,000	117,856	24.3	180,250	125,000
Home equity (second home)	5.5	0	9,937	2.0	179,155	100,000
Other real estate	7.2	0	20,634	4.2	286,954	55,000

Business assets	4.2	0	12,438	2.6	292,913	200,000
Personal retirement accounts	27.6	0	26,042	5.4	94,199	41,000
IRAs and Keoghs	27.6	0	26,022	5.4	94,127	41,000
401(k)s and similar plans	0.2	0	20	0.0	12,500	12,500
Social Security	97.8	119,406	123,086	**25.3**	125,834	121,259
Defined-benefit pension	49.7	0	56,229	11.6	113,231	64,384
Nonannuity net worth	90.7	127,000	306,323	63.1	337,868	160,000
Net worth	100	302,751	485,638	100.0	485,638	302,751
Married couples						
Financial assets	92.8	70,500	309,775	24.7	333,758	84,000
Nonmortgage debt	19.2	0	−1,451	−0.1	−7,578	−4,900
Home equity (primary home)	85.5	136,000	210,697	16.8	246,798	*160,000*
Home equity (second home)	16.2	0	35,185	2.8	216,879	*65,000*
Other real estate	14.4	0	72,070	5.7	501,400	125,000
Business assets	9.6	0	58,127	4.6	604,378	280,000
Personal retirement accounts	50	0	110,193	8.8	220,558	73,000
IRAs and Keoghs	49.3	0	103,496	8.2	210,026	72,000
401(k)s and similar plans	3	0	6,697	0.5	222,938	110,000
Social Security	98.7	262,814	282,989	**22.6**	286,814	263,889
Defined-benefit pension	61.4	51,693	177,233	14.1	288,665	141,651
Nonannuity net worth	95.1	371,500	794,595	63.3	835,385	400,000
Net worth	99.8	748,356	1,254,817	100.0	1,257,291	748,875

Source: Authors' tabulations using Health and Retirement Survey, Wave 9 (2008).

Table 1A.5   **Balance sheets for households aged eighty-five or older in 2008**

Asset category	Percent of households with asset	Median holding	Mean holding	Share of total wealth	Values conditional on positive holding	
					Mean	Median
All households						
Financial assets	88.7	29,000	177,611	33.2	200,293	48,000
Nonmortgage debt	9.4	0	−757	−0.1	−8,070	−2,000
Home equity (primary home)	60.9	63,000	125,883	23.5	206,935	140,000
Home equity (second home)	6.5	0	14,358	2.7	222,543	100,000
Other real estate	8.4	0	29,243	5.5	346,127	150,000
Business assets	5.4	0	26,752	5.0	500,032	350,000
Personal retirement accounts	20.9	0	15,096	2.8	72,396	33,387
IRAs and Keoghs	20.7	0	15,031	2.8	72,626	35,000
401(k)s and similar plans	0.2	0	65	0.0	41,803	2,500
Social Security	98	77,587	99,613	18.6	101,678	78,026
Defined-benefit pension	49.8	0	47,853	8.9	96,114	45,257
Nonannuity net worth	92.6	153,000	388,186	72.5	419,435	179,000
Net worth	99.8	291,832	535,652	100.0	**536,739**	**293,342**
Single-person households						
Financial assets	88.1	19,000	143,704	35.2	163,115	30,000
Nonmortgage debt	9.2	0	−572	−0.1	−6,226	−2,000
Home equity (primary home)	54.1	35,000	101,728	24.9	188,223	130,000
Home equity (second home)	4.4	0	9,805	2.4	223,061	125,000
Other real estate	6.5	0	19,064	4.7	293,103	150,000

Business assets	4.5	0	16,997	4.2	375,286	275,000
Personal retirement accounts	15.6	0	9,255	2.3	59,211	25,000
IRAs and Keoghs	15.6	0	9,255	2.3	59,211	25,000
401(k)s and similar plans	0	0	0	0.0		
Social Security	98	69,352	73,500	18.0	75,024	70,373
Defined-benefit pension	47.8	0	35,082	8.6	73,462	35,319
Nonannuity net worth	91	116,500	299,980	73.4	329,835	148,000
Net worth	99.7	214,371	408,562	100.0	**409,628**	214,511
Married couples						
Financial assets	90.7	98,000	296,971	30.2	327,416	125,000
Nonmortgage debt	10.1	0	–1,411	–0.1	–13,961	–2,000
Home equity (primary home)	84.8	125,000	210,917	21.5	248,919	*150,000*
Home equity (second home)	13.7	0	30,388	3.1	221,957	*100,000*
Other real estate	15.3	0	65,075	6.6	425,514	155,000
Business assets	8.2	0	61,094	6.2	741,382	500,000
Personal retirement accounts	39.2	0	35,660	3.6	90,885	51,000
IRAs and Keoghs	38.5	0	35,365	3.6	91,783	51,000
401(k)s and similar plans	0.7	0	295	0.0	41,803	2,500
Social Security	98	170,162	191,539	**19.5**	195,504	173,503
Defined-benefit pension	56.9	23,633	92,809	9.4	162,990	87,063
Nonannuity net worth	98.2	362,000	698,693	71.1	711,635	378,200
Net worth	100	674,965	983,042	100.0	**983,042**	**674,965**

Source: Authors' tabulations using Health and Retirement Survey, Wave 9 (2008).

References

Adams, P., M. D. Hurd, D. McFadden, A. Merrill, and T. Ribeiro. 2003. "Healthy, Wealthy and Wise? Tests for Direct Causal Paths between Health and Socioeconomic Status." *Journal of Econometrics* 112 (1): 3–56.

Attanasio, Orazio, and Carl Emmerson. 2003. "Mortality, Health Status, and Wealth." *Journal of the European Economic Association* 1 (4): 821–50.

Bernheim, B. Douglas. 1992. *Is the Baby Boom Generation Preparing Adequately for Retirement?* Summary Report. Princeton, NJ: Merrill Lynch.

Case, Anne, and Angus Deaton. 2005. "Health and Wealth among the Poor: India and South Africa Compared." *American Economic Review* (Papers and Proceedings) 95 (2): 229–33.

Engen, Eric, William Gale, and Cory Uccello. 1999. "The Adequacy of Household Saving." *Brookings Papers on Economic Activity* 2:65–187.

Haveman, Robert, Karen Holden, Barbara Wolfe, and Andrei Romanov. 2005. "Assessing the Maintenance of Savings Sufficiency over the First Decade of Retirement." Center for Economic Studies and Ifo Institute for Economic Research (CESIFO) Working Paper no. 1567, October.

Hurd, Michael, Daniel McFadden, and Angela Merrill. 2001. "Predictors of Mortality among the Elderly." In *Themes in the Economics of Aging,* edited by David A. Wise, 171–99. Chicago: University of Chicago Press.

Hurd, Michael, and Susann Rohwedder. 2008. "The Adequacy of Economic Resources in Retirement." MRRC-Working Paper No. 2008-184.

Hurd, Michael, and David Wise. 1989. "The Wealth and Poverty of Widows: Assets Before and After the Husband's Death." In *The Economics of Aging,* edited by David A. Wise, 177–99. Chicago: University of Chicago Press.

Johnson, Richard, Cori Uccello, and Joshua Goldwyn. 2005. "Who Forgoes Survivor Protection in Employer-Sponsored Pension Annuities." *The Gerontologist* 45 (1): 26–35.

Love, David, Paul Smith, and Lucy McNair. 2008. "A New Look at the Wealth Adequacy of Older U.S. Households." Federal Reserve Board Finance and Economics Discussion Paper no. 2008-20.

Michaud, P.-C., and A. van Soest. 2008. "Health and Wealth of Elderly Couples: Causality Tests Using Dynamic Panel Data Models." *Journal of Health Economics* 27 (5): 1312–25.

Mitchell, Olivia, and James Moore. 1998. "Can Americans Afford to Retire? New Evidence on Retirement Saving Adequacy." *Journal of Risk and Insurance* 65 (3): 371–400.

Munnell, Alicia, Anthony Webb, and Francesca Golub-Sass. 2007. "Is There Really a Retirement Saving Crisis? An NRRI Analysis." Center for Retirement Research (CRR) Boston College no. 7-11, August.

Poterba, James M., Steven F. Venti, and David A. Wise. 2010a. "The Asset Cost of Poor Health." NBER Working Paper no. 16389. Cambridge, MA: National Bureau of Economic Research, September.

———. 2010b. "Family Status Transitions, Latent Health, and the Post-Retirement Evolution of Assets?" NBER Working Paper no. 15789. Cambridge, MA: National Bureau of Economic Research, February.

Rohwedder, Susann, Steven J. Haider, and Michael D. Hurd. 2006. "Increases in Wealth among the Elderly in the Early 1990s: How Much is Due to Survey Design?" *Review of Income and Wealth* 52 (4): 509–24.

Scholz, John Karl, Ananth Seshadri, and Surachai Khitatrakun. 2006. "Are Americans Saving Optimally for Retirement?" *Journal of Political Economy* 114 (4): 607–47.

Sevak, Purvi, David Weir, and Robert Willis. 2003. "The Economic Consequences of a Husband's Death: Evidence from the HRS and AHEAD." *Social Security Bulletin* 65 (3): 31–44.

Smith, James P. 1999. "Healthy Bodies and Thick Wallets: The Dual Relation between Health and Economic Status." *Journal of Economic Perspectives* 13 (2): 145–66.

———. 2004. "Unraveling the SES-Health Connection." *Population and Development Review Supplement: Aging, Health and Public Policy* 30:108–32.

———. 2005. "Consequences and Predictors of New Health Events." In *Analyses in the Economics of Aging*, edited by David A. Wise, 213–40. Chicago: University of Chicago Press.

VanDerhei, Jack, and Craig Copeland. 2010. "The EBRI Retirement Readiness Rating: Retirement Income Preparation and Future Prospects." Employee Benefit Research Institute (EBRI) Issue Brief no. 344, July.

Venti, Steven F. 2011. "Economic Measurement in the Health and Retirement Study." *Forum for Health Economics and Policy* 14 (3): 1–18.

Venti, Steven F., and David A. Wise. 2002. "Aging and Housing Equity." In *Innovations in Retirement Financing*, edited by Olivia S. Mitchell, Zvi Bodie, P. Brett Hammond, and Stephen Zeldes, 254–81. Philadelphia: University of Pennsylvania Press and the Pension Research Council.

———. 2004. "Aging and Housing Equity: Another Look." In *Perspectives on the Economics of Aging*, edited by David A. Wise, 127–80. Chicago: University of Chicago Press.

Weir, David, and Robert Willis. 2000. "Prospects for Widow Poverty in the Finances of Married Couples in the HRS." In *Forecasting Retirement Needs and Retirement Wealth*, edited by O. Mitchell, B. Hammond, and A. Rappaport, 208–34. Philadelphia: University of Pennsylvania Press.

Wu, Stephen. 2003. "The Effects of Health Status Events on the Economic Status of Married Couples." *Journal of Human Resources* 38 (1): 219–30.

Comment   David Laibson

Poterba, Venti, and Wise (PVW) provide a wealth of analysis that insightfully and painstakingly describes the financial state of aging US households. Their chapter uses the Health and Retirement Study (HRS), a biannual longitudinal survey of middle-aged and older adults. Poterba, Venti, and Wise cut the data in many different ways, revealing a grim picture of financial vulnerability for the bottom half of the population of US households. In this discussion, I summarize some of their most important findings and then ask whether the ongoing expansion of the defined-contribution savings system holds out hope for improvement among future cohorts of retirees. I reach

David Laibson is Harvard College Professor and the Robert I. Goldman Professor of Economics at Harvard University and a research associate of the National Bureau of Economic Research.

For acknowledgments, sources of research support, and disclosure of the author's material financial relationships, if any, please see http://www.nber.org/chapters/c12430.ack.

the disappointing conclusion that the picture that PVW paint for the current cohort will continue to apply for generations of retirees to come.

A Perspective on Savings Adequacy

Poterba, Venti, and Wise provide several perspectives on the financial state of retired households. First, they look at balance sheet information, incorporating all sources of household claims, including financial wealth, net housing wealth, the net present value of Social Security claims, and the net present value of other defined-benefit claims. Their net worth variable is a comprehensive measure of claims that support consumption.[1] Among single-person households aged sixty-five to sixty-nine (surveyed in the 2008 wave of the HRS), median net worth is $414,435 (all quantities are in 2008 dollars). Assuming a 4 percent expenditure rate,[2] this amounts to annual expenditure of $16,577. Among single-person households aged sixty-five to sixty-nine, the twenty-fifth percentile of net worth is $237,154. Assuming a 4 percent expenditure rate, this amounts to annual expenditure of $9,486. To provide context, the 2008 poverty threshold for a one-person household is $10,326.[3]

By comparison, two-person households are better off. Among two-person households aged sixty-five to sixty-nine, median household net worth is $1,015,317. Assuming a 4 percent expenditure rate, this amounts to annual per capita expenditure of $20,306. Among two-person households aged sixty-five to sixty-nine, the twenty-fifth percentile of household net worth is $609,949. Assuming a 4 percent expenditure rate, this amounts to annual per capita expenditure of $12,199.

While these absolute expenditure equivalents are informative, it is important to evaluate retirement resources relative to the life cycle benchmark of pre-retirement expenditure/income. The authors do this toward the end of the chapter. Specifically, the authors compare annualized total income[4] in retirement (at the last biannual observation wave before death) to pre-retirement labor income (ages fifty-seven to sixty-two). To do this, the authors use Social Security linkages (focusing on the HRS subsample with these linkages). These comparisons are fraught with both conceptual and measurement issues, including the problem that consumption can be supported by income as well as asset sales (if there are assets left to sell), so

1. Two important exceptions should be highlighted: intergenerational transfers (which flow both to and away from these households), and antipoverty programs (especially Medicaid).
2. At the time of this writing, a competitive real annuity (with no survivor benefits and no period-certain payout) for a sixty-five-year-old had a 4 percent payout rate. Many financial advisors also advocate a 4 percent payout rule among retirees who have not annuitized.
3. US Census Bureau.
4. Total income includes benefits from Social Security and defined-benefit pension plans, government transfer income, and dividends, interest payments, rent received, and other income from assets.

income will be lower than consumption for some elderly households. However, the authors point out other problems that lead to a *downward* bias in measured pre-retirement labor income, which would create an upward bias in the implied income replacement ratio.

Although the tug of war among dueling biases makes interpretation difficult, the results of this analysis are nevertheless eye-opening. For example, consider men who (a) are in single-person households in the HRS, and (b) have matched Social Security records. Before retirement, their median labor income is $25,604. Deep into retirement (in essence, a couple of years before they die), their median total income is $15,213, representing a 40.6 percent decline. Tables 1.2 and 1.6 provide more tabulations of this sort. However, these kinds of calculations need to be interpreted with a grain of salt, since the method for inferring "pre-retirement income" involves many approximating assumptions and since expenditure and income are not necessarily one and the same.

Poterba, Venti, and Wise also evaluate wealth trajectories over the course of retirement. As one would expect, low levels of retirement income in the last few years of life coincide with low levels of retirement assets in those years. Indeed, many households hold no assets other than their Social Security claims. For example, among single-person households, 57.0 percent are last observed with less than $10,000 in financial assets. Of these households, 61.2 percent also have no home equity. Aggregating across all types of families, 46.1 percent are last observed with less than $10,000. Of these households, 51.7 percent also have no home equity.

These results raise fundamental questions about the health of the US retirement savings system. On one hand, economic models can rationalize the low wealth/income levels of retirees. Households may be optimally spending down their assets because of (a) predictable mortality events, (b) Medicaid means testing, (c) standard time preference effects[5] (and some reason for resisting annuitization), (d) lower expenditure needs in retirement relative to pre-retirement, and (e) an expectation of financial support from their children. On the other hand, steep life cycle declines in expenditure may result from less sanguine mechanisms, like bounded rationality or self-control problems. The identification of mechanisms will be advanced by papers like the current chapter, which characterize the key data that needs to be explained.

Will the Modern 401(k) Increase Wealth Accumulation?

I now turn to a related question. How will these patterns change for younger cohorts who are spending most of their working lives in firms with

---

5. In a classical model without liquidity constraints, a high rate of time preference (relative to the rate of interest) implies a falling level of consumption and wealth.

Table 1C.1   Net worth excluding Social Security and DB claims, Survey of
                    Consumer Finances

	Median ($)	Mean ($)
1983	123.4	450.4
1992	142.8	414.6
1995	150.0	471.4
1998	186.5	594.2
2001	207.9	793.5
2004	208.8	758.8
2007	239.4	1,015.7

Note: Households age sixty-five to seventy-four at time of survey; 2007 dollars.

401(k) plans? Will these new "DC cohorts" have more to retire on? The new cohorts are likely to look different in many ways, since defined-benefit (DB) pensions are rapidly shrinking as a fraction of the total pool of retirement assets. At year-end 2010, DC retirement accounts represented over two-thirds of the total pool of US retirement assets ($16.6 trillion).[6]

A first glance, the answer is not encouraging. Table 1C.1, derived from the Federal Reserve's triannual Survey of Consumer Finances, reports net worth (this time excluding DB and Social Security wealth) for households with a head aged sixty-five to seventy-four (all in 2007 dollars).[7] From 1983 to 2007,[8] mean net worth has more than doubled, but it has only kept pace with real GDP. Moreover, median net worth has not kept pace with real GDP. The final numbers are taken from year-end 2007, just before household net worth fell very sharply. In conclusion, looking across cohorts, recently retired cohorts look no better off (scaled by income) than cohorts that retired a generation ago.

There is also no ground for optimism if one studies the US gross and net savings rates, which have been trending down since the 1960s. The gradual switch from DB to DC systems (from 1980 to the present day) has done nothing to perturb this forty-five-year trend. For example, the net national savings rate was negative in 2009 (as well as 2010), for the first time since 1934 (see fig. 1C.1).

Finally, one can use a simple simulation model to see why 401(k)s probably will not change the patterns that PVW have documented. This simula-

6. Investment Company Institute.
7. These numbers are similar to the numbers in the 2008 HRS, which reports median net worth (excluding SS and DB wealth) of $221,700 and average net worth (excluding SS and DB wealth) of $567,500. The HRS numbers are lower partly because of the timing of the survey. By 2008, the financial crisis was under way and asset markets (including the housing market) had fallen considerably from the levels of one year earlier.
8. At the time of writing, the 2010 data was not yet available.

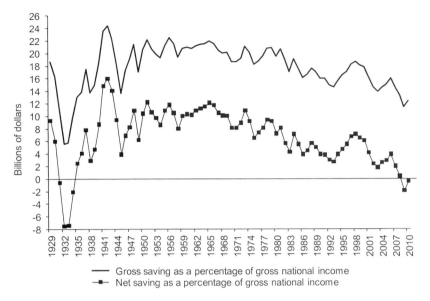

Fig. 1C.1   **Gross and net saving as a percentage of gross national income**

tion model shows why 401(k)s will not make a big difference unless they are reengineered in the future.

To begin this analysis, consider an illustrative benchmark case. We will soon see that this benchmark is far too optimistic. I make the following assumptions for the benchmark:

- 6.5 percent guaranteed nominal return (risk-adjusted rate of return)
- 2 percent inflation rate
- All employees contribute 6 percent of their income to a 401(k) (or equivalent individual account)
- 100 percent employer match of this 6 percent contribution
- No leakage before retirement
- Everyone starts working at age twenty-two (and starts participating at the same age)
- Starting job pays $35,000 (2011 dollars)
- 1 percent real wage growth until retirement at age sixty-seven
- 50 percent Social Security replacement rate
- 4 percent expenditure rule (i.e., retiree spends 4 percent of his accumulated financial assets)

These assumptions imply a total inflation-adjusted accumulation of 401(k) assets of $719,275 (2011 dollars), and a total replacement rate of 103 percent of final income. At this point, the situation looks promising.

Now let's make the simulation more realistic, by incorporating the following assumptions that better characterize the "representative" US worker:

1. Each year, 3.5 percent of the money in retirement accounts of *nonretirees* is withdrawn.[9] In practice, these *pre-retirement* withdrawals are comprised of cash distributions after an employer-employee separation, 401(k) loan defaults, 401(k) hardship withdrawals, and all types of IRA withdrawals (including nonpenalized withdrawals—e.g., certain expenditures on health, education, or home purchase—as well as penalized withdrawals).

2. Savings flows do not start until age thirty (instead of age twenty-two).

3. Forty percent of US workers do not have workplace access to a DC savings plan. I assume that these "no-access" workers have only a 33 percent participation rate—i.e., in any given year, one-third of these households make self-directed IRA contributions—and those who do contribute to IRAs save 5 percent of their income.

4. Among workers with a workplace DC plan, the match rate is 50 percent, not 100 percent.

5. Among workers with a workplace DC plan, 20 percent of workers (thirty years old and above) do not participate.

6. The (risk-adjusted, net-of-fees) return is 5.5 percent, not 6.5 percent.

7. The Social Security replacement rate will eventually be 45 percent, not 50 percent (for the representative worker that we are studying).

With all of these assumptions, total (real) savings falls drastically from the benchmark case. Specifically, total inflation-adjusted accumulation of 401(k) assets falls from $719,275 (2011 dollars) to $86,732, and the total replacement rate (including Social Security) falls from 103 percent to 51 percent of final labor income. This representative scenario implies very little wealth accumulation, and generates accumulation patterns that look remarkably like the financial wealth claims of the current cohort of retirees. For example, in the 2007 Survey of Consumer Finances, the median holding of financial assets is $68,100 (2007 dollars).

Many of the quantitative assumptions in this "representative" simulation are debatable, but tweaking them within the range of empirical plausibility barely affects the result. Moreover, these assumptions are probably still too rosy, since the calculations gloss over new challenges that will confront later cohorts of retirees, including rising longevity (which will decrease the

---

9. See Victoria L. Bryant, Sarah Holden, and John Sabelhaus, "Qualified Retirement Plans: Analysis of Distribution and Rollover Activity," mimeo 2010. See also "Leakage of Participants' DC Assets: How Loans, Withdrawals, and Cashouts Are Eroding Retirement Income," Aon Hewitt, 2011. http://www.aon.com/attachments/thought-leadership/survey_asset_leakage .pdf. See also, "401(k) Plans: Policy Changes Could Reduce the Long-Term Effects of Leakage on Workers' Retirement Savings," GAO-09-715, August 28, 2009. http://www.gao .gov/products/GAO-09-715.

sustainable payout rate) and rising out-of-pocket health costs (which will increase the optimal income replacement rate).

If policymakers want to address the financial vulnerabilities that PVW document, they are going to need to change the DC savings system going forward. Leading candidates include: (a) raising the net rate of return by reducing asset management and record-keeping fees (e.g., by agglomerating smaller plans and thereby exploiting scale economies); (b) raising participation within firms that offer 401(k)s; (c) raising the fraction of firms that offer workplace savings plans; (d) raising the typical 401(k) contribution rate by adopting more aggressive default contribution rates and using default auto-escalation; (e) reducing leakage by making defined contribution plans more illiquid.[10]

The important financial vulnerabilities that PVW have documented are likely to characterize generations to come, unless firms and policymakers revamp the retirement savings system.

10. For example, consider the following adjustments to the "representative" case described earlier: (a) raising the nominal (after-fee, risk-adjusted) return from 5.5 percent to 5.75 percent; (b) raising the participation rate from 80 percent to 95 percent in firms with 401(k) plans; (c) raising the fraction of workers that have a workplace 401(k) from 60 percent to 85 percent; (d) raising the worker contribution at firms with 401(k)s from 6 percent to 10 percent, and (e) cutting leakage from 3.5 percent to 0.5 percent. These five changes would jointly raise (inflation adjusted) 401(k) wealth accumulation to $463,673, implying a 74 percent income replacement ratio.

Economic Preparation for Retirement

Michael D. Hurd and Susann Rohwedder

2.1 Introduction

The most common metric for assessing the adequacy of economic preparation for retirement is the income replacement rate, the ratio of income after retirement to income before retirement. This metric is usually applied without regard to family circumstances or the complete portfolio of economic resources, particularly wealth. Thus, it is stated that a single person or a couple is adequately prepared if their post-retirement income is in some fixed ratio (such as 80 percent) to their pre-retirement income. However, both economic theory and common sense say that someone is adequately prepared if she is able to maintain her level of economic well-being, which is not the same as maintaining her level of income or some fixed proportion of income because of the accumulation and decumulation of wealth.

Consumption is a better measure of well-being or utility than the level of income at some particular point in time. But the relationship of consumption after retirement to consumption before retirement is not at all well measured by the relationship of income after retirement to income before retirement,

Michael D. Hurd is principal senior researcher and director of the Center for the Study of Aging at the RAND Corporation, a research fellow of NETSPAR, and a research associate of the National Bureau of Economic Research. Susann Rohwedder is senior economist and associate director of the Center for the Study of Aging at the RAND Corporation and a research fellow of NETSPAR.

We gratefully acknowledge research support from the Social Security Administration via the Michigan Retirement Research Center (UM06-03 and UM09-08), from the Department of Labor (J-9-P-2-0033), and from the National Institute on Aging (P01AG08291 and P01AG022481). We thank Joanna Carroll for excellent programming assistance. For acknowledgments, sources of research support, and disclosure of the authors' material financial relationships, if any, please see http://www.nber.org/chapters/c12431.ack.

which is the income replacement ratio. Consumption before retirement will typically be substantially less than income before retirement because of taxes (and Social Security contributions) and work-related expenses, but most importantly because of saving for retirement. Consumption after retirement will typically be greater than income because of the ability to spend out of saving. Furthermore, many retired households pay little or no taxes and make no Social Security contributions. The implication is that income could change by a great deal at retirement, yet consumption could be maintained.[1]

The overall goal of this chapter is to assess economic preparation for retirement in a way that addresses many of the deficiencies of the income replacement rate concept. We will find whether shortly after retirement households have the financial resources needed to finance a consumption plan from retirement through the end of life. The consumption plan begins at an observed starting value for each household and follows a path whose shape is determined by observed consumption change with age in panel data. We classify a single person as being adequately prepared if he or she dies with positive bequeathable wealth. A married person is adequately prepared if he or she dies with positive wealth where he or she may die as a married person or as a surviving spouse.

Because the age of death is unknown and because wealth is not completely annuitized, someone who dies unexpectedly early may have been adequately prepared ex post, yet someone who survives to extreme old age will not have been adequately prepared ex post. To account for this randomness we find via simulation the fraction of times ex post a household was adequately prepared.

Economic resources are a combination of post-retirement income, housing wealth, and nonhousing wealth. The estimations and simulations account for mortality risk, and, in the case of couples, the lifetime of the couple and the subsequent loss of returns-to-scale in consumption at the death of the first spouse. They recognize that consumption need not be constant with age. They incorporate the risk of large out-of-pocket spending on health care. We account for taxes, which for some households substantially reduce resources available for consumption.

Our main result is that about 70 percent of individuals age sixty-six to sixty-nine are adequately financially prepared for retirement. However, some individuals identified by education, sex, and marital status are not financially prepared, most notably single females who lack a high school education: just 29 percent of that group is adequately prepared.

---

1. An additional complicating factor is whether individuals have had children: if so, they will want to spend relatively more of their lifetime income during their working lives and thus will reach retirement with less wealth than someone who did not have children.

2.2   Data

Our analyses are based on data from the Health and Retirement Study (HRS) and data from the Consumption and Activities Mail Survey (CAMS). The HRS is a biennial panel. Its first wave was conducted in 1992. The target population was the cohorts born in 1931 to 1941 (Juster and Suzman 1995). Additional cohorts were added in 1993 and 1998 so that in 1998 it represented the population from the cohorts of 1947 or earlier. In 2004 more new cohorts were added, making the HRS representative of the population fifty-one or older. The HRS is very rich in content. In this study we take advantage of the detailed information on economic resources, out-of-pocket medical expenditures, and longitudinal information on survival.

The CAMS is a supplemental survey to the HRS that is administered to a random subsample of HRS households. One of its main objectives is to elicit total household spending over the preceding twelve months, which can be linked to the rich information collected in the HRS core survey on the same individuals and households. The first wave of CAMS was collected in the fall of 2001, and longitudinal follow-up surveys have been conducted every two years since then. When HRS inducts a refresher cohort into the survey, a random subsample of households that are part of the refresher group are also inducted into the CAMS. In this study we use data on household spending from the first four waves of CAMS, spanning the period from 2001 through 2007.[2] In the first two waves the unit response rate in CAMS was in the high seventies and it was 72 percent in waves 3 and 4. This yields spending data for just under 3,700 HRS households on average in each wave of CAMS.

With the CAMS, the HRS is the only general-purpose survey to attempt collecting a detailed measure of total spending. The fact that CAMS is longitudinal and that the spending data can be linked to the rich background information in the HRS core survey make the data unique. While the HRS cannot afford the level of detail asked about in the Consumer Expenditure Survey (CEX)—the survey in the United States that collects the most detailed and comprehensive information on total spending—CAMS nevertheless is notable for a number of design features that enhance data quality of the spending information.[3] These features have generated high item response rates so that relatively little information needs to be imputed to arrive at a measure of total spending for all households.

A natural validation exercise for the spending data in CAMS is to compare them to the CEX. As we show in Hurd and Rohwedder (2009b), the totals are almost identical among those fifty-five to sixty-four. At older ages the

2. We do not use data from CAMS 2009 because of the financial crisis. Observed consumption in CAMS 2009 was unusually low and that low level is unlikely to be maintained in the future. Anchoring baseline consumption to that temporarily low level would underestimate actual future spending and, hence, overestimate economic preparation for retirement.

3. See data appendix for details.

CEX shows lower spending than the CAMS, implying a much higher rate of saving for the older population than is consistent with actual rates of change in wealth as observed in HRS panel data. We therefore believe that the statistics from CAMS for the older population have greater validity.[4]

2.3 Methods

Our approach relies on simulating consumption paths over the remaining lifetime for a sample of households observed shortly after retirement. We construct life cycle consumption paths for each household. Whereas a model based on a particular utility function would specify that the slope of the consumption path depends on the interest rate, the subjective time rate of discount, mortality risk, and utility function parameters, we estimate these slopes directly from the data. Thus our estimations use the framework of lifetime utility maximization, but they are essentially nonparametric in that we allow the consumption path to be determined directly by the data.

We estimate the consumption trajectories from the initial level of consumption near retirement, which we observe directly in the CAMS data, and observed panel transitions in consumption in CAMS waves 1 to 2, 2 to 3, and 3 to 4 (three transitions). Economic resources at retirement consist of bequeathable wealth and annuities (Social Security benefits, defined-benefit [DB] pensions benefits, and actual annuities). We ask: Can the resources support the projected consumption path? Because lifetime is uncertain, and wealth is not typically annuitized, we perform multiple simulations making random draws from mortality tables. We find whether the resources will sustain the path at least until advanced old age where the probability of survival is small. If that is the case, the household will not have undersaved ex ante. We investigate whether any shortfalls in resources are large or small by finding the fraction of the sample that would have to reduce consumption by a large percentage to meet the adequacy criterion of being able to finance consumption to advanced old age.

We account for consumption of health care services on average in the CAMS data. This category of consumption is part of the CAMS measurement; consequently, it helps us determine a single person's initial total level of consumption and the rate of change in consumption with age. If there were no spending risk, out-of-pocket spending for health care would need no further treatment. However, because of spending risk, a single person's actual consumption of health care services will differ from the average level by a spending shock that has an expected value of zero, but which could

---

4. Panel wealth change shows slowly declining wealth among couples after age seventy. Among single persons, wealth declines after age seventy but at a greater rate. The CEX spending, when combined with HRS after-tax income would, in contradiction, predict steadily increasing wealth for couples and too little wealth decline among single persons.

be quite large. We construct that shock from HRS data on out-of-pocket spending for health care services.

We do these calculations of the consumption trajectory modified by simulated health care spending shocks for each single person in our CAMS sample who is in his or her early retirement years.

For couples the basic method is similar. However, the consumption path followed while both spouses survive will differ from the consumption path of single persons, so it is separately estimated from the CAMS data. The couple will follow that consumption path as long as both spouses survive, and then the surviving spouse will switch to the consumption path of a single person. The shape of the single's path is estimated as described earlier, but the level of consumption by the surviving spouse will depend on returns-to-scale in consumption by the couple. At the death of the first spouse, the surviving spouse reduces consumption to the level specified by the returns-to-scale parameter. We assume a returns-to-scale parameter that is consistent with the literature and with practice. For example, the poverty line specifies that a couple with 1.26 times the income of a single person who is at the poverty line will also be at the poverty line. This implies that consumption by the surviving spouse should be 79 percent of consumption by the couple to equate effective consumption. Knowing the consumption path of the surviving spouse, we find the expected present value of consumption for the lifetime of the couple and surviving spouse.

We assess adequacy of retirement resources in three ways. First, we compare population averages of the expected present value of consumption with average resources at retirement to find whether the cohort can finance the expected consumption path. Second, we move from the cohort level to the household level to determine the fraction of households that can finance with high probability their expected consumption path. Third, we find by how much a household would have to adjust consumption to keep the chances of running out of wealth toward the end of the life cycle small.

2.4   Model for Singles

In this section we more formally develop the ideas discussed previously. Suppose a single person retires at age R. Call that $t = 0$. He or she retires with real annuity S_0 and nominal annuity P_0, the inflation rate is f, and the nominal interest rate F, which implies a real interest rate $r = F - f$. Then the real annuity at some later time t is $A_t = S_0 + P_0/(1 + f)^t$. When the only source of uncertainty is mortality risk (and ignoring any bequest motive), according to the life cycle model a single person will choose optimal consumption to satisfy

$$(1) \qquad \frac{d \ln c_t}{dt} = \frac{1}{\gamma_t}(r - \rho - h_t),$$

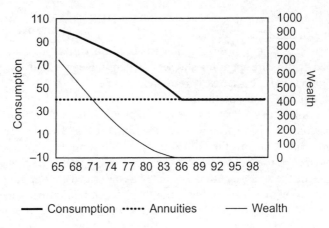

Fig. 2.1   Optimal spending: Single person

as long as bequeathable wealth is positive, where γ_t is local risk aversion (which in general need not be constant), r is the fixed real interest rate, ρ is the subjective time rate of discount, and h_t is mortality risk. Because h_t is approximately exponential, at some (relatively young) age consumption will decline with age. The optimal consumption level will be determined by adjusting the consumption path so that at the age when consumption has declined to equal annuity income, age T, bequeathable wealth is zero. At that point consumption will not drop further: it will equal annuities at all subsequent ages. Figure 2.1 has an example of an optimal path. Initial consumption is 100, initial wealth is 700 (right scale), annuities are 40. The consumption path is determined by equation (1) for the values $r = 0.01$, $\rho = 0.01$, and $\gamma_t = \gamma = 1.3$. Mortality risk is that of men from the year 2000 life table. The area under the consumption path but above the annuity path equals initial bequeathable wealth and consumption equals annuities at age $T = 86$, when wealth becomes zero.

Figure 2.2 shows the consumption path that is also determined by equation (1), but where initial consumption is 110. Wealth reaches zero at age seventy-eight, but consumption at that age is seventy-six so the lifetime budget constraint requires a discontinuous drop in consumption to 40, which is not optimal. Conditional on survival to at least seventy-nine, the single person undersaved, or equivalently, overconsumed at age sixty-five.

Figure 2.3 shows the consumption path when initial consumption is 94. At age $T = 86$ when consumption equals annuities, wealth is positive. Because consumption equals annuity income at greater ages, wealth will grow at the interest rate. This person could increase initial consumption and in this sense she has oversaved.

In the empirical application we construct the consumption path $\{c_t\}$ such that initial consumption, c_0, is given by observed consumption at or near retirement and the change in consumption from one period to the next. The

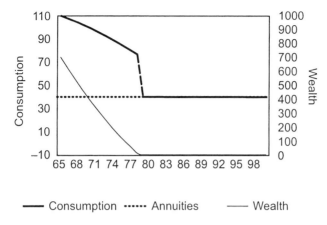

— Consumption ⋯⋯ Annuities   — Wealth

Fig. 2.2   Overspending: Single person

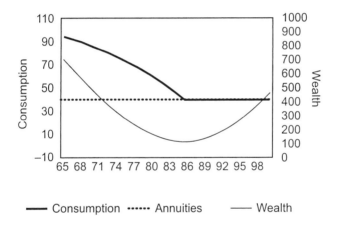

— Consumption ⋯⋯ Annuities   — Wealth

Fig. 2.3   Underspending: Single person

fraction $\Delta c/c$ is estimated over four waves of CAMS panel data by age band, education, and sex. The present value of spending in excess of annuities is $PV_T = \sum_{t=1}^{T}[(c_t - A_t)/(1 + r)^t]$. If PV_T is less than initial wealth the person will die with positive wealth. We would say that this person is adequately prepared for retirement. If PV_T is greater than initial bequeathable wealth, the empirical consumption path is not feasible should the individual survive to T: at some prior age consumption would have to drop discontinuously.

2.5   Model for Couples

The life cycle model for couples is considerably more complicated than the model for single persons. Under the same assumptions as for the singles model the first-order condition for consumption by a couple is

$$\frac{d \ln C_t}{dt} = \frac{1}{\gamma}(r - \rho - h_t) + \frac{1}{\gamma}\frac{\Omega_t}{C_t^{-\gamma}},$$

where h_t = the couple's mortality risk (the probability density that one of them will die at t given that neither has died before t), C_t is consumption by the couple, γ is the risk aversion parameter in the couple's constant relevant risk aversion (CRRA) utility function, r is the fixed real interest rate, and ρ is the subjective time rate of discount of the couple. The last term accounts for "bequests" to the surviving spouse: Ω_t is the expected marginal utility of wealth should one of the spouses die. It is composed of two terms: the marginal utility of wealth of the widower weighted by the mortality hazard of the wife and the marginal utility of wealth of the widow weighted by the mortality hazard of the husband. Variable Ω_t varies from couple to couple according to the marginal utility of wealth of the survivor should one of the spouses die. The marginal utility of wealth of the survivor varies by the wealth of the couple (which the survivor will "inherit"), the mortality risk of the survivor, and the level of pension and Social Security benefits that the survivor will have. Predictions about the slope and level of the consumption path are complex because of Ω_t. But consumption should decline if both spouses are old because the marginal utility of wealth will be small for an old surviving spouse. The slope of the consumption path should be greater algebraically (flatter) when one spouse is young because the marginal utility of wealth is large for a young spouse.

To find the predicted consumption path of a couple we begin with C_0, which is observed consumption by a couple at baseline. Then we project consumption to the next period by $C_{t+1} = C_t(1 + G_t)$, where G_t is the annual growth rate of consumption by couples. We estimate G_t by age and education bands between waves 1 and 2, 2 and 3, and 3 and 4 of CAMS in a nonparametric manner directly from the spending data, just as we did for singles. The associated wealth path is $W_{t+1} = W_t(1 + r) - C_t + A_t$, where r is an assumed real rate of interest. The couples model differs from the singles model in that one spouse will die before the other and the surviving spouse will continue to consume, but the consumption level will change according to returns-to-scale. Suppose the husband dies. Then the widow will "inherit" the wealth of the couple, an annuity that is some fraction of A_t, and a consumption level that reflects returns-to-scale. According to the poverty line, the widow would need $1/1.26 = 0.794$ of the consumption of the couple; according to scaling of the wife's and widow's benefits in Social Security, the widow would need $1/1.5 = 0.667$. From that point on the widow will follow the singles model, taking as initial conditions the inherited wealth, the reduced annuities, and the reduced consumption level.

Figure 2.4 has an example under the assumption that both spouses are initially sixty-five and that the husband dies at age eighty. Initial consumption is 100 and initial wealth is 925. Prior to age eighty consumption by the

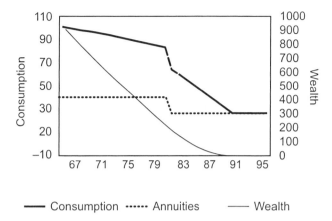

— Consumption ⋯⋯ Annuities —— Wealth

Fig. 2.4   Optimal spending by couple and subsequent survivor: Widowing at age 80

couple follows $C_{t+1} = C_t(1 + G_t)$. The household's consumption declines when the husband dies because of returns-to-scale, and then it follows the path of singles.[5] In the case shown, the couple and surviving spouse could just exactly afford the initial consumption. Should the widow survive to ninety-one or beyond, wealth would be exhausted.

If initial consumption were greater than 100 the surviving spouse would be forced to reduce consumption discontinuously should that spouse survive to age ninety. If initial consumption were less than 100 the surviving spouse would die with positive wealth.

The foregoing assumes widowing at eighty, but we implement random widowing. Take the same couple, where both are initially sixty-five. Randomly choose whether both, one, or neither spouse survives with probabilities given by life table survival hazards. If both survive we continue calculating the couple's consumption and wealth path. If the husband dies, we switch to the widow's consumption path and apply the estimated consumption growth rates of a single female. We find the expected present value of spending in excess of annuities. If the wife dies we perform the same calculation, except that we use the rate of change in consumption estimated for single males. If both die, we stop the calculations.

The outcomes of one simulation are: Did the household die with positive wealth? If so, how much compared with initial wealth? If not, what is the wealth shortfall?

By repeating the simulations a number of times for the same household we can find the probability that the household will die with positive wealth

---

5. Note that we refer to household-level variables throughout our exposition. When one spouse dies, household consumption declines, but consumption per capita increases because of returns-to-scale in consumption when both spouses are alive.

or negative wealth and the distribution of those excesses or shortfalls in wealth.

2.6   Inputs into Simulations

2.6.1   Differential Mortality

A large literature on the gradient between socioeconomic status (SES) and health documents that individuals with high SES such as high education live longer than those with low SES (Kitagawa and Hauser 1973; Marmot et al. 1991; Adams et al. 2003). Because households are not fully annuitized, long-lived households have to be prepared to finance consumption over a longer remaining time horizon. We take this into account in our simulations by applying survival probabilities that differentiate by education as well as by age, sex, and marital status.

We obtain our estimates of differential mortality based on eight waves of HRS data spanning the years 1992 to 2006. We estimate the probability of 2-year survival to time $t + 2$, conditional on being alive at time t, pooling the seven transitions we observe in the HRS. The logit model yields the estimates shown in table 2.1 for males and females as a function of age, marital status, and education. For single males the odds of survival for college graduates between waves is 44 percent higher than the odds of survival for high school dropouts. For both men and women the survival odds increase in education, and for both there is a substantial interaction between completing college and being married.

From these estimates we construct survival curves by sex, marital status,

Table 2.1   Logistic estimates of the effects of personal characteristics on 2-year survival

	Males ($N = 37,797$)			Females ($N = 49,224$)		
	Coefficient	Standard error	P-value	Coefficient	Standard error	P-value
Married	0.290	0.043	0.000	0.271	0.043	0.000
Education						
Less than high school	—	—	—	—	—	—
High school	0.139	0.044	0.001	0.268	0.040	0.000
Some college	0.234	0.055	0.000	0.388	0.051	0.000
College or more	0.363	0.106	0.001	0.338	0.075	0.000
Couple*college or more	0.196	0.120	0.102	0.290	0.131	0.027
Age spline: age <64	−0.079	0.061	0.197	−0.150	0.073	0.040
Age 64–73	−0.083	0.008	0.000	−0.072	0.009	0.000
Age 74–83	−0.094	0.006	0.000	−0.103	0.006	0.000
Age 84+	−0.109	0.009	0.000	−0.116	0.006	0.000
Constant	7.836	3.898	0.044	12.824	4.648	0.006

Source: Authors' calculations.

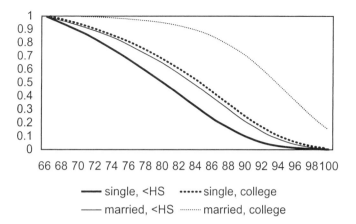

Fig. 2.5   Fitted survival curves: Women by marital status and education (< high school or college graduate)

and education and normalize these to life tables so that the average survival probability given age and sex equals that given in the life tables. Figure 2.5 has examples of the estimated survival curves for females. A single female lacking a high school education has a 50 percent chance of surviving to age eighty, while a single female with a college education has a 50 percent change of surviving to age eighty-four. For married women the difference by education is considerably larger: the age at which survival chances fall below 50 percent is about ten years greater among women with a college education than among women lacking a high school degree. These survival differences translate into large differences in life expectancy. For example, married men with a college degree have a life expectancy that is 39 percent greater than single men who lack a high school degree. Such long-lived men need correspondingly greater bequeathable wealth to finance their retirement years.

Figure 2.6 has similar survival curves for males. The survival chances for males are lower than for females, but the patterns by education and by marital status are similar.

2.6.2   Estimation of Consumption Paths

Because survival differs by age, sex, and education the slope of the consumption path should vary by those characteristics according to equation (1). Therefore we estimate the model

(2) $$\frac{c_{t+1} - c_t}{c_t} = \alpha_i + \beta_j + \theta_k + u,$$

where i indicates the age category, j indicates sex, and k indicates the education category. We have four education categories: less than high school, high school, some college, and college graduate. For singles we have five age

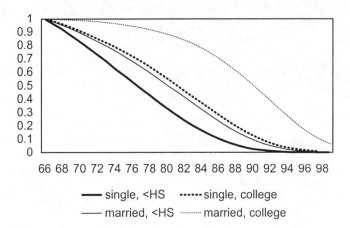

Fig. 2.6   **Fitted survival curves: Men by marital status and education (< high school or college graduate)**

categories: sixty-five to sixty-nine, seventy to seventy-four, seventy-five to seventy-nine, eighty to eighty-four, and eighty-five or over. We observed 2,037 consumption transitions among singles sixty-five or older between the four waves of CAMS. For couples we have just four age categories because of small sample size in the top age category. In addition we entered categorical variables for the age of the spouse. We observed 4,593 consumption transitions among couples where both spouses were sixty-two or older and at least one spouse was sixty-six to sixty-nine or older. We estimated by median regression because observation error on consumption produces large outliers in the left-hand variable, which makes ordinary least squares (OLS) estimates unreliable. We restricted the sample to those with observed positive wealth because consumption change cannot be freely chosen if a household has no wealth.

Table 2.2 shows the predicted one-year change in consumption by single persons based on equation (2). It is notable that almost all the changes are negative, indicating reductions in consumption with age. Table 2.3 has similar results for married persons. It has a separate panel for couples where the husband is older than the wife by five years or more because theory predicts the slope of the consumption path will be algebraically larger when the wife is young. In the estimation that turns out not to be the case: for example, when the husband is sixty-five to sixty-nine and the wife's age differs from the husband's by less than five years, the slope is –0.86 (less than high school education), but when the wife's age differs by five years or more the slope is –2.31. A possible explanation might be that households with a large age difference between spouses differ in some other ways from other households. The prediction from theory assumes that all else is held the same except the age difference.

Table 2.2   **Estimated one-year change in consumption: Single persons (N = 2,037)**

		Education			
	N	Less than high school	High school graduate	Some college	College and above
Female age					
65–69	403	–3.35	–2.29	–2.31	–1.09
70–74	366	–2.49	–1.44	–1.46	–0.23
75–79	316	–4.08	–3.02	–3.05	–1.82
80–84	296	–6.14	–5.08	–5.11	–3.88
85 or over	283	–4.53	–3.47	–3.50	–2.27
Male Age					
65–69	114	–1.89	–0.83	–0.85	0.37
70–74	79	–1.03	0.02	0.00	1.23
75–79	73	–2.62	–1.56	–1.59	–0.36
80–84	67	–4.68	–3.62	–3.65	–2.42
85 or over	40	–3.07	–2.01	–2.04	–0.81

Source: Authors' calculations.

Table 2.3   **Estimated one-year change in consumption: Couples (N = 4,593)**

			Education			
Male age – female age	Male age	N	Less than high school	High school graduate	Some college	College and above
<5 years	62–64	92	3.59	3.59	3.18	3.23
	65–69	1,227	–0.86	–0.86	–1.28	–1.23
	70–74	1,060	–1.40	–1.40	–1.81	–1.77
	75–79	689	–1.38	–1.38	–1.79	–1.75
	80+	379	–2.38	–2.38	–2.79	–2.75
5+ years	65–69	143	–2.31	–2.31	–2.72	–2.68
	70–74	381	–2.85	–2.85	–3.26	–3.21
	75–79	315	–2.83	–2.83	–3.24	–3.20
	80+	307	–3.83	–3.83	–4.24	–4.19

Source: Authors' calculations.

To see the implications of these differing slopes for lifetime consumption, we show in figure 2.7 examples of fitted consumption paths for single women. The paths are normalized at 100 at age sixty-five. College graduates have flatter consumption paths than those with less education as would be expected from their greater survival chances. There is little difference among those with high school or some college (their consumption paths are on top of each other in the graph). Those lacking a high school degree have still greater rates of decline. This group has a 50 percent chance of surviving to age eighty, at which time consumption will have dropped to about 60 percent of its level at age sixty-five. For comparison we have graphed the optimal consumption

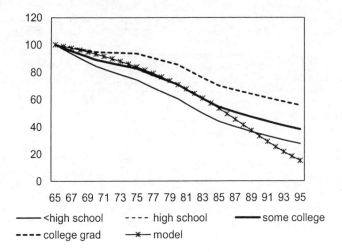

Fig. 2.7   **Fitted life cycle consumption paths: Single females**

path based on CRRA utility, where the path is generated by equation (1). Risk aversion, γ, is 1.12, which Hurd (1989) estimated on wealth change data in the Retirement History Survey. In this simulation, $r = \rho$. We use life table mortality risk of women. The paths generated by the CAMS consumption changes for those with a high school degree or some college are practically identical to the path generated by the model up to about the age of eighty-five.[6]

Figure 2.8 shows consumption paths of couples where both spouses are the same age. The most obvious difference from the consumption paths of single women is that consumption by couples shows less decline. This is to be expected because the couple has a strong desire to leave wealth to a surviving spouse, as reflected in substantial marginal utility of wealth to the surviving spouse. There is little difference in the paths by education.[7] Because of the high mortality risk of the couple, the most relevant part of the consumption path is up to about age eighty. Over this age range consumption declines slowly, to about 80 percent of initial consumption.

2.6.3   Future Earnings

In our analytical sample, 24 percent of sixty-six to sixty-nine-year-old single persons and 23 percent of married persons are working for pay at baseline. Among married persons, those still working are mostly younger spouses. To forecast the future earnings of workers we first predict the probability of working for pay in the next period, conditional on working in the

6. The trajectories of consumption by single men have a similar pattern but are flatter. Single men comprise 18 percent of single persons in our sample.
7. Education is the education of the respondent to the CAMS survey, which for couples was chosen at random.

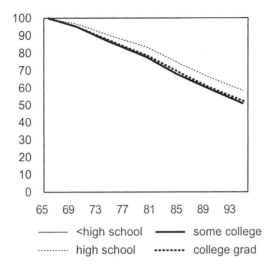

Fig. 2.8   Fitted life cycle consumption paths: Married persons

Note: Age is husband's age. Age difference between husband and wife is five years or less.

current period. We obtain these predictions from panel data estimations regressing working for pay in the HRS on covariates, including age, sex, marital status, and education. We then multiply this probability of working with the respondent's observed baseline earnings adjusted for earnings growth. Earnings growth by gender and marital status is also estimated on HRS panel data among respondents of the relevant age and with positive earnings in adjacent survey waves. See the data appendix for further details.

For those who are not working for pay at baseline, we assume that they will not work in the future.

2.6.4   Taxes

Taxes influence economic preparation for retirement via four routes. The first is federal and state tax paid on ordinary income such as earnings, capital income, and pension income. The second is Social Security contributions paid on earnings. The third is that Social Security income is only partially counted as taxable income and the fraction depends on the level of other taxable income and on the amount of Social Security income. The fourth is that withdrawals from tax-advantaged accounts such as IRAs are taxed and minimum withdrawals become mandatory at age 70 1/2. We have accounted for these taxes in a somewhat simplified manner, which nonetheless addresses all of these elements. See the data appendix for further details.

Because low income groups pay very little, if any, taxes in retirement, accounting for taxes for them has little impact on the assessment of whether the household is economically prepared for retirement. For example, the median tax rate among those in the lowest annuity income quartile (pension plus Social Security) is zero, and it is just 1 percent in the second annuity income quartile. In addition, those who pay some income tax often pay no tax at all on Social Security benefits. However, among high-income groups the situation is very different. They tend to have sizable pretax retirement assets (IRAs) and they are most likely to have 85 percent of their Social Security benefits taxed. As a result, taking into account the effect of taxation is likely to have a greater effect on economic preparation for retirement for those with more education than for those with less education.

2.6.5   Housing

Older households tend to retain their housing wealth, or more precisely their primary residence, until advanced old age (Venti and Wise 2004). In terms of financing spending in retirement it appears that housing wealth is often not used until other assets are exhausted. To approximately replicate these patterns, we separate housing wealth held in the primary residence from other assets. We assume that this form of housing wealth is not depleted until all other wealth has been drawn down. This matters for taxation, because it requires that IRA balances are withdrawn and subject to taxation before housing equity is accessed. We assume that housing wealth appreciates at a real rate of return of 2.5 percent, which is approximately the rate observed from 1985 to 2006.[8] We assume that capital gains in housing accumulate tax free, which is the case for the great majority of households because of the large federal tax exemption ($500,000 lifetime capital gains on primary residence per person) that most people would not exhaust.

2.6.6   Health Care Spending Risk

To account for health care spending risk we draw from the distribution of out-of-pocket health care spending in HRS 2008. We use that year for two reasons. When we compared the level and distribution of out-of-pocket spending for health care in HRS 2004 with similar measures in the Medical Expenditure Panel Survey (MEPS) and the Medicare Current Beneficiary Survey (MCBS), we found that mean out-of-pocket spending in the HRS was about 60 percent greater than in the MCBS or MEPS (which were similar); yet, HRS medians were practically the same as in MCBS and in MEPS (Hurd and Rohwedder 2009a). The discrepancy in means is due to some very large values in HRS. For example, the ninety-ninth percentile of spending in 2004 HRS was $24,600 (expressed in 2003 prices). The ninety-ninth percentile in the 2003 MCBS was $11,400 and $9,300 in the 2003 MEPS. Thus the risk of out-of-pocket spending for health care is substantially greater in HRS than in MCBS or in MEPS. We determined that the main source of the difference is in the measurement of spending for prescription drugs. The

---

8. Based on the Federal Housing Finance Agency quarterly house price index adjusted by the CPI (http://www.fhfa.gov/Default.aspx?Page=87, accessed 6/17/2011).

HRS modified in 2006 the questions about spending on prescription drugs, which brought HRS back in line with MEPS and MCBS.[9]

The second reason we use HRS 2008 is the introduction of Medicare Part D in 2006, which reduced the risk of large out-of-pocket spending for some retirees. This reduction should have an impact on economic preparation for retirement that we want to take into account.

2.6.7   Serial Correlation in Out-of-Pocket Spending for Health Care

People who have chronic conditions are likely to have greater than average spending on health care each year, which induces serial correlation in out-of-pocket spending. Serial correlation increases the likelihood that someone will have several successive years of high spending, increasing the risk of not being adequately economically prepared for retirement.

To account for serial correlation at the household level we estimate a model of out-of-pocket spending by marital status specified as follows:

$$\ln(s_{ijk,t}) = (\alpha_i + \alpha_j + \alpha_k) + (\beta_i + \beta_j + \beta_k)\ln(s_{ijk,t-1}),$$

where i indexes age, j indexes sex, and k indexes education. Thus the correlation between spending at $t - 1$ and t will depend in an additive manner on those personal characteristics. The categories of age and education are the same as those we have used in the specifications for the consumption trajectories and for mortality.

We estimated this model on MCBS 2004 and 2005. We chose MCBS for several reasons. First, we could not use HRS because our model has one-year transitions, and HRS is a two-year panel. Second, MEPS specializes in measuring health care spending, including out-of-pocket spending, but we could not use it because it does not cover the institutionalized population. Third, MCBS spends a considerable amount of interviewing resources to collect out-of-pocket spending data, and it compares well with MEPS for the noninstitutionalized population.

Table 2.4 shows estimated serial correlation in health care spending based on the regression of out-of-pocket spending in 2005 on out-of-pocket spending in 2004. There is strong persistence in spending: for example, among sixty-five to sixty-nine-year-old single males in the lowest education band the coefficient on lagged spending is 0.56, which implies that spending in the current year is comprised of 46 percent of last year's out-of-pocket spending and 54 percent of a new draw on out-of-pocket spending from HRS.[10] Although the increase is not monotonic in age, serial correlation tends to increase with age so that in the age band eighty-five or older 56 percent of the current year's spending is from last year's spending and just 44 percent is

---

9. See Hurd and Rohwedder (2009a) for further details.

10. Current year out-of-pocket spending is a weighted average of last year's spending and a new draw from HRS. The weight on last year's spending is ρ, which is the serial correlation coefficient in year-to-year spending; the weight on the new draw from HRS is $\sqrt{1 - \rho^2}$. See the data appendix for more detail.

Table 2.4   Serial correlation in out-of-pocket medical expenditures

	Education			
	Less than high school	High school	Some college	College or more
Single males				
Age 65–69	0.559	0.490	0.454	0.435
70–74	0.682	0.613	0.577	0.558
75–79	0.680	0.610	0.574	0.556
80–84	0.702	0.633	0.597	0.578
85+	0.701	0.632	0.596	0.577
Single females				
Age 65–69	0.590	0.521	0.484	0.466
70–74	0.713	0.644	0.608	0.589
75–79	0.711	0.641	0.605	0.587
80–84	0.733	0.664	0.627	0.609
85+	0.732	0.663	0.627	0.608
Couples				
Age 62–69	0.529	0.460	0.423	0.405
70–74	0.652	0.583	0.547	0.528
75–79	0.650	0.580	0.544	0.526
80+	0.672	0.602	0.566	0.548

Source: Authors' calculations.

from a new HRS draw. This increase is likely due to the increase in chronic conditions with age. Serial correlation declines in education, which is likely due to fewer chronic conditions among the better educated.

We incorporate the serial correlation coefficients in out-of-pocket spending for health care, which increases the variance in spending and, hence, the likelihood of running out of wealth prior to death. The details of the simulations can be found in the data appendix.

2.7   Results

To obtain the initial conditions for the simulations we need a population-representative sample in which we observed all or almost all of the relevant data. Because we want to observe Social Security and pension income we select a sample shortly after retirement and of a sufficient age that they are likely to be receiving Social Security if they are eligible. We select couples where one spouse is sixty-six, sixty-seven, sixty-eight, or sixty-nine, and the other is sixty-two or older; they were respondents in CAMS wave 1, 2, 3, or 4; and they were a couple in the HRS surrounding waves. We make the age restriction on the younger spouse because spouses younger than sixty-two would likely not yet be receiving Social Security benefits even by the time we observe them in the latest available HRS wave of 2008, and so we might miss a significant fraction of retirement resources. We select singles who

Table 2.5   Comparison of simulation sample with HRS 2008

	Single persons		Married persons		All		
	Simulation sample	HRS 2008	Simulation sample	HRS 2008	Simulation sample	HRS 2008	HRS weighted
Female (%)	76.6	73.5	61.4	53.5	67.0	60.6	58.2
Married (%)	—	—	—	—	63.3	64.6	63.8
Education (% distn)							
Less than high school	25.9	27.2	17.1	20.3	20.3	22.8	19.0
High school	39.2	35.6	43.4	39.0	41.9	37.8	37.7
Some college	20.9	21.4	20.4	20.0	20.6	20.5	21.8
College or more	14.1	15.8	19.0	20.7	17.2	18.9	21.5
N	633	831	1,092	1,519	1,725	2,350	2,350

Source: Authors' calculations.

were sixty-six to sixty-nine who were respondents to CAMS wave 1, 2, 3, or 4. Our simulation sample comprises 633 single persons and 1,092 married persons.

Table 2.5 compares the distributions of some characteristics of our simulation sample with distributions from HRS using the same age selections. With few exceptions, the distributions of characteristics are similar in the two samples.

We perform 100 simulations of the consumption and wealth paths of each person who is in the age range sixty-six to sixty-nine. By consumption we mean the consumption by the couple as long as both spouses survive and also the consumption by the survivor. Although we begin with 866 couple households, we only have 1,092 married persons who are age-eligible (sixty-six to sixty-nine), the other spouses being outside the given age range. The economic circumstances of the 1,092 age-eligible persons will enter the tables. In these simulations we use the poverty line for returns-to-scale in consumption (0.794) and assume that the annuity of the survivor is 0.67 times the annuity of the couple.

Tables 2.6 and onward have the results of the simulations, incorporating differential mortality and differential rates of consumption change by education level, age, sex and marital status, random serially correlated out-of-pocket health care spending, taxes, and a "last out" treatment of housing wealth. Table 2.6 shows population averages of the simulations for single persons. In 63 percent of the simulations individuals die with positive wealth, but among the least educated just 46 percent die with positive wealth. The sum of initial average wealth, the average present value of earnings and the average present value of annuities for single persons is about $463,000. The present value of consumption and taxes is about $331,000, so that average excess wealth is $132,000. At least as measured by average resources and spending (including taxes), single persons are well-prepared financially

Table 2.6   Economic resources and expenditures: Single persons, thousands (2008$)

	N	Percent positive (%)	Mean initial wealth	Mean PV of earnings	Mean PV annuities	Mean PV taxes	Mean PV consumption	Mean excess wealth	Median excess wealth
Less than high school	164	45.6	60.2	6.0	106.8	3.2	201.3	−30.9	−7.7
High school	248	68.0	232.2	13.8	193.0	23.3	266.8	149.5	74.4
Some college	132	66.6	317.5	20.1	226.1	41.4	353.3	170.8	96.7
College and above	89	75.8	538.2	44.0	329.2	95.3	490.9	325.1	201.3
All	633	63.0	248.4	17.4	196.7	32.0	299.4	131.9	50.6

Source: Authors' calculations.

for retirement. The median of the household-level amount of excess wealth is about $51,000, indicating that the household of the median person is well-prepared, but not with a large margin of adjustment. Excess wealth increases strongly with education: among the least educated even average resources fall short of average outflows by about $31 thousand.

Couples are much better prepared on average (table 2.7). Their average resources are about $1.2 million. The sum of taxes and consumption is $681,000, resulting in $525,000 in excess wealth. As with single persons, there is a strong gradient with respect to education.

Tables 2.6 and 2.7 show population averages, not the situation of individuals. The fraction of simulations in which wealth is positive at death does not provide the risk of any individual or household outliving resources. For example, the 63 percent in the case of single persons would be achieved if every single person had a 63 percent chance or if 63 percent of single persons had a 100 percent chance of dying with positive wealth and 37 percent had no chance. Because we are interested in the fraction of individuals that runs out of resources at the end of the life cycle, we have arranged all subsequent tables at the individual level. They show the characteristics and results for sixty-six to sixty-nine-year-olds living in couple households and in single households at baseline.

Our individual-level metric for the probability of dying with positive wealth is based on the fraction of simulations for which an individual in a couple or a single person dies with positive wealth. In this metric we say that the individual is adequately prepared if the chances of dying with positive wealth are 95 percent or greater. Table 2.8 shows that among single persons about 49 percent are adequately prepared. In the lowest education category only 27 percent of women are adequately prepared, compared with 61 percent of men. Overall about 77 percent of married persons are adequately prepared. The average for males and females is about the same. As would be predicted from the wealth and consumption averages in table 2.7, those with more education are better prepared.

The preceding tables measured adequate preparation for retirement in terms of residual wealth at death. This measure does not distinguish whether the required adjustment to a household's consumption path is large or small relative to current consumption. For example, a household with generous annuities, say of $80,000 per year, may have similar shortfalls in excess wealth as a household with very low annuity entitlements. Yet the consumption floor that either of these households faces is very different and so are the welfare implications. If a household with a consumption level of $10,000 per year has to reduce consumption by $1,000 to keep the probability of running out of wealth sufficiently low, this implies a drop in consumption of 10 percent at an already very low level of consumption. For a household with a consumption level of $80,000 per year a drop in consumption by $1,000 is equivalent to a drop of only 1.25 percent at a much higher level of

Table 2.7   Economic resources and expenditures: Couples, thousands (2008$)

	N	Percent positive (%)	Mean initial wealth	Mean PV of future earnings	Mean PV annuities	Mean PV taxes	Mean PV consumption	Mean excess wealth	Median excess wealth
Less than high school	187	75.1	284.6	14.0	265.4	27.9	321.2	215.0	137.2
High school	474	84.3	499.2	16.5	395.7	75.7	441.9	394.2	261.5
Some college	223	85.3	1,024.5	22.7	477.6	227.9	595.9	701.4	337.9
College and above	208	88.9	1,406.7	56.7	651.0	319.2	880.4	913.9	572.3
All	1,092	83.8	742.6	25.0	438.7	145.0	536.2	525.2	287.6

Source: Authors' calculations.

Table 2.8   **Percent adequately prepared: 95 to 100 percent chance of dying with positive wealth**

	Single persons			Married persons		
	All	Males	Females	All	Males	Females
Less than high school	33.5	60.6	26.7	66.8	65.5	68.0
High school	54.4	61.9	51.9	77.4	74.7	78.8
Some college	50.8	62.5	47.0	76.2	73.4	77.8
College and above	61.8	65.0	60.9	85.1	83.3	86.6
All	49.3	62.2	45.4	76.8	74.6	78.2

Source: Authors' calculations.

Table 2.9   **Percent adequately prepared: 95 to 100 percent chance of dying with positive wealth after reducing consumption by 10 percent**

	Single persons			Married persons		
	All	Males	Females	All	Males	Females
Less than high school	36.0	63.6	29.0	70.1	70.2	69.9
High school	62.1	66.7	60.5	79.5	77.2	80.8
Some college	53.8	62.5	51.0	80.7	77.2	82.6
College and above	68.5	65.0	69.6	88.5	86.5	90.2
All	54.5	64.9	51.3	79.9	77.9	81.1

Source: Authors' calculations.

consumption. Due to the concavity of the utility function, the welfare loss for the latter household will be even smaller in comparison.

A household would be far from adequately prepared if it had to reduce initial consumption by a substantial amount in order to reduce the chances of running out of wealth to 5 percent or less. To assess the sensitivity of adequate preparation to the initial consumption level, we reduce initial consumption by each household by 10 percent and define adequate preparation as before. Table 2.9 shows that among single persons the overall rate is 55 percent. An especially inadequately prepared group is females in the lowest education category: just 29 percent are adequately prepared. Among married persons about 80 percent are adequately prepared, and females are slightly more likely to be prepared than men. Even among married high school dropouts about 70 percent are adequately prepared.

A comparison of tables 2.8 and 2.9 shows that the reduction of 10 percent in initial consumption increases economic preparation by 5.2 percentage points among single persons and 3.1 percentage points among couples, which in view of the relatively large reductions in consumption are rather small changes. The implication is that a substantial number of persons are overconsuming by an amount that places them fairly far from being prepared.

Table 2.10   Sensitivity of adequacy assessment to thresholds

	Reduction in initial consumption					
	Singles			Married persons		
Percent chances of dying with positive wealth	5 (%)	10 (%)	15 (%)	5 (%)	10 (%)	15 (%)
≥ 95	51.8	54.5	57.2	78.3	79.9	81.4
≥ 90	55.3	58.0	61.1	79.8	81.2	83.0
≥ 85	57.8	60.8	63.5	80.7	82.3	84.6
≥ 80	59.7	62.1	64.9	81.5	83.0	86.1

Source: Authors' calculations.
Note: Percent of persons adequately prepared based on variation in chances of dying with positive wealth and reduction in initial consumption.

Our definition of adequate preparation makes some ad hoc choices regarding the cut-off points for the chances of running out of wealth and the allowable reduction in initial consumption. We have presented results for a cut-off of 5 percent or less for the chances of running out of wealth, but some might argue that this could also be higher or possibly smaller. Similarly, we have chosen a reduction of initial consumption by 10 percent or more to signal inadequate preparation. Table 2.10 shows the sensitivity of economic preparation to these cut-off points. For singles the results range from a minimum of 51.8 percent adequately prepared to a maximum of 64.9 percent adequately prepared. The minimum arises when limiting the reduction of initial consumption to less than 5 percent and the chances of running out of wealth to less than 5 percent. The maximum arises when imposing the most generous thresholds in the adequacy assessment. For couples the range is 78.3 percent adequately prepared to 86.1 percent, and the results are less sensitive to the choice of thresholds. The reason is that most couple households either fall substantially short of the thresholds of adequacy or they exceed them by a large margin, resulting in floor and ceiling effects in the statistics for preparedness.

2.7.1   Planning Horizon and Economic Preparation for Retirement

The HRS asks about an individual's financial planning horizon, which might be taken to be a measure of the propensity for forward-looking behavior. The question in the HRS is as follows:

In deciding how much of their (family) income to spend or save, people are likely to think about different financial planning periods.

In planning your (family's) saving and spending, which of the following time periods is most important to you (and your [husband/wife/partner]), the next few months, the next year, the next few years, the next 5–10 years, or longer than 10 years?

Table 2.11   **Percent with adequate resources by financial planning horizon**

	Single persons			Married persons		
	All	Males	Females	All	Males	Females
Next few months	37.1	32.4	38.6	70.0	68.9	70.7
Next year	46.7	58.3	42.4	82.2	83.0	81.7
Next few years	67.7	81.1	63.7	78.7	79.0	78.6
Next 5 to 10 years	63.1	82.8	58.3	81.6	76.9	84.9
Longer than 10 years	60.0	80.0	53.3	86.2	84.3	87.5
Total	55.2	64.9	51.3	79.7	77.9	81.1

Source: Authors' calculations.
Note: Percent adequately prepared: 95 to 100 percent chance of dying with positive wealth after reducing consumption by 10 percent by financial planning horizon.

Table 2.11 shows the percentage adequately prepared as a function of the respondent's planning horizon.[11] Among single persons with a horizon of the next few months, just 37 percent are adequately prepared. Especially for single males the variation by planning horizon is sharply increasing from 32 percent to 80 percent. However, for both males and females the major difference is between a horizon of a year or less and more than a year. Among married persons the pattern is approximately the same but with less variation.

The results in table 2.11 are consistent with a lack of forward-looking behavior contributing to the mismatch between spending and available economic resources that leads to an elevated probability of outliving wealth. An alternative interpretation is that households with little or no savings have no need to engage in financial planning beyond the next few months or the next year.

2.7.2   Health and Preparation for Retirement

Table 2.12 has the percentage adequately prepared stratified by self-rated health. Those who rate their health as fair or poor at baseline are much less likely to be adequately prepared for retirement: the difference is about 25 percentage points among single persons and 14 percentage points among married persons. One potential explanation is that those in worse health have reduced subjective survival probabilities, and so they are consuming at a higher rate than would be consistent with the survival curves we have used in our simulations.

---

11. See, for example, HRS 2006 Core question KP041 in HRS Codebook for section P (http://hrsonline.isr.umich.edu/modules/meta/2006/core/codebook/h06p_ri.htm). This question is not asked in every wave of HRS (only in 1992, 1998, 2000, 2002, 2004, and 2006); and if asked then it is not always queried of all respondents. For each respondent we use the earliest report, which would usually pertain to the pre-retirement years of the individual.

Table 2.12   Percent with adequate resources by self-rated health

	Single persons			Married persons		
	All	Males	Females	All	Males	Females
Fair or poor	37.7	44.1	35.2	68.9	68.1	69.5
Good to excellent	62.5	78.7	58.2	83.3	81.5	84.4
Total	54.5	64.9	51.3	79.9	77.9	81.1

Source: Authors' calculations.

Note: Percent adequately prepared: 95 to 100 percent chance of dying with positive wealth after reducing consumption by 10 percent by self-rated health.

2.7.3 Scenario: Eliminate Risk of Out-of-Pocket Expenditures for Health Care

Health care spending risk is incorporated in our previous tables via random draws from the observed distribution of out-of-pocket spending in HRS 2008. After adjusting for serial correlation and normalizing to mean zero, we add the shocks to spending by the single person or couple. On average, spending with the shocks will be the same as spending in the absence of the shocks as long as wealth is positive. However, the shocks will increase the variance of spending, and, therefore, the variance of predicted wealth, increasing the chances of running out of wealth before death.[12] To find how important the variance in out-of-pocket health care spending is in preparation for retirement, we put spending risk to zero and resimulated. Table 2.13 shows adequacy assessments when the variance in out-of-pocket medical expenditures is zero but the average spending on health care is unchanged (columns labeled "no out-of-pocket risk") along with results from table 2.9 that include health care spending risk (columns labeled "with out-of-pocket risk"). Overall, the health spending shocks reduce economic preparation for retirement among single persons by about 7 percentage points. But the effect is considerably larger for some groups. For example, health care spending risk reduces preparation for retirement by 13 percentage points among women with some college education.

The effect of risk of out-of-pocket spending is considerably smaller for married persons, reducing economic preparation by about 3 percentage points.

2.7.4 Scenario: Social Security Benefit Cut of 30 Percent

A method of assessing the importance of Social Security for adequacy of economic preparation for retirement is to find how preparation changes

12. We assume that if wealth is driven to zero by a spending shock, that person or household will consume at the level of annuity income. This implicitly assumes that future health care spending shocks are paid for by a public program such as Medicaid once wealth is depleted.

Table 2.13   **Effect of out-of-pocket medical expenditure risk on adequacy assessment**

	No out-of-pocket risk			With out-of-pocket risk		
	All	Males	Females	All	Males	Females
Single persons						
Less than high school	43.3	63.6	38.2	36.0	63.6	29.0
High school	66.9	66.7	67.0	62.1	66.7	60.5
Some college	63.6	62.5	64.0	53.8	62.5	51.0
College and above	74.2	65.0	76.8	68.5	65.0	69.6
All	61.1	64.9	60.0	54.5	64.9	51.3
Married persons						
Less than high school	72.7	73.8	71.8	70.1	70.2	69.9
High school	82.3	80.2	83.3	79.5	77.2	80.8
Some college	86.1	81.0	88.9	80.7	77.2	82.6
College and above	89.4	86.5	92.0	88.5	86.5	90.2
All	82.8	80.5	84.2	79.9	77.9	81.1

Source: Authors' calculations.
Note: Percent adequately prepared: 95 to 100 percent chance of dying with positive wealth after reducing consumption by 10 percent.

Table 2.14   **Effect of Social Security benefit cut of 30 percent on adequacy assessment**

	30 percent benefit cut			No benefit cut		
	All	Males	Females	All	Males	Females
Single persons						
Less than high school	23.8	48.5	17.6	36.0	63.6	29.0
High school	48.4	55.6	45.9	62.1	66.7	60.5
Some college	47.0	59.4	43.0	53.8	62.5	51.0
College and above	62.9	65.0	62.3	68.5	65.0	69.6
All	43.8	56.1	40.0	54.5	64.9	51.3
Married persons						
Less than high school	59.9	58.3	61.2	70.1	70.2	69.9
High school	71.1	68.5	72.4	79.5	77.2	80.8
Some college	73.5	69.6	75.7	80.7	77.2	82.6
College and above	83.7	82.3	84.8	88.5	86.5	90.2
All	72.1	69.8	73.5	79.9	77.9	81.1

Source: Authors' calculations.
Note: Percent adequately prepared: 95 to 100 percent chance of dying with positive wealth after reducing consumption by 10 percent.

when benefits are reduced. Table 2.14 has the results from a reduction in Social Security benefits by 30 percent. Compared with table 2.9, economic preparation of single persons is reduced by 10.7 percentage points. The reduction is especially large for those with less education, ranging from 11 to 15 percentage points. Even among married persons who have considerably more economic resources than single persons, the reduction in Social Security benefits has a noticeable impact on preparation for retirement, causing a drop in preparation of 7.8 percentage points.

These results suggest that by providing longevity insurance Social Security has an important role in economic preparation for retirement. While large among single persons and the less educated, it is nonetheless important for all the groups we have studied.

2.8   Conclusions

Our main finding is that a substantial majority (about 71 percent) of those just past the usual retirement age are adequately prepared for retirement in that they will be able to follow a path of consumption that begins at their current level of consumption and then follow an age-pattern similar to that of current retirees with positive wealth holdings. Thus we do not find inadequate preparation for retirement on average. This is not true, however, for all groups in the population. In particular, many singles who lack a high school education are not well-prepared: even were they to reduce initial consumption by 10 percent, about 64 percent would still face a probability of running out of wealth greater than 5 percent. Economic preparation by couples is much better than preparation by singles. Nonetheless, there is substantial variation by education with some 89 percent of college graduates being prepared compared with 70 percent among those lacking a high school education.

The demographic groups that are less well financially prepared—singles, those with low education, and particularly single women—are more likely to have experienced financial shocks in the past, including marital disruption. However, in a forward-looking life cycle framework past shocks should have led to adjustments in spending so that the updated lifetime budget constraint holds. The fact that we find these groups to be underprepared means that their spending is too high in view of their available resources, or, said differently, these households have not fully adjusted consumption downward to compensate for past shocks.

Our method of assessing the adequacy of retirement resources involves comparing resources with spending levels and spending patterns that we observe in today's data. If spending requirements increase substantially faster than they have in the past, then resources ex post will look inadequate whereas ex ante they looked adequate. Out-of-pocket spending on health care is an obvious area where this could happen. Accounting for this would require a sound method of forecasting what future health care expenses will be on average and in variance. We note, however, that the consumption slopes that form the basis of our forecasts have imbedded in them adjustments to spending that resulted from out-of-pocket health care spending trends and shocks during the period 2001 to 2007. Such shocks would have flattened the consumption paths (i.e., less decline in consumption with age), resulting in higher predicted lifetime spending in our simulations. Thus future increases would have to be greater than those that occurred over our sample period in order for the actual future spending trajectory to be flatter than our estimated trajectory, and for actual future spending to be greater than predicted spending.

Our assessment of the adequacy of economic preparation for retirement is more optimistic than those of the National Retirement Risk Index published by the Center for Retirement Research at Boston College. The National Retirement Risk Index measures the share of American households "at risk" of being unable to maintain their pre-retirement standard of living in retirement. It finds that 51 percent of working-age households are at risk (Munnell, Webb, and Golub-Sass 2010). Among the early baby boomers 41 percent are at risk, with the implication that 59 percent are not at risk or are adequately prepared. Our estimate from a slightly older cohort is that 71 percent are adequately prepared. Our sample comes from people born in the mid-1930s to early 1940s, which is an earlier cohort than the early baby boomers. However, comparisons of the economic resources of those fifty-one to fifty-six in HRS 1992, 1998, and 2004 shows approximately constant real economic resources among singles and increasing economic resources among couples.[13] Thus we would expect that the early baby boomers, who were fifty-one to fifty-six in 2004, will have greater resources when they reach sixty-six to sixty-nine than our sample had. The implication is that more than 71 percent of early baby boomers are on track to be adequately prepared.

Our assessment of economic preparation for retirement is somewhat more pessimistic than that of Scholz, Seshadri, and Khitatrakun (2006). Based on a life cycle model that accounts for lifetime earnings they estimate that "[f]ewer than 20 percent of households have less wealth than their optimal targets, and the wealth deficit of those who are undersaving is generally small."

Our chapter uses a very different approach from these two papers. The most obvious difference is that our estimated spending paths are based on rates of change in spending as observed in panel data, rather than on the assumption of constant spending as in Munnell, Webb, and Golub-Sass, or on model-based estimates as in Scholz, Seshadri, and Khitatrakun. A second aspect is our treatment of mortality. It recognizes that a married household will naturally reduce spending at widowing; and it classifies some low-wealth households as adequately prepared because of their reduced survival chances. Whether these or other differences are primarily responsible for the differing outcomes is beyond the scope of this chapter to investigate.

---

13. Authors' calculations based on HRS. Pension wealth as reported in Hurd and Rohwedder (2007). Particularly pertinent is that DB pension entitlements at the household level were not lower in the early baby boom cohort than in earlier cohorts because an increased entitlement among wives offset a decline in entitlements among husbands.

Data Appendix

The starting point for almost all variable derivations is RAND HRS version K.[14] All amounts are expressed in 2008 dollars.

Measurement of Household Spending in CAMS and Derivation of the Variable "Household Consumption" Used in the Analyses

Survey Design Features of CAMS Enhancing Data Quality

First, CAMS asks separate questions about spending in a relatively large number of categories (six big-ticket items and thirty-three other categories that mostly refer to nondurable spending, with some exceptions such as home furnishings, or home repair or vehicle repair). This level of detail is designed to help respondents to remember all categories of household spending, while keeping respondent burden acceptable. Second, CAMS is a self-administered survey (paper-and-pencil format) which allows respondents to take the time they need to reflect upon their answers or possibly consult records or other members of the households. Third, the instructions requested that for the spending part of the survey the person most knowledgeable about this topic be involved in answering the questions. Fourth, CAMS reduces recall error—the tendency to forget to report spending amounts, especially those lying further in the past—by offering a choice of recall period for more regular or more often occurring spending items. Depending on the category, respondents can choose the reference period as "last week," "last month," or for the "last 12 months." For example, it would be difficult for many respondents to give an estimate of food spending over the last twelve months, but much easier to report food spending of the household over the last week or last month.[15]

Imputation of Missing Information

Item nonresponse rates in the CAMS spending categories are mostly less than 10 percent, many even less than 5 percent, which is low in comparison to other economic variables in the HRS. In imputing missing observations we take advantage of information from the HRS core for informed logical imputations wherever possible. For example, in the spending categories with the highest rate of nonresponse, we have information from the HRS core that we can use for imputation. Rent has almost the highest rate of nonre-

14. The RAND HRS data file is an easy to use longitudinal data set based on the HRS data. It was developed at RAND with funding from the National Institute on Aging and the Social Security Administration.

15. There has been some variation in the recall periods offered to respondents across the CAMS waves reflecting survey experience. In the later waves, the "last week" option has only been offered for three high-frequency categories of spending (food in, food out, and gasoline).

sponse. However, we have data in the HRS about homeownership that we can use with considerable confidence to impute rent to many nonresponders: most of the nonresponders were homeowners and so we imputed zero rent. At the end of this process 63.5 percent of CAMS wave 1 respondents are complete reporters over all categories of spending. For the remaining missing observations we imputed the average amount observed among nonmissing responses for a particular spending category. An exception are the big-ticket items for which we imputed zero if there was no entry for whether the household bought that big-ticket item over the last twelve months. When the respondent reported that there was a purchase of the big-ticket item and only the amount was missing, then we used for imputation the prediction from a simple regression of the purchase price on some basic household characteristics.

Identification and Adjustment of Extreme Values

We also applied some cleaning of outliers, following a systematic algorithm. We used cross-wave comparisons to identify outliers in the case of those spending categories that tend to be regular and fairly flat over time, such as utilities. We only changed a value when there was evidence that the respondent had mixed up the recall period (e.g., one entry being twelve times the amount of the other entry), then the outlier would be brought in line by multiplying or dividing by 12. We also checked whether the outlier could be explained by a slippage in the decimal (multiples of 10 or 100), in which case we would change the value also. Finally, we winsorized the top and bottom five values in each category. We applied the same cleaning and imputation methods to all four waves of CAMS.

Derivation of Total Household Consumption

Total household consumption is defined as the sum of all annualized spending categories elicited in CAMS, subject to some adjustments to those categories of spending that have a savings component. For big-ticket items that are consumed over multiple periods we estimate consumption services derived from durables as described in the next section of this appendix. For mortgage and car payments we only count the interest as part of consumption, because payments toward the principal are part of the household's saving. For observations using CAMS 2001 data, the consumption measure is adjusted to reflect the lower number of spending categories that was collected in CAMS 2001 compared to subsequent waves.

Estimating Consumption Services Derived from Durables

For five of our big-ticket items (excluding automobile purchases) our general strategy is to estimate in CAMS the probability of a purchase and the expected value conditional on a purchase as functions of important covariates, such as income, wealth, age, and marital status. Then we impute an annual purchase amount which, in equilibrium, will be equal to the annual consumption with straight-line depreciation. In particular we make the following assumptions and calculations. We assume straight-line depreciation and that average annual consumption is equal to average annual depreciation. We estimate logistic functions for the probability of annual purchase. Covariates are age, income, marital status, and number of household residents. We estimate spending conditional on purchase using the same covariates as for purchase. Then predicted average annual consumption on five big-ticket items is calculated as:

$$\text{average annual consumption on five big-ticket items} = \sum_{i=1\ldots5} (\text{probability of purchasing item } i) \times (\text{expected amount given purchase of item } i).$$

To give an example of the resulting consumption services from durables that we obtain in this manner, the mean consumption in 2001 of the five big-ticket items is estimated to be $282 per year, with a range of $70 to $2,682.

Because we have the value of automobiles and other vehicles used for transportation in the HRS in 2000 and 2002, we calculate the flow of services from the actual values. This calculation will more accurately estimate the flow of services for low-income households. We make these assumptions and calculations: The value of transportation (almost all automobiles) is measured in the HRS core; user cost is the sum of interest on the value, depreciation on a twelve-year schedule, and observed maintenance costs from CAMS. We find that the mean flow of services is $2,912 per year, with a range of $0 to $41,040.

We follow a similar strategy to estimate the flow of consumption services from owner-occupied housing by estimating a rental equivalent: the amount the housing unit would rent for in a competitive market in equilibrium. In particular, we make the following assumptions and calculations: (a) The interest cost is the value of housing multiplied by the prevailing interest rate. We use the observed house value from the HRS core and assume an interest rate of 7.16 percent, which was the average thirty-year mortgage interest rate in 2001. (b) We estimate depreciation from maintenance costs which are observed in CAMS and from the observed house value: we assume depreciation of 2.14 percent per year, which is equivalent to a depreciation period of forty-seven years. The flow of housing services is the sum of these items, amounting to $13,500 at the mean among home owners and $10,000 at the median.

Details of the Measurement and Definition of Key Variables

Consumption

We use the observations on household consumption in two ways. First, to measure initial consumption for each household in our simulations; that is, the level of spending from which we project out the subsequent spending path. It is critical to minimize observation error in this measure of initial consumption, because observation error would affect our adequacy assessments. Therefore, to compute baseline consumption for each household we average observed total consumption, as derived earlier, over all adjacent waves where marital status is constant.[16] For example, if marital status was constant from 2000 to 2008, then consumption in 2001, 2003, 2005, and 2007 is averaged. Likewise, if marital status was constant from 2002 to 2006, then consumption in 2003 and 2005 is averaged for baseline consumption. Second, we use longitudinal observations on household consumption to estimate the shape of the life cycle consumption path, stratified by sex, marital status, and education (see "Estimation of Consumption Path" in section 2.6.2 of this chapter).

Income from Pensions and Annuities

We use the annualized measure of income from pension and annuities. We assume that this income stream is not indexed to inflation. To reduce measurement error we average the observations across adjacent waves where available, provided marital status does not change. More specifically, if marital status is constant in the two HRS waves following the baseline observation, then baseline pensions are the average of pension income in the following two HRS waves. If marital status is not constant in the two HRS waves following the baseline observation, then baseline pension income is equal to the following HRS wave's reported pension. In the case of couples, we use the sum of income from pensions and annuities for the respondent and spouse. Once one of the spouses dies, pension and annuity income is assumed to be reduced to two-thirds, reflecting the fact that most pension and annuities have some survivor provisions.

Income from Social Security

To measure income from Social Security for the respondent (and the spouse in the case of couples) we use the latest report available in the HRS. This way we capture Social Security income also for those individuals who claim late. In projecting Social Security income out into the future for each household, we take into account that Social Security is indexed to inflation. In the case of widowing among couples, total Social Security income of the household is reduced to two-thirds.

Current and Future Earnings

The latest available reported income from earnings is used as baseline earnings. To forecast future earnings we first predict the probability of working for pay in the next period, conditional on working in the current period.

---

16. Holding marital status constant is important so that changes in spending are not due to household dissolutions, widowing, or marriage.

We obtain these predictions from a logistic regression estimated over nine waves of HRS panel data (1992 to 2008). The left-hand variable is working for pay at time $t + 2$, conditional on working for pay at time t. The estimation sample is therefore restricted to those working for pay at time t. The right-hand variables are age at time t, sex, marital status, and education. We then multiply the predicted probability of working with the respondent's observed baseline earnings adjusted for earnings growth. (Real) earnings growth by gender and marital status is also estimated on two-year transitions observed in the HRS 1992 to 2008 panel data, but the estimation sample is restricted to those working in consecutive waves (t to $t + 2$). Because the time unit in our simulations is one year, both the predicted probability of working at time $t + 2$ and the two-year growth rate in earnings are converted into one year rates.

Wealth

Our measure of total bequeathable assets includes the value of all assets (primary residence, secondary residence, other real estate, transportation, business or farm, individual retirement accounts [IRAs and similar], stocks and stock mutual funds, checking and savings accounts, CDs, bonds, other assets) minus all debt (mortgage on primary residence, other home loans on primary residence, mortgage on secondary residence, other debt [RANDHRS variable HxATOTB]). Baseline wealth for each household is calculated as the average of the two adjacent HRS waves' total of all assets. Averaging achieves two things: first, it reduces measurement error in bequeathable wealth. Second, it approximates bequeathable wealth in the baseline period anchored to a certain wave of CAMS that lies between two HRS waves. For example, for an observation anchored to CAMS 2005 we average wealth from HRS 2004 and HRS 2006.

Taxation

We account for federal taxes, state taxes, partial taxation of Social Security benefits as a function of total taxable income, and the taxation of IRA withdrawals. In the simulations, we calculate the total taxes owed by each household in each period.

Federal Taxes

We calculate gross taxable income as the sum of income from pensions and annuities, the taxable portion of Social Security benefits, interest income, and earnings. We subtract all applicable deductions to obtain adjusted gross income (AGI). Every household is assumed to claim the standard deduction ($5,350 for singles and $10,700 for couples). Additional deductions are applied if the respondent and/or spouse is age sixty-five or older. To the adjusted gross income, we apply the tax brackets implied by the federal tax law, taking into account marital status for determining the bend points.

State Taxes

We approximate the amount in state taxes owed by each household in any one simulation period by applying an average state tax rate that is stratified by age band and marital status. We obtained these average state tax rates from running all relevant information available for the HRS 2004 sample through the NBER TAXSIM calculator (see Feenberg and Coutts 1993). The NBER TAXSIM calculations return for each HRS 2004 household an estimate of state taxes and federal taxes for each of the fifty states (plus Puerto Rico). We first calculate an average state tax rate for each HRS 2004 household by taking the ratio of the average of state taxes owed across the fifty-one states divided by the average of federal taxes owed across the fifty-one states. In a second step, we average the resulting household-level state tax rate by age band and marital status.

Taxation of Social Security Benefits

According to federal tax law, the fraction of Social Security benefits that is subject to taxation depends on the household's total taxable income. The household only pays tax on Social Security benefits if the sum of total other income plus half of the household's Social Security income is greater than the base amount, which is $32,000 for couples and $25,000 for singles. Depending on by how much the base amount is exceeded, between 50 percent and 85 percent of Social Security benefits are subject to tax (again with different thresholds for singles and couples). At most, 85 percent of Social Security benefits are taxable. In the simulations, we implemented these rules exactly in the computation of taxable income for each household in each period.

IRA Withdrawals

For each household and each simulation period we calculate the amount of IRA withdrawals using the following algorithm. First we calculate after-tax income of the household, taking into account any applicable required minimum IRA distributions at ages greater than seventy. We check whether the household's after-tax income (including any mandatory IRA withdrawals) is sufficient to finance the household's consumption in that period. If after-tax income is greater than consumption then there is no need for the household to draw down any other savings. However, if consumption is greater than after-tax income we calculate how much of that period's consumption a household needs to finance out of savings. We assume that housing assets are depleted last (see discussion of housing). Therefore, withdrawals from savings are assumed to come proportionally from IRA assets and from nonhousing, non-IRA assets for as long as these are not depleted. We recalculate the tax liability to take into account that a larger withdrawal from IRA assets increases the household's tax liability and may even lead to an increased marginal tax rate.

Serial Correlation in Out-of-Pocket Spending on Health Care

To simulate serially correlated out-of-pocket spending we use the following simple model of serial correlation

$$u_t = \rho u_{t-1} + v_t$$

where the v_t are i.i.d. $(0, \sigma^2)$. Then the u are identically distributed $(0, \sigma^2/(1-\rho^2)$. In our spending data from HRS 2008 we have observations on the u and so we can calculate the variance of u and the variance of v as $V(v) = V(u)(1-\rho^2)$.

Let s_{at} be actual out-of-pocket spending as observed in HRS, and let s_t be spending assigned to a person. Then we can simulate the estimated serial correlation and preserve the distribution of out-of-pocket spending by drawing from the actual distribution in the first period of the simulation, s_{a1}, and assigning that to out-of-pocket spending in period 1: $s_1 = s_{a1}$. In the next period we draw from the actual distribution, s_{a2}, and then assign out-of-pocket s_2 as

$$s_2 = \rho s_1 + s_{a2}\sqrt{1-\rho^2},$$

then $V(s_2) = V(s_a)$. We continue in this manner:

$$s_{t+1} = \rho s_t + s_{at+1}\sqrt{1-\rho^2}.$$

This ignores that we want to only modify wealth by health care spending shocks; that is, deviations from means. The shock in any period would be

$$s_t - \bar{s}_a,$$

where $\bar{s}_a$ is the mean of spending in the HRS. It does not have a t subscript because we are always drawing from the same distribution (2008 HRS).

The preceding applies to each group defined by age, education, sex, and marital status: each group has its own distribution of s_a and its own value of ρ, as shown in table 2.4.

References

Adams, P., M. D. Hurd, D. McFadden, A. Merrill, and T. Ribeiro. 2003. "Healthy, Wealthy, and Wise? Tests for Direct Causal Paths between Health and Socioeconomic Status." *Journal of Econometrics* 112 (1): 3–56.
Feenberg, Daniel Richard, and Elisabeth Coutts. 1993. "An Introduction to the TAXSIM Model." *Journal of Policy Analysis and Management* 12 (1): 189–94.
Hurd, Michael D. 1989. "Mortality Risk and Bequests." *Econometrica* 57:779–813.
Hurd, Michael D., and Susann Rohwedder. 2007. "Trends in Pension Values around Retirement." In *Redefining Retirement,* edited by Brigitte Madrian, Olivia Mitchell, and Beth Soldo, 234–47. New York: Oxford University Press.

————. 2009a. "The Level and Risk of Out-of-Pocket Health Care Spending." Michigan Retirement Research Center Working Paper 2009-218.
————. 2009b. "Methodological Innovations in Collecting Spending Data: The HRS Consumption and Activities Mail Survey." *Fiscal Studies* 30 (3/4): 435–59.
Juster, F. Thomas, and Richard Suzman. 1995. "An Overview of the Health and Retirement Study." *Journal of Human Resources* 30 (Supplement): S7–S56.
Kitagawa, E., and P. Hauser. 1973. *Differential Mortality in the United States: A Study in Socioeconomic Epidemiology.* Cambridge, MA: Harvard University Press.
Marmot, M. G., G. D. Smith, S. Stanfeld, C. Patel, F. North, J. Head, I. White, E. Brunner, and A. Feeney. 1991. "Health Inequalities among British Civil Servants: The Whitehall II Study." *Lancet* 337:1387–93.
Munnell, A., A. Webb, and F. Golub-Sass. 2010. "How Will Higher Tax Rates Affect the National Retirement Risk Index?" Center for Retirement Research at Boston College. IB#10-19. http://crr.bc.edu/images/stories/Briefs/IB_10-19.pdf.
RAND HRS Data. 2011. "Version K." Produced by the RAND Center for the Study of Aging, with funding from the National Institute on Aging and the Social Security Administration, March. Santa Monica, CA: RAND Corporation.
Scholz, John Karl, Ananth Seshadri, and Surachai Khitatrakun. 2006. "Are Americans Saving 'Optimally' for Retirement?" *Journal of Political Economy* 114 (4): 607–43.
Venti, Steven F., and David A. Wise. 2004. "Aging and Housing Equity: Another Look." In *Perspectives on the Economics of Aging,* edited by David A. Wise, 127–80. Chicago: University of Chicago Press.

Comment   Robert J. Willis

Hurd and Rohwedder's chapter presents an important alternative to other approaches for measuring the adequacy of preparation for retirement. It asks whether a couple's or individual's pre-retirement consumption path can be sustained with the financial wealth and rights to future pension and Social Security income that have been accumulated by the time of retirement plus potential future labor income. Most studies of adequacy focus on the proportion of pre-retirement income that can be replaced by income flows from retirement resources. If the replacement rate falls below an arbitrary threshold, typically between 70 and 85 percent, preparation is deemed inadequate. Studies using a replacement rate criterion have typically found alarmingly high fractions of households who are on a track that will leave them with too little wealth at retirement, forcing them either to suffer a lower standard of living during retirement, to reduce their pre-retirement

Robert J. Willis is professor of economics and a research professor at the Institute for Social Research and the Population Studies Center at the University of Michigan and a research associate of the National Bureau of Economic Research.

For acknowledgments, sources of research support, and disclosure of the author's material financial relationships, if any, please see http://www.nber.org/chapters/c12432.ack.

standard of living by saving more (and consuming less), or to work longer by delaying retirement.

While replacement rates continue to be used extensively by financial advisers, at best they provide a crude rule of thumb that adjusts the level of income that a household needs to maintain its pre-retirement standard of living during retirement for the lower tax rates, reduced work-related expenses, and reduced savings rates that it will face after retirement. Even if these adjustments were perfect, Scholz, Seshadri, and Khitatrakun (2008) point out that household-specific measurement error in lifetime income or standard of living is likely to lead to an understatement of the degree to which households are adequately prepared for retirement. For example, consider two households that have each saved exactly the optimal amount for retirement, have identical measured incomes, but differ in true lifetime income. Using the replacement rate methodology, one of these households will appear to have more than enough wealth for retirement while the other will be deemed inadequately prepared. Such measurement errors would tend to push an estimated "inadequacy rate" toward 50 percent, resulting in an overestimate if the true rate is less than 50 percent.

Of course, the degree to which a household is able to smooth consumption—or, more precisely, smooth the marginal utility of wealth—between the pre- and post-retirement phases of the life cycle is the theoretically relevant criterion for retirement adequacy. Scholz, Seshadri, and Khitatrakun (2006) have conducted the most ambitious attempt to date to calculate the optimal level of household retirement resources using a dynamic programming model based on life cycle theory and longitudinal data from the HRS linked to administrative earnings data from Social Security. They find that only about 16 percent of households have accumulated a smaller amount of wealth than the optimal level, as compared, for example, to an estimate by Munnell, Webb, and Delorme (2006), using a replacement rate criterion, that nearly 45 percent of households are at risk of being unable to maintain their standard of living following retirement.

The current chapter by Hurd and Rohwedder (hereafter HR) takes up where Scholz, Seshadri, and Khitatrakun (hereafter SSK) leave off. They exploit longitudinal data on consumption from the CAMS self-administered mail survey which they designed. The CAMS measures the consumption expenditures of about half of HRS households during odd numbered years in which the HRS core survey is not in the field and provides the only source of longitudinal consumption data in the United States. Hurd and Rohwedder first calculate an expected life cycle consumption path for each household, conditional on survival of each member to a given age, using the initial level of consumption at the time of retirement and mean percentage rates of change in consumption for couples or singles, as appropriate. The level and shape of these consumption paths are estimated nonparametrically. It is of independent interest to consider what insight these consumption paths provide for the theoretical determinants of consumption suggested by life cycle theory. I shall return to this point later.

The adequacy of retirement resources is judged by whether the resources available to the household at the time of retirement are sufficient to pay for the simulated consumption profile. If not, the household will run out of discretionary wealth before the last survivor dies and will be forced to subsist on their annuity income from Social Security, DB pensions, or purchased annuities. The answer to this question depends, of course, on the date of death of single persons or the dates of death of each spouse in a couple. Since mortality is random, HR simulate the distribution of outcomes using survival probabilities based on survival functions for men and women estimated from data on actual mortality in the HRS. This is an important innovation in this chapter because it allows the adequacy of retirement resources to be judged in light of variation in education and marital status that affect longevity but are not measured in standard actuarial life tables. It would be of interest to push this approach further by incorporating measures of each person's health status at the time of retirement into the survival model.

In addition, after presenting results in which out-of-pocket medical expenses are only incorporated as expected values, HR add stochastic, serially correlated shocks to medical expenses to their simulation model to gauge the sensitivity of their results to the economic effects of uninsured health shocks. These simulations also incorporate variation in spending shocks by the same factors used in the survival model and, again, I would suggest that it would be interesting to introduce initial health into these simulations.

One key output of this simulation exercise is the probability of dying with positive wealth. As a measure of the adequacy of wealth, HR calculate the fraction of persons in a given group who have a 95 percent or greater chance of dying with positive wealth. Given this criterion, 77 percent of married and 49 percent of single people are adequately prepared for retirement. Single females constitute the only subgroup in which a majority is unprepared.

Earlier, I discussed the potential sensitivity to measurement error of adequacy measures based on the replacement rate. It is worth thinking about whether and how HR's measure is sensitive to measurement error. While error could occur in a number of ways, for simplicity I consider only error in the level of consumption at the time of retirement, c_0. Given the way that HR calculate the expected present discounted value of retirement consumption, a given percentage error in c_0 will lead to the same percentage error in the present value of retirement consumption.

In justifying their 95 percent threshold, HR write:

The fraction of simulations in which wealth is positive at death does not provide the risk of any individual or household outliving resources. For example, the 63 percent in the case of single persons would be achieved if every single person had a 63 percent chance or if 63 percent of single persons had a 100 percent chance of dying with positive wealth and 37 percent had no chance.

Continuing with this example, imagine a truly homogeneous group of single persons who all have common values of c_0 and all other economic magnitudes in the model and assume that they each face a 63 percent chance of dying with positive resources. In this case, zero percent are adequately prepared for retirement, according to the 95 percent criterion that HR use. Obviously, individual-specific errors in measuring c_0 will induce a spread in the simulated probabilities within this homogeneous group. With large enough error, some fraction of those with positive errors will have calculated probabilities of dying with positive resources that are 95 percent or greater. Thus, this measurement error has the effect of upwardly biasing HR's index of adequacy whereas measurement error creates bias with the opposite sign when using a threshold based on replacement rates, as I discussed earlier.

The potential of measurement errors to create bias in measures of adequacy of retirement preparation suggests the need to seek ways to correct for these errors or, alternatively, use measures that are resistant to error. It would not be too difficult to investigate the sensitivity of the fraction satisfying the 95 percent criterion for different plausible values of the error in c_0 or even to think of a way to estimate the variance of the error. Since there are many possible sources of error on both the consumption and income/wealth side of the model, however, it is not clear how useful such an approach would be. It would be helpful, however, to have some analysis of the sensitivity of the results from the simulations to measurement error. A more direct approach to measuring the risk of dying without assets by age at death would be to use data on estates from the HRS postmortem "exit interviews" following the death of the last surviving spouse.

The nonparametric consumption profiles estimated by HR are an important and innovative contribution of this chapter. If households were fully annuitized, theory implies that these consumption profiles should be flat, apart from slope imparted by a difference between the rate of interest and rate of time preference. However, because few households are fully annuitized, HR point out that economic theory implies that consumption profiles should be downward sloping. While this holds true, the negative slope is substantially less for married persons. For example, in figure 2.4 consumption by couples declines by 1.4 percent per year, but at widowing that rate increases to 5.1 percent per year. This difference brings to mind a result of Kotlikoff and Spivak (1981), who show that sharing of resources by a small number of family members—even just a husband and wife—creates an implicit annuity market that provides a substantial fraction of the longevity insurance that a full annuity would provide. Their point is reinforced if one considers the implicit disability insurance that one spouse provides for the other through caregiving. The relatively flat consumption profile of married couples when both are living is consistent with the hypothesis of considerable risk pooling by couples.

In sum, I highly recommend this chapter both as an innovative addition to literature on the adequacy of retirement preparation and in pointing the way toward a rich new line of research on the implications of the life cycle model and related economic theories of marriage and the family for behavior after retirement. This work is made possible by the addition of longitudinal consumption data to the HRS pioneered by the authors. An interesting extension would be for the authors to team up with Scholz and Seshadri to create a dynamic programming model that covers the full life cycle of saving, covering pre-retirement preparation for retirement and post-retirement management of wealth and consumption.

References

Kotlikoff, Laurence J., and Avia Spivak. 1981. "The Family as an Incomplete Annuities Market." *Journal of Political Economy* 89 (2): 372–89.

Munnell, Alicia H., Anthony Webb, and Luke Delorme. 2006. "A New National Retirement Risk Index." An Issue in Brief, Center for Retirement Research at Boston College, no. 8, June.

Scholz, John Karl, Ananth Seshadri, and Surachai Khitatrakun. 2006. "Are Americans Saving 'Optimally' for Retirement?" *Journal of Political Economy* 114 (4): 607–43.

How Well Are Social Security
Recipients Protected from Inflation?

Gopi Shah Goda, John B. Shoven, and
Sita Nataraj Slavov

3.1 Introduction

Social Security is widely believed to protect its recipients from a number of risks, including uncertainty regarding length of life and inflation, due to the inflation-indexed life annuity form of the benefit. The inflation protection comes from the fact that Social Security benefits are indexed to the Consumer Price Index for Urban Wage Earners and Clerical Workers (CPI-W). The CPI-W is based on the spending patterns of a broad group of workers, representing approximately 32 percent of the US population. However, the CPI-W may not accurately reflect the experience of retirees for two reasons. First, retirees generally have higher medical expenses than workers, and medical costs in recent years have tended to rise faster than the prices of other goods. Second, even if medical costs did not rise faster than

Gopi Shah Goda is research scholar and postdoctoral fellow program coordinator at the Stanford Institute for Economic Policy Research, Stanford University, and a faculty research fellow of the National Bureau of Economic Research. John B. Shoven is the Charles R. Schwab Professor of Economics at Stanford University and a research associate of the National Bureau of Economic Research. Sita Nataraj Slavov is associate professor of economics at Occidental College.

This research was supported by the US Social Security Administration (SSA) through grant #10-M-98363-1-01 to the National Bureau of Economic Research as part of the SSA Retirement Research Consortium. The findings and conclusions expressed are solely those of the authors and do not represent the views of the SSA, any agency of the federal government, or the NBER. The authors would like to thank Isabella Tang for superb research assistance. For acknowledgments, sources of research support, and disclosure of the authors' material financial relationships, if any, please see http://www.nber.org/chapters/c12433.ack. This paper was previously published as Gopi Shah Goda, John B. Shoven, and Sita Nataraj Slavov (2011), "How Well Are Social Security Recipients Protected from Inflation?," *National Tax Journal* 64 (2): 429–49. Permission to reprint this article was granted by the National Tax Association.

the prices of other goods, individual retirees would still, on average, need to devote a larger share of income to medical spending as they age. This means that individual retirees would still see a decline in the real income they have available for nonmedical spending. In this chapter, we explore both of these factors, quantify the extent to which they undermine the inflation protection provided by the indexation of Social Security benefits, and explore the implications of alternative methods of indexing benefits.

Our analysis is related to the literature on cost-of-living indices for the elderly. Most recently, Burdick and Fisher (2007) and Stewart (2008) compare the CPI-W to the CPI-E, an experimental consumer price index based on the spending patterns of the elderly, produced but not published by the Bureau of Labor Statistics (BLS). Since the CPI-E is intended to reflect the experience of Americans aged sixty-two and older, the main difference between the CPI-E and the CPI-W is in the weights for the various expenditure categories. The CPI-E has increased faster than the CPI-W over the past twenty years, due primarily to the relative rise in health care costs, and the fact that the elderly spend more on health care than the nonelderly, even after taking into account the availability of Medicare. Hobijn and Lagakos (2003) suggest that if Social Security benefits were indexed to the CPI-E instead of the CPI-W, the Trust Fund depletion date would be moved forward by about five years. This result demonstrates that there are important differences between the two indices, and that the choice between them is consequential. Other relevant research includes Boskin and Hurd (1982), who compute separate price indices for elderly and nonelderly households even before the CPI-E was constructed, and List (2005), who reviews the issues regarding cost-of-living indices for the elderly, but without as much of a focus on health care spending.

In carrying out our analysis, we examine two major components of medical costs. First, most Social Security recipients are also participants in Medicare Part B. The monthly premiums for Part B, which recently became means-tested, go up with the increasing costs of health insurance as they account for approximately 25 percent of the cost of providing benefits. These premiums are automatically deducted from Social Security retirement benefits and have increased much faster than Social Security benefits. The dramatic difference in growth rates is shown in figure 3.1, which illustrates that the monthly premium of Part B has gone up approximately 1,600 percent between 1975 and 2011 (i.e., the amount is seventeen times higher than it was), while the automatic cost-of-living adjustments have accumulated to just over 300 percent. Moreover, with means-adjusted Part B premiums introduced in 2007, very high-income individuals (with modified adjusted gross income of more than $214,000 in 2011) saw their Medicare Part B monthly premiums go from $45.50 in 2000 to $369.10 in 2011. The increase for these very high-income people clearly eroded the real value of their

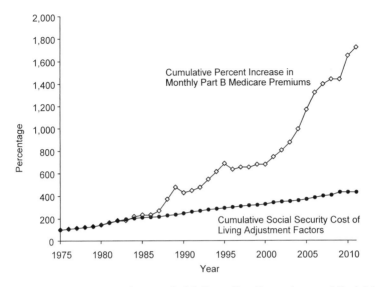

Fig. 3.1   Cumulative percent increase in Medicare Part B premiums and Social Security cost-of-living adjustment factors, 1965–2011

Note: Medicare Part B premiums and cost-of-living adjustment normalized to 100 in 1975.

monthly Social Security benefit. Second, retirees often have substantial out-of-pocket medical expenses, including Medicare deductibles and copayments, and payments for services with limited Medicare coverage, such as nursing home care.

We show that, after subtracting both of these components of health spending from Social Security benefits, available income net of medical expenses for a Social Security participant with average out-of-pocket medical spending has, in fact, been increasing more slowly than a price index of nonmedical goods and services. For example, the average man born in 1918 has seen his monthly Social Security benefit, net of medical expenses, rise from $527.85 at the end of 1983 (when he was sixty-five) to $866.80 at the end of 2007 (when he was eighty-nine). However, if his net-of-medical-expenses benefit had kept pace with inflation in the prices of nonmedical goods over that time period, he would have had $1,086.13 per month in 2007 after medical expenses. That is, his net-of-medical-spending benefit has declined by around 20 percent, relative to the nonmedical goods price index. Similarly, the average woman born in 1918 has seen her net-of-medical-expenses benefit decline by around 27 percent relative to the nonmedical goods price index. Of course, these results assume no other income besides Social Security, but a sizable fraction of the elderly depend on Social Security for the majority of their income: 64 percent of beneficiaries rely on Social Security for 50 percent or more of their income, and 34 percent of beneficiaries rely on Social Security for 90 percent or more of their income.[1]

We also show that if Social Security benefits had been indexed to the CPI-E instead of the CPI-W, men born in 1918 would have $961.20 net of medical expenses, falling only 11.5 percent short of the $1,086.13 needed to hold nonmedical expenditures constant in real terms; similarly, women born in 1918 would fall only 18.1 percent short. The reason indexing to the CPI-E does not fully compensate retirees for inflation is that, even if medical costs remained constant over time for the elderly, they tend to spend more on out-of-pocket medical expenses as they age, crowding out nonmedical spending. Thus, each cohort's Social Security benefit net of average out-of-pocket medical spending would tend to decline in real terms even if the price of medical care rose at the same rate as the prices of other goods, or alternatively, even if the average retiree's real net Social Security benefit remained constant.

Both the CPI-W and CPI-E are subject to the usual criticisms of consumer price indices. In particular, neither accounts adequately for technological progress or for consumer substitution among goods. The CPI-E is subject to additional criticisms, including the fact that it overlooks senior citizen discounts and differences in the retail shopping patterns of the elderly, and is based on a relatively small sample.[2] The failure to account properly for technological progress can be quite serious when it comes to health care. Higher medical costs may reflect the consumption of better quality medical care, and retirees may be better off even if they are left with less to spend on other nonmedical goods. Therefore, we emphasize that we cannot draw any conclusions about changes in the utility of Social Security recipients from this analysis. All we show is that Social Security benefits may not be fully inflation-indexed in the sense that recipients with average out-of-pocket medical spending cannot, from one year to the next, purchase the same bundle of nonmedical goods with their Social Security benefits.

Our methodology and results are described in more detail in sections 3.2 and 3.3. Section 3.4 discusses the policy implications of changing the method of indexation, and section 3.5 offers concluding remarks.

3.2 Methodology

Our analysis proceeds in several steps. First, we estimate a model to predict average out-of-pocket medical spending as a function of age, gender, and race. Second, we estimate average Social Security benefits broken down by age, gender, and race. Third, we subtract Medicare Part B premiums, as

---

1. US Social Security Administration, Office of Retirement and Disability Policy, "Fast Facts and Figures About Social Security," http://www.ssa.gov/policy/docs/chartbooks/fast_facts/2010/fast_facts10.html.
2. See Stewart (2008) and Budrick and Fisher (2007) for a more detailed discussion.

well as our estimates of average out-of-pocket medical expenses, from these average benefits. Finally, we compare the rate of increase in the remaining amount (nonmedical spending) to the CPI-E for all items less medical expenses. Each of these steps is detailed in the following subsections.

3.2.1   Out-of-Pocket Spending

We use Health and Retirement Study (HRS) data from 1995, 1996, 1998, 2000, 2002, 2004, and 2006 to model the age profile of out-of-pocket medical expenses.[3] Our analysis is limited to these years because the definition of out-of-pocket expenses is relatively consistent across interviews starting in 1995. The sample includes all individuals aged sixty-five to eighty-nine. The HRS collects data on a wide range of out-of-pocket medical expenses, including payments for doctor and dentist visits, hospital and nursing home stays, outpatient surgery, prescription drugs, home health care, and special facilities. Respondents are asked about their total out-of-pocket spending over the two years prior to the interview; we divide this amount by twenty-four to arrive at monthly out-of-pocket spending. One shortcoming of the HRS data is that it does not include health insurance premiums in out-of-pocket medical expenses, including those for Medicare Part B. Later in the analysis, we add Part B premiums to predicted out-of-pocket expenditures.

We regress monthly total out-of-pocket spending (the sum of all the components just listed) on a variety of demographic variables, including age, age-squared, gender, and race (white non-Hispanic, black non-Hispanic, or other race). The results from our three basic specifications are shown in table 3.1.[4] Specification 1 does not include any controls for race, but allows the level and shape of the age profile of spending to vary by gender by including a gender dummy interacted with the age variables. Specification 2 adds race dummies, allowing the level, but not the shape, of the age profile to vary by race. Specification 3 includes a full set of interactions among race, age, and gender, allowing each race-gender combination to have a different level and shape. All specifications include a set of year dummies, which allow the age profiles to shift (generally upwards) over time.

We use specification 1 to construct a preliminary age profile of out-of-pocket spending for men and women aged sixty-five to eighty-four in each year from 1983 to 2007. Predicted values for years not covered by our HRS data are assigned the intercept for the closest year in the HRS; for example,

---

3. University of Michigan, Institute for Social Research, Health and Retirement Study, http://hrsonline.isr.umich.edu/.
4. Other studies use the log of medical expenses as the dependent variable (e.g., French and Jones 2004). Although we also estimated regressions using the log of out-of-pocket spending as our dependent variable, we prefer the linear specifications because, when aggregated, they produce results that most closely match the actual aggregate values of out-of-pocket spending. The semi-log regression results are available from the authors upon request.

Table 3.1   Predicting out-of-pocket medical spending

Specification	(1)	(2)	(3)
Age	−20.4*	−21.5*	−22.3*
	(11.3)	(11.3)	(12.6)
Age-squared	.155**	.161**	.169**
	(.074)	(.0739)	(.0824)
Female	1,500***	1,568***	2,236***
	(557)	(557)	(627)
Female*Age	−40.4***	−42.1***	−60***
	(14.6)	(14.6)	(16.5)
Female*Age-squared	.273***	.284***	.404***
	(.0956)	(.0955)	(.107)
Black		−40.4***	−280
		(6.01)	(1,341)
Other race		−61.1***	−700
		(7.08)	(1,592)
Interactions	No	No	Yes
R^2	0.011	0.013	0.014

Notes: All specifications include year dummies. Standard errors are in parentheses. Specification 3 also includes all three-way interaction terms between age, gender, and race. The number of observation is $N = 58{,}004$.

***Significant at the 1 percent level.
**Significant at the 5 percent level.
*Significant at the 10 percent level.

1985 is given the intercept for 1995 (the earliest year in our HRS sample), and 1997 is given the intercept for 1996. Clearly we would expect our predicted profiles to be more accurate for the years covered by the HRS data. However, as long as the predicted *relative* values of spending for the age-gender groups are accurate, we can scale the levels to match the overall level of out-of-pocket expenditures. We do this by aggregating our predicted values using population counts for men and women of each age group, and then dividing actual aggregate expenditures for the sixty-five to eighty-four age group in each year by our predicted aggregate expenditures.[5] These ratios of actual to predicted aggregate expenditures are our "scaling factors." We then multiply our preliminary predicted age profiles by the scaling factor for the appropriate year. Figure 3.2 shows the predicted and actual aggregate expenditures for the sixty-five to eighty-four age group, as well as the scaling

5. Population counts were obtained by request from the Social Security Administration, and actual aggregate expenditures from the Centers for Medicare and Medicaid Services, National Health Expenditure Data, https://www.cms.gov/NationalHealthExpendData/. Aggregate out-of-pocket expenditures by age are reported for years 1987, 1996, 1999, 2002, and 2004. To impute out-of-pocket expenditures for additional years, the 2004 values were adjusted by the rate of growth of aggregate out-of-pocket payments for all ages. This procedure yielded values that closely match the actual values in the years where expenditures by age were reported.

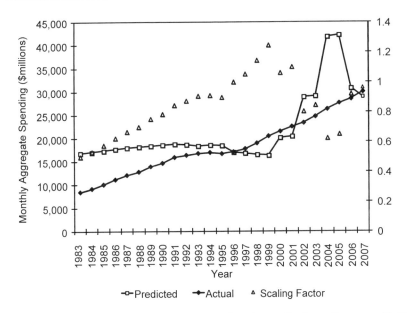

Fig. 3.2   Actual and predicted aggregate out-of-pocket medical spending, ages 65–84

factors for each year. The scaling factors are quite close to 1 for most of the years covered by the HRS data.

For example, actual aggregate expenditures in 2006 were 1.06 times the aggregate amount predicted by our regression model for 2006. Our model also predicts that a seventy-year-old male has average out-of-pocket expenses of $125.64 per month in 2006. We multiply this amount by the scaling factor of 1.06 to obtain $133.21, our final predicted value for average out-of-pocket expenditures of seventy-year-old males in 2006. Thus, we construct our age profiles by using our regression to predict the relative values of average out-of-pocket expenditures for the age-gender groups, and then choosing the levels to match actual aggregate expenditures in the sixty-five to eighty-four age group.

We repeat this procedure for specification 3 to obtain the age profiles of out-of-pocket spending for four groups: white males, white females, black males, and black females.[6] For the breakdown by race, we chose specification 3 rather than 2 because there appear to be substantial differences in the

6. The procedure is identical to that for specification 1, except that we scale our model's predicted out-of-pocket expenditures to match aggregate expenditures for individuals aged sixty-five to seventy-four. This is because our population counts by race, gender, and age come from the Current Population Survey, http://www.census.gov/cps/, in which age is top-coded at eighty for many years in our sample period. As we cannot know whether an individual with a top-coded age is younger than eighty-five, we cannot use the aggregate amounts for the sixty-five to eighty-four age group.

shapes of the age profiles across races, and the interactions are jointly significant at the 1 percent level. Our results—the scaled, predicted age profiles—are presented and discussed in the next section.

3.2.2   Social Security Benefits

The Social Security Administration's Statistical Supplement for 2008, http://www.ssa.gov/policy/docs/statcomps/supplement/2008/index.html, contains data on the average Social Security benefit received by retired workers in December 2007, broken down by race, gender, and single year of age. We include retired worker benefits only, not disability, survivor, or spouse benefits. We then use the CPI-W to "backtrack" these average benefits to the year in which the group was aged sixty-five. That is, the benefit for a group aged i in 2007 in any year $t \geq 2007 - i$ is

$$(1) \qquad B_t^i = \frac{B_{2007}^i}{\prod_{s=t}^{2006}(1+\text{COLA}_s)},$$

where B_t^i is the benefit received by group i in year t, and COLA_s is the cost-of-living adjustment, or the percentage by which the benefit in year s is increased to arrive at the benefit in year $s + 1$. These amounts are taken to represent what the individuals who are currently in group i would have received in previous years.

Clearly, there is a potential for sample selection bias. Our analysis for each cohort is based on individuals who survived until 2007. There is evidence to suggest that there are substantial differentials in mortality rates across income groups (Waldron 2007; Cristia 2007). Thus, the individuals in our sample are likely to be among the higher earners in their cohort, who are receiving above-average Social Security benefits. This effect is more likely to be important for older cohorts. Additionally, not all of the individuals in the 2007 groups would have started receiving benefits at age sixty-five; some may have delayed until age seventy and received a credit. A final issue is that, by assuming that the benefit received in 2007 is the benefit received at retirement plus the subsequent COLAs, we do not account for individuals who may have switched from receiving a retirement benefit to receiving a survivor's benefit upon the death of a spouse. It is possible that a retiree who experienced the death of a spouse might have switched to receiving a survivor's benefit (two-thirds of the deceased spouse's primary insurance amount) if the survivor's benefit was larger than the initial worker-only benefit. While these three factors affect the level of benefits we use as our benchmark, they do not affect our main conclusions of the relative differences in benefits from different types of benefit indexation policies.

3.2.3   Net-of-Medical-Expense Benefits

From the average benefits by race, age, and gender, we subtract the premiums paid for Medicare Part B and our predicted out-of-pocket spending on medical care for the relevant age-race-gender group. Medicare Part B premiums are automatically deducted from Social Security payments for those Medicare beneficiaries who do not opt out of Part B (inpatient insurance). This includes the vast majority of Medicare beneficiaries. We ignore the means testing for Part B that became effective in 2007 and assume everyone pays the standard Part B premium, a reasonable assumption given our focus on individuals who depend primarily on Social Security for their retirement income.[7] This allows us to track the growth of nominal benefits net of average out-of-pocket medical expenses over time for each cohort within a race-gender group. We compare this to the growth in the CPI-E for all items less medical expenses.[8] The CPI-E net of medical expenses tells us what our groups would need for nonmedical expenses at the end of 2007 in order to have the same purchasing power as they did when they were age sixty-five. Additionally, we compute the path of each group's Social Security benefit, starting at age sixty-five, if benefits had been indexed to the CPI-E instead of the CPI-W. This tells us the extent to which indexation to the CPI-E would have protected retirees from inflation.[9]

3.3   Results

3.3.1   Predicted Out-of-Pocket Expenses

Figures 3.3 and 3.4 show our simulated average out-of-pocket medical spending for all men and all women. Figures 3.5 through 3.8 show simulated average out-of-pocket medical spending for black men, black women, white men, and white women separately. The two solid lines represent the age profiles of spending in 1987 and 2007. However, as a particular cohort ages, it moves from the curve for one year to the curve for the next year. Therefore, the age profile for a particular cohort is steeper than the age profile across

---

7. Means testing was in effect in 2007 for individuals with a modified adjusted gross income over $80,000.

8. We are grateful to Ken Stewart of the BLS for providing us with unpublished CPI-E data. We have the CPI-E for all items less medical care for 1987 to 2007. We estimate the values for 1983 to 1986 as follows. Using the weights for medical care in the CPI-E for 1987, 2007, and 2008 (the BLS did not retain historical weights for other years), we fit a quadratic equation through these three values (with year as the independent variable), and use this equation to predict the weights for the other years. Using the fitted weights, we solve for the growth rate of the CPI-E for all items less medical care in the formula $g_t = w_{t-1}g_t^m + (1 - w_{t-1})g_t^{nm}$, where g_t is the growth in the CPI-E from year $t - 1$ to year t, g_t^m is the growth in the CPI-E for medical care from year $t - 1$ to year t, g_t^{nm} is the growth in the CPI-E for all items less medical care from year $t - 1$ to year t, and w_{t-1} is the weight on medical care in year $t - 1$. Using the same procedure for the CPI-W yields estimates of the CPI-W for all items less medical care that are fairly close to the actual values.

9. The COLAs applied by the SSA are based on the change in the CPI-W from the third quarter (Q3) of the previous year and Q3 of the current year. For the CPI-E, we only have the December-to-December (rather than the Q3-to-Q3) changes; therefore, all our analysis using the CPI-E uses December-to-December changes. While these may vary from the Q3-to-Q3 changes for particular years, the cumulative effect over the years should be approximately the same.

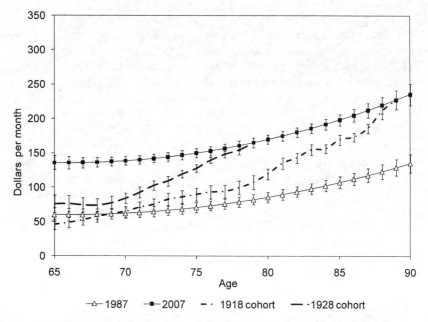

Fig. 3.3   Simulated out-of-pocket medical spending by year and age, all males

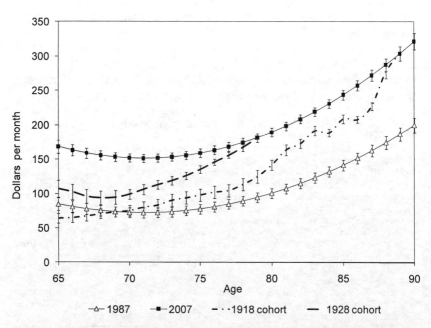

Fig. 3.4   Simulated out-of-pocket medical spending by year and age, all females

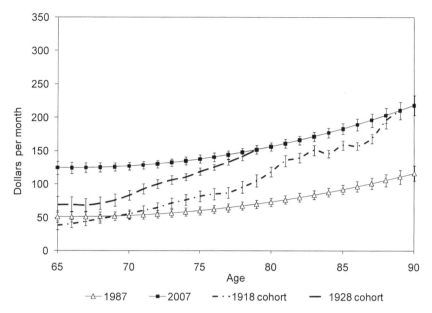

Fig. 3.5   Simulated out-of-pocket medical spending by year and age, white males

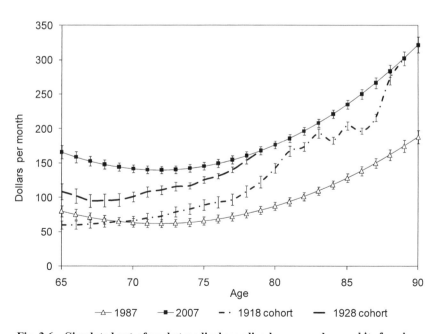

Fig. 3.6   Simulated out-of-pocket medical spending by year and age, white females

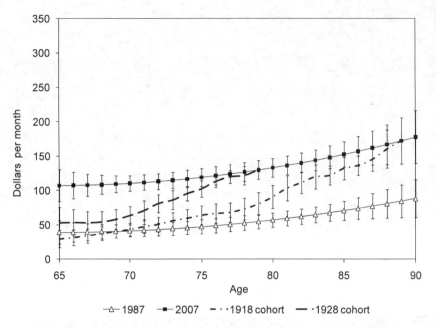

Fig. 3.7   Simulated out-of-pocket medical spending by year and age, black males

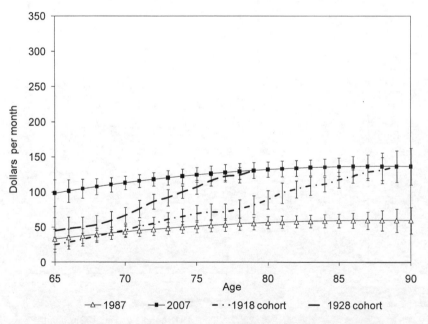

Fig. 3.8   Simulated out-of-pocket medical spending by year and age, black females

cohorts in a given year. The average out-of-pocket medical spending of the cohorts born in 1918 and 1928 are depicted by the dashed lines. The vertical bars represent the standard errors of our predicted values.[10]

Overall, average out-of-pocket expenses are higher—and rise faster—for women than for men. This result is consistent with other studies of medical expenditures (French and Jones 2004; Di Nardi, French, and Jones 2009). Di Nardi, French, and Jones (2009) show that, after controlling for age, income, and health status, men spend about 20 percent less than women on medical care. Our results suggest that this relationship appears to be driven primarily by white men and women; black women tend to have a lower and flatter profile of expenses than black men.

It is not clear why women overall seem to have higher and steeper expense profiles than men. One possibility is that, because women tend to outlive men and husbands tend to be older than their wives, there are more elderly widows than widowers. Older retirees living alone may have higher out-of-pocket medical expenses because, to some extent, a spouse can substitute for paid caregivers. In our 2006 sample, 56 percent of men aged eighty-five and above are married, compared to only 17 percent of women in the same age group. Men aged eighty-five and above had mean out-of-pocket medical expenses of $197 per month, compared with $276 per month for women in the same age group. However, married women aged eighty-five and above had monthly expenses of only $181, compared to $295 for single women. Single men's expenses were only slightly higher than those of married men—$198 versus $196 per month.[11] This provides some support for the hypothesis that differences in marital status can partly explain the observed gender differences.

One possible explanation for the flatness of the profiles for African Americans relative to whites is that elderly African Americans tend to have lower incomes than elderly whites. Current Population Survey data, http://www.census.gov/cps/, suggest that 7.9 percent of whites aged sixty-five and older are living in poverty, in comparison to 22.7 percent of African Americans aged sixty-five and older. Thus, elderly whites are more likely to have income and assets that can be used to finance high medical expenses. Indeed, Di Nardi, French, and Jones (2009) show that the age profile of medical expenses is much steeper for higher-income individuals, with differences in spending across income groups becoming far more pronounced at older

10. We assume that the standard error of the adjusted prediction is equal to the scaling factor multiplied by the standard error of the original prediction.
11. For this calculation, married is defined as either married with a spouse present, or partnered. Single is defined as married with an absent spouse, separated, divorced, widowed, or never married. We classify individuals who are married with an absent spouse as single because we are trying to capture the impact of living alone. There are 410 men and 768 women aged eighty-five and above in the 2006 sample.

ages. For individuals in their mid-seventies, medical expenses do not vary much with income; however, at age 100, individuals in the top quintile of lifetime income spend more than ten times as much as individuals in the bottom quintile.

We also note that our simulations of average out-of-pocket medical spending mask a large amount of variation in actual out-of-pocket medical spending experienced by the elderly. For example, French and Jones (2004) show that individuals face considerable risk of catastrophic health costs. Our regression results show that only a small part of the variation in out-of-pocket medical spending is explained by age, gender, and race. The level of out-of-pocket medical expenditures for any one individual may vary greatly from our predictions, and any given individual is also likely to experience more variation from year to year than our averages by race, gender, and age suggest.

3.3.2   Benefits Net of Average Out-of-Pocket Medical Expenses

To summarize our results, we focus on the experience of two cohorts—individuals born in 1918, and individuals born in 1928. The former cohort is eighty-nine at the end of 2007, and the latter is seventy-nine at the end of 2007.

Figures 3.9 and 3.10 depict the experience of the 1918 cohort of men

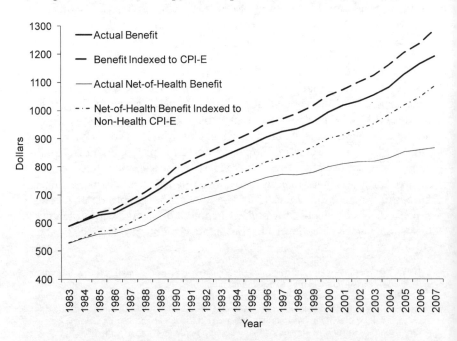

Fig. 3.9   Difference in monthly benefits using CPI-W and CPI-E, men aged 89 in December 2007

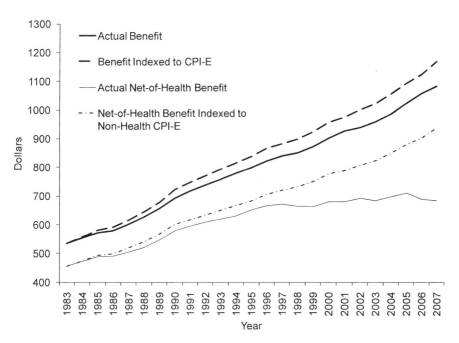

Fig. 3.10 Difference in monthly benefits using CPI-W and CPI-E, women aged 89 in December 2007

and women. In each graph, the solid black line shows the evolution of the cohort's actual Social Security benefit. The dashed black line shows the evolution of the cohort's Social Security benefit if the benefit had been indexed to the CPI-E. The solid gray line shows the actual benefit net of average out-of-pocket medical spending received by the cohort. Finally, the dashed gray line shows the benefit net of average out-of-pocket medical spending that would be required to keep pace with inflation in the prices of nonmedical goods (as measured by the CPI-E for all goods less medical care).

These graphs suggest that benefits net of average out-of-pocket medical spending have risen more slowly than the price index for nonhealth spending. The same pattern emerges for the four race-gender groups (the graphs are not shown), and for the 1928 birth cohort. The results for these other groups are summarized in table 3.2. The second column of the table shows, for each group, the actual monthly benefit net of average out-of-pocket medical expenses at age 65. The third column shows the actual monthly benefit net of average out-of-pocket medical expenses in December 2007. The third column shows the monthly benefit net of average out-of-pocket medical expenses that would be needed in December 2007 to reflect growth in the nonmedical component of the CPI-E. The last two columns show the percentage difference between columns (3) and (4), expressed relative to

Table 3.2   Comparison of actual net-of-medical-care benefit and benefit needed to maintain ability to purchase nonmedical care bundle

Cohort, age in Dec. 2007	Benefit at age 65	Dec. 2007, actual	Dec. 2007, needed	Percent shortfall (%)	Percent increase needed (%)
All men, 79	713.01	924.74	1028.93	10.1	11.3
All men, 89	527.85	866.80	1086.13	20.2	25.3
White men, 79	736.14	961.57	1062.30	9.5	10.5
White men, 89	542.75	898.97	1116.79	19.5	24.2
Black men, 79	598.75	763.91	864.04	11.6	13.1
Black men, 89	448.92	729.05	923.73	21.1	26.7
All women, 79	512.29	666.14	739.27	9.9	11.0
All women, 89	456.05	682.57	938.40	27.3	37.5
White women, 79	520.24	692.63	750.74	7.7	8.4
White women, 89	468.49	700.76	963.99	27.3	37.6
Black women, 79	511.09	626.16	737.54	15.1	17.8
Black women, 89	406.75	670.33	836.95	19.9	24.9

both the actual 2007 benefit ("Percent increase needed") and the 2007 benefit needed to keep up with inflation ("Percent shortfall").

For example, men born in 1918 have seen their average Social Security benefit, net of out-of-pocket medical expenses, rise from $527.85 at the end of 1983 (at age sixty-five) to $866.80 at the end of 2007 (at age eighty-nine). However, if this cohort's average benefit net of out-of-pocket medical expenses had kept pace with the nonmedical CPI-E over that time period, this amount would have been $1,086.13 in 2007. That is, the average benefit net of out-of-pocket medical expenses has declined by around 20 percent relative to the nonmedical CPI-E. Similarly, women born in 1918 have seen their average benefit net of out-of-pocket medical expenses decline by around 27 percent relative to the nonmedical CPI-E.

Table 3.3 shows the benefit net of average out-of-pocket medical expenses that retirees in both cohorts would be receiving in December 2007 if their benefits had been indexed to the CPI-E rather than the CPI-W. The last two columns, again, compare these amounts to the amounts that would be needed to offset inflation in nonmedical goods prices. This table suggests that retirees would have been more protected from inflation if cost-of-living adjustments had been based on the CPI-E. However, there is still a shortfall of 10 to 20 percent for the older cohort and 6 to 7 percent for the younger cohort. As noted previously, the reason indexing to the CPI-E does not fully compensate retirees for inflation is that, even if medical costs remained constant over time for the elderly, they tend to need additional medical care as they age, and the additional medical spending crowds out nonmedical spending. Thus, Social Security benefits net of average out-of-pocket medical expenses would tend to decline for each individual even if the price of

Table 3.3   Comparison of CPI-E indexed net-of-medical-care benefit and benefit needed to maintain ability to purchase net-of-medical-care bundle

Cohort, age in Dec. 2007	Dec. 2007, indexed with CPI-E	Dec. 2007, needed	Percent shortfall (%)	Percent increase needed (%)
All men, 79	961.14	1028.93	6.6	7.1
All men, 89	961.20	1086.13	11.5	13.0
All women, 79	695.12	739.27	6.0	6.4
All women, 89	768.45	938.40	18.1	22.1

medical care rose at the same rate as the prices of other goods. This idea is illustrated graphically in figures 3.3 through 3.8, in the contrast between the solid and dashed lines. A price index for medical care reflects the vertical shift over time in the solid line (the age profile of spending in any given year); it does not pick up the horizontal movement that occurs as an individual ages. In fact, each cohort is moving diagonally—to a higher curve as time passes, and to a point further to the right on that curve as its members age.

Because actual out-of-pocket medical expenditures are subject to a great deal of uncertainty, particular individuals may be more or less protected against inflation than shown here. We emphasize again that we are not claiming retirees are worse off than they were when they were sixty-five. Our analysis does not allow us to make any such utility comparisons. The CPI does not adequately account for the fact that higher medical costs may reflect the consumption of better quality medical care, and retirees may be better off even if they are left with less to spend on other nonmedical goods. All we have shown is that Social Security benefits may not be fully inflation-indexed in the sense that recipients cannot, from one year to the next, purchase the same bundle of nonmedical goods with their Social Security benefits.

3.4   Policy Implications

Our results suggest that retirees who depend primarily on Social Security have fallen behind substantially in terms of inflation-adjusted nonmedical spending. However, indexing Social Security benefits to the CPI-E—or alternatively, indexing benefits to keep real nonmedical spending constant—would clearly have an adverse impact on Social Security's finances.

To provide a back-of-the-envelope estimate of the impact on Social Security's finances, we begin with our estimates of the rate of increase in aggregate monthly benefit amounts required from 2006 to 2007 if (a) Social Security benefits had been indexed to the CPI-E, and (b) Social Security benefits had been adjusted to keep the real net-of-health benefit constant for the average retiree. We construct these estimates by using the number of retired workers in December 2006 and December 2007 by age and gender, actual average monthly benefits in December 2006 and December 2007 by age and gender, and our projections of average monthly benefits under scenarios (a) and (b).[12]

We find that aggregate benefits for individuals aged sixty-five to eighty-nine would have risen by 8.3 percent between December 2006 and December 2007 if benefits had been indexed to the CPI-E. Using the same methodology, if benefits had instead been adjusted to keep the real net-of-medical benefit constant, aggregate benefits for individuals aged sixty-five to eighty-nine would have risen by 12.4 percent over the same period. By contrast, actual aggregate benefits for this age group rose by only 5.6 percent between December 2006 and December 2007.[13]

The 2010 Social Security Trustees' report provides projections of the Old Age and Survivor's Insurance (OASI) program's income and cost rates through 2085. The income rate is defined as OASI tax revenue (from payroll taxes and taxation of benefits) as a percentage of taxable payroll, and the cost rate is defined as the cost of the OASI program as a percentage of taxable payroll. Using these income and cost rates, combined with the trustees' projections of gross domestic product (GDP) and taxable payroll as a fraction of GDP, we can project OASI's total income and costs through 2085. Under the trustees' projections of current law using intermediate assumptions, total OASI costs are projected to grow at an average rate of 5.6 percent per year between 2006 and 2085, in line with our estimate of the increase in aggregate benefits between 2006 and 2007. Consistent with our calculations for the growth in aggregate benefits between 2006 and 2007, we assume that indexation to the CPI-E would increase this growth rate by 2.6 percentage points in each year, and that indexation to maintain the real value of non-medical spending would increase this growth rate by 6.7 percentage points in each year.[14]

Figure 3.11 depicts the income and cost rates of the OASI program under

12. Beneficiary counts by age and gender were obtained from the US Social Security Administration, Annual Statistical Supplement, 2008, Table 5.A.1, "Number and average monthly benefit, by type of benefit and race, December 2007," http://www.ssa.gov/policy/docs/statcomps/supplement/2008/5a.html#table5.a1; and the US Social Security Administration, Annual Statistical Supplement, 2007, Table 5.A.1, "Number and average monthly benefit, by type of benefit and race, December 2006," http://www.ssa.gov/policy/docs/statcomps/supplement/2007/5a.html#table5.a1.

13. The actual rate of increase between December 2006 and December 2007 is considerably larger than the rate of increase in the CPI-W during this time period of 2.3 percent. This discrepancy is due to the fact that the composition of beneficiaries also changes over time and, because of differential mortality by income, beneficiaries with lower Social Security benefits tend to die earlier than beneficiaries with higher Social Security benefits.

14. Our analysis of net-of-medical-cost spending uses only retired worker benefits, and applies only to workers between the ages of sixty-five and eighty-five. We compute estimates of the increase in the aggregate retired worker benefits paid to this age group under the status quo and alternative policies. Thus, our estimated growth rates for aggregate benefits are not strictly comparable to the trustees' estimates of OASI cost increases, as OASI costs include retired worker, spouse, and survivor benefits for individuals of all ages, as well as administrative

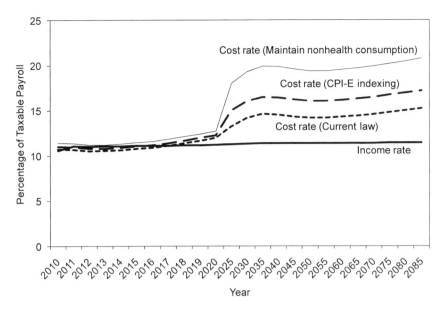

Fig. 3.11   Social Security income and cost rates as percentage of taxable payroll under alternative cost-of-living adjustments

current law, as well as the cost rate under each of these alternative indexing schemes, assuming the alternative indexing took effect in 2010. Under current law, persistent deficits begin in 2018. If benefits were indexed to the CPI-E, persistent deficits would begin two years earlier, in 2016, and if benefits were indexed to keep real nonmedical spending constant, persistent deficits would begin in 2015.

Starting with the assets of the OASI trust fund in 2009 ($2.2 trillion), we project the trust fund assets under each of our alternative indexing schemes. For 2010 to 2019, we assume that assets in the OASI trust fund earn the interest rates implied by the Social Security Trustees' short-term intermediate projections of the OASI trust fund ratio and interest income.[15] For 2020 and beyond, we assume that the interest rate paid on trust fund assets is 5.7 percent, which is the trustees' intermediate projection for the long-term nominal interest rate.[16] Under current law, the OASI trust fund is projected to become exhausted in 2040. Exhaustion of the trust fund would occur five

---

costs. However, our back-of-the-envelope calculation assumes that the *differences* in the growth rates of aggregate costs across policies should be similar regardless of whether we look at retired worker benefits for workers aged sixty-five to eighty-five, or total OASI costs.

15. These projections are available in the US Social Security Administration, *The 2010 OASDI Trustees' Report,* Table IV.AI, "Operations of the OASI Trust Fund, Calendar Years 2005–19," http://www.ssa.gov/OACT/TR/2010/IV_SRest.html#280816.

16. See the US Social Security Administration, *The 2010 OASDI Trustees' Report,* Table V B2, "Additional Economic Factors," http://www.ssa.gov/OACT/TR/2010/V_economic .html#205214.

to ten years earlier (between 2030 and 2035) if benefits were indexed to the CPI-E, and between ten and fifteen years earlier (between 2025 and 2030) if benefits were indexed to maintain the real value of nonmedical spending.

Given the state of Social Security's long-term finances, switching to one of these alternative indexing schemes is unrealistic from a policy perspective. While changes in benefits indexation can be done in ways that are revenue-neutral (e.g., by reducing initial benefits and increasing the rate of increase), reforms of this nature would raise distributional concerns and would rely on the assumption that such a policy would be preferred to one where benefits indexation remained constant and beneficiaries utilized other savings vehicles to ensure the adequacy of benefits for later medical expenses. Social Security reform proposals generally take into account the need to protect low-income retirees from benefit cuts, and many proposals in fact increase benefits to low-income earners (e.g., National Commission on Fiscal Responsibility and Reform, 2010). In this spirit, it might be reasonable for policy makers to consider an alternative indexing scheme to protect very low-income retirees as part of a more comprehensive Social Security reform package.

3.5   Conclusion

We have shown that Social Security benefits may not be as safe from inflation as commonly believed. Because medical costs have been rising over time, and because the elderly spend a larger fraction of their income on medical care than workers do, the CPI-W does not properly reflect the inflation experience of Social Security beneficiaries. This is partly reflected in the fact that premiums for Medicare Part B, in which most retirees participate, have risen much faster than Social Security benefits. It is compounded by the fact that retirees often have substantial out-of-pocket medical expenses, which increase as they age. Even experimental measures like the CPI-E may not fully compensate for inflation because they are intended to reflect the inflation experience of the average elderly person from year to year, rather than the experience of a given cohort. Given the state of Social Security's finances, it would not be fiscally prudent to raise legislated benefits for all retirees to keep pace with the CPI-E or to maintain average real net-of-medical benefits. However, most Social Security reform proposals attempt to protect very low-income retirees, and the alternative indexing schemes discussed in this chapter can provide guidance on how to accomplish this goal.

References

Boskin, Michael J., and Michael D. Hurd. 1982. "Are Inflation Rates Different for the Elderly?" NBER Working Paper no. 0943. Cambridge, MA: National Bureau of Economic Research, February.

Burdick, Clark, and Lynn Fisher. 2007. "Social Security Cost-of-Living Adjustments and the Consumer Price Index." *Social Security Bulletin* 67 (3): 73–88.
Cristia, Julian P. 2007. "The Empirical Relationship between Lifetime Earnings and Mortality." CBO Working Paper 2007-11. Washington, DC: Congressional Budget Office.
Di Nardi, Mariacristina, Eric French, and John Bailey Jones. 2009. "Why Do the Elderly Save? The Role of Medical Expenses." NBER Working Paper no. 15149. Cambridge, MA: National Bureau of Economic Research, July.
French, Eric, and John Bailey Jones. 2004. "On the Dynamics and Distribution of Health Care Costs." *Journal of Applied Econometrics* 19 (6): 705–21.
Hobijn, Bart, and David Lagakos. 2003. "Social Security and the Consumer Price Index for the Elderly." *Current Issues in Economics and Finance* 9 (5): 1–7.
List, Matthew Patrick. 2005. "Inflation and the Elderly." Unpublished Manuscript. Boston College, Chestnut Hill, MA.
National Commission on Fiscal Responsibility and Reform. 2010. "The Moment of Truth: Report of the National Commission on Fiscal Responsibility and Reform." Washington, DC: National Commission on Fiscal Responsibility and Reform. http://www.fiscalcommission.gov/sites/fiscalcommission.gov/files/documents/TheMomentofTruth12_1_2010.pdf.
Stewart, Kenneth J. 2008. "The Experimental Consumer Price Index for Elderly Americans (CPI-E): 1982–2007." *Monthly Labor Review* 131 (4): 19–24.
Waldron, Hilary. 2007. "Trends in Mortality Differentials and Life Expectancy for Male Social Security-Covered Workers, by Socioeconomic Status." *Social Security Bulletin* 67 (3): 1–28.

Comment   Michael D. Hurd

In the mid-1980s Boskin and Hurd calculated a separate Laspeyres price index for the older population using weights that reflected the different consumption pattern by the older population (Boskin and Hurd 1985). Of particular interest was the higher budget share for health care (fraction of total spending for health care): in the population less than age sixty the budget share was 4.9 percent, whereas in the population age seventy-five or older it was 9.8 percent. A higher rate of inflation for health care services interacted with a greater weight on them would result in a higher inflation index for the older population. However, Hurd and Boskin found that "the inflation experience of the elderly from 1961–1981 was quite similar to the general population both cumulatively and year-by-year." Table 3C.1 gives their prices levels in 1961 and 1981 by age group, and, indeed, the cumulative price increases are almost identical across the age groups. One reason for this somewhat surprising outcome is that the rate of inflation for health

Michael D. Hurd is principal senior researcher and director of the Center for the Study of Aging at the RAND Corporation, a research fellow of NETSPAR, and a research associate of the National Bureau of Economic Research.
For acknowledgments, sources of research support, and disclosure of the author's material financial relationships, if any, please see http://www.nber.org/chapters/c12434.ack.

Table 3C.1   Age-specific Laspeyres price indices

		Age category		
	<55	60–64	70–74	75+
1961	90.5	90.4	90.5	90.5
1981	250.1	252.1	251.4	250.8

Source: Boskin and Hurd (1985).

Table 3C.2   Budget shares for health care services (%) 2009

	Age category			
	All	55–64	65–74	75+
Total	6.4	7.4	11.4	15.1
Health insurance	3.6	3.8	7.1	9.5
Medical services	1.5	2.0	1.9	2.6
Drugs	1.0	1.3	2.0	2.5
Medical supplies	0.2	0.3	0.4	0.5

Source: Bureau of Labor Statistics, Consumer Expenditure Survey.

care services was not systematically greater than the overall rate of inflation, and, in fact, for some years it was lower. For example, between 1976 and 1981 the Consumer Price Index-All Urban Consumers (CPI-U) increased by 70 percent, whereas the medical care inflation rate was just 59 percent.

The situation today is quite different. The budget shares for health care are higher for everyone, but much higher for the older population, as shown in table 3C.2. In addition, the rate of inflation in health care services is persistently higher than the overall rate: between year 2000 and 2007 the CPI-U increased by 20 percent, whereas the medical care component increased by 35 percent. Thus there are good reasons to expect that the prior finding by Boskin and Hurd would no longer hold.

The BLS has calculated an experimental price index for the older population, the CPI-E.[1] Between 1997 and 2009 the CPI-U increased by 33.9 percent, whereas the CPI-E increased by 36.1 percent. Had Social Security benefits been indexed to the CPI-E over that period, benefits would have been about 6 percent higher than they actually were, at least partially protecting the older population from increases in health care spending, such as the increase in Part B premiums.

The chapter by Goda, Shoven, and Slavov has two main topics. What would be the consequences for Social Security benefits were the CPI-E to be used for indexing? By how much would Social Security benefits have to

1. See Stewart, referenced in chapter 3.

be increased with age so as to cover the increased costs of health care spending that are associated with age? According to their calculations, over the twenty-four years from 1983 to 2007 Social Security benefits would have increased by 8 percent more had the benefits been indexed to the CPI-E rather than to the CPI-U. While this difference is not as large as one might think due to the large increases in the medical component of the CPI over this time period,[2] it would have added a noticeable increase to the Social Security benefits of someone who claimed benefits in 1983 and survived to 2007. This result should rightfully enter the debate about the adequacy of Social Security benefits and potential reforms to the Social Security system.

The second and longest part of the chapter calculates the increases in Social Security benefits that would be required to fully cover age-related increases in health care spending over the period. Or said differently, by how much would Social Security benefits have to be increased to prevent health care spending from crowding-out non-health care spending? My reservations about this part of the chapter center around two issues. The first is that under the simplest life cycle model in old age total spending will decline with age, so that we would expect the level of spending on non-health care categories to decline with age. Further, the share of the budget devoted to non-health care categories will likely not be constant but will vary with the level of spending, as reflected in Engel-type curves.[3] Some goods are necessities, where the budget share will decline as total spending increases, and some are superior goods, where the budget share will increase. Whether the budget share would increase or decrease would depend on weighted spending responses of the various components.

My second reservation is based on the more realistic situation where tastes or production efficiencies change with age. As people age and health deteriorates, the marginal utility of spending on health care increases, so that quite naturally we would expect that spending on health care would increase with age. As a consequence, spending on other categories would decrease holding total spending constant. But, in addition, because of deteriorating health, declines in the marginal utility of spending on some non-health care categories are certainly plausible. For example, Börsch-Supan and Stahl (1991) speculated that the high German saving rate post-retirement comes from that fact that Germans are pretty well-protected from out-of-pocket spending on health care, and that declining health makes it hard to spend for non-health care. While it is difficult to generalize about total non-health care spending, it would seem that spending on at least some components is likely to decrease. Examples might be spending on private transportation,

---

2. The medical component of the CPI increased by about 250 percent, versus 107 percent for the CPI-U.

3. I say Engel-type curves because the budget constraint is not income within a time period but a within-period spending constraint determined by life cycle spending considerations.

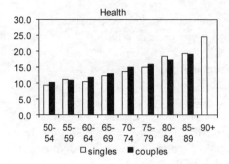
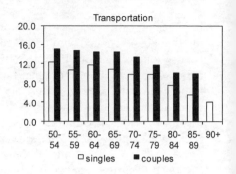
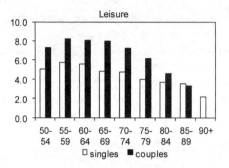
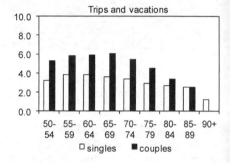
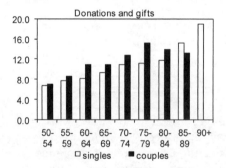

Fig. 3C.1   Budget shares
Source: Hurd and Rohwedder (2010).

where health limitations may reduce the quantity of driving, or spending on travel, where health makes travel more difficult. These and further examples are in figure 3C.1, which shows budget shares by age and marital status calculated from data from the Consumption and Activities Mail Survey. Accompanying the large increase in budget shares for health care are sharp declines for transportation (from about 12 percent to 4 percent for single persons), leisure (from about 8 percent to 3 percent for married persons), and trips and vacations (from about 6 percent to 2 percent for married persons).

The last category, donations and gifts, implies that the budget constraint is not forcing reductions in spending on transportation, leisure, and trips and vacations because donations and gifts are largely discretionary.

In our leading model of life cycle spending neither the level of spending nor the budget share of a category of spending should be constant with age. That basic model can be augmented from the observation that changes in health are likely to increase spending on health care and reduce spending on some other categories of spending because of changes in the marginal utility of consumption in those categories. These considerations lead to the conclusion that spending on non-health care will decline in level as people age, and likely also in budget shares. Thus a policy that aims to keep non-health care spending constant as people age would be odd indeed.

References

Börsch-Supan, Axel, and Konrad Stahl. 1991. "Life Cycle Savings and Consumption Constraints." *Journal of Population Economics* 4:233–55.
Boskin, Michael, and Michael D. Hurd. 1985. "Indexing Social Security Benefits: A Separate Price Index for the Elderly?" *Public Finance Quarterly* 13:436–49.
Hurd, Michael, and Susann Rohwedder. 2010. "Spending Patterns in the Older Population." In *The Aging Consumer: Perspectives from Psychology and Economics,* edited by Aimee Drolet, Norbert Schwarz, and Carolyn Yoon, 25–50. New York: Routledge.

4

The Availability and Utilization of 401(k) Loans

John Beshears, James J. Choi, David Laibson, and Brigitte C. Madrian

Borrowing from defined contribution savings plans, including 401(k) plans, has long been permissible. Nevertheless, the impact of this borrowing on economic outcomes has only recently begun to attract attention in the academic and policy worlds. The growth of 401(k) loans, coupled with the introduction of the 401(k) debit card,[1] motivated Senators Herb Kohl and Michael Enzi to propose legislation that would limit the number of outstanding 401(k) loans to three per participant and ban 401(k) debit cards

John Beshears is assistant professor of finance at the Graduate School of Business, Stanford University, and a faculty research fellow of the National Bureau of Economic Research. James J. Choi is associate professor of finance at Yale School of Management and a faculty research fellow of the National Bureau of Economic Research. David Laibson is Harvard College Professor and the Robert I. Goldman Professor of Economics at Harvard University and a research associate of the National Bureau of Economic Research. Brigitte C. Madrian is the Aetna Professor of Public Policy and Corporate Management at the Kennedy School of Government, Harvard University, and codirector of the Household Finance Working Group and a research associate of the National Bureau of Economic Research.

The research reported in this chapter was supported by a grant from the US Social Security Administration (SSA), administered by the Retirement Research Consortium (RRC). Additional financial support from the National Institute on Aging (grants R01-AG021650 and T32-AG00186) is gratefully acknowledged. The findings and conclusions expressed are solely those of the authors and do not represent the views of the SSA, the NIA, any other agency of the federal government, the NBER, or the RRC. See the authors' websites for a list of their outside activities. We thank Gopi Shah Goda for useful comments on the chapter. We also thank Aon Hewitt for providing data and insights into 401(k) loans from the perspective of a plan administrator. We are particularly grateful to Pam Hess, Yan Xu, and Kirsten Bradford for their feedback. We are also indebted to Yeguang Chi, Eric Zwick, Anna Blank, Patrick Turley, John Klopfer, Jung Sakong, Gwendolyn Reynolds, and Chelsea Zhang for their research assistance. For acknowledgments, sources of research support, and disclosure of the authors' material financial relationships, if any, please see http://www.nber.org/chapters/c12435.ack.

1. See Burton (2008) on the 401(k) debit card.

outright.[2] The concern is that easy access to one's retirement nest egg will lead to excessive consumption in the present at the expense of future financial security.

This chapter is the first step in a research agenda on how the availability of 401(k) loans affects retirement wealth accumulation. The aims of the current chapter are descriptive. We document both the widespread availability and utilization of 401(k) loans. About 90 percent of 401(k) participants are in plans that offer a loan option. Within those plans, about one in five eligible participants has a loan outstanding at a given point in time. Loan utilization rates follow hump-shaped patterns with respect to age, tenure, compensation, and plan balances, reaching peaks for participants in their forties, those with ten to twenty years of tenure, those earning $40,000 to $60,000 per year, and those with $20,000 to $30,000 in plan balances. Conditional on having a loan, the loan balance to 401(k) balance ratio is declining in age, tenure, compensation, and 401(k) plan balance.

Despite the prevalence of 401(k) loans, they constitute only 2.5 percent of total plan assets among plans with a loan option (Profit Sharing/401(k) Council of America 2010). For some individuals, however, 401(k) loans can be an important source of credit. Our empirical analysis finds that 401(k) loan utilization is correlated with the types of loan rules adopted by firms. Loans are more likely to be used in plans that charge low interest rates, and conditional on taking a loan, loan sizes are larger when multiple loans are allowed to be outstanding simultaneously, the maximum loan duration allowed is long, and the loan interest rate is high.

The rest of the chapter is organized as follows. In section 4.1, we describe the various sources of data that we use. Section 4.2 discusses the availability of 401(k) loans. In section 4.3, we explain how 401(k) loans work and describe the loan features that plan sponsors offer. Section 4.4 assesses how savings plan participants utilize 401(k) loans. Section 4.5 concludes.

4.1   Data on 401(k) Loans

We exploit several different sources of data on 401(k) loans in this chapter: published statistics, household survey data, firm-level 401(k) plan documents, and participant-level 401(k) administrative data. We briefly describe each primary data source and its strengths and weaknesses.

The first source of data is published statistics from a joint data collection effort by the Employee Benefit Research Institute (EBRI) and the Investment Company Institute (ICI). The EBRI/ICI database contains administrative data on 401(k) participants and their 401(k) plans from thousands of firms

---

2. The Savings Enhancement by Alleviating Leakage in 401(k) Savings Act of 2011 (SEAL) was submitted to the Senate on May 18, 2011 (http://www.govtrack.us/congress/bill .xpd?bill=s112-1020).

that are affiliated with either EBRI or ICI. In 1996, the first year for which such data were collected, the EBRI/ICI database included almost 28,000 401(k) plans with over 6.5 million plan participants, representing 9 percent of all 401(k) plans, 18 percent of all 401(k) participants, and 31 percent of all 401(k) assets (VanDerhei et al. 1999). Over time, the coverage of the EBRI/ICI database has expanded: in 2009, it included almost 52,000 plans covering twenty-one million participants, representing 10 percent of all plans, 42 percent of all participants, and 44 percent of all assets (Holden, VanDerhei, and Alonso 2010). Although the EBRI/ICI database is not a random or stratified random sample of either 401(k) plans or 401(k) participants, its distributions of total plan assets and number of plan participants are very similar to those of the entire universe of 401(k) plans,[3] making the data fairly representative at least on those dimensions. The 401(k) loan statistics published for the EBRI/ICI database include the fraction of firms offering 401(k) loans, the fraction of 401(k) participants utilizing such loans, and the average outstanding balance of 401(k) loans, all reported separately by plan size and by participant demographic characteristics. The strengths of the EBRI/ICI statistics include their broad coverage of the 401(k) market and their consistent reporting over the 1996 to 2009 time period. Their weakness is that the sample of firms included in the calculations is neither constant nor completely representative over time, so it is never clear whether differences over time and across plan and participant characteristics represent true differences or just different selection into the sample.

The second source of data is published tabulations from the Employee Benefits Surveys (EBS) conducted by the Bureau of Labor Statistics. These surveys, which have been conducted periodically since the early 1980s, were designed to be nationally representative of certain types of occupations in certain types of firms. The number of firms surveyed is substantially smaller than the number of firms in the EBRI/ICI database (totaling in the low thousands rather than the tens of thousands). The strength of these data is their representativeness for the population covered by the survey design. The weaknesses of the EBS data are several: (a) the survey population covered is somewhat limited;[4] (b) there is a high nonresponse rate both for firms and for the questions specific to retirement plans among the firms that did respond;[5]

---

3. Holden, VanDerhei, and Alonso (2009) benchmark the representativeness of the EBRI/ICI database to data published by Cerulli Associates on the entire universe of 401(k) plans.

4. The survey population is limited to certain occupations in private, nonagricultural, non-household establishments with one hundred or more employees. The published numbers on savings plans with a loan option are limited to full-time workers. The Bureau of Labor Statistics (1998) reports that 33.4 million full-time workers fell within the scope of the 1995 survey tabulations, which is much less than half of the full-time private sector labor force in 1995.

5. The Bureau of Labor Statistics (1998) reports that 60 percent of the establishments selected for the 1995 survey responded. Among responding establishments, 30 percent of the retirement plan participants represented in the data had their retirement plan provisions imputed due to missing data.

(c) the only statistic reported related to 401(k) loans is the fraction of 401(k) plan participants who are in plans with a loan option;[6] and (d) this statistic was only reported in the 1993, 1995, and 1997 surveys.

The third source of data is published statistics from the Profit Sharing/ 401(k) Council of America (PSCA). The PSCA data are derived from a survey of employers offering either profit-sharing or 401(k) plans and have two advantages over other data. First, they offer a long historical perspective on loan availability, loan provisions, and loan utilization, with data going back to 1990 for 401(k) loans.[7] Second, the PSCA surveys collect extensive information on the loan provisions at sampled firms. As with the EBRI/ICI data, the primary weakness of this data source is that the sample of firms included is neither representative nor constant over time.

The fourth source of data we use is the Survey of Consumer Finances (SCF), a triennial survey of households. The primary advantages of these data are that the sampling is designed to be nationally representative (when appropriately weighted), the data are publicly available at the individual level (as opposed to available only at the aggregate level in the form of summary statistics, as is the case with the previous three data sources), the data include information about portions of the household balance sheet other than the employer-sponsored savings plan, and the data include questions on savings plan loans going back to 1989. The primary disadvantage of the SCF is that the questions on savings plan loans are asked only of savings plan participants (and not of those eligible to participate but not currently participating) and are fairly limited. Nonetheless, it is the only source of information on the reasons why individuals borrow from their savings plans.

Our final two sources of data come from Aon Hewitt, a firm that administers many 401(k) plans. The first consists of plan descriptions from years ranging from 2002 to 2004 for eighty-seven 401(k) plans that offer loans at seventy-nine large companies. The primary advantage of these data is the level of detail they give about the loan provisions in these 401(k) plans. The primary disadvantages are the limited number of firms in the sample and the fact that they are not representative of the universe of firms offering 401(k) loans, although they may be somewhat representative of large firms that offer 401(k) loans.

Our second source of data from Aon Hewitt is a series of year-end cross-sections from 2002 to 2008. The cross-sections include individual-level data on all employees eligible to participate in their companies' 401(k) plans.

---

6. A handful of loan-related provisions for other categories of defined contribution savings plans (e.g., savings and thrift plans, deferred profit-sharing plans) are reported. These include whether loans are restricted to cases of hardship, whether participants' full account balances are available to be borrowed, and the length of the repayment period. The vast majority of savings and thrift plans are also 401(k) plans, but the converse is less likely to be true.

7. The PSCA first began surveying firms offering profit-sharing plans in 1957. Over time, as regulatory changes led many profit-sharing plans to incorporate a 401(k) component, the survey framework was adjusted to incorporate 401(k) plans as well as profit-sharing plans.

They contain demographic information such as birth date, hire date, gender, and compensation.[8] They also contain information on each individual's 401(k), including participation status in the plan at year-end, date of first participation, monthly contribution rates, asset allocation, plan balances, and 401(k) loans outstanding at the end of the year. For participants with a loan, we know the date on which each loan was taken out, the loan terms (interest rate, amount due per payment, scheduled payment frequency, and total number of payments due), and whether the loan was delinquent or had been converted to a taxable withdrawal due to nonpayment. The primary advantage of this data source is the amount of information on loans and other aspects of individuals' 401(k) accounts. This allows us to examine in greater detail how 401(k) participants utilize 401(k) loans.

4.2 Availability of 401(k) Loans

The regulation of 401(k) loans is shared by the Department of the Treasury and the Department of Labor, the two agencies that jointly regulate tax-favored savings plans.[9] Under the Internal Revenue Code, qualified retirement savings plans may (but are not required to) provide plan participants with the option of obtaining one or more loans against their plan balances.[10] If plans do make loans available, they must be made available to all participants on a reasonably equivalent basis.

There are two sources of data on the fraction of 401(k) plans with a loan option: the EBRI/ICI database and the PSCA surveys. Using the EBRI/ICI database (which covers many more firms than the PSCA surveys), Holden, VanDerhei, and Alonso (2010) calculate that 61 percent of plans in 2009 include a loan provision. Loan availability is much higher in the PSCA data, with 88 percent of plan respondents offering a loan option in 2009 (Profit Sharing/401(k) Council of America 2010). Both data sources indicate some increase in the availability of loans over time (figure 4.1). Large plans are more likely to offer a loan provision than small plans (figure 4.2). In the 2009 EBRI/ICI data, 94 percent of plans with more than 10,000 participants offered loans, compared to only 35 percent of plans with ten or fewer participants (Holden, VanDerhei, and Alonso 2010). The patterns in the PSCA surveys are similar, although the gradient with respect to plan size is much smaller.

Because most individuals work in large companies and large plans are more likely to offer loans, the fraction of 401(k) participants whose plan offers loans is much higher than the fraction of 401(k) plans that offer loans.

---

8. The data on compensation are not reported for all companies.
9. See US GAO (2009) for a summary of the laws that regulate 401(k) loans.
10. Qualified plans are those that satisfy the requirements of I.R.C. 401(a), annuity plans that satisfy 403(a) or 403(b), and governmental plans (Internal Revenue Service 2011). Loans are not permitted from IRAs, SEPs, or other similar plans.

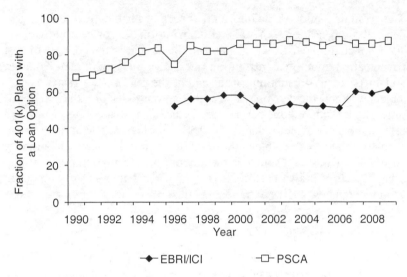

Fig. 4.1   Fraction of 401(k) plans with a loan option (1990–2009)

Notes: EBRI/ICI statistics come from a series of Investment Company Institute reports starting in 1999, including the first report by VanDerhei et al. (1999) and the most recent report by Holden, VanDerhei, and Alonso (2010). PSCA statistics come from various issues of the Profit Sharing/401(k) Council of America's "Annual Survey of Profit Sharing and 401(k) Plans."

In the most current EBRI/ICI data year (2009), 89 percent of 401(k) participants belong to a plan offering loans, even though only 61 percent of the plans in the data offer loans (Holden, VanDerhei, and Alonso 2010). The fraction of plans with a loan provision has increased only slightly in the past decade, but the EBRI/ICI data suggest that the fraction of participants whose savings plan offers a loan option has increased substantially during that time, from 70 percent in 1996 to 89 percent in 2009 (figure 4.3). The EBS also collected data on the fraction of 401(k) participants with a loan option during the 1990s. Although the prevalence of loans in the EBS is much lower than in the EBRI/ICI data, the EBS also shows an increase in loan access from 43 percent of participants in 1993 to 51 percent in 1997 (Bureau of Labor Statistics 1995, 1998, and 1999).

Note that in 1997, the one year when the two data sources overlap, there is a sizable discrepancy in the fraction of participants reported to belong to a plan with a loan option: 51 percent in the EBS data versus 79 percent in the EBRI/ICI data. It is not obvious how to interpret this discrepancy. Neither sample is completely representative of all 401(k) plans. The EBS is designed to be representative of certain occupations in private establishments with at least one hundred employees, so small employers (and thus small savings plans) and workers in several occupations are necessarily excluded. The EBRI/ICI database, while not designed to be representative, does include

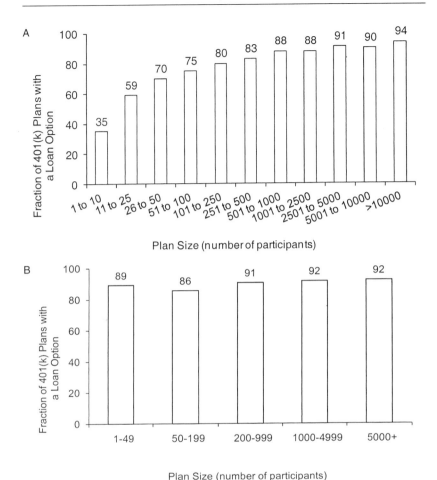

Fig. 4.2   401(k) loan availability by plan size: *A*, EBRI/ICI (2009); *B*, PSCA (2009)
Notes: See Holden, VanDerhei, and Alonso (2010); Profit Sharing/401(k) Council of America, "Annual Survey of Profit Sharing and 401(k) Plans."

small plans and appears to be fairly representative of the 401(k) plan universe on several dimensions; it also covers a sizable share of the total market. The fact that the EBRI/ICI number is higher than the EBS number is puzzling given the exclusion of smaller firms from the EBS data, since loans are less likely to be offered in smaller plans than in larger ones. If the EBS survey had included smaller firms, the gap between the EBS and EBRI/ICI estimates of loan availability would have been even larger. Both data sources indicate that 401(k) loan availability has grown over time, but what is less clear is exactly how many participants had a loan option available at any particular point in time.

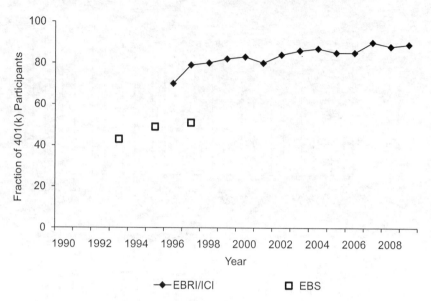

Fig. 4.3   Fraction of 401(k) participants in a plan with a loan option (1990–2009)

Notes: EBRI/ICI statistics come from a series of Investment Company Institute reports starting in 1999, including the first report by VanDerhei et al. (1999), and the most recent report by Holden, VanDerhei, and Alonso (2010). EBS statistics come from various issues of the Department of Labor's "Employee Benefits in Medium and Large Private Establishments."

4.3   401(k) Loan Provisions

The terms of a 401(k) loan are set by individual savings plans within certain regulatory bounds. When a loan is made to a 401(k) participant, the plan liquidates some of its assets to make the loan disbursement. The participant is then responsible for the timely repayment of the loan. Loan payments, which include both principal and interest, are made with after-tax dollars and are credited to the participant's account, transferring principal back into the participant's investments.

There are no regulatory restrictions on how the proceeds from a 401(k) loan may be used, nor are borrowers required to demonstrate financial need.[11] Plan sponsors have discretion to impose such restrictions if desired, but most do not. The PSCA (1999) reports that among savings plans with a loan option, 82 percent place no restrictions on how loan proceeds may be

---

11. In contrast, hardship withdrawals—which plans are allowed but not required to offer—are limited by regulation to be used for "immediate and heavy" expenditures for which no other resources are available. Allowable expenditures include medical expenses, educational expenses, burial or funeral expenses, expenditures related to the purchase of a home, and payments necessary to forestall eviction or foreclosure.

utilized.[12] Of the 18 percent of plans with restrictions, most allow loans for home purchases, education, and medical expenses.

There are, however, regulations on the maximum size of 401(k) loans. The total outstanding principal of all unpaid loans can be no larger than the minimum of 50 percent of a participant's vested account balance and $50,000 (employers can place additional size limits).[13] The only information we have on the actual maximum limits that plan sponsors place on 401(k) loan size comes from our sample of Aon Hewitt plan descriptions. In this sample, all plans adhere to the statutory limits, although some do so with minor modifications.[14]

Plans can also place restrictions on the minimum loan size. In the 2009 PSCA annual survey, only 3 percent of plans report having no minimum loan limit. Twelve percent of plans report a positive limit of $500 or less; 84 percent report a limit between $501 and $1,000; and the remaining 2 percent report some other limit. In our sample of Aon Hewitt plan descriptions (table 4.1), the minimum loan amounts are roughly in line with those in the PSCA survey: 28 percent have a minimum loan amount of $500 or less;[15] 69 percent have a minimum loan amount between $501 and $1,000; and 3 percent have a minimum loan amount greater than $1,000.

Plans are allowed to charge both an application fee and an annual service fee for each 401(k) loan. Survey data from the PSCA suggest that such fees are becoming more common. In the 1990 PSCA survey, only 26 percent of plans reported having loan fees; in the 2009 survey, this number had risen to 90 percent. The most common fee is a loan origination or application fee, which 85 percent of 2009 PSCA plans report having; among these plans, the median application fee is $75. Twenty-eight percent of plans report charging an annual maintenance fee, with a median amount of $25. Ten percent of plans report charging some other sort of fee. In our sample of Aon Hewitt plan descriptions, 43 percent either report having no fees or make no mention of any fees (table 4.1). Of the remaining plans, none report having any

---

12. Restrictions are more common in profit-sharing plans (27 percent) than in 401(k) plans (16 percent), and are more common in smaller plans than in larger ones (Profit Sharing/401(k) Council of America). Similarly, data from the EBS suggest that only 7 percent of savings and thrift plans place restrictions on how loan proceeds may be used (most savings and thrift plans are 401(k) plans).

13. The regulatory language also suggests that employers have discretion to allow loans of up to $10,000, even if this exceeds the limit of 50 percent of a participant's vested balance. Conversations with plan administrators suggest that in practice this is rarely allowed because of concerns that doing so could violate regulatory provisions in the Employee Retirement Income Security Act (ERISA). Participants affected by the 2005 hurricanes Katrina, Rita, or Wilma face a higher limit: the lesser of $100,000, or 100 percent of the participant's account balance.

14. Other restrictions included additional limits on loan amounts for participants with assets allocated to a self-directed brokerage window or employer stock.

15. Only one firm in the Aon Hewitt sample has a loan minimum of less than $500.

Table 4.1   Firm-level 401(k) loan provisions (2002–2004)

General provisions		*Loan duration*	
Offers a 401(k) loan option		Minimum, general purpose	
For general purpose	100.0%	≤1 month	13.8%
For a primary residence	73.6%	> 1 to 6 months	16.1%
Maximum number of loans outstanding		> 6 to 12 months	65.5%
1	33.3%	Not specified	4.6%
2	56.3%	Maximum, general purpose	
≥3	10.4%	< 5 years	21.8%
Application fee, general purpose		5 years	73.6%
$0	5.8%	Not specified	4.6%
> $0 to $25	5.8%	Minimum, primary residence	
> $25 to $50	34.5%	≤1 month	10.5%
> $50 to $75	13.8%	> 1 to 6 months	9.0%
> $75	3.5%	> 6 to 12 months	34.3%
Not specified	36.8%	> 12 to 60 months	16.4%
Minimum loan amount, general purpose		> 60 to 72 months	25.4%
< $500	1.1%	Not specified	4.5%
$500	26.4%	Maximum, primary residence	
> $500 to $1,000	69.0%	< 10 years	3.0%
> $1,000	3.4%	10 years	31.3%
Interest rate provisions		15 years	46.3%
Interest rate		20 to 25 years	6.0%
Prime	25.3%	30 years	9.0%
> Prime to prime + 1	59.8%	Not specified	4.5%
> Prime + 1 to prime + 2	5.8%		
Other	5.8%		
Not specified	3.5%		
Interest rate update frequency			
Daily	4.6%		
Monthly	54.0%		
Quarterly	33.3%		
Annually	1.1%		
Other frequency	1.1%		
Not specified	5.8%		

Source: Authors' calculations from the Aon Hewitt plan documentation for eighty-seven plans at seventy-nine companies for which we have documentation from one year between 2002 and 2004. Percentages sometimes do not add up to 100 percent due to rounding.

fees other than application fees, which range from $25 to $100 for general purpose loans, with a median of $50.[16]

Employers may allow participants to have more than one loan outstanding simultaneously, although the loans would in total be subject to the maximum loan size restrictions noted previously. In the latest PSCA survey, about

16. Two of the plans in the Aon Hewitt sample have a higher fee for primary residence loans than for general purpose loans. One company has a higher fee for loans requested through a benefits representative than for loans requested on the benefits website, and we use the lower fee for table 4.1.

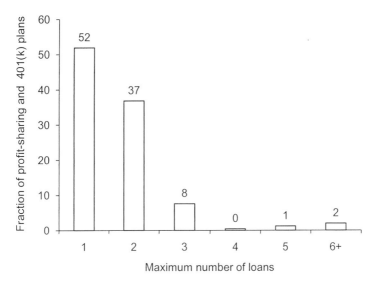

Fig. 4.4   Maximum number of loans allowed: PSCA (2009)
Notes: PSCA statistics come from the Profit Sharing/401(k) Council of America's "Annual Survey of Profit Sharing and 401(k) Plans."

half of plans allow participants to have more than one loan outstanding. Large plans are much more likely to allow multiple loans than small plans: for example, 38 percent of plans with fewer than fifty participants allow multiple loans, while 57 percent of plans with over 5,000 participants do. Figure 4.4 shows the distribution of the maximum number of loans allowed in the 2009 PSCA survey.[17] Most (52 percent) allow only one loan, 37 percent allow two loans, and 8 percent allow three loans. Only 3 percent of plans allow four or more loans. In our sample of Aon Hewitt plan descriptions, 33 percent restrict participants to only one loan, 56 percent allow participants to take out two loans, and 10 percent allow three or more loans (table 4.1).

Employers have some discretion in establishing loan repayment procedures. Regulations require that loan payments be made at least quarterly and pay down both principal and interest. In practice, many companies use automatic payroll deduction for loan repayments, so loan payments are made on a monthly or biweekly basis. The amortization period for a 401(k) loan can typically be chosen by participants within a set of constraints established by the plan. These constraints are dictated in part by regulatory requirements. One such requirement is that general purpose loans must be repaid within five years, although employers can choose a shorter maximum repayment

17. This figure includes both profit-sharing and 401(k) plans, as the PSCA does not report the distribution of permissible loans separately by defined contribution plan type. The fraction of plans that allow more than one loan is reported separately by plan type, and this fraction is similar for both types of plans.

horizon. Employers can establish a longer repayment period for loans taken for investment in a primary residence. Early repayment of loans (potentially with a prepayment penalty) is also allowed.[18]

Our source of information on the distribution of both minimum and maximum loan amortization periods is the sample of Aon Hewitt plan descriptions (table 4.1). In this sample, about two-thirds of plans have a minimum duration of more than six months for general purpose loans; the rest either do not specify a minimum repayment period or specify a shorter minimum repayment period (usually one or six months). Almost three-quarters of plans have a maximum repayment period of five years for general purpose loans, the statutory maximum; the remaining quarter either do not specify a maximum repayment period or specify a shorter repayment period, usually between four and five years.

Of the plans in the Aon Hewitt plan description sample, all offer general purpose loans, and 74 percent allow both primary residence and general purpose loans (table 4.1). The main distinction between general purpose and primary residence loans is that the latter can have a longer repayment period and the plan must verify that the loan is being used for a primary residence. Primary residence loans require both additional documentation from applicants and additional processing by plan sponsors.[19] As with general purpose loans, the modal minimum repayment period for primary residence loans is twelve months, but plans often stipulate a longer minimum loan duration. Forty-two percent of the Aon Hewitt plans have a minimum repayment period exceeding twelve months for a primary residence loan, and a minimum repayment period of five to six years is the most common within this subset of plans. The maximum repayment period for primary residence loans varies widely across plans, ranging from 117 months to 360 months. The modal maximum repayment duration is 180 months (fifteen years).

Loan repayments are made with after-tax dollars and are not counted as plan contributions (and thus do not count against annual plan contribution limits), even though both the principal and interest payments are credited to participants' accounts. Interest payments are not tax deductible, even if the purpose of the loan was for a primary residence, because the loan is not secured by the residence, as the IRS requires for mortgage interest tax deductibility.

Plans have discretion in determining the interest rate for 401(k) loans, although the interest rate chosen must be reasonable, meaning that it must be similar to what other financial institutions are charging for similar types

18. Prepayment penalties appear to be rare. None of the plans in our Aon Hewitt sample of plan descriptions imposes a prepayment penalty.
19. In plans that do not offer both general purpose and primary residence loans, participants can apply for a general purpose loan and use the proceeds for their primary residence. Such a loan would not require additional documentation regarding its purpose and would have to be repaid in five years (or less, if the plan has a shorter maximum loan duration).

of loans. In practice, most savings plans that allow loans peg their interest rate to the prime rate. In the most recent PSCA survey that reports how plans determine their 401(k) loan interest rate, 86 percent of plans report pegging their interest rate to the prime rate. In our sample of Aon Hewitt plan descriptions, 91 percent of plans peg their interest rate to the prime rate (table 4.1). There is, however, variation in the spread between the prime rate and the 401(k) loan rate. Twenty-five percent of Aon Hewitt plans set their interest rate equal to the prime rate, 60 percent set it to the prime rate plus 0 to 1 percent (not including 0), and 6 percent set it to the prime rate plus 1 to 2 percent (not including 1). There is also some variation in the frequency with which 401(k) loan interest rates are updated. Most (54 percent) of the Aon Hewitt plans adjust their interest rate monthly, but 33 percent adjust only quarterly, 5 percent adjust daily, and the rest adjust at some other frequency (including one plan that adjusts only once a year). This increases variation in 401(k) loan interest rates across plans during periods when the prime rate is changing frequently.

We can look at the participant-level data from our sample of Aon Hewitt plans to get a sense for how 401(k) interest rates vary across firms and how they have evolved over time. We use the set of twenty-seven plans at twenty-five companies for which we have year-end data in every year from 2002 to 2008. For each company, we calculate the modal interest rate of loans originated in each month.[20] Because we have data not only on newly originated loans, but also on all loans outstanding at year-end, we can examine interest rates prevailing before the initial 2002 cross-section to the extent that loans taken out before that time have not yet been fully repaid by year-end 2002. This gives us a long time series of interest rates. Figure 4.5 shows, across these twenty-seven plans, the median, twenty-fifth, and seventy-fifth percentile of firm-level modal interest rates by loan origination month. The difference between the twenty-fifth and seventy-fifth percentile interest rates across firms is almost always 100 basis points. As expected, given how 401(k) loan interest rates are set, the median interest rate tracks the prime interest rate fairly closely, as seen in figure 4.6.

If a participant defaults on his or her loan, the outstanding balance at the time of default is treated as a taxable distribution from the plan and is subject to the 10 percent early withdrawal penalty for participants under the age of fifty-nine-and-a-half.[21] If a participant's employment is terminated,

20. There tends to be little heterogeneity in interest rates among loans originated in a particular plan in a given month. However, loan interest rates can vary within a plan for a given month due to within-month movements in the prime rate, differential delays between loan application and disbursement, and participants of acquired firms who took out loans under their former plans. This is why we use the modal interest rate, which is almost always identical to the median interest rate (and often is also the fifth percentile and ninety-fifth percentile interest rate) among loans originated in a particular plan-month.

21. Plans may suspend loan payments for employees on active military duty. They may also suspend payments for employees on nonmilitary leave for up to one year.

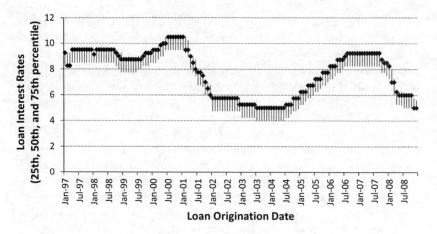

Fig. 4.5   Distribution of 401(k) loan interest rates: 1997–2008

Notes: Authors' calculations using the Aon Hewitt loan-level data on 531,126 loans from twenty-seven plans at twenty-five companies for which we have data at every year-end from 2002 to 2008. The year 1997 is the origination year for the oldest general-purpose loans in the data set. Individuals with zero or missing account balances are excluded.

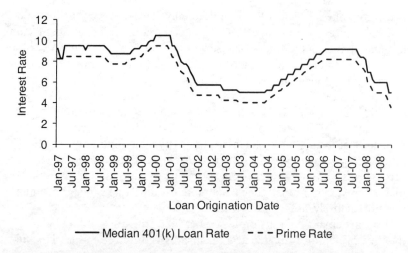

——— Median 401(k) Loan Rate   - - - Prime Rate

Fig. 4.6   Median 401(k) loan interest rates and the prime rate (1997–2008)

Notes: Authors' calculations using the Aon Hewitt loan-level data on 531,126 loans from twenty-seven plans at twenty-five companies for which we have data at every year-end from 2002 to 2008. The year 1997 is the origination year for the oldest general-purpose loans in the data set. Individuals with zero or missing account balances are excluded.

most companies stipulate that the loan must be repaid in full within a reasonable period of time, or the outstanding loan balance is treated as a taxable distribution from the plan. Some companies, however, may allow terminated employees to continue repaying their 401(k) loans over a longer period of time. The Aon Hewitt plan descriptions show some heterogeneity across firms as to when a loan is deemed to be in default and when it becomes a taxable distribution, but generally, terminated participants have sixty to ninety days to repay a loan before it becomes a taxable distribution. Current employees of the company have a similar amount of time to become current on a loan whose payments are in arrears.

4.4   401(k) Loan Utilization

We now turn to an assessment of how individuals use 401(k) loans. Figure 4.7 plots the fraction of 401(k) participants in plans with a loan option who have at least one outstanding 401(k) loan, as reported by the PSCA, as reported by the Investment Company Institute (using the EBRI/ICI data), and from our own calculations using the Aon Hewitt participant-level data.

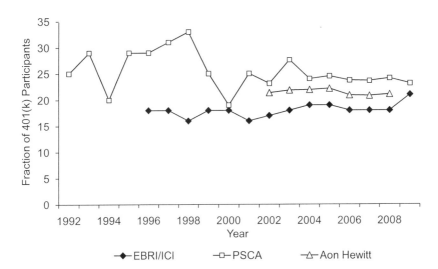

Fig. 4.7   Fraction of participants with an outstanding 401(k) loan (1992–2009)

Notes: EBRI/ICI statistics come from a series of Investment Company Institute reports starting in 1999, including the first report by VanDerhei et al. (1999), and the most recent report by Holden, VanDerhei, and Alonso (2010). PSCA statistics come from various issues of the Profit Sharing/401(k) Council of America's "Annual Survey of Profit Sharing and 401(k) Plans." Aon Hewitt statistics come from the authors' calculations using 3,896,412 employee-year observations from twenty-seven plans at twenty-five companies for which we have data at every year-end from 2002 to 2008. Individuals with zero or missing account balances are excluded.

In the EBRI/ICI data, the fraction of participants with a loan has been relatively stable over time, ranging between 16 percent and 21 percent. The fraction of participants with a loan is somewhat higher in the PSCA surveys, ranging from 19 percent to 33 percent, although it stabilized around 24 percent during the past several years. In the Aon Hewitt data, a nearly constant 21 percent to 22 percent of participants have an outstanding loan at year-end between 2002 and 2008.[22] If we restrict the Aon Hewitt sample to participants who remain employed at the same company for all seven years, an average of 31 percent have a loan in any given year, but a much higher 44 percent have a loan at some point during the entire seven-year period. Annual loan utilization figures are thus likely to substantially understate the fraction of participants who could be affected by a change in plan loan policies or federal regulations of 401(k) loans.

In the first two columns of table 4.2, we report, separately by demographic characteristics, the fraction of participants who have a 401(k) loan in 401(k) plans that allow loans. The numbers in the first column are from the EBRI/ICI data for calendar year 2008, and the numbers in the second column are from the Aon Hewitt participant-level data at year-end 2008. Loan utilization follows a hump pattern with respect to age, peaking in the forties at 22 percent in the EBRI/ICI data and 26 percent in the Aon Hewitt data. Employees in their twenties or sixties have substantially lower loan utilization rates (between 10 percent and 14 percent). Loan utilization also follows a hump pattern with respect to tenure, peaking at 26 percent in the EBRI/ICI data and 33 percent in the Aon Hewitt data for employees with ten to twenty years of tenure. Employees with two or fewer years of tenure have very low utilization rates, likely reflecting the fact that employees must accumulate some balances in their savings plan before they can take out a loan. Loan utilization rates are fairly flat, around 25 percent (EBRI/ICI) and 30 percent (Aon Hewitt) across much of the distribution of plan assets, but show a marked decline once plan balances exceed $200,000 or fall below $10,000. For low-balance participants, loan utilization is limited by institutional constraints. First, in most firms, taking out a loan is not feasible until participants have reached a certain level of balances due to restrictions on the minimum loan size (see table 4.1). Second, loans are restricted to be no more than 50 percent of vested balances. This restriction, coupled with application fees, means that a 401(k) loan may be economically unattractive for participants with low plan balances. Loan utilization rates are highest for middle-income participants ($40,000 to $60,000 in annual compensation) and lower for those with very low incomes or very high incomes.

Figure 4.8 plots the time series of average total outstanding loan balances

---

22. These numbers are very similar to the results of internal calculations by Aon Hewitt on the fraction of their plan participants with a 401(k) loan over the same time period (Aon Hewitt 2011).

Table 4.2   401(k) loan utilization and balances by demographic characteristics (2008)

	Fraction of participants with a 401(k) loan		Average loan balance as a fraction of balances	
	EBRI/ICI (%)	Aon Hewitt (%)	EBRI/ICI (%)	Aon Hewitt (%)
Overall	18	21	16	23
Age				
20s	10	10	29	28
30s	20	23	25	26
40s	22	26	18	23
50s	19	23	13	20
60s	11	14	11	22
Tenure (years)				
0 to 2	6	3	25	27
> 2 to 5	15	13	26	27
> 5 to 10	23	28	24	26
> 10 to 20	26	33	17	23
> 20 to 30	25	30	12	16
> 30	18	26	9	14
Plan balance				
≤$10,000	12	13	39	30
> $10,000 to $20,000	26	31	33	25
> $20,000 to $30,000	26	32	29	23
> $30,000 to $40,000	26	31	26	22
> $40,000 to $50,000	25	31	24	21
> $50,000 to $60,000	24	30	21	20
> $60,000 to $70,000	23	31	19	19
> $70,000 to $80,000	22	29	18	19
> $80,000 to $90,000	21	29	16	18
> $90,000 to $100,000	20	28	15	16
> $100,000 to $200,000	18	25	11	12
> $200,000	12	17	5	6
Compensation				
≤$40,000	19	15	21	23
> $40,000 to $60,000	27	23	19	22
> $60,000 to $80,000	24	23	17	20
> $80,000 to $100,000	20	23	14	19
> $100,000	14	16	11	17
Participants	—	638,902	—	134,584

Notes: EBRI/ICI statistics come from Holden, VanDerhei, and Alonso (2009). Aon Hewitt statistics come from the authors' calculations using the Aon Hewitt individual-level data in 2008 from twenty-seven plans at twenty-five companies for which we have data at every year-end from 2002 to 2008. Individuals with zero or missing account balances are excluded. Seven plans at five companies are dropped from the salary range rows due to missing salary data. A small number of individuals are dropped from the age and tenure rows due to missing age or tenure data. The first two columns show the fraction of 401(k) participants with an outstanding loan at year-end. The last two columns show outstanding loan balances as a fraction of total 401(k) balances at year-end among participants with an outstanding loan. In the Aon Hewitt data, we winsorize the top and bottom 0.5 percent of the loan-to-balance observations in order to reduce the impact of outliers.

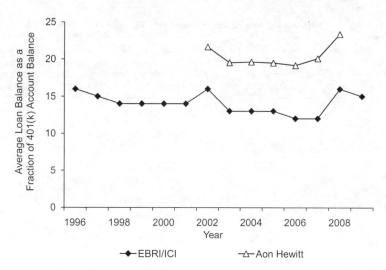

Fig. 4.8   Outstanding loan balances as a fraction of 401(k) balances (1996–2009) (conditional of having loan balances)

Notes: EBRI/ICI statistics come from a series of Investment Company Institute reports starting in 1999, including the first report by VanDerhei et al. (1999), and the most recent report by Holden, VanDerhei, and Alonso (2010). Aon Hewitt statistics come from the authors' calculations using 833,433 employee-year observations from twenty-seven plans at twenty-five companies for which we have data at every year-end from 2002 to 2008. Individuals with zero or missing account balances are excluded. In the Aon Hewitt data, we winsorize the top and bottom 0.5 percent of the loan-to-balance observations in order to reduce the impact of outliers on the average.

divided by plan balances among participants who have an outstanding 401(k) loan.[23] In the EBRI/ICI data, loan balances as a fraction of balances have varied between 12 percent and 16 percent over the 1996 to 2009 time period but exhibit no clear trend. Our sample of Aon Hewitt participants shows a similar pattern during the years it overlaps with the EBRI/ICI data, although the average loan-to-balance ratio is higher, ranging from 19 percent to 23 percent.

As with loan utilization, there are significant differences in the size of outstanding loan balances relative to 401(k) balances across different demographic groups. These are shown in the third column of table 4.2 using the EBRI/ICI data from 2008 and in the fourth column using the Aon Hewitt data at year-end 2008. In both data sets, loan balances relative to plan balances decrease with age, tenure, plan balances, and salary.

Figure 4.9 shows the average nominal dollar value of outstanding 401(k)

---

23. For participants with more than one 401(k) loan outstanding at a given time, the numerator sums loan balances across all the participant's outstanding loans. The denominator reflects total plan balances that do not net out outstanding loan balances. Private correspondence with Jack VanDerhei indicates that the Investment Company Institute reports erroneously describe the EBRI/ICI denominator as netting out loan balances.

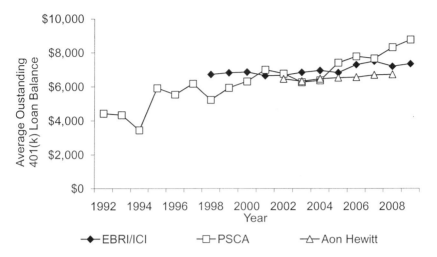

Fig. 4.9   Average outstanding 401(k) loan balances (1992–2009)

Notes: EBRI/ICI statistics come from a series of Investment Company Institute reports starting in 1999, including the first report by VanDerhei et al. (1999), and the most recent report by Holden, VanDerhei, and Alonso (2010). PSCA statistics come from various issues of the Profit Sharing/401(k) Council of America's "Annual Survey of Profit Sharing and 401(k) Plans." Aon Hewitt statistics come from the authors' calculations using 833,433 employee-year observations from twenty-seven plans at twenty-five companies for which we have data at every year-end from 2002 to 2008. Individuals with zero or missing account balances are excluded.

loan balances as reported by the PSCA, reported by the Investment Company Institute (using the EBRI/ICI data), and from our own calculations using the Aon Hewitt data. Average outstanding balances are very similar across all three data sources and are about $7,500 in 2008. They have increased slightly over time in the EBRI/ICI data and somewhat more substantially in the PSCA data.

Table 4.3 shows the distribution of the number of loans per participant in our 2008 Aon Hewitt participant-level sample, separately by the maximum number of loans allowed by the plan. There is no clear relationship between the number of loans allowed by a plan and the fraction of participants with an outstanding loan; loan utilization is highest in the plans that allow a maximum of two loans. The last two columns of table 4.3 show the average total outstanding loan-to-balance ratio and the average total outstanding loan balance by the number of outstanding loans held by participants. Both the loan-to-balance ratio and the total outstanding loan balance increase with the number of loans outstanding. Among participants with only one outstanding loan, loans represent 16 percent to 19 percent of total balances; among participants with two outstanding loans, loans represent 24 percent to 27 percent of total balances; and among participants with three outstanding loans, loans represent 29 percent of total balances. Average outstanding

Table 4.3   Number of loans outstanding by maximum number of loans allowed (2008)

Maximum number of loans allowed in plan	Number of loans outstanding	Fraction of participants (%)	Average total loan balance/401(k) balance (%)	Average total outstanding loan balance
1	0 loans outstanding	85.7	0.0	$0
	1 loan outstanding	14.3	16.3	$5,305
2	0 loans outstanding	74.5	0.0	$0
	1 loan outstanding	12.4	19.1	$6,212
	2 loans outstanding	13.1	27.3	$8,529
3	0 loans outstanding	88.5	0.0	$0
	1 loan outstanding	5.7	18.6	$11,225
	2 loans outstanding	2.2	23.5	$14,066
	3 loans outstanding	3.6	29.2	$16,779

Notes: Authors' calculations using the Aon Hewitt individual-level data in 2008 from twenty-seven plans at twenty-five companies for which we have data at every year-end from 2002 to 2008. Individuals with zero or missing account balances were excluded. Thirty-eight individuals were dropped whose account and loan records did not match, leaving a sample size of 638,864.

loan balances range from $5,305 to $11,225 among participants with only one loan to $16,779 among participants with three loans.

Because many of the demographic characteristics associated with loan utilization and the size of loan balances are highly correlated with each other, table 4.4 reports results from regressions of loan utilization and loan balances as a fraction of total balances (conditional on having a loan outstanding) on demographic and plan characteristics using the Aon Hewitt participant-level data from the year-end closest to the date of the plan description that we have (2002, 2003, or 2004).[24] The sample in these regressions—participants in eighty-seven plans at seventy-nine companies that offer loans—is much larger than in our previous analysis because we do not require continuous data coverage from 2002 to 2008. The first two columns show linear probability regression coefficients and standard errors where the dependent variable is a dummy for having a 401(k) loan outstanding and the only explanatory variables are dummies for demographic characteristics. The third and fourth columns add a set of plan loan feature dummy variables: whether the plan offers primary residence loans, the maximum number of loans permitted by the plan, how the loan interest rate is set, whether there is an application fee, whether the minimum loan amount for a general purpose loan is greater than $500, the minimum loan duration for a general purpose loan, and whether the maximum loan duration for a general purpose loan is less than five years. In the fifth and sixth columns,

24. Because plans change their provisions over time, restricting the data to the year-end extract that is closest to the plan description date reduces measurement error in the plan variables. This means that the data in the regression come from different years. The statistics on loan utilization in the Aon Hewitt and EBRI/ICI data are fairly stable over time, so some mixing across the relatively short span of three years should not be problematic.

Table 4.4   The association of demographic characteristics and plan features with 401(k) loan utilization (2002–2004)

	Has a 401(k) loan outstanding				Loan balance as a fraction of total balances			
	Coefficient	SE	Coefficient	SE	Coefficient	SE	Coefficient	SE
Constant	0.0449**	(0.0177)	0.0846**	(0.0391)	0.2806***	(0.0113)	0.2301***	(0.0193)
			Demographic controls					
Age								
20s (omitted)								
30s	0.0308***	(0.0059)	0.0334***	(0.0043)	0.0079***	(0.0025)	0.0074***	(0.0021)
40s	0.0166**	(0.0082)	0.0202***	(0.0065)	0.0095***	(0.0033)	0.0096***	(0.0031)
50s	−0.0249**	(0.0121)	−0.0192*	(0.0114)	0.0037	(0.0038)	0.0047	(0.0036)
60s	−0.1131***	(0.0141)	−0.1045***	(0.0131)	−0.0073	(0.0051)	−0.0032	(0.0044)
Tenure (years)								
0 to 2 (omitted)								
> 2 to 5	0.1094***	(0.0107)	0.1114***	(0.0114)	−0.0272***	(0.0074)	−0.0177**	(0.0071)
> 5 to 10	0.2244***	(0.0208)	0.2283***	(0.0194)	−0.0310***	(0.0103)	−0.0152*	(0.0084)
> 10 to 20	0.2933***	(0.0271)	0.2986***	(0.0256)	−0.0306**	(0.0120)	−0.0147	(0.0089)
> 20 to 30	0.3187***	(0.0262)	0.3196***	(0.0253)	−0.0234**	(0.0106)	−0.0109	(0.0090)
> 30	0.3101***	(0.0286)	0.3038***	(0.0289)	−0.0273**	(0.0106)	−0.0167*	(0.0090)
Plan balance								
≤$10,000 (omitted)								
> $10,000 to $20 000	0.0896***	(0.0091)	0.0852***	(0.0099)	−0.0397***	(0.0038)	−0.0430***	(0.0034)
> $20,000 to $30 000	0.0778***	(0.0108)	0.0722***	(0.0106)	−0.0570***	(0.0050)	−0.0632***	(0.0042)
> $30,000 to $40 000	0.0604***	(0.0135)	0.0538***	(0.0129)	−0.0702***	(0.0061)	−0.0781***	(0.0052)
> $40,000 to $50 000	0.0443***	(0.0155)	0.0374**	(0.0146)	−0.0799***	(0.0064)	−0.0889***	(0.0055)
> $50,000 to $60 000	0.0291*	(0.0174)	0.0218	(0.0160)	−0.0908***	(0.0068)	−0.1010***	(0.0057)
> $60,000 to $70 000	0.0210	(0.0187)	0.0129	(0.0170)	−0.0997***	(0.0071)	−0.1107***	(0.0057)
> $70,000 to $80 000	0.0074	(0.0206)	−0.0010	(0.0189)	−0.1091***	(0.0077)	−0.1204***	(0.0060)

(*continued*)

Table 4.4 (continued)

	Has a 401(k) loan outstanding				Loan balance as a fraction of total balances			
	Coefficient	SE	Coefficient	SE	Coefficient	SE	Coefficient	SE
Plan balance								
> $80,000 to $90,000	0.0054	(0.0227)	-0.0031	(0.0204)	-0.1188***	(0.0076)	-0.1309***	(0.0060)
> $90,000 to $100,000	-0.0065	(0.0221)	-0.0162	(0.0204)	-0.1282***	(0.0077)	-0.1408***	(0.0064)
> $100,000 to $200,000	-0.0332	(0.0271)	-0.0450*	(0.0252)	-0.1621***	(0.0083)	-0.1758***	(0.0067)
> $200,000	-0.1166***	(0.0323)	-0.1294***	(0.0307)	-0.2186***	(0.0094)	-0.2341***	(0.0073)
Compensation								
≤$40,000 (omitted)								
> $40,000 to $60,000	-0.0367	(0.0244)	-0.0364*	(0.0211)	0.0053	(0.0127)	0.0050	(0.0094)
> $60,000 to $80,000	-0.0126	(0.0114)	-0.0174*	(0.0095)	0.0101**	(0.0047)	0.0102***	(0.0032)
> $80,000 to $100,000	-0.0306*	(0.0174)	-0.0395***	(0.0146)	0.0198***	(0.0065)	0.0205***	(0.0045)
> $100,000	-0.0544***	(0.0207)	-0.0641***	(0.0172)	0.0244***	(0.0067)	0.0249***	(0.0046)
Missing	-0.0890***	(0.0214)	-0.0970***	(0.0197)	0.0341***	(0.0072)	0.0322***	(0.0050)
Plan loan features								
Primary residence loans			-0.0643***	(0.0213)			0.0051	(0.0081)
Maximum number of loans								
1 (omitted)								
2			0.0896***	(0.0213)			0.0239***	(0.0074)
≥3			-0.0101	(0.0301)			0.0683***	(0.0111)
Interest rate								
Prime (omitted)								
> Prime to prime + 1			-0.0277	(0.0212)			0.0059	(0.0081)
> Prime + 1 to prime + 2			-0.1015***	(0.0317)			0.0399***	(0.0132)
Other			0.0366	(0.0397)			-0.0093	(0.0138)

Application fee	-0.0097 (0.0203)			-0.0068 (0.0072)
Minimum loan amount				
> $500	0.0009 (0.0191)			0.0100 (0.0097)
Minimum loan duration				
≤ 1 month (omitted)				
> 1 to 6 months	-0.0332 (0.0406)			0.0232 (0.0163)
> 6 to 12 months	-0.0127 (0.0310)			0.0202 (0.0141)
Maximum loan duration				
< 5 years	0.0072 (0.0186)			-0.0167** (0.0066)
Participants	1,376,025	1,376,025	314,033	314,033
Plans	87	87	87	87
Companies	79	79	79	79
R^2	0.0755	0.0856	0.1787	0.2002

Notes: Authors' calculations from the Aon Hewitt individual-level data for eighty-seven plans at seventy-nine companies for which we have data in one year between 2002 and 2004. Individuals with zero or missing account balances are excluded. A small number of individuals are dropped from the regression due to missing age or tenure data. Standard errors are clustered at the plan level. We winsorize the top and bottom 0.5 percent of the loan-to-balance observations in order to reduce the impact of outliers.

***Significant at the 1 percent level.

**Significant at the 5 percent level.

*Significant at the 10 percent level.

the dependent variable is loan balances as a fraction of total balances, and the only explanatory variables are demographic variables; the seventh and eighth columns add plan feature controls.

Some of the coefficients on the demographic variables show patterns that differ from those shown in table 4.2. Instead of following a hump shape, the probability of having a loan increases with tenure and decreases with compensation. The loan-to-total balance ratio is hump-shaped with respect to age and increasing with respect to compensation, rather than decreasing with respect to these variables. Using administrative data from Vanguard, Lu and Mitchell (2010) find similar relationships between demographic characteristics and loan utilization. The patterns of the demographic coefficients do not change much when the plan feature controls are added.

A few interesting patterns emerge from the coefficients on the 401(k) loan features in the third and seventh columns of table 4.4. Conditional on demographic characteristics, the probability of having a loan outstanding decreases with the loan interest rate; participants in plans that charge more than prime plus one are 10 percentage points less likely to borrow against their balances than participants in plans that charge only the prime rate. However, the size of loans that do get taken out are slightly larger (4 percent of total balances) in plans that charge more than prime plus one than in plans that charge the prime rate. Lu and Mitchell (2010) also find that a higher loan interest rate is related to a lower probability of having a 401(k) loan, but a higher loan balance conditional on having a loan. Imposing a maximum general purpose loan duration of less than five years is associated with a decrease in loan size of 2 percent of total balances, and allowing more loans outstanding is associated with larger loan-to-balance ratios. Surprisingly, the probability of having a loan is highest in plans that allow up to two loans outstanding as compared to plans that allow either only one or more than two loans outstanding. It is difficult to think of a causal mechanism running from number of loans allowed to loan utilization that would generate this pattern. Similarly, the negative correlation between the probability of loan utilization and the option to take out a primary residence loan seems unlikely to be caused by the loan rule.

Table 4.5 reports the distribution of characteristics for 401(k) loans originated from 2002 to 2008 in our Aon Hewitt participant-level data. The sample is again restricted to the twenty-seven plans for which we have continuous data coverage over the entire time span. The vast majority of loans—97 percent—are general purpose loans rather than primary residence loans.[25] The administrative data give no further insights into the purposes for which individuals take out 401(k) loans. The Survey of Consumer

---

25. Utkus and Young (2010) and Lu and Mitchell (2010) report that a similarly high fraction of loans in Vanguard-administered savings plans are general purpose loans.

Table 4.5   **Characteristics of originated 401(k) loans (2002–2008)**

	2002	2005	2008	2002–2008
Loan type				
General purpose	96.3%	97.2%	97.6%	97.1%
Primary residence	3.7%	2.8%	2.4%	2.9%
Loan amount				
5th percentile	$1,000	$1,000	$1,050	$1,000
25th percentile	$1,800	$1,761	$1,792	$1,800
Median	$3,983	$4,000	$4,000	$4,000
75th percentile	$8,500	$9,000	$9,750	$9,000
95th percentile	$23,000	$25,000	$26,000	$25,000
Loan duration				
< 1 year	2.4%	1.8%	1.5%	1.7%
1 to < 2 years	17.0%	17.2%	17.0%	16.9%
2 to < 3 years	18.8%	18.1%	17.7%	18.1%
3 to < 4 years	14.5%	14.7%	12.7%	13.8%
4 to < 5 years	22.8%	24.4%	25.7%	24.7%
≥5 years	24.5%	23.8%	25.5%	24.9%
Loan interest rate				
5th percentile	4.75%	5.18%	5.00%	4.00%
25th percentile	4.75%	6.25%	5.20%	5.00%
Median	5.75%	6.75%	6.00%	5.81%
75th percentile	5.75%	7.25%	6.25%	8.25%
95th percentile	5.82%	7.75%	8.25%	9.25%
Payment (monthly)				
5th percentile	$32	$30	$31	$31
25th percentile	$73	$74	$74	$74
Median	$127	$130	$130	$129
75th percentile	$233	$246	$254	$245
95th percentile	$538	$587	$603	$576
Loans	54,860	61,166	59,876	430,984

Notes: Authors' calculations using the Aon Hewitt loan-level data from twenty-seven plans at twenty-five companies for which we have data at every year-end from 2002 to 2008. Individuals with zero or missing account balances are excluded.

Finances, however, does collect more detailed information on the reasons why individuals borrow from their retirement savings plans. These are presented in table 4.6 for 1998, 2001, 2004, and 2007. Note that there is quite a bit of variability over time in the reasons for taking out a 401(k) loan.[26] Interestingly, in some years up to one-third of 401(k) loan recipients report using a 401(k) loan for either a home purchase or home improvement, uses that would potentially qualify for a longer-term primary residence loan. This far exceeds the fraction of individuals in the Aon Hewitt administrative data who take out a primary residence loan. These findings are not necessar-

26. Li and Smith (2010) find similar variability in the reasons for 401(k) loan taking.

Table 4.6   Reasons for obtaining a 401(k) loan (1998–2007)

Reason	1998	2001	2004	2007
Home purchase/improvement	35.1%	35.9%	23.4%	14.3%
Investments and other real estate	1.6	5.9	1.6	3.4
Vehicles, appliances, and other durables	11.2	23.4	20.0	10.2
Education and medical expenses	15.9	4.6	12.7	11.8
Occasional expenses (e.g., wedding, divorce)	7.8	6.0	6.1	11.7
Other	28.5	24.3	36.2	48.7

Note: Authors' calculations from the Survey of Consumer Finances.

ily inconsistent. Individuals could take out a general purpose loan and use the proceeds for a primary residence; in this case, they would simply have to repay the loan within the five-year maximum legal time limit (or sooner, if their plan specifies a shorter maximum repayment period). The advantage of doing this is that a general purpose loan requires less documentation and, in some plans, also has a lower application fee. Other significant reasons cited for obtaining a 401(k) loan include the purchase of a vehicle or other durable goods (10 percent to 23 percent); education and medical expenses (5 percent to 16 percent); and occasional expenses, like a wedding or divorce (6 percent to 12 percent).

Utkus and Young (2010) analyze the use of loan proceeds in a 2008 survey of savings plan participants and find broadly similar results. They find that 40 percent of respondents borrow from their savings plan for investment purposes (including home purchases or improvements, vehicle purchases, and educational expenses), while 39 percent report borrowing to consolidate bills or pay off other bills. Few report using 401(k) loans purely for consumption reasons. Many of the loan expenditure categories in table 4.6 and in Utkus and Young (2010) represent items frequently financed with loans, suggesting that 401(k) loans may be substituting for other sources of credit at potentially better terms.[27]

As shown in table 4.5, the median size of a newly originated loan in 2008 was $4,000, with a fifth percentile amount of $1,050 and a ninety-fifth percentile amount of $26,000. Over the 2002 to 2008 time period covered by our data, less than 1 percent of loans were made for $50,000, the maximum legal amount. More were surely made at the 50 percent of plan balances threshold, although we cannot assess how binding that constraint is on loan size since we do not have balance data at exactly the time each participant took out a loan.

27. Li and Smith (2010) argue that households could be even more aggressive in substituting 401(k) loans for other sources of credit. According to their estimates, such substitutions could save households with 401(k) loans available to them $200 to $275 per year on average.

Despite the fact that most plans do allow participants to take out a general purpose loan for the full legal maximum duration of five years, most participants choose a much shorter repayment period. In 2008, 19 percent of loans were taken out with a repayment period of less than two years; another 18 percent had a repayment period of two to three years. Only 26 percent had a repayment period of five years or more.

The distribution of interest rates for new loans originated between 2002 and 2008 is also shown in table 4.5.[28] Over the entire 2002 to 2008 period, interest rates largely fall in the range of 4.00 percent to 9.25 percent. The median monthly repayment amount for new loans is $130 in 2008, but the fifth percentile repayment amount is just $31 per month, whereas the ninety-fifth percentile repayment amount is $603 per month.

4.5   Conclusion

This chapter has documented the types of loan provisions in 401(k) savings plans and how participants use 401(k) loans. While a minority of savings plan participants use 401(k) loans at any given point in time—about 22 percent in our calculations based on participant-level data from Aon Hewitt—a much higher fraction will use a 401(k) loan over a longer period of time—slightly fewer than half of those whom we observe over a seven-year period from 2002 through 2008.

The loan utilization rate varies with demographic characteristics. The fraction of participants with a loan at a point in time follows a hump-shaped pattern with respect to age, tenure, salary, and plan balances, whereas the size of outstanding loan balances as a fraction of plan balances (conditional on having a loan outstanding) is decreasing in these characteristics. When these variables are controlled for simultaneously in a regression, the probability of having a loan is still hump-shaped with respect to age and balances, but it is increasing in tenure and decreasing in compensation; normalized loan size conditional on having a loan is still decreasing with respect to tenure and balances, but hump-shaped with respect to age and increasing with respect to compensation. Some plan characteristics are also correlated with loan utilization. Participants are less likely to use a loan in plans that charge a higher interest rate, and conditional on having a loan, total loan balances are smaller as a fraction of plan balances when fewer loans can be outstanding at once, the interest rate is low, and the maximum loan duration allowed is short. However, these correlations must be interpreted with caution, since some of them—such as the negative correlation between a plan offering a

---

28. This distribution differs from that shown in figures 4.5 and 4.6 in that figures 4.5 and 4.6 count each plan-month mode as one observation, whereas table 4.5 counts each loan as one observation.

primary residence loan and the probability that its participants take out a loan—seem inconsistent with a causal mechanism running from the plan feature to loan utilization.

References

Aon Hewitt. 2011. "Leakage of Participants DC Assets: How Loans, Withdrawals, and Cashouts are Eroding Retirement Income." Accessed May 26, 2011. http://www.aon.com/attachments/thought-leadership/survey_asset_leakage.pdf.
Burton, Jonathan. 2008. "Critics Detail the Ills of 401(k) Debit Cards." *Wall Street Journal,* July 22. Accessed August 1, 2008. http://online.wsj.com/article/SB121668972397572373.html.
Bureau of Labor Statistics. 1995, 1998, 1999. "Employee Benefits in Medium and Large Private Establishments." Washington, DC: US Department of Labor, Bureau of Labor Statistics.
Holden, Sarah, Jack VanDerhei, and Luis Alonso. 2009. "401(k) Plan Asset Allocation, Account Balances, and Loan Activity in 2008." *Investment Company Institute Research Perspective* 15 (2). Accessed September 27, 2010. http://www.ici.org/pdf/per15-02.pdf.
———. 2010. "401(k) Plan Asset Allocation, Account Balances, and Loan Activity in 2009." *Investment Company Institute Research Perspective* 16 (3). Accessed April 27, 2011. http://www.ici.org/pdf/per16-03.pdf.
Internal Revenue Service, United States Department of Treasury. 2011. "Retirement Plans FAQs Regarding Loans." Accessed April 20, 2011. http://www.irs.gov/retirement/article/0,,id=162415,00.html.
Li, Geng, and Paul A. Smith. 2010. "401(k) Loans and Household Balance Sheets." *National Tax Journal* 63 (3): 479–508.
Lu, Timothy Jun, and Olivia S. Mitchell. 2010. "Borrowing from Yourself: The Determinants of 401(k) Loan Patterns." University of Michigan Retirement Research Center Working Paper no. 2010-221.
Profit Sharing/401(k) Council of America. 1999. "Plan Loan Restriction Study." Accessed July 10, 2008. http://www.psca.org/RESEARCHDATA/PlanLoanRestrictionStudy/tabid/176/Default.aspx.
———. "401(k) Loans: When You Need Your Money NOW." Accessed July 10, 2008. http://www.401k.org/401kloans.html.
———. Various years. "Annual Survey of Profit Sharing and 401(k) Plans." Chicago: Profit Sharing/401(k) Council of America.
US Government Accountability Office. 2009. "401(k) Plans: Policy Changes Could Reduce the Long-Term Effects of Leakage on Workers' Retirement Savings." GAO-09-715.
Utkus, Stephen P., and Jean A. Young. 2010. "Financial Literacy and 401(k) Loans." Pension Research Council Working Paper WP2010-28.
VanDerhei, Jack, Russell Galer, Carol Quick, and John Rea. 1999. "401(k) Plan Asset Allocation, Account Balances, and Loans." *Investment Company Institute Perspective* 5 (1). Accessed July 9, 2008. http://www.ici.org/perspective/per05-01.pdf.

Comment   Gopi Shah Goda

The transition from defined-benefit (DB) pension plans to defined-contribution (DC) savings plans, including 401(k) plans, has involved employees making a variety of choices regarding their retirement saving decisions. Employees who work at firms that offer DC plans decide whether to enroll in their employer's plan, how much of their salary they wish to contribute, and how they wish to invest their plan assets.

The chapter by Beshears, Choi, Laibson, and Madrian investigates the parameters of another choice that is often available to 401(k) plan participants: whether they wish to take a loan against their 401(k) balance. The authors perform this analysis by collecting an impressive array of data sets from several sources to describe: (a) the prevalence of 401(k) loan availability and stipulations that govern their use, and (b) how utilization of 401(k) loans varies across plan characteristics and individuals. Understanding the basic landscape of 401(k) loans is an important first step in assessing the broader implications of the ability of plan participants to take loans against their retirement savings accounts.

The ability to borrow against 401(k) account balances provides some implicit insurance to eligible workers against negative shocks. While participants may have other sources of credit, borrowing 401(k) assets can be attractive because the process to borrow funds is typically simpler and does not involve an evaluation of credit. In addition, the financial costs of a 401(k) loan may dominate the costs of alternative sources of credit depending on the borrower's rate of return on assets in the savings plan, the 401(k) loan interest rate, the market borrowing cost, and the borrower's marginal tax rate. Finally, while defaulting on a 401(k) loan affects the accumulation of retirement wealth and may trigger penalties and tax consequences, it does not affect credit ratings. It is worth noting that this type of implicit insurance is not available to employees with DB pensions, representing another important difference between DB and DC pension plans.

The chapter documents the terms of 401(k) loans in terms of restrictions regarding the use of the proceeds from the loan, minimum and maximum loan amounts, fees associated with loan origination, restrictions on the number of loans, loan repayment procedures, and the loan interest rate. A typical firm does not restrict the use of loan proceeds and restricts loan amounts to be between approximately $1,000 and $50,000 (or 50 percent of the participant's vested account balance, if lower). Loan application fees tend to be

Gopi Shah Goda is a research scholar and postdoctoral fellow program coordinator at the Stanford Institute for Economic Policy Research, Stanford University, and a faculty research fellow of the National Bureau of Economic Research.

For acknowledgments, sources of research support, and disclosure of the author's material financial relationships, if any, please see http://www.nber.org/chapters/c12436.ack.

between $25 and $50 and participants are often limited to having only one or two loans outstanding at any given time. A typical interest rate charged is the prime rate plus 1 percentage point. Loan durations are often limited to five years but may be longer if the loan is for a primary residence. Users of 401(k) loans are more likely to be in their thirties and forties and have moderate plan balances and income.

The chapter motivates two basic questions about 401(k) loan provision and utilization: (1) what determines whether firms allow 401(k) loans and the stipulations governing their use, and (2) what factors influence whether employees take loans against their 401(k) plan? The chapter suggests that loan provision is related to firm characteristics that tend to be correlated with richer employee benefits, such as employer size, and that loan availability has been increasing over time. However, it is unclear how the provision of 401(k) loans correlates with firm characteristics other than plan size. For instance, conditional on offering a 401(k) plan, are firms with other types of employee benefits more likely to allow 401(k) loans? Are the costs of administering loans levied against the borrowers (through the application fee) or spread across all plan participants? Finally, once an employer decides to offer a 401(k) loan provision, how are the terms of the loan determined?

Understanding how rules dictating 401(k) loans affect loan utilization is important because employers and policymakers might be able to affect loan utilization by adjusting various plan features. The chapter shows that there are some correlations between utilization and the maximum number of loans and the interest rate. However, the causal impact of different plan features is difficult to tease out because loan features may not be exogenous to loan utilization. For instance, the pool of workers contributing into a 401(k) plan at a firm where the rules governing 401(k) loans are lax may be different from the pool who contributes into a 401(k) plan with strict rules.

Despite the richness of the data, the authors face several data limitations in their ability to address certain important features of 401(k) loan availability and utilization. For instance, the authors are not able to link the data on plan features with data describing the reasons for obtaining 401(k) loans. Therefore, it is difficult to conclude whether loan proceeds from the minority of plans that restrict how loan proceeds may be utilized differ from plans without such restrictions. The authors are also not able to determine the account balance at the time the loan is initiated. This information would be useful to assess whether the maximum loan amount is a binding constraint and would provide suggestive evidence of the effect of changing the maximum loan amount on loan utilization. Finally, the multiple data sources the authors use often show the same trends over time but very different levels in the fraction of 401(k) plans that allow loans, the fraction of 401(k) participants in plans with a loan option, and outstanding loan balances as a fraction of 401(k) balances.

This work on 401(k) loans opens up several interesting directions for future research. While media attention has focused on the potential of 401(k) loans to deplete one's retirement resources, the effect of 401(k) loan provision on retirement wealth accumulation is not clear. By employers offering relatively easy access to borrow against retirement accounts, wealth accumulation could be reduced because funds used for loans do not earn investment returns and defaulting on a 401(k) loan can reduce retirement wealth permanently. On the other hand, employees may find participating in the plan more appealing if a loan provision exists and contribute a higher amount than they would in the absence of a loan provision. In addition, the effect of 401(k) loan provision on retirement wealth accumulation may vary across workers. The workers induced to contribute more into their 401(k) plan may not be the same as those whose savings could be reduced by the ability to borrow against 401(k) assets. Therefore, assessing the heterogeneity of the effects of 401(k) plans on saving and retirement wealth accumulation could have important implications.

Another interesting line of research is related to consumer financial decision making more generally. It is possible that 401(k) loans are *underutilized* relative to alternative ways to finance current consumption. If participants with sufficient account balances are accessing funds through alternative, higher-cost sources (such as credit cards with high interest rates), it would be important to understand the factors that lead participants to access funds through these alternative sources rather than against their 401(k) accounts. Such a finding may suggest that eligible participants are not fully aware of the availability of 401(k) loans. Indeed, recent work suggests that the average household could reduce borrowing costs by approximately $200 to $275 by accessing loans via their 401(k) accounts rather than more costly sources (Li and Smith 2010).

Finally, 401(k) loans may have an impact on other employee outcomes such as turnover. Leaving the firm (either voluntarily or involuntarily) requires the employee to pay back their loan within a specified time period to avoid a default; therefore, there could be a "job lock" effect on employees with loans outstanding or employees who value the option of taking a loan against their 401(k) balance with their current employer.

The results of these analyses would inform the general welfare effects of 401(k) loans. As mentioned before, 401(k) loans offer some insurance value because they provide access to credit that may be less costly relative to alternative sources. While it may be optimal for plan participants to reduce their retirement wealth and increase current consumption, myopic participants may be more likely to access funds for current consumption because of the ease of the 401(k) loan process and be left unprepared for retirement. Therefore, the welfare implications of 401(k) loan availability are unclear.

Overall, the chapter helps us understand the availability and utilization of 401(k) loans. The findings of this chapter and future work on this topic will help inform how 401(k) loans affect retirement wealth accumulation and how loans may be structured to improve the adequacy of retirement income while still offering 401(k) participants the ability to borrow against an important component of their household assets.

References

Li, Geng, and Paul A. Smith. 2010. "401(k) Loans and Household Balance Sheets." *National Tax Journal* 63 (3): 479–508.

II

Health and Health Care

5

Dimensions of Health
in the Elderly Population

David M. Cutler and Mary Beth Landrum

Understanding changes in the health of the elderly is a central policy issue. A healthier elderly population is able to work to later ages, spends less on medical care each year, and requires less informal care from family and friends. Efforts to promote population health are therefore central to many health reform proposals (Pardes et al. 1999).

By many metrics, the health of the elderly has improved over time. For example, the share of elderly people with basic physical impairments such as difficulty walking around the home or bathing has declined markedly over the past two decades. By other metrics, however, the health of the elderly is worsening. Problems with more advanced functional measures such as stooping and walking moderate distances have increased over time, and obesity among the elderly has soared along with weight in the nonelderly population.

Researchers have attempted to combine indicators of the health of the elderly into a single summary measure, but these summaries are generally ad hoc and lacking in nuance. The most common single measure of disability is whether the person has any impairments in Activities of Daily Living (ADLs, such as bathing or dressing) or Instrumental Activities of Daily Living (IADLs, such as doing light housework or managing money). In the Medicare Current Beneficiary Survey, which we analyze in this chapter,

David M. Cutler is the Otto Eckstein Professor of Applied Economics at Harvard University and a research associate of the National Bureau of Economic Research. Mary Beth Landrum is associate professor of health care policy, with a specialty in biostatistics, in the Department of Health Care Policy at Harvard Medical School.

We are grateful to Marcelo Coca, Yunfan Gong, and Kaushik Ghosh for research assistance and the National Institutes on Aging for research support. For acknowledgments, sources of research support, and disclosure of the authors' material financial relationships, if any, please see http://www.nber.org/chapters/c12437.ack.

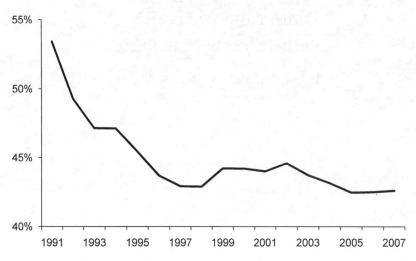

Fig. 5.1   Disability among the elderly

Notes: Disability is measured as the share of people reporting at least one impairment in ADLs and IADLs. Data are from the MCBS Access to Care sample. Tabulations use sample weights and are adjusted to the age/sex composition of the elderly population in 2000.

the share of the elderly population that is disabled by this definition has declined from 53 percent in 1991 to 42 percent in 2007 (figure 5.1). This summary measure exhibits somewhat different trends in different surveys and for different measures of health (Schoeni, Freedman, and Wallace 2001; Manton and Gu 2001), however, and ignores measures of functional impairment (e.g., can the person walk a reasonable distance), cognitive problems such as memory loss, and sensory impairments such as difficulty seeing and hearing.

At the same time, there is a history of more theoretically grounded measures of disability—as with the Grade of Membership (GOM) model proposed by Ken Manton and colleagues (Lamb 1996; Manton, Stallard, and Corder 1998; Woodbury, Clive, and Garson 1978; Manton, Woodbury, and Tolley 1994). But these models met resistance because of their complexity. Perhaps as a result, they have not been widely pursued.

In this chapter, we characterize the multifaceted health of the elderly and understand how health along multiple dimensions has changed over time. Our data are from the Medicare Current Beneficiary Survey (MCBS), a rotating panel of nearly 12,000 elderly people annually. The survey started in 1991; we employ data through 2007. The MCBS has the virtue that it is a person-based sample, not a housing-unit based sample. Thus, it samples and follows people when they move into nursing homes and records death.

We first consider how to optimally combine different measures of health into a smaller number of summary measures. Of course, the best way to summarize multiple measures of health depends on the question being asked. The optimal measure to predict medical spending may be somewhat different than the optimal measure to predict health transitions, for example. We use a somewhat ad hoc approach and estimate factor models for nineteen indicators of health in the community-based population. These measures include specific ADL impairments, IADL impairments, functional impairments, and sensory impairments.

We show that these nineteen dimensions can be compressed into three broad summary measures. The dominant factor is impairment in very basic physical and social tasks such as dressing, eating, transferring in and out of bed, preparing meals, doing light housework, and managing money. This encompasses many of the ADLs and IADLs, but not all. The second factor loads heavily on functional limitations and includes measures such as walking moderate distances, stooping, and reaching. The third dimension is sensory impairments—trouble seeing and hearing.

After determining these factors, we analyze the evolution of these health dimensions over time. We show that the set of physical and social limitations and sensory impairments have declined rapidly over time. Functional ability was flat or increasing, after declining early in the time period.

These results suggest many possible patterns. One possibility is that the community-dwelling population is increasingly concentrated among the less severely ill, with more severely ill individuals in nursing homes or having died. We show, however, that composition changes—both people leaving the sample and new people entering the sample—cannot explain a change in the health of the community-dwelling population. In a second scenario, it may be that people are recovering from severe disability more frequently in later years in the sample, thanks to better medical care or other environmental changes.

We investigate the evolution of health states in the final part of the chapter. In particular, we estimate models explaining within-person health trends over time, controlling for demographic characteristics and year dummy variables. We examine health trends in the early years in the sample (1991–1996), middle years in the sample (1997–2001), and later years in the sample (2002–2007). We show that health deteriorates less rapidly in later years of the sample than in earlier years. This sets up an exploration of what shocks to health are occurring less rapidly, which is the subject of ongoing research.

This chapter is structured as follows. The first section describes the data we employ. The second section presents information on trends in elderly health and reports the results of factor analyses for the 1991 to 2007 period. The third section shows the evolution of summary health measures of health over time, and the fourth section examines within-person changes. The last section concludes.

5.1   The Data

Our primary data source is the Medicare Current Beneficiary Survey (MCBS). The MCBS, sponsored by the Centers for Medicare and Medicaid Services (CMS), is a nationally representative survey of aged, disabled, and institutionalized Medicare beneficiaries that oversamples the very old (aged eighty-five or older) and disabled Medicare beneficiaries. Since we are interested in disability among the elderly, we restrict our sample to the population aged sixty-five and older.

While a number of surveys have measures of disability in the elderly population (Freedman, Martin, and Schoeni 2002), including the National Health Interview Study and the Health and Retirement Study, the MCBS has a number of advantages. First, the sample size is large, about 10,000 to 18,000 people annually. In addition, the MCBS samples people regardless of whether they live in a household or a long-term care facility, or switch between the two during the course of the survey period. Finally, the set of health questions are very broad, encompassing health in many domains.

The MCBS started as a longitudinal survey in 1991. In 1992 and 1993, the only supplemental individuals added were to replace people lost to attrition and to account for newly enrolled beneficiaries. Beginning in 1994, the MCBS began a transition to a rotating panel design, with a four-year sample inclusion. About one-third of the sample was rotated out in 1994, and new members were included in the sample. The remainder of the original sample was rotated out in subsequent years. We use all interviews that are available for each person from the start of the survey in 1991 through the 2007 survey.

The MCBS has two samples: a set of people who were enrolled for the entire year (the Access to Care sample) and a set of ever enrolled beneficiaries (the Cost and Use sample). The latter differs from the former in including people who die during the year and new additions to the Medicare population. The primary data that we use are from the health status questionnaire administered in the fall survey, which defines the Access to Care sample. We thus use the Access to Care data. We supplement this with information about death in the year following the fall interview, taken from the Cost and Use data. Because the Cost and Use data are only available through 2006, our analysis of deaths, nursing home transitions, and loss to follow-up go only through that year. Other data go through 2007.

Table 5.1 shows the number of individuals in the sample by year or interview and wave (number of interviews for that person). The sample of new beneficiaries is low in 1992 and 1993, rises throughout the 1990s, and then declines in the early 2000s. The difference between the number of people in one wave in year t and the next wave in year $t + 1$ is an approximate death and attrition rate across years.

The health questions asked about in the MCBS are shown in table 5.2. The questions are generally the same for the community population and the institutional population, with the exception that the institutionalized are not asked about three IADLs limitations—light housework, preparing meals, and heavy lifting. The tabulations in table 5.1 are for people interviewed in 1991 to 2007. On average, 5 percent of people are in a nursing home.

Table 5.1   Sample size for MCBS

| | Wave | | | | | | |
Year	1	2	3	4	5	6	Total
1991	10,495						10,495
1992	1,685	8,495					10,180
1993	1,795	1,516	7,391				10,702
1994	4,011	1,510	1,408	6,472			13,401
1995	4,250	3,270	1,244	809	3,411		12,984
1996	6,494	3,443	2,803	1,037	277	1,046	15,100
1997	6,274	3,764	3,036	2,450	—	—	15,524
1998	8,069	3,698	3,370	2,678	—	—	17,815
1999	5,341	3,545	3,289	2,958	—	—	15,133
2000	4,274	3,572	3,115	2,861	—	—	13,822
2001	4,279	3,563	3,172	2,709	—	—	13,723
2002	4,207	3,479	3,142	2,770	—	—	13,598
2003	4,160	3,437	2,996	2,741	—	—	13,334
2004	4,055	3,292	2,961	2,556	—	—	12,864
2005	4,195	3,302	2,916	2,617	—	—	13,030
2006	4,317	3,308	2,838	2,523	—	—	12,986
2007	4,203	3,411	2,910	2,485	—	—	13,009

Note: The sample is the elderly population in the Access to Care survey. Dashed cells indicate no observations.

Functional limitations are most common. Sixty-nine percent of the community-dwelling population report difficulty stooping, crouching, or kneeling, along with 93 percent of the institutionalized. For other questions, positive responses are reported by a quarter to a half of the population. Very severe physical impairments, such as help needed bathing or toileting, are very common for the institutionalized, but rare in the community. The same is true about social indicators such as managing money and shopping, with the exception that there is significant difficulty doing heavy housework among people living in the community. About one-third of both groups report difficulties seeing or hearing.

Figure 5.2 shows the trend in health for each of the dimensions identified in table 5.2, along with the share of people living in a nursing home. For each dimension, we determine the share of people who report having being impaired in at least one specific item, in each year of the data. For example, our ADL trend is the share of people in each year who report at least one ADL impairment. In this analysis, we do not distinguish between one or more than one impairment. Our models in the next section will do so.

There are very different patterns for the different dimensions of health. The share of people who are in a nursing home, who have an ADL or IADL impairment, or who have a sensory impairment has declined over time. The decline in nursing home residence is about 30 percent. The reduction in ADL impairment is also about 30 percent, while the reduction in IADL

Table 5.2   Health questions in MCBS

		Prevalence	
Num	Question	Community (95%)	Institutionalized (5%)
	Functional limitations: Difficulty		
1	Stooping/crouching/kneeling	69	93
2	Lifting/carrying 10 pounds	37	92
3	Extending arms above shoulder	27	68
4	Writing/handling object	26	63
5	Walking 1/4 mile or 2–3 blocks	44	90
	Activities of Daily Living: Says difficulty doing by himself/herself because of a health or physical problem		
6	Bathing or showering	11	91
7	Going in or out of bed or chairs	7	80
8	Eating	3	48
9	Dressing	13	65
10	Walking	24	66
11	Using the toilet	5	70
	Instrumental Activities of Daily Living: Difficulty doing the following activities by yourself because of a health or physical problem		
12	Using the telephone	7	61
13	Doing light housework (like washing dishes, straightening up, or light cleaning)	12	—
14	Doing heavy housework (like scrubbing floors or washing windows)	31	—
15	Preparing own meals	9	—
16	Shopping for personal items	14	85
17	Managing money (like keeping track of expenses or paying bills)	7	85
	Sensory problems		
18	Trouble seeing	35	44
19	Trouble hearing	40	39

Note: Tabulations are from the MCBS Access to Care sample for 1991–2007 and use sample weights. Dashed cells indicate that questions were not asked of those individuals.

impairment is about 20 percent. Sensory impairments declined by 24 percent. The share of the population with functional limitations, in contrast, was relatively flat.

The appendix shows the specific items that contribute to the trends for each dimension. There is surprisingly little variation within the specific items in each domain. Almost all of the ADL and IADL impairments have declined, as have both of the sensory impairments. Most of the functional limitations have been relatively flat, as have the two cognitive measures. This suggests that the grouping shown in figure 5.1 may be relatively accurate as a true description of elderly health. We turn to this next.

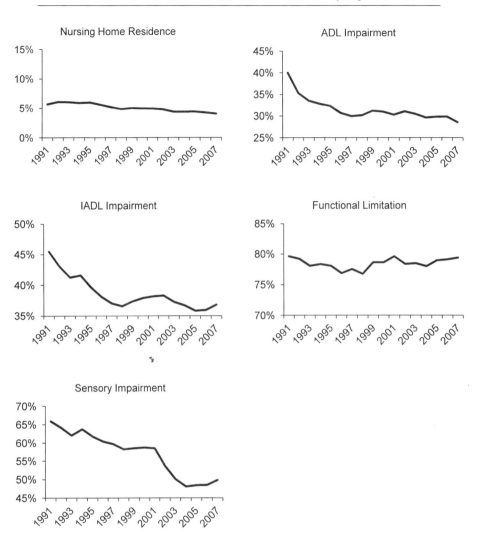

Fig. 5.2   Summary health measures by domain
Notes: Data are from the MCBS Cost and Use sample. Percentages use sample weights and are adjusted to the age/sex composition of the population in 2000.

5.2   The Dimensions of Elderly Health

As noted before, most research defines disability as a binary variable based on the self-report of any ADL or IADL impairment. While simple to implement, this measure lacks a theoretically rigorous foundation. More-over, a binary measure does not capture heterogeneity in the population. For many purposes, we care about the distribution of health in addition to the proportion with any specific limitation. At the same time, there is a literature (e.g., Verbrugge and Jette 1994) arguing for a distinction between functional status (measures of specific physical functioning) and disability (the ability to engage in the activities typically expected of a person). Within this latter spirit, we examine the different dimensions of health among the elderly.

The optimal way to combine the different measures depends on the purpose for which the data are being used. If one were interested in forecasting medical spending, for example, one would weight the questions by how much they are associated with medical service use. We propose a less structural version and simply ask the question: How many domains summarize the health impairments that people have? Those domains can then be used to assess the health status of the elderly. To do this, we will use factor analysis to characterize responses into different domains of functioning.

Formally, denote y_{ij} as the response to question j for individual i. Suppose there are J questions total ($J = 19$ in our setting). We imagine that these health states are a linear function of K different unobserved or latent factors, denoted F_{ik}. We fit a latent variable model of the form (e.g., Bartholomew 1987; Knol and Berger 1991):

(1) $$y_{ij} = \gamma_{0j} + \gamma_{1j}F_{i1} + \gamma_{2j}F_{i2} + \gamma_{3j}F_{i3} + \ldots + \gamma_{Kj}F_{iK},$$

where y_{ij} is a 0 or 1 outcome variable, γ_{0j} is a threshold parameter that accounts for varying prevalence of limitations in the population (for example, limitations climbing stairs are more common than limitations in bathing), and the γ_{kj}'s are factor loadings that describe the relationship between unobserved factor k and question j. Unobserved factors are assumed to follow a Multivariate Normal distribution. The latent variable model described by (1) is similar to the factor analyses and Grade of Membership models that have been previously used to describe dimensions of disability (Lamb 1996; Manton, Stallard, and Corder 1998; Woodbury, Clive, and Garson 1978; Manton, Woodbury, and Tolley 1994).

We can fit this model provided $K < J$. Empirically, because the data tend to be highly correlated and we have nineteen dimensions of health, a small number of factors is associated with a wide range of variation in the data.

Table 5.3 shows the results of the factor analysis on community-dwelling elderly over the 1991 to 2007 time period. By the usual criterion of eigenvalues greater than 1, there are three significant factors. These three also have natural economic and demographic interpretations. We thus work with those three.

To aid in interpretation, we consider rotations of the factors that maximize the loading of individual measures into single factors while also allowing correlation between latent factors. Specifically, we use an oblique rotation of the three factor scores (promax = 3). The predicted factor scores are positively correlated. The correlation between factors 1 and 2 is .428, between 1 and 3 is .251, and between 2 and 3 is .242.

Figure 5.3 shows plots of the (rotated) first factor against factors 2 and 3. These plots are primarily useful to see the individual items that are loading most highly on each dimension. The first factor encompasses largely ADL and IADL limitations, with heavy loading on all of the ADLs and IADLs such as shopping, light housework, and preparing meals. The second factor is largely associated with functional limitations and related IADLs, including difficulty walking, lifting, stooping, reading, and doing heavy housework. The third factor is concentrated in sensory impairments, including both vision and hearing.

For each individual, we predict their score on each of the three dimensions. Figure 5.4 shows trends in factor scores over the 1991 to 2006 time period. By definition, the factor scores are normalized to mean 0 and standard deviation 1. Thus, a decline of .1 is a reduction of .1 standard deviation. Corresponding to figure 5.2, there are large declines in factor 1 (ADL and IADL limitations) and factor 3 (sensory impairment) over time. Factor 2 declines in the early years of the sample, picking up the reduction in IADLs and ADLs that enter factor 2.

Table 5.3   **Factor analysis for MCBS data**

	Eigenvalue	Proportion	Cumulative
1	6.90	.363	.363
2	1.75	.092	.455
3	1.17	.062	.517
4	0.98	.051	.568
5	0.89	.047	.615
6	0.82	.043	.658

Note: The results are from factor analyses using the MCBS community-dwelling sample from 1991–2007. The sample includes 211,952 observations.

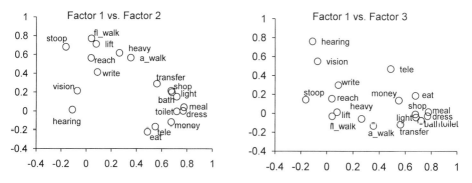

Fig. 5.3   Factor loadings
Notes: Data are from the MCBS Access to Care sample. The factor analysis is for people surveyed in 1991–2007. Table 5.3 has details.

Factor 1: ADL/IADL Impairment

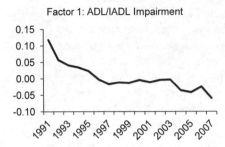

Factor 2: Functional Limitations

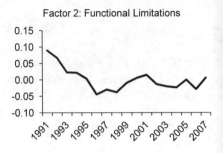

Factor 3: Sensory Impairment

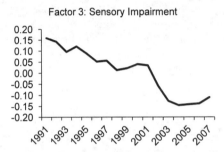

Fig. 5.4   Trends in factor scores

Notes: Data are from the MCBS Access to Care sample. The factor analysis is for people surveyed in 1991–2007. Table 5.3 has details.

We next plot the factor scores by age. If all of the health improvement were at younger elderly ages, the explanation would likely fall in the medical and environmental factors that influence health of the working age population. Conversely, improvements in health at older ages raise the possibility that conditions at those older ages are the driving factor (though they do not prove it, as the literature on the impact of in utero conditions shows; Barker 1992).

Figure 5.5 shows the trend in each of the three factor scores by age. Health improvements in factors 1 and 3 are prevalent at all ages. For example, the reduction in factor 1 is 0.1 (.1 standard deviation) for people aged sixty-five to sixty-nine and 0.38 for people aged eighty-five and over.

Since there are more young elderly than old elderly, the contribution of the older elderly to the reduction in total disability is perhaps overstated. Another metric is to evaluate the share of the total improvement in the health of the elderly that is accounted for by improvements in the health of each age group. At any time period t, $F(t) = \Sigma_a pct(a,t) * F(a,t)$, where $pct(a,t)$ is the percent of the population at time t that is in age group a. The contribution of age group a to the total change in health between two time

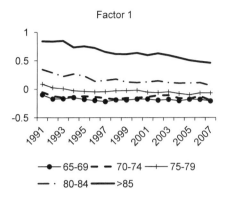

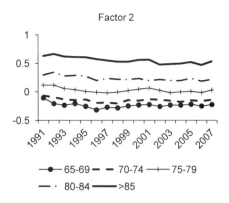

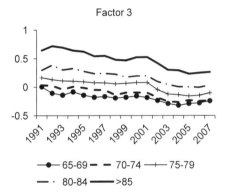

Fig. 5.5   Factor scores by age

Notes: Data are from the MCBS Access to Care sample. The factor analysis is for people surveyed in 1991–2007. Table 5.3 has details.

periods is then $pct(a,0) * \Delta F(a)$, and the total change in the population is $\Sigma_a pct(a,0) * \Delta F(a)$. The ratio of those two, $pct(a,0) * \Delta F(a) / \Sigma_a pct(a,0) * \Delta F(a)$, is the contribution of health improvements at age group a to the total change in population health.

Figure 5.6 shows these contribution shares for factors 1 and 3, the dimensions on which health is improving most significantly, along with the population distribution by age. For both factors 1 and 3, the oldest old contribute disproportionately to health improvements. People aged eighty-five and older are 14 percent of the population in 1991 but account for 30 to 50 percent of the health improvement. This suggests that late life health and social conditions may be important contributors to population health. At minimum, any theory of health improvement will have to account for this age differential.

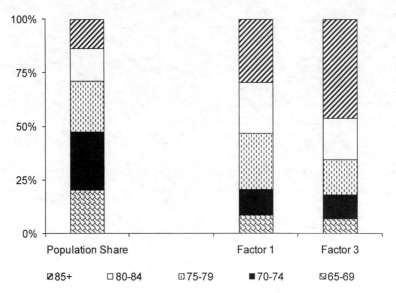

Fig. 5.6   Contribution of different ages to health improvement
Note: Calculations are based on the trends shown in figure 5.5.

5.3   Explaining the Improvement in Health

The central economic challenge is to understand why health improves in so many dimensions. We consider two explanations for improved health. The first explanation is composition change: people with severe health impairments may be more likely to die or transition into a nursing home over time. Alternatively, new entrants to the survey may be healthier than the people they replace. Either of these situations would improve the health of the community-dwelling population because of selection. Second, people may be impaired along the same dimensions, but impairment may not progress to more severe stages as frequently as it did formerly, either because of person-specific aging trends (e.g., richer people can manage their chronic conditions better), or because of population-wide shocks (a new treatment for vision impairment).

Figure 5.7 shows a schematic of the model that we estimate. We start off with the community-dwelling population in year t. Between t and $t + 1$, two things happen. First, the sample changes. Some people leave the sample, either through death, loss to follow-up, or nursing home entry, and others enter. The combination of these two transitions is the composition effect. Second, new health shocks occur (for example, a heart attack or diagnosis of cancer) and old health conditions exert an effect on health. An example of the latter is a continued deterioration that might occur from untreated arthritis. The combination of composition changes and health changes among the existing population yields the new population health at $t + 1$.

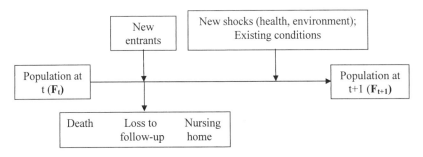

Fig. 5.7   Schematic of estimation model

5.3.1   Composition Change

We now show the equations that we model, starting with the composition change. Denote F_{kit} as the factor score in dimension k for person i in year t; F_{it} is the vector of factor scores for person i in year t. The equations for nursing home entry (NH), death (Die), and loss to follow-up (Loss) are given by:

$$(2) \qquad NH_{it+1} = F_{it}\alpha^{NH} + X_{it+1}\theta^{NH} + \mu^{NH}_{it+1}$$

$$(3) \qquad Die_{it+1} = F_{it}\alpha^{Die} + X_{it+1}\theta^{Die} + \mu^{Die}_{it+1}$$

$$(4) \qquad Loss_{it+1} = F_{it}\alpha^{Loss} + X_{it+1}\theta^{Loss} + \mu^{Loss}_{it+1}$$

where i denotes individuals and t is year. In a general specification, the μ_{it} error terms might be correlated. For simplicity, we assume they are not.

For new entrants, the issue is whether people who are new to the survey are healthier than those who continue. We estimate this as follows:

$$(5) \qquad F_{kit} = X_{it}\theta^k + \pi_1^k Wave1 + \mu_{it}^k$$

where Wave1 is a dummy for the first year in the survey. To the extent that new entrants at any age are more or less healthy than people of the same age but who are continuing in the survey, the coefficient π_1 will be different from zero.

5.3.2   Health Trends within Individuals

We then consider the model for health of the continuing population. We describe the evolution of health for the surviving, community-dwelling population as:

$$(6) \qquad F_{kit} = \alpha_{0ik} + \alpha_{1ik}t + \alpha_{2ik}h_{it} + Year_t\gamma_k + \varepsilon_{kit}.$$

The factor score for an individual depends on their demographics (α_{0ik}), aging (t), new and ongoing health shocks (h_{it}), and year dummy variables (γ_k).

It is natural for α_{0ik} to vary in the population, for both measurable reasons (older people are sicker than younger people) and unmeasurable reasons (random differences across individuals). Similarly, aging and health shocks may affect people differently. Generally, we parameterize α_{jik} ($j = 0, 1$, and 2—corresponding to the three α terms in equation [6]) as follows:

$$(7) \qquad \alpha_{jik} = \beta_{j0k} + X_{it} \beta_{j1k} + \text{Period}_{it} \beta_{j2k} + \xi_{jik}.$$

Equation (7) relates the level and trend in health to a constant, person-specific factors, and the time period.

In principle, the ε_{kit} errors may be correlated (factor scores in different domains), as might the ξ_{jik} errors (coefficients on different control variables). A general formulation would model these as $\varepsilon \sim N(0, \Sigma)$ and $\xi \sim N(0, \Psi)$. For this analysis, we assume that the ε's are independent, as are the ξ's. Also for simplicity, we assume that the only coefficients that vary over people are α_{0ik} and α_{1ik}—the constant term and the coefficient on the time trend. We parameterize α_{0ik} as depending on demographics and an error term (i.e., $\alpha_{0ik} = \beta_{00k} + X_{it} \beta_{01k} + \xi_{0ik}$) and the β_{12k} as differing in three time periods: 1991–1996; 1997–2001; and 2002–2007 (i.e., $\alpha_{1ik} = \beta_{10k} + \text{Period}_{it} \beta_{12k} + \xi_{1ik}$). Finally, for this analysis, we leave out the health measures h_{it}. We do this not because they are unimportant, but because we wish to focus on the aging effect α_{1ik}. We therefore estimate β_{00k}, β_{01k}, β_{10k}, β_{12k}, var(ξ_{0ik}), and var(ξ_{1ik}).

Our **X** vector consists of basic demographics. We include dummy variables for age and gender (a dummy for aged sixty-five to sixty-nine, seventy to seventy-four, seventy-five to seventy-nine, eighty to eighty-four, and eighty-five and older interacted with gender), and a dummy for nonwhites. We also include year dummy variables. Future work could naturally incorporate a richer array of variables, including health shocks to the individual and other family members, changes in socioeconomic status such as reductions in income or wealth, and environmental conditions.

5.4   Composition Change

All three exits from the community sample are common. About 1.5 percent of the elderly population transitions into a nursing home in any year. This is smaller than the share of people who are living in a nursing home at a point in time (around 5 to 6 percent) because of the long-stayers. We also exclude from this analysis people who died between one survey wave and the next, since we do not know about nursing home utilization for them. About 4 percent of the population dies in any year (this is among the community-dwelling sample; a larger share of the institutionalized population dies). Finally, about 12 percent of the population is lost to follow-up each year. This share is particularly high early in the sample, when the initial population was purposely phased out. Outside of those years, the average loss to follow-up is about 10 percent.

The primary question we explore is whether people who are sicker (that is, score higher on the factor score) depart the sample more frequently, and whether this is particularly likely to occur over time. Thus, we interact the factor scores in equations (2) through (4) with the period dummies noted before: 1991 to 1996, 1997 to 2001, 2002 to 2006. We then test whether being sick has a greater effect on sample exit in later years of the sample.

Table 5.4 shows the estimates of death, transitions to a nursing home, or loss to follow-up. Since we have repeat observations on the same individual, we cluster the standard errors by individual—as we do in table 5.5 as well. In the first column, factor 1 is particularly predictive of mortality. An increase of 1 standard deviation raises mortality rates by 3 percent. Factor 1 is mildly more predictive of death in the later years of the sample than

Table 5.4   **Transitions out of the community sample**

Independent variable	Die	Enter a nursing home	Loss to follow-up
Factor 1			
1991–1996	.028**	.021**	.006**
	(.001)	(.001)	(.002)
1997–2001	.031**	.020**	.007**
	(.002)	(.001)	(.002)
2002–2006	.032**	.016**	.011**
	(.002)	(.001)	(.002)
Factor 2			
1991–1996	.009**	−.001	.000
	(.001)	(.001)	(.002)
1997–2001	.010**	.000	.002
	(.001)	(.001)	(.002)
2002–2006	.010**	.000	.003
	(.001)	(.001)	(.002)
Factor 3			
1991–1996	.000	.003**	−.008**
	(.001)	(.001)	(.002)
1997–2001	.001	.002**	−.009**
	(.001)	(.001)	(.002)
2002–2006	.001	.002*	−.006*
	(.001)	(.001)	(.002)
Demographics	Yes	Yes	Yes
Wave dummies	Yes	Yes	Yes
Year dummies	Yes	Yes	Yes
N	153,214	123,270	153,214
R^2	.053	.045	.032
Dependent variable mean	.035	.013	.125

Notes: Data are from the MCBS. Demographic controls include age-sex dummies (ages sixty-five to sixty-nine, seventy to seventy-four, seventy-five to seventy-nine, eighty to eighty-four, eighty-five and over, by gender), and a dummy for nonwhite. Standard errors are clustered by individual.

**Significant at the 5 percent level.

*Significant at the 10 percent level.

the earlier years. An F-test rejects that that the coefficients in later years are the same as in earlier years. But the quantitative difference is not large at .4 percentage points.

We determine the quantitative impact of this change on the health of survivors using a simulation model. Specifically, we simulate for each person death under the coefficients in the early time period, and then again using the coefficients in the later time period, but keeping the X's the same as in the early time period. We then average health of the survival group in each case. We estimate that the average score on factor 1 would decline by .004 because of the increased propensity of the sick to die. Given an overall decline in factor 1 of .072 between the early and late time periods, mortality selection can explain only 5 percent of the decline in factor 1 over time.

In the models for nursing home entry, shown in the second column, factor 1 is particularly predictive of transitions into a nursing home. This corresponds to severe physical or social impairment. Factors 2 and 3 (functional limitations and sensory impairment), in contrast, have relatively little impact on nursing home transitions. The coefficient on factor 1 declines a bit, implying that sicker people are more likely to be in the community in later years of the sample.

The third column shows the model for loss to follow-up. If appropriate effort is put into follow-up, loss to follow-up should be approximately random. Somewhat surprisingly, this is not true in the data. Higher scores on factor 1 (that is, worse health) predicts loss to follow-up, while those with sensory impairments are somewhat less likely to be lost to follow-up. These coefficients are relatively small, however, and do not vary much over time.

We evaluate the combined impact of these three sources of sample attrition using the simulation noted earlier. We draw random variables to predict death, nursing home entry, and loss to follow-up and then simulate the community-dwelling population under the coefficients in the early years of the sample and the later years of the sample. The simulation shows that factor 1 for the community-dwelling population would decline by .006 as a result of selection, or 8 percent of the total decline. For factor 3, the predicted change is only 1 percent of the total improvement.

The regressions in table 5.4 have year dummies included, and these year dummies are graphed in figure 5.8. Generally, the year dummies are relatively flat—death and nursing home entry are no more or less likely over time, conditional on health status and demographics. As noted before, loss to follow-up is high in two years of the sample (1991 and 1994) and constant in other years.

The final component of composition change is the changing health of new enrollees to the survey. We estimate equation (5) interacting the wave 1 dummy variable with dummy variables for early, middle, and late periods of the sample. We then examine whether people in the first wave of the survey are increasingly healthy over time.

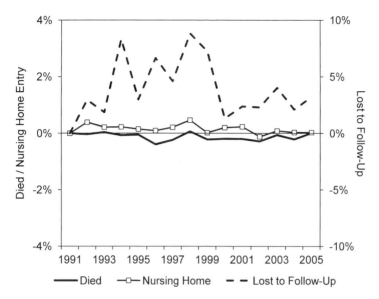

Fig. 5.8   Year effects for leaving the sample

Notes: Figure shows the year dummy variables for models of death, nursing home entry, and loss to follow-up. Data are from the MCBS Cost and Use sample. Table 5.4 describes the model.

Table 5.5   The health of new entrants

Independent variable	Factor 1	Factor 2	Factor 3
Coefficient on Wave 1 dummy			
1991–1996	.013	−.009**	−.008
	(.009)	(.012)	(.009)
1997–2001	.029**	−.021**	.006
	(.007)	(.008)	(.008)
2002–2007	.021**	−.021**	.060**
	(.007)	(.007)	(.007)
Demographics	Yes	Yes	Yes
Year dummies	Yes	Yes	Yes
N	211,952	211,952	211,952
R^2	.072	.085	.062

Notes: Data are from the MCBS. Demographic controls include age-sex dummies (ages sixty-five to sixty-nine, seventy to seventy-four, seventy-five to seventy-nine, eighty to eighty-four, eighty-five and over, by gender), year dummies, and a dummy for nonwhite. Standard errors are clustered by individual.

**Significant at the 5 percent level.

Table 5.5 shows the results. The three columns show averages for factors 1, 2, and 3, respectively. New entrants to the survey are less healthy than existing members along factor 1, but healthier in the second dimension. In both cases, the coefficients are relatively small. Furthermore, the factor 1 and 3 coefficients are somewhat increasing over time. That is, health of new entrants is on average deteriorating relative to the health of existing members across the years.

The implication of these transition models is therefore that the improving health of the community-based population is not attributable to changes in the sample of people living in the community, or picked up by the MCBS. By residual, then, it must be the case that the same population is increasingly healthy over time.

5.5   The Evolution of Health among Community Dwellers

In this section, we turn to the evolution of health among the community-dwelling population. Specifically, we estimate the model given by equations (6) and (7). Given the aforementioned results, our primary focus is on the time trend, and how that varies in the early, middle, and later years of the sample.

Table 5.6 shows the models' health trends. The three columns correspond to models for the three different factors. Within each model, we present the

Table 5.6   The evolution of health

Independent variable	Factor 1	Factor 2	Factor 3
Average effects			
t^*(1991–1996)	.065**	.041**	.019**
	(.004)	(.003)	(.004)
t^*(1997–2001)	.035**	.037**	.010**
	(.003)	(.003)	(.003)
t^*(2002–2007)	.034**	.031**	−.016**
	(.003)	(.002)	(.003)
Standard deviation of average			
t^*(1991–1996)	.192	.087	.101
t^*(1997–2001)	.137	.076	.089
t^*(2002–2007)	.128	.063	.092
Demographics	Yes	Yes	Yes
Year dummies	Yes	Yes	Yes
N	211,952	211,952	211,952

Notes: Data are from the MCBS. Demographic controls include age-sex dummies (ages sixty-five to sixty-nine, seventy to seventy-four, seventy-five to seventy-nine, eighty to eighty-four, eighty-five and older, by gender) and a dummy for nonwhite. Standard errors are clustered by individual.

**Significant at the 5 percent level.

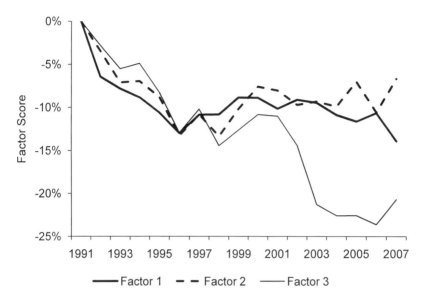

Fig. 5.9   Year effects in factor scores

average aging effect (β_{10k}) and the standard deviation of that coefficient. There are also year dummies in the model, and these are shown in figure 5.9.

The averages show considerable decline in health as a person ages. For example, factor 1 increases by .065 each year (.065 standard deviations) during the early phase of the sample, and factor 3 increases by .019 each year.

The rate of decline in health has slowed over time. Relative to the increase in factor 1 of .065 each year, as shown in the first time period, the increase is only .034 in the more recent time period. This reduction, which occurs after 1997, accounts for a large change in health over time. Had the decrement to health stayed the same after 1996 as before 1996, health in 2007 would have been one-third of a standard deviation worse. Another way to show the impact of this change is to consider the year effects in figure 5.9. While there are strong year trends in factors 1 and 2 up through 1996, there are no consistent year trends afterwards.

Health in the third dimension also deteriorates less rapidly over time, with roughly the same pattern. Factor 3 increases by 0.019 per year in the early time period, and then declines by .016 per year in the later time period. There is an unexplained year trend in the early time period and again between 2001 and 2003. Other than those time periods, there is little aggregate drift.

Not only does the rate of decline in health slow, but health is actually estimated to improve for many people. The standard deviations of health trends, shown in the middle rows of table 5.6, are large. The standard deviation of .19 for factor 1 in the early time period implies that the 95 percent interval for the impact of aging is –.32 to +.44. There are clearly many people whose health is improving, even while health is deteriorating on average.

5.6   Conclusions and Next Steps

Our results provide important evidence on the well-noted decline in disability in the elderly population. We show that health has several dimensions: one that is largely severe physical and social impairment; a second that is less severe physical limitations; and a third that encompasses sensory impairments. The first and third of these dimensions are improving over time, while the second is not.

The reason for the improvement in health is complex. On the one hand, the health improvement is not a result of sample or demographic changes. Younger people are healthier than younger people used to be, but the same is true of older people. Rather, health is improving because individual health deteriorates less rapidly now than in the past. We do not know exactly why this occurs, but we show that the average trend masks significant heterogeneity. Even as health deteriorates overall as people age, health is improving for a significant minority of people.

The next step is to develop a richer model of the change in health over time. To what extent is the improvement in health a result of fewer new conditions developing, existing problems being cared for better, or changes in the social and environmental circumstances that the elderly face? Considering these questions is a fruitful area for further study.

Appendix

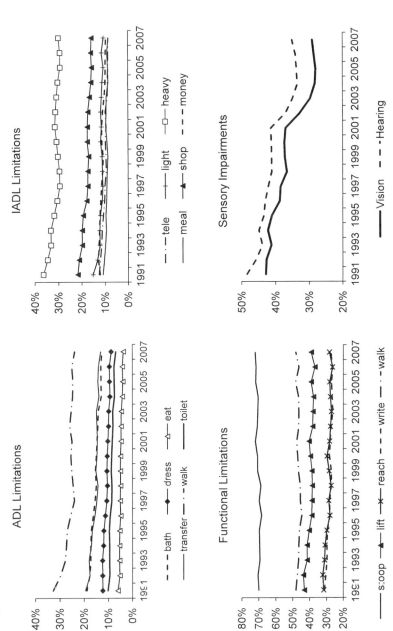

Fig. 5A.1 Plots of individual health measures

Notes: See table 5.2 for the specific items graphed. All tabulations use weighted data, with the population adjusted for changes in the age/sex mix of the population over time.

References

Barker, D. J. P. 1992. *The Fetal and Infant Origins of Adult Disease.* London: BMJ Books.

Bartholomew, D. J. 1987. "Latent Variable Models and Factor Analysis." New York: Oxford University Press.

Freedman, V. A., L. G. Martin, and R. F. Schoeni. 2002. "Recent Trends in Disability and Functioning Among Older Adults in the United States: A Systematic Review." *Journal of the American Medical Association* 288 (24): 3137–46.

Knol, D. L., and M. P. Berger. 1991. "Empirical Comparison between Factor Analysis and Multidimensional Item Response Models." *Multivariate Behavioral Research* 26:457–77.

Lamb, V. L. 1996. "A Cross-National Study of Quality of Life Factors Associated with Patterns of Elderly Disablement." *Social Science and Medicine* 42 (3): 363–77.

Manton, K. G., and X. Gu. 2001. "Changes in the Prevalence of Chronic Disability in the United States Black and Nonblack Population above Age 65 from 1982 to 1999." *Proceedings of the National Academy of Sciences* 98 (11): 6354–59.

Manton, K. G., E. Stallard, and L. S. Corder. 1998. "The Dynamics of Dimensions of Age-Related Disability 1982 to 1994 in the U.S. Elderly Population." *J Gerontol A Biol Sci Med Sci* 53 (1): B59–70.

Manton, K. G., M. A. Woodbury, and H. D. Tolley. 1994. *Statistical Applications Using Fuzzy Sets.* New York: Wiley.

Pardes, H., K. G. Manton, E. S. Lander, H. D. Tolley, A. D. Ullian, and H. Palmer. 1999. "Effects of Medical Research on Health Care and the Economy." *Science* 283 (5398): 36–37.

Schoeni, R. F., V. A. Freedman, and R. B. Wallace. 2001. "Persistent, Consistent, Widespread, and Robust? Another Look at Recent Trends in Old-Age Disability." *Journal of Gerontology, Series B* 56 (4): S206–18.

Verbrugge, L. M., and A. M. Jette. 1994. "The Disablement Process." *Social Science Medicine* 38:1–14.

Woodbury, M., J. Clive, and A. Garson. 1978. "Mathematical Typology: A Grade of Membership Technique for Obtaining Disease Definition." *Computers and Biomedical Research* 11:277–98.

Comment   David R. Weir

The chapter by Cutler and Landrum is concerned with trends in the health of the elderly population over the past twenty years. Health here is physical functioning and limitations; the chapter does not examine trends in disease prevalence or severity. It is rather an examination of the trend toward declining disability first identified by Kenneth Manton and colleagues using the National LongTerm Care Survey, and subsequently confirmed in a number

David R. Weir is research professor and director of the Health and Retirement Study at the University of Michigan.

For acknowledgments, sources of research support, and disclosure of the author's material financial relationships, if any, please see http://www.nber.org/chapters/c12438.ack.

of other data sets by Linda Martin, Robert Schoeni, and colleagues. This chapter focuses exclusively on the Medicare Current Beneficiary Survey (MCBS) from 1992 to 2007. The MCBS has advantages for some of the chapter's aims, disadvantages for others, and some unexploited advantages that are discussed later.

The key contribution of the chapter is to consider the appropriate level of aggregation of components of physical functioning to better understand the multidimensionality of this concept of health and in particular to better understand somewhat conflicting time trends of different dimensions. Survey self-reports of physical functioning and disability typically ask about a number of different specific physical actions (e.g., walking, stooping, lifting, hearing) and a number of different activities (e.g., dressing, bathing, managing money). An item-by-item accounting would be unnecessarily detailed, but the authors show that aggregating all of these items into a single index of health misses importantly distinct dimensions.

The authors use factor analysis to identify important higher-order dimensions within the set of items. This analysis largely confirms the conventional groupings into (a) limitations in activities and instrumental activities of daily living, (b) functional limitations, and (c) sensory impairments. This makes the subsequent analysis of trends in these dimensions easily interpretable to most readers familiar with the disability literature but it does not say whether the estimated factors deviate in any significant way from the traditional aggregates. All three factors show declines in the early 1990s, to about 1998. From that point decline continues and perhaps accelerates in sensory impairments, slows down in ADL/IADL difficulties, and essentially stops in functional limitations. These trends are generally similar for all age groups, but an interesting decomposition of the contributions of different age groups to the overall trends shows that the oldest-old (eighty-five and over) contribute disproportionately to the gains.

The authors spend a great deal of effort demonstrating that neither changes in selective recruitment into nor attrition from the MCBS can account for the trends they see. This is comforting but not surprising considering that MCBS can sample from the entire population of Medicare beneficiaries with knowledge of their health from the Medicare claims data. The analysis actually contributes more than a vindication of MCBS. By separating exits from the study into three very distinct events—death, institutionalization, and dropping out of the study—they shed light on population trends as well as survey performance. Sensory impairments have no influence on death and small influence on nursing home entrance but reduce the risk of dropout, which might seem surprising given the need to hear and see to participate. This is not a model of change in impairment affecting participation—it merely says that conditional on having done the study once with an impairment you are less likely to drop out than someone without one. Functional limitations predict death, but not nursing home use or attrition.

The ADL/IADL difficulties predict all three outcomes. More importantly for the topic at hand, the coefficients in these relationships do not change very much over time. That means that the population trend to lower disability is not due to the disabled dying at greater rates, which is a more interesting finding than that MCBS is not getting (much) worse at keeping the disabled in the study.

The final stage of the analysis is to model year trends within time periods. This is given the interpretation of an aging effect even though age itself is in the model, presumably because age is fixed at age at entry into the study. The identification of this aging effect thus comes from the relatively short period of time in which individuals remain in MCBS. The pace of deterioration in health with age slowed across the time periods examined, accounting for a substantial part of the gains in average health by age.

The underlying goal of the chapter is to understand the reasons for changing health and to relate that to policy goals for the health care system. The MCBS had advantages for the basic demonstration of trends in different dimensions because it has similar items over the entire time period and covers the entire community-dwelling sixty-five and over population in each year. It is much less desirable for the kinds of longitudinal analysis the authors put it through to study changes over time in individual trajectories because participants are only in the study for a short time. Other studies, like the Health and Retirement Study (HRS), would be better for that purpose. Ultimately, though, this structure does not really help to narrow the range of explanations, which should include better health behaviors in the population, better environmental accommodation of physical limitations, and better medical care. Both the HRS and the MCBS are linked to Medicare claims, which could be used to identify the disease conditions and health shocks that contribute to disability. With that kind of data, one could ask whether disability decline was related to lower incidence of disability-producing health shocks, or to reduced disability consequences of those health shocks. Similarly, one could ask why the decline in disability seems to have stalled.

6

The Value of Progress against Cancer in the Elderly

Jay Bhattacharya, Alan M. Garber,
Matthew Miller, and Daniella Perlroth

6.1 Introduction

Cancer remains one of the most common causes of death in the elderly despite large investments in early detection and better treatments over the last forty years (Cutler 2008). The number of cancer deaths in the United States began falling in the early 2000s—the first decline since reliable cancer mortality statistics were collected (Lenzer 2006). This trend of improved overall survival, including for the most common types of cancers—breast, prostate, lung and colorectal cancers—continued at least through the end of the last decade, when the latest national statistics were available (National Cancer Institute 2010).

Jay Bhattacharya is associate professor at the Center for Primary Care and Outcomes Research (PCOR), Stanford University School of Medicine, and a research associate of the National Bureau of Economic Research. Alan M. Garber is provost of Harvard University, the Mallinckrodt Professor of Health Care Policy at Harvard Medical School, professor of economics in the faculty of arts and sciences, and professor of public policy in the Harvard Kennedy School of Government. He is also a research associate of the National Bureau of Economic Research. Matthew Miller was a research associate at the Center for Health Policy/Center for Primary Care and Outcomes Research (CHP/PCOR) at Stanford University and a medical student at the University of California, Los Angeles, during the course of this work. He is currently an engagement manager with McKinsey and Company's southern California office. Daniella Perlroth is an instructor at the Center for Health Policy/Center for Primary Care and Outcomes Research (CHP/PCOR) at Stanford University.

This work was supported by National Institute on Aging Grants AG17253 and AG05842, K02-AG024237, and by National Cancer Institute Grant HS09121. We thank participants at the American Economics Association meetings and at the National Institute on Aging Roundtable at the Center for Medicare and Medicaid Services for helpful suggestions. We especially thank Amitabh Chandra and the rest of the participants at the 2011 NBER Program Project meeting on aging. We also thank Grant Miller and Nicole Smith for their suggestions and comments. For acknowledgments, sources of research support, and disclosure of the authors' material financial relationships, if any, please see http://www.nber.org/chapters/c12439.ack.

Before these recent gains, some analysts questioned whether substantial progress had been made against cancer despite numerous innovations in methods to prevent, detect, and treat the conditions (Bailar and Gornik 1997). Among the innovations were policies to discourage cigarette smoking, campaigns to promote screening for cervical, breast, and colorectal cancer, better imaging technologies, and advances in treatment with new chemotherapeutics and next-generation radiation therapy (e.g., intensity-modulated radiation therapy). More recent treatment innovations have included costly antibody and immune therapies, such as bevacizumab (Avastin) for colorectal cancer and sipuleucel-T (Provenge) for prostate cancer (Chambers and Neumann 2011).

Because cancer is prevalent in the elderly, and Medicare expenditure growth is a critical policy challenge (2008), it is likely that costly treatment advances will increasingly need to demonstrate value (Elkin and Bach 2010). One approach for assessing the value in technology advances has been the application of cost-effectiveness analysis to medical decision making (Garber and Phelps 1997; Owens et al. 2011). Other credible definitions of value are essentially variations of the cost-benefit framework (Porter 2010). Cost-effectiveness analysis of individual physician-patient decision making has made advances in research methodology and is now an accepted methodology in the medical literature to guide medical decision making.

The evidence that outcomes have improved for some medical conditions is clear. Over the past twenty-five years, mortality from heart disease has declined substantially (Rodriguez et al. 2006), effective treatment for HIV disease has become available, the microbial basis for peptic ulcers has been elucidated and resulted in more effective treatment, and new classes of drugs have improved care for serious psychiatric, cardiac, and rheumatologic diseases. Some economists have estimated that new medical technologies have led to large gains in survival and health, with extraordinary economic value (Murphy and Topel 2003, 2005). According to one analysis, "between 1970 and 2000 increased longevity added about $3.2 trillion per year to national wealth" (Murphy and Topel 2006, 871).

These health gains have come at a time of unsustainable growth in health expenditures, particularly for Medicare (Medicare Trustees 2008). Consequently, a debate has arisen about whether these benefits are worth the costs they require. Some have argued that outcomes for myocardial infarction patients have improved so greatly that increased expenditures on these new technologies are justified (Cutler 2004; Cutler and McClellan 2001) Others have argued that many new technologies raise costs without conferring significant health benefits (Meltzer 2003; Siegler, Weisfeld, and Cronin 2003). Indeed, the medical care subsidy embedded in health insurance and other market distortions create incentives for the adoption of new medical technologies even when their benefits exceed their costs (Fuchs and Garber 2003,

1990). Further, there is evidence from the literature on regional variations in the standards of medical care that the early adoption of new medical technology may not translate into improved health (Skinner, Staiger, and Fisher 2006).

We extend these attempts to assess the value of medical progress at the population level by matching changes in survival for cancer with changes in spending for those conditions. This has been done in the past, most notably by Cutler and McClellan (2001), who evaluated aggregate outcomes and expenditures on Medicare patients and found that advances in acute heart attack care and cataract surgery were highly likely to have met conventional cost-effectiveness criteria in the past. In their evaluation of breast cancer care in the 1990s, they were unable to rule out cost-ineffective advances in breast cancer treatment with their approach. Thus, the aggregate population approach to estimating value in medical progress has been attempted before, and could be useful to policymakers, for example, when considering changes to public health programs or prioritizing population health investments.

With this research, we compare improvements in overall survival after a cancer diagnosis with changes in the cost of medical care for the cancer patient. We begin by evaluating the relative contribution of changes in diagnosis and treatment to changes in survival after a diagnosis of breast, prostate, lung, or colorectal cancer, separately for men and women. We combine these estimates (survival, expenditures) into a traditional cost-effectiveness approach by estimating the marginal cost-effectiveness of improvements in the detection and treatment of cancer for two periods: 1986 to 1994 and 2000 to 2004.

We run two versions of this analysis. In one, we measure trends in survival and expenditures among diagnosed cancer patients, not adjusted for trends in staging. These trends presumably represent changes in these outcomes due to changes in treatment technology and in diagnostic and staging technology. In the second version, we present survival and expenditure trends holding fixed staging at a fixed date. We do this because diagnostic improvements will influence survival by shifting diagnosis to less advanced stages of disease. These stage-adjusted trends presumably represent changes in these outcomes due to changes in treatment technology alone, though there are some important subtleties in this interpretation which we will discuss shortly.

We study four cancers (prostate, breast, colorectal, and lung) that together account for over half of all new cancer cases in the elderly, and for which the elderly represent 70 percent of new cases (Potetz and DeWilde 2009). Understanding the relative effectiveness of early diagnosis and treatment advances for these cancers is important in deciding where increasingly limited anticancer resources should be allocated.

6.2   Methods

We evaluate the two periods of analysis using similar methodologies for assessing increases in expenditures and changes in survival for cancer patients. The first period (1986–1994) represents a time of screening innovation and higher rates of mammography, Prostate-Specific Antigen (PSA) testing, and colon cancer screening exams. The second period (2000–2004) had mostly flat rates of screening for breast (with a slight decline starting in 2003), with modest increases in the rates of colorectal cancer screening and PSA screening for prostate cancer (National Cancer Institute 2010). During this second period, we evaluate breast, prostate, colorectal, and lung cancer survival and expenditure changes. We refer to each cancer type and gender diagnosed during each period separately as a cohort.

6.2.1   1986 to 1994 Data

Our data during this period are drawn from the 20 percent random sample of the Centers for Medicare and Medicaid Services Health Insurance Skeleton Eligibility Write-off (HISKEW) files, the basic data set used to track Medicare eligibility. Only elderly men and women enrolled in the traditional (fee-for-service) Medicare program are included, because accurate diagnostic information is not available for Medicare managed care enrollees in claims files. Beneficiaries who are eligible based upon disability or end-stage renal disease are also excluded.

We identified all men and women with a diagnosis of breast, prostate, or colorectal cancer, using diagnosis and procedure fields from each claim, noting the first date that a diagnostic code for cancer was recorded for the individual. These claims were then linked to all subsequent claims for these patients.

From this final sample, we calculated Medicare expenditures and survival in the five years after the initial diagnosis year for each cohort of newly diagnosed cancer patients. We characterized the experiences of beneficiaries with breast cancer, prostate cancer, and colorectal cancer, the latter separately for men and women.

Early reports from the Institute of Medicine suggested that using claims to infer diagnosis is error-prone (Institute of Medicine 1977), while more recent reports suggest that error rates are lower (Fisher, Wennberg et al. 1994; Fisher, Whaley et al. 1992; Mark 1994; McBean, Warren, and Babish 1994). As one test of reliability, we compared mortality rates in our sample to mortality in the Surveillance, Epidemiology, and End-Results (SEER) database, which contains detailed information on a nationally representative sample of US cancer patients. We found that mortality rates for breast, prostate, and colorectal cancer in the two samples matched closely.

We calculated one-year, three-year, and five-year survival probabilities for each group using date of first diagnosis and date of death. We estimated patient life expectancy by fitting these survival data to standard statistical models of mortality. We also calculated medical expenditures in each year following initial cancer diagnosis. We calculate the net present value (NPV) of five years of Medicare expenditures after cancer diagnosis, including the diagnosis year. We include all medical care costs, not only cancer-related costs, the appropriate approach to cost-effectiveness analysis under most circumstances (Garber and Phelps 1997). Annual expenditures were calculated as the sums of expenditures for all claims over each twelve month period after the diagnosis, from anniversary to anniversary of the diagnosis date. Expenditures include Part A (inpatient hospital), Part B (outpatient), physician, home health, and hospice services. These totals include chemotherapy and inpatient pharmaceutical expenditures but exclude outpatient prescription drugs, which Medicare did not cover during the periods in question. Claims in each category were available for everyone in the 20 percent sample, except for physician services, which were only available for a one-quarter random subset of the 20 percent sample. We adjusted all results for inflation, reporting results in constant year 2000 US dollars.

The SEER data were used to adjust the survival and expenditure estimates for age-specific trends in staging, which is not recorded in claims files. We merged SEER data to the appropriate Medicare claims by cohort and age and calculated estimates of cohort-specific five-year survival and Medicare expenditures adjusted for age and stage at diagnosis. We performed nonlinear regressions of five-year survival and expenditures (separately) on flexible functions of age and cohort as well as on the proportion of each age-cohort diagnosed at the various stages of disease (Garber and MaCurdy 1993).

6.2.2   2000 to 2004 Data

For this period, our basic approach was the same as the aforementioned, with a few modifications. First, we used the Surveillance, Epidemiology, and End Results (SEER) Program case files directly linked to Medicare claims data. The main advantage of this directly linked data is that we are able to calculate stage-specific survival and expenditure trends, rather than just stage-adjusted trends. We selected newly diagnosed patients with breast, prostate, colorectal, and lung cancer from 2000 to 2004 based on the SEER files. The SEER incorporates seventeen geographic regions including Seattle/Puget Sound, California, Utah, New Mexico, Alaska, Hawaii, Louisiana, Iowa, Kentucky, Atlanta and rural Georgia, Detroit, New Jersey, and Connecticut. Table 6.1 reports the sizes of each cohort based on year of diagnosis. We obtained linked SEER-Medicare claims data through 2009 to ensure five years minimum of claims data for all patients. Similar exclusionary criteria to the aforementioned period were used, including enrollment in Part C at any time during this period. We evaluated endpoints of one-, three-, and five-year survival probabilities and mean health expenditures adjusted for dummy stage, dummy age, and year of diagnosis (excluding outpatient phar-

Table 6.1   Cancer cohort sizes (2000–2004)

	2000	2001	2002	2003	2004	Total cases
Prostate	12,175	12,944	13,549	12,258	19,119	70,045
Breast	15,069	15,889	16,188	15,414	15,286	77,846
Lung—Men	9,367	9,889	10,220	10,604	9,679	49,759
Lung—Women	7,550	8,239	8,768	9,025	8,603	42,185
Colorectal—Men	7,293	7,540	7,756	7,694	7,267	37,550
Colorectal—Women	8,253	8,330	8,629	8,358	7,754	41,351

maceutical, or Part D expenditures). For this time period only, we calculated five-year survival rates by stage of disease for each annual cancer cohort. The calculation of stage-specific survival rates is not possible with the data from the previous time period.

We calculated life expectancy using hazard rates calculated from the one-, three-, and five-year survival probabilities by assuming the hazard rate was constant over time. We need such an assumption for life expectancy calculations since we do not observe the whole sample through its whole life span.

We follow the approach of Cutler and McClellan in calculating the marginal cost-effectiveness ratios of Medicare expenditures on medical care for cancer (Cutler and McClellan 2001). These should not be interpreted as cost-effectiveness ratios corresponding to any specific clinical intervention or policy. These are calculated by dividing the change in the NPV of Medicare expenditures between two periods by the change in life expectancy between those same periods; the interpretation as cost-effectiveness ratios is based on an assumption that changes in treatment and screening for patients during this period are solely responsible for changes in expenditures and survival. The stage-adjusted numbers can be similarly interpreted (under an analogous assumption) as cost-effectiveness ratios corresponding to changes in treatment regimens over the specified periods. We perform these calculations annually and for the overall periods 1986 to 1994 and 2000 to 2004.

For the analysis of 2000 to 2004 data, we included a terminal value for the cost of medical care beyond the five years of Medicare claims. We did this for breast, prostate, and colorectal cancer patients because their average life expectancy was greater than the five years of expenditure data. We estimated the terminal cost component by assuming that observed average medical costs in the fifth year after diagnosis continue for each cohort. We adjusted future annual expenditures for inflation by applying the medical Consumer Price Index (CPI) in 2000 (4.1 percent) for the remaining average years of life expected based on the calculation from observed five-year survival. We then discounted all years of expenditures back to 2000 US dollars at 5 percent and summed to estimate the final terminal component for medical expenditures past the five years of data (and for the remaining average life expectancy left for each cohort).

6.2.3   Cancer Staging Systems

For stage evaluation, we rely on data from Surveillance Epidemiology and End Results (SEER) Program Registry. The SEER data report staging using two different, though related, staging classification systems. The first is a historical staging system that relies on a consistent staging system definition that did not change during the years we analyze. The second system is called the American Joint Committee on Cancer (AJCC) staging system, which is periodically updated. The AJCC was founded by the American College of Surgeons in 1959 to establish a national standard for cancer staging (Fleming 2001). Both systems rely on the "TNM" system, according to the extent of the primary tumor "T," the involvement of lymph nodes "N," and the presence of distant or metastatic, "M," disease. Since 1982, the TNM criteria have become the single major approach to cancer staging throughout the world (Hutter 1984). Every five years, the AJCC makes minor updates to the TNM staging manual to reflect interim changes in the management of cancer diagnosis and treatment.

6.3   Results

6.3.1   Age and Survival Trends

For each period, we investigated trends in survival and age at diagnosis. Figure 6.1 shows that age-adjusted cancer survival rates increased substantially between 1986 and 1994 for breast and prostate cancer patients. This is true whether survival rates are measured at one, three, and five years after diagnosis, and the change between 1986 and 1994 is statistically significant at $p < 0.01$. Men with colorectal cancer experienced a small and statistically insignificant rise in age-adjusted survival, while survival in women with colorectal cancer did not increase. That cancer deaths and age-adjusted survival rates can increase at the same time should not be surprising: the size of the elderly population grew over this period and falling mortality rates from competing causes of death such as heart disease also left a larger pool at risk for cancer. During the later period, 2000 to 2004 (fig. 6.2), age- and stage-adjusted three- and five-year survival increased for all cancer cohorts, again with the greatest increases in prostate and breast cancer, followed by men and women with lung cancer and women with colorectal cancer. Men with colorectal cancer had only slight survival gains.

Figure 6.3, which plots the probability that new diagnoses are found at an early stage adjusted for age, shows a shift toward earlier diagnosis at a time when surveillance efforts, such as mammography, colonoscopy, sigmoidoscopy, and prostate cancer screening were increasingly used in the Medicare

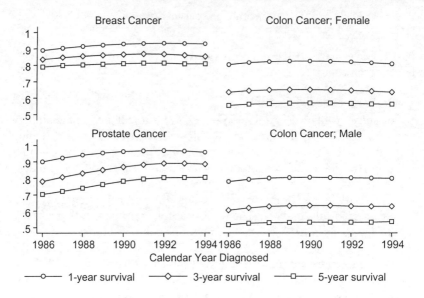

Fig. 6.1 Age-adjusted survival probabilities by year of diagnosis (1986–1994)

Notes: Trends in survival probabilities were smoothed; the figures show predicted survival probabilities, adjusted for age, for 65-year-olds in each year.

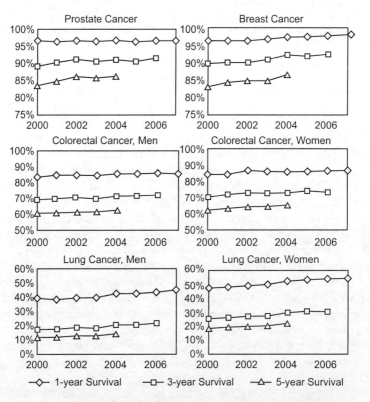

Fig. 6.2 Age-adjusted survival probabilities by year of diagnosis (2000–2004)

Note: Survival adjusted for age 65 to 69-year-olds with stage mix of 2000 cohorts.

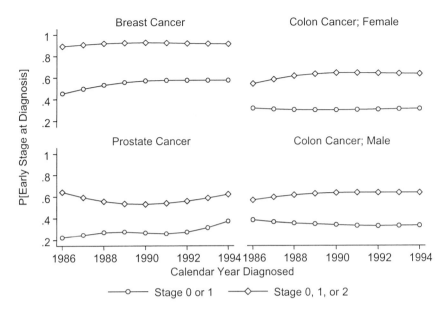

Fig. 6.3   Age-adjusted trends in stage at diagnosis (1986–1994)
Notes: Trends in survival probabilities were smoothed; the figures show predicted survival probabilities, adjusted for age, for 65-year-olds in each year.

population (1986–1994). In 1986, 45 percent of sixty-five-year-old women diagnosed with breast cancer had stage 0 or 1 cancer. By 1994, 60 percent had stage 0 or 1 breast cancer. For prostate cancer patients the probability of a stage 1 diagnosis for a sixty-five-year-old male increased from 20 percent to 40 percent between 1986 and 1994. For colorectal cancer patients, though the probability of finding a stage 1 cancer remained flat through the period, the probability of finding either a stage 1 or 2 cancer went up for both men and women. For the later period (fig. 6.4), the portion of early stage cancers for lung, colorectal, and breast cancer changed little, reflecting small increases in colorectal cancer screening over this period, and flat to declining rates in the use of mammography (an estimated 4 percent decline in mammography occurred between 2000 and 2005; Breen et al. 2007). The proportion of early stage prostate cancer did grow, reflecting continued adoption and increased frequency of PSA testing for cancer screening during this period. During this period, Medicare also began reimbursing providers for annual prostate screening examinations (digital rectal examinations and PSA blood tests) starting in 2000, and routine screening colonoscopies every ten years for individuals with normal cancer risk starting in 2001 (Freeman et al. 2002).

The effect of shifts in diagnosis on cancer survival can be seen in figure 6.5, which compares the change in age-adjusted five-year survival probabilities from 1986 levels when those probabilities are and are not adjusted for

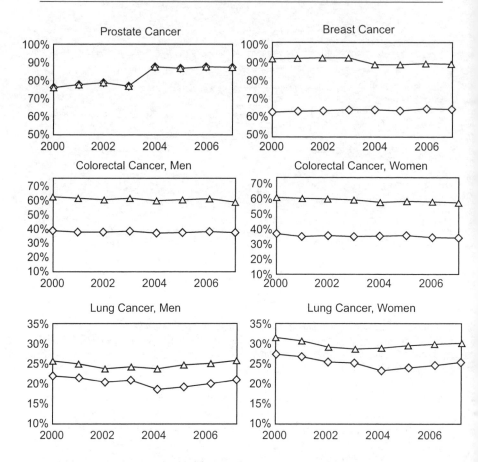

*Adjusted for age 65 year of age at diagnosis.

—◇— Stage 0 or 1   —△— Stage 0, 1 or 2

Fig. 6.4   Age-adjusted trends in stage at diagnosis (2000–2004)
Note: Adjusted for age 65, year of age at diagnosis.

staging trends. Stage adjustment has a dramatic effect on estimated breast cancer survival. A patient diagnosed in 1994 had a 10 percentage point lower probability of five-year survival than a patient with the same stage and at the same age diagnosed in 1986; survival rates not adjusted for stage show little improvement over the same period. By contrast, for men with colorectal cancer, stage-adjusted survival probability improved substantially between 1986 and 1994. Stage-adjustment has little effect for either prostate or colorectal cancer in women during this period.

During the 2000 to 2004 period, stage-adjusted five-year survival increased

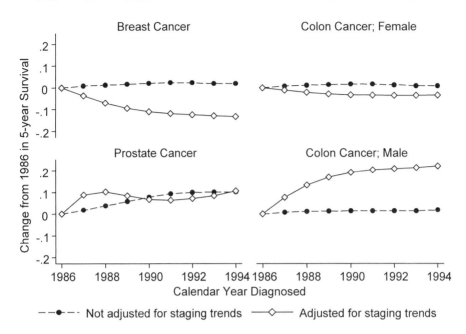

Fig. 6.5   Adjusted average changes in 5-year survival (1984–1996)
Notes: Trends in survival probabilities were smoothed; the figures show predicted survival probabilities, adjusted for age, for 65-year-olds in each year.

each year for all cancer cohorts compared to 2000 survival (fig. 6.6). The survival gains during this period were greater for women, with a 3 to 4 percent absolute gain in five-year survival for all cancer cohorts adjusted for stage and age of disease between 2004 and 2000, compared to a 2 to 3 percent increase for men during the same period.

6.3.2   Expenditure Trends

Figure 6.7 shows mean Medicare expenditures by year from diagnosis (in 1986–1994). Costs were highest during the first year after diagnosis; even after adjustment for inflation, costs increased for each successive cohort. These trends were also found in the 2000 to 2004 period (fig. 6.8). We find that expenditures are highest in the diagnosis (and presumed treatment) year, fall precipitously soon after, and then grow gradually as survivors age, as has been observed in other studies. Initial year costs for the 2000 to 2004 period were greatest for colorectal cancer, followed by lung cancer, followed by breast and prostate cancer. Expenditures for men and women were roughly equal in the year following diagnosis for both colorectal and lung cancers.

Figure 6.9 plots age-adjusted expenditure trends alongside age- and stage-adjusted expenditure trends. The figure confirms the expectation that

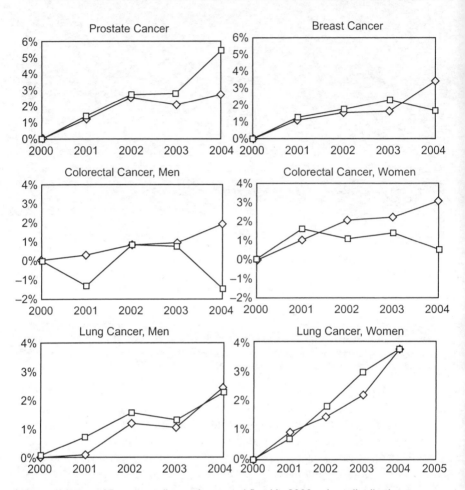

*Adjusted for age 65 years at diagnosis, staged fixed in 2000 cohort distributions.

——◇—— Stage Fixed   ——□—— Stage Not Fixed

Fig. 6.6   Adjusted average change in 5-year survival from 2000 (2001–2004)
Note: Adjusted for age 65 years at diagnosis, staged fixed in 2000 cohort distributions.

shifting toward earlier stages at diagnosis will reduce medical expenditures, especially during the year following diagnosis, since early stage cancer tends to be less expensive to treat than later stage cancer. In each case, the age- and stage-adjusted expenditure trends lie below the age-adjusted trends. For prostate cancer and colorectal cancer patients, the age- and stage-adjusted expenditures in the diagnosis year rose by about $10,000 between 1986 and 1994. For breast cancer, analogous expenditures rose by about $2,000 over the same period.

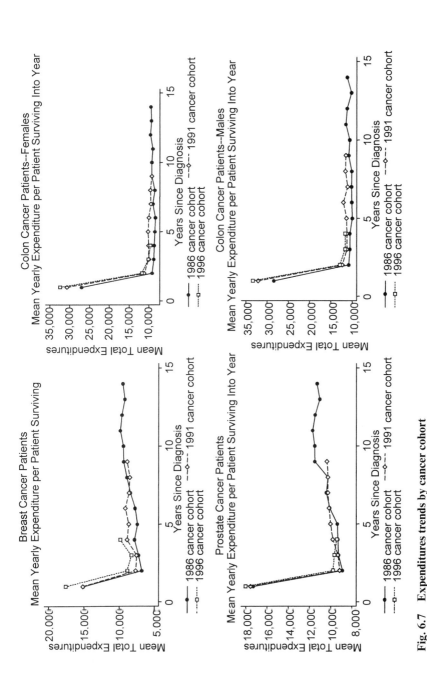

Fig. 6.7   Expenditures trends by cancer cohort
Note: All entries are in real year 2000 US$ (CPI-U deflator).

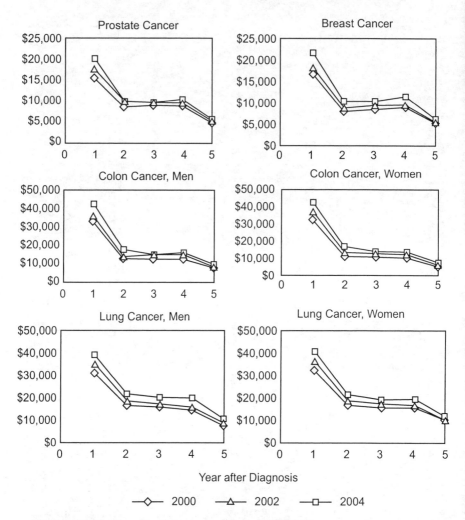

Fig. 6.8   Expenditure trends by cancer cohort (2000–2004)
Note: Expenditures adjusted to 2000 US$ using GDP deflator.

Figure 6.10 shows the same analysis for the 2000 to 2004 cohort. This demonstrates similar trends except in the case of prostate cancer, where age- and stage-adjusted expenditure estimates are lower than age-only adjusted average expenditures. Stage- and age-adjusted expenditure growth during this period was the highest for men with lung cancer, with an NPV of $20,000 more to treat similar age and stage of disease in 2004 over 2000. Breast and prostate cancer cases showed the lowest age- and stage-adjusted growth in expenditures during this period, with about $5,000 more spent per case treated in 2004 for these conditions, compared with 2000.

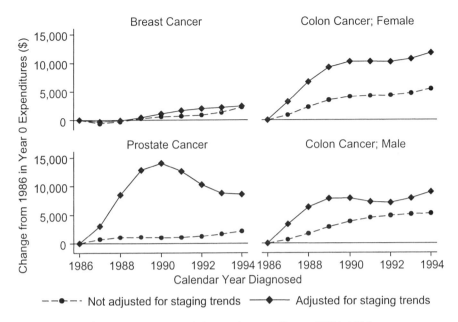

Fig. 6.9   **Adjusted average annual changes in expenditures (1984–1996)**
Notes: Trends in survival probabilities were smoothed; the figures show predicted survival probabilities, adjusted for age, for 65-year-olds in each year. All entries are in real year 2000 US$ (CPI-U deflator).

6.3.3   Incremental Cost-Effectiveness of Medical Progress for Cancer in the Elderly

Table 6.2 shows life expectancy and the net present value (NPV) of expenditures for successive cohorts of women diagnosed with breast and colorectal cancer in the 1986–1994 period. Table 6.3 shows analogous numbers for men with prostate and colorectal cancer. Included are estimates unadjusted and adjusted for age and stage at diagnosis. These trends parallel the findings for changes in cancer outcomes over time. Unadjusted life expectancy increased for all groups, while adjusted life expectancy increased for men with prostate and colorectal cancer, fell for breast cancer patients, and stayed roughly flat for women with colorectal cancer. Unadjusted expenditures increased sharply for all four cancer groups, while adjusted expenditures changed little for men with colorectal cancer and increased for breast, prostate, and for colorectal cancer in women.

During this period, advances in medical care of patients with prostate cancer cost an additional $44,466 when diagnosed in 1994 as compared with 1986, and these costs were associated with an incremental cost per life-year gained of $13,500 adjusted for changes in age and stage of disease. For colorectal cancer in women, it actually cost less to treat a case in 1986

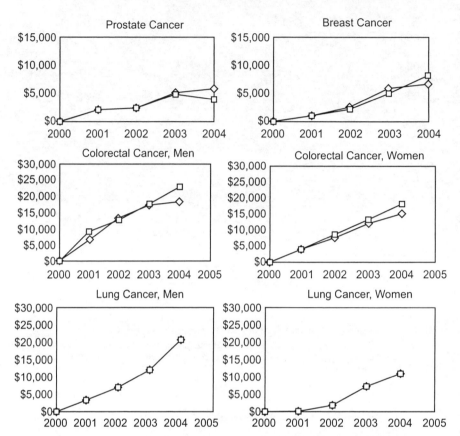

*Change in 5-year NPV from year of diagnosis compared to 2000. These show predicted probabilities for 65-69 year olds with stage proportions fixed at 2000 levels. All expenditures are in 2000 US dollars.

—◇— Stage Fixed   —□— Stage Not Fixed

Fig. 6.10   Adjusted average annual changes in expenditures (2000–2004)

at $43,409, as compared to care in 1994 costing $68,870, and was associated with an estimated loss of 0.6 years of life (when diagnosed in 1994 versus 1986). Breast cancer improvements in care cost an additional $16,600 in 1994 compared with 1986, and resulted in an age- and stage-adjusted loss of 2.6 life-years.

Tables 6.4 and 6.5 show life expectancy, five-year costs, and terminal lifetime costs of medical care for patients in the 2000 to 2004 period. These results show the greatest increase in life expectancy for patients with breast and prostate cancers, at 7.6 and 6.1 years, respectively, of additional life

Table 6.2   **Incremental cost-effectiveness of changes in cancer therapy for women (1986–1994)**

	Unadjusted					Adjusted for stage and age[a]				
	Change in LE	Change in 5-year NPV ($)	ICER (5-year costs) ($)	Delta terminal cost ($)	ICER (with terminal) ($)	Change in LE	Change in 5-year NPV ($)	ICER (5-year costs) ($)	Delta terminal cost ($)	ICER (with terminal) ($)
Breast cancer										
1987	0.69	(643)	Improved			−0.86	3,250	Dominated		
1988	0.46	99	217			−0.67	2,700	Dominated		
1989	0.35	1,430	4,107			−0.45	2,350	Dominated		
1990	0.25	1,180	4,737			−0.27	2,080	Dominated		
1991	0.15	1,016	6,942			−0.14	1,800	Dominated		
1992	0.06	570	9,230			−0.09	1,480	Dominated		
1993	0.05	1,470	27,150			−0.07	1,360	Dominated		
1994	0.16	1,100	6,729			−0.06	1,600	Dominated		
1987–1994	2.20	6,215	2,825	17,400	10,700	−2.60	16,600	Dominated	(16,300)	Dominated
Colorectal cancer										
1987	0.19	2,400	12,670			−0.20	3,250	Dominated		
1988	0.11	3,230	28,950			−0.20	2,700	Dominated		
1989	0.06	850	15,100			−0.13	2,350	Dominated		
1990	0.02	1,600	65,500			−0.06	2,080	Dominated		
1991	0.00	1,600	Dominated			−0.02	1,800	Dominated		
1992	−0.03	210	Dominated			−0.02	1,480	9,730		
1993	−0.03	960	Dominated			−0.02	1,360	Dominated		
1994	0.01	2,150	153,400			0.02	1,600	54,900		
1987–1994	0.40	13,000	32,500	9,200	55,500	−2.60	16,600	Dominated	(60)	Dominated

Notes: ICER = incremental cost-effectiveness ratio; LE = life expectancy; NPV = net present value. All dollar figures are 2000 USD. "Dominated" means worse outcomes and greater costs in the later year. Delta terminal cost represents the lifetime expected medical expenditures for survivors beyond five years for each cohort (but not applicable to lung cancer, with shorter than five year average survival).

[a] Adjusted for 2000 stage distribution and age 65 years.

Table 6.3   **Incremental cost-effectiveness of changes in cancer therapy for men (1986–1994)**

	Unadjusted					Adjusted for stage and age[a]				
	Change in LE	Change in 5-year NPV ($)	ICER (5-year costs) ($)	Delta terminal cost ($)	ICER (with terminal) ($)	Change in LE	Change in 5-year NPV ($)	ICER (5-year costs) ($)	Delta terminal cost ($)	ICER (with terminal) ($)
Prostate cancer										
1987	0.62	1,860	2,980			2.61	11,230	4,300		
1988	0.74	800	1,070			0.54	20,500	37,700		
1989	0.83	(50)	Improved			-0.66	17,120	Dominated		
1990	0.89	(125)	Improved			-0.58	6,760	Dominated		
1991	0.81	(755)	Improved			-0.11	(2,720)	24,460		
1992	0.60	840	1,400			0.24	(6,030)	Improved		
1993	0.34	(520)	Improved			0.45	(3,320)	Improved		
1994	0.03	1,175	36,230			0.85	930	1,100		
1987–1994	4.9	3,200	650	29,560	6,170	3.3	44,460	13,475	21,900	10,700
Colorectal cancer										
1987	0.17	1,380	8,185			1.13	(1,990)	Improved		
1988	0.10	2,500	24,160			1.04	(1,550)	Improved		
1989	0.07	830	12,370			0.83	(700)	Improved		
1990	0.04	2,630	59,480			0.56	200	360		
1991	0.03	460	13,780			0.31	800	2,560		
1992	0.02	(905)	Dominated			0.15	920	6,130		
1993	0.04	2,260	62,930			0.13	660	5,270		
1994	0.09	2,900	31,165			0.27	300	1,130		
1987–1994	0.50	12,065	24,130	9,300	66,900	4.40	(1,300)	Improved	46,900	10,600

Notes: ICER = incremental cost-effectiveness ratio; LE = life expectancy; NPV = net present value. All dollar figures are 2000 USD. "Dominated" means worse outcomes and greater costs in the later year. Delta terminal cost represents the lifetime expected medical expenditures for survivors beyond five years for each cohort (but not applicable to lung cancer, with shorter than five year average survival).

[a] Adjusted for 2000 stage distribution and age 65 years.

Table 6.4 Incremental cost-effectiveness of changes in cancer therapy for women (2000–2004)

	Unadjusted					Adjusted for stage and age[a]				
	Change in LE	Change in 5-year NPV ($)	ICER (5-year costs) ($)	Delta terminal cost ($)	ICER (with terminal) ($)	Change in LE	Change in 5-year NPV ($)	ICER (5-year costs) ($)	Delta terminal cost ($)	ICER (with terminal) ($)
Breast cancer										
2000										
2001	3.71	1,020	275			2.16	1,190	551		
2002	0.55	1,100	1,870			0.92	1,290	1,400		
2003	0.28	3,225	11,570			0.07	3,440	49,100		
2004	2.68	1,600	600			4.45	655	150		
2000–2004	7.25	6,940	950	73,575	11,100	7.59	6,575	865	75,500	10,800
Colorectal cancer										
2000										
2001	0.84	4,550	5,410			0.38	4,065	10,775		
2002	0.38	4,020	10,700			0.40	3,589	8,960		
2003	-0.40	4,180	(10,450)			0.08	4,430	56,920		
2004	0.17	4,175	25,160			0.36	3,100	8,600		
2000–2004	0.98	16,935	17,225	17,630	35,160	1.22	15,175	12,480	19,200	28,300
Lung cancer										
2000										
2001	0.06	4,550	78,100			0.09	4,065	45,640		
2002	0.09	4,020	42,735			0.05	3,590	72,945		
2003	-0.02	4,185	Dominated			0.07	4,430	64,650		
2004	0.18	4,175	22,970			0.15	3,100	20,140		
2000–2004	0.31	16,935	54,430	n/a		0.36	15,175	42,110	n/a	

Notes: ICER = incremental cost-effectiveness ratio; LE = life expectancy; NPV = net present value. n/a = not applicable. All dollar figures are 2000 USD. "Dominated" means worse outcomes and greater costs in the later year. Delta terminal cost represents the lifetime expected medical expenditures for survivors beyond five years for each cohort (but not applicable to lung cancer, with shorter than five year average survival).

[a] Adjusted for 2000 stage distribution and age bracket 65–69 years.

gained when diagnosed in 2004 as compared to 2000. Lung cancer advances lead to the lowest life expectancy improvements, with approximately 2.6 to 4.3 months gained in life expectancy between 2004 and 2000.

The average life expectancy for breast, lung, and colorectal cancer was greater than the five years of expenditures in the data. Thus, to match medical costs to life expectancy, we estimated a terminal component for medical costs for these cohorts; the difference in terminal costs for medical care between cohorts diagnosed in 2004 and 2000 is shown in a separate column in tables 6.4 and 6.5. Incremental cost-effectiveness ratios were calculated with and without the terminal cost component. Adjusted expenditures increased across all cohorts, resulting in an incremental cost-effectiveness ratio greatest for lung cancer, at $94,110 for men diagnosed with lung cancer in 2004 as compared to 2000, adjusted for age and stage of disease. Women with lung cancer were treated at an additional $42,110 per life-year gained in 2004 compared with 2000. Colorectal cancer had the next highest marginal cost-effectiveness ratios for treatment advances, with $54,000 per life-year gained for men and $28,300 per life-year gained for women. The medical care for men with prostate cancer resulted in an adjusted $10,300 per life-year gained. Advances in the treatment of women with breast cancer resulted in an additional $10,800 per life-year gained when diagnosed in 2004 as compared with 2000. We compared adjusting for both AJCC and historical stage of disease to calculate incremental cost-effectiveness ratios but, given the close similarity of findings, report only AJCC-adjusted estimates in tables 6.4 and 6.5.

6.3.4 Stage-Specific Survival Trends

We also explored stage-specific survival trends between cohorts diagnosed in 2004 and 2000, adjusted for age sixty-five to sixty-nine years in figures 6.11 and 6.12. Improvements in the stage-specific survival rates differed for each cancer cohort. Overall survival improvements were not evenly distributed across stages in most cancer cohorts. Breast cancer survival showed the largest gain for stage 3 disease (14 percent), but essentially no gain for stage 4 disease. Women with colorectal cancer showed a more consistent 4.0 to 4.8 percent increase in survival for stages 2 to 4 disease during this time period. Women and men with stage 1 lung cancer experienced the largest gain in survival—7.7 percent for women and 9.1 percent for men, when diagnosed in 2004 as compared with 2000. For prostate cancer, survival for men with distant disease declined by 2.6 percent, and increased modestly for local and regional disease. Our findings for prostate cancer, breast cancer, and men with lung cancer strongly argue against the Will Rogers phenomenon (see discussion in subsection 6.4.3).

Table 6.5   Incremental cost-effectiveness of changes in cancer therapy for men (2000–2004)

	Unadjusted for stage					Adjusted for stage and age[a]				
	Change in LE	Change in 5-year NPV ($)	ICER (5-year costs) ($)	Delta terminal cost ($)	ICER (with terminal) ($)	Change in LE	Change in NPV ($)	ICER (5-year costs) ($)	Terminal costs ($)	ICER (with terminal) ($)
Prostate cancer										
2000										
2001	1.11	1,875	1,690			2.50	2,210	880		
2002	2.78	222	80			3.12	110	35		
2003	-0.71	2,900	Dominated			-1.10	2,870	Dominated		
2004	3.80	(800)	Improved			1.55	520	340		
2000–2004	6.99	4,200	600	52,375	8,100	6.07	5,700	940	56,600	10,300
Colorectal cancer										
2000										
2001	-0.19	7,460	Dominated			0.09	6,800	75,690		
2002	0.36	6,150	16,985			0.17	6,410	38,760		
2003	0.71	3,870	5,450			0.05	4,340	81,130		
2004	-0.28	2,030	Dominated			0.35	840	2,410		
2000–2004	0.60	19,510	32,750	17,500	62,200	0.66	18,400	27,910	17,210	54,030
Lung cancer										
2000										
2001	-0.06	2,960	Dominated			0.01	3,340	482,110		
2002	0.09	4,160	47,820			0.10	3,730	36,350		
2003	0.03	4,830	149,100			-0.01	5,110	Dominated		
2004	0.11	8,900	79,100			0.12	8,440	68,040		
2000–2004	0.17	20,850	123,570	n/a		0.22	20,620	94,110	n/a	

Notes: ICER = incremental cost-effectiveness ratio; LE = life expectancy; NPV = net present value. n/a = not applicable. All dollar figures are 2000 USD. "Dominated" means worse outcomes and greater costs in the later year. "Improved" means costs fell and outcomes improved in the later year. Delta terminal cost represents the lifetime expected medical expenditures for survivors beyond five years for each cohort (but not applicable to lung cancer, with shorter than five year average survival).

[a] Adjusted for 2000 stage distribution and age bracket 65–69 years.

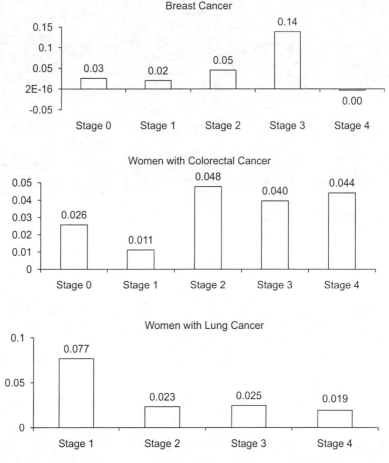

Fig. 6.11   Change in 5-year survival probability (2000–2004) for women by
AJCC stage

6.4   Discussion

6.4.1   Summary and Interpretation of Results

Our analysis suggests that advances in the medical care of cancer patients
were not uniformly cost-effective during the periods of analysis, but varied
based upon gender and cancer cohort. First, we found that medical progress
in the treatment of women with breast and colorectal cancer was generally
not cost-effective during the earlier period 1986 to 1994. For women with
these cancers, earlier years dominate later ones, since adjusted survival
declined while expenditures increased. During the early 2000s, this trend
reversed, with advances in treatment for breast cancer now highly cost ef-

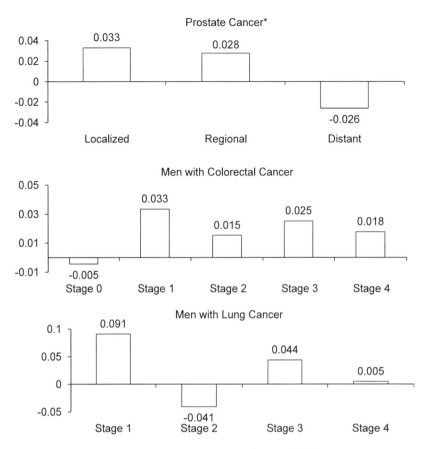

Fig. 6.12   Change in 5-year survival probability (2000–2004) for men by AJCC stage

Notes: Prostate cancer* AJCC stages combined stage 1 and 2 for Localized, stage 3 for Regional, and stage 4 for Distant. This was done because the *AJCC Cancer Staging Manual Sixth Edition,* released in 2003, reclassified almost all previous prostate cancer stage 1 disease into stage 2 disease beginning in 2004 (less than 0.5 percent of prostate cancer patients are classified as stage 1 after 2004).

fective, and advances for women with colorectal cancer slightly less cost-effective but still within a generally accepted range for cost per life-year gained (below $50,000 to 100,000 per life-year gained—assuming these years were mostly of high quality, which may not necessarily be the case).

The results for men with cancer diagnosed from 1986 to 1994 contrast sharply with the results for women. For prostate cancer, the adjusted cost-effectiveness ratios imply that the changes were cost-effective (except in 1989 and 1990, when adjusted survival fell). For some years, like 1992 and 1993, costs actually fell while survival rose. For men with colorectal cancer, there were highly cost-effective changes in every year between 1986 and 1994.

Between 1986 and 1994, the stage of breast, prostate, and colorectal cancer at the time of diagnosis among Medicare beneficiaries shifted to more limited, earlier disease. Although we do not address the issue directly, other authors have found that some cancer screening strategies are cost-effective in elderly populations. Our results from this era show that some cancers are diagnosed at earlier stages in Medicare beneficiaries, as would be expected with intensified screening. The findings do not suggest, however, that earlier diagnosis was consistently associated with improvement in the outcomes of treatment. While survival rates for men with prostate and colorectal cancer rose between 1986 and 1994, adjusted survival for women fell even at this time when more screening techniques were being recommended. The change in probability of earlier stage diagnosis was relatively flat for the 2000 to 2004 era, implying small to flat changes in screening rates, as we discuss next.

6.4.2   Lead and Length-Time Bias

Lead and length-time bias may contribute to observed survival gains. These biases are well-known to be associated with cancer screening programs (Duffy et al. 2008). Prostate and breast cancer are particularly prone to overdiagnosis—an extreme form of length-time bias—from intensive screening efforts. Prostate cancer screening programs and mammography for breast cancer can increase the diagnosis of indolent, very slow growing, early stage tumors (such as ductal carcinoma in situ, or DCIS breast cancer) which, if left undetected, would have been unlikely to clinically present or lead to death (Yen et al. 2003). Lead-time bias is perhaps most studied in regards to prostate cancer, where estimates of a lead-time of six years for a man diagnosed at age seventy-five is generally accepted for men diagnosed in the PSA-screening era as opposed to the prescreening era (Draisma et al. 2003). During the 2000 to 2005 time period, PSA screening rates have been reported in the Medicare population. Drazer et al. (2011) report modest age-based changes in screening rates between 2000 and 2005. They report that PSA screening rates increased by 3.1 percent (from 43 to 46.1 percent) of the population aged sixty-five to sixty-nine years, 3.8 percent for the population aged seventy to seventy-four years, 0 percent for population aged seventy-five to seventy-nine years, and a dramatic 15 percent increase for the population aged eighty to eighty-five years (Drazer et al. 2011). Overall, we found an age- and stage-adjusted six additional years of life for men diagnosed with prostate cancer in 2004. We find that given the small changes in PSA screening between these years, our results are unlikely to be entirely, or even mostly, accounted for by lead- and length-time bias due to improved prostate cancer screening (Duffy et al. 2008).

Interestingly, the results of our stage-specific survival trends for lung cancer might suggest a role for lead- or length-time bias for men and women diagnosed with stage 1 disease. The five-year probability of survival increased dramatically for both men and women with stage 1 lung cancer (by

9.1 percent and 7.7 percent, respectively). As lung cancer screening is not a population-based recommendation at this time, we postulate that perhaps this increase in stage 1 disease reflects increased use of CT imaging with an incidental diagnosis of early-stage lung cancer in the population. We do not understand the cause for this finding, which to our knowledge, has not yet been reported.

6.4.3   Will Rogers Phenomenon

One possible explanation for our finding of increased stage-adjusted survival among some groups of cancer patients is that they are caused by changes over time in the classification of cancer patients to a more advanced stage even though the underlying disease of patients has not changed over time. The idea is that "up-staging" classifications could move patients with a better prognosis over time to previously poorer prognostic groups. With that move, measured survival for lower stage patients will improve (since these stages no longer include patients who truly have more advanced disease), as will measured survival for higher stage patients (since presumably the patients who are upstaged have less advanced disease than the typical patient who would be diagnosed with advanced cancer regardless of when the staging took place). In the literature, this explanation is called the Will Rogers phenomenon (Feinstein, Sosin, and Wells 1985). Will Rogers once quipped, "When the Okies left Oklahoma and moved to California, they raised the average intelligence level in both states." The Will Rogers phenomenon has particularly been postulated to impact advanced stages of disease (Chee et al. 2008).

Other authors have suggested that long-term historical comparisons of cancer staging may lead to erroneous conclusions regarding survival based on the Will Rogers phenomenon (Gofrit et al. 2008). For example, in the case of prostate cancer, researchers compared grade (Gleason score) classifications from 1990 to 1992 with re-reading by pathologists in 2002 to 2004, blinded to the original readings (Albertsen et al. 2005). They found that the contemporary Gleason scores were significantly higher when read according to 2002 to 2004 pathologic criteria. They estimated that consequently, the contemporary prostate-cancer adjusted mortality rate would be 28 percent lower than standard historical rates without any apparent change in actual outcomes (Albertsen et al. 2005).

Another analysis evaluated the effect of new technology (positron emission tomography, or PET scanning) on stage migration in the post-PET era (1999–2004) and pre-PET (1994–1998) (Chee et al. 2008). The authors found a 5.4 percent decline in patients with stage 3 disease and an 8.4 percent increase in stage 4 disease between these periods. The authors argue that retrospectively, the PET period was associated with a marginally better overall survival (hazard ratio of 0.95 compared with pre-PET survival), which was entirely limited to those with stage 3 (HR 0.77) and stage 4

(HR 0.64) disease, as opposed to patients with stage 1 or 2 disease. Though we analyze two different eras for stage-adjusted survival within each era, we do not make comparisons between these eras.

The causal pathway for the Will Rogers phenomenon rests mostly on improved sensitivity of imaging modalities over time. If imaging technologies for cancer staging did not improve substantially over time, then it is inappropriate to read the results we present here as consistent with the Will Rogers phenomenon. We believe that the literature on imaging and cancer staging does not support the idea that there have been clinically substantial advances in cancer imaging over this period.

While an extensive literature is devoted to marginal improvements in sensitivity or specificity for cancer staging of imaging advances (Cooper et al. 2011; Gould et al. 2003)—CT-PET over conventional CT, MRI over CT or PET-CT—actual evidence for improved outcomes (survival) with these technologies is nonexistent. In fact, at least one highly publicized study, a randomized trial of combined PET-CT imaging versus conventional imaging enrolled during 2002 through 2007, did not find an effect on overall mortality for the use of the advanced imaging modality (Fischer et al. 2009). Furthermore, higher false positive rates have been documented with PET-CT for lung cancer, which could lead to erroneous conclusions regarding the utility of surgical management (and potential for cure) (Darling et al. 2011). These types of studies demonstrate that better outcomes should not necessarily be assumed simply because technology is next-generation.

In summary, the Will Rogers phenomenon remains an interesting theoretical phenomenon in regards to cancer staging and survival. Yet the weight of evidence does not support that it occurs along time horizons relevant to this analysis. Furthermore, improved outcomes based on advances in today's imaging technologies, as the presumed causal pathway for the Will Rogers phenomenon, is not supported by evidence for superior outcomes based on a review of today's medical literature.

6.4.4   Competing Risks

The possibility of competing risks is an important caveat to interpreting our results as directly measuring the cost-effectiveness of technological change in cancer therapy or cancer screening. Patients with cancer are naturally in the age group most at risk of cardiovascular disease. It is plausible that some of our findings for improvements in life expectancy (particularly for prostate cancer patients) occur because of improved care for important competing risks for death, not necessarily due to improvements in cancer treatments. This is particularly true for prostate cancer patients—who even after prostate cancer diagnosis, are still more likely to suffer a death from cardiovascular disease as opposed to prostate cancer-specific causes. There is extensive evidence that heart disease treatment in the population we study has results in improved outcomes for patients over the relevant period (Cutler and McClellan 2001; Lichtenberg 2004; Rodriguez et al. 2006; Skinner, Staiger, and Fisher 2006).

Authors publishing based on SEER data have consistently reported 100 percent five-year prostate-cancer-specific survival rates for patients diagnosed with localized disease (National Cancer Institute 2010). However, there is significant difficulty with correctly identifying causes of death in the elderly population. For example, if a patient diagnosed with localized prostate cancer is given androgen deprivation therapy and subsequently dies of a heart attack when androgen deprivation therapy has been shown to increase risk for such cardiac events (D'Amico et al. 2007; Keating, O'Malley, and Smith 2006), does this clearly constitute a death unrelated to prostate cancer?

Lastly, our claim that technological innovations may have been cost-effective in some cases requires an assumption that there is a direct causal relationship between the expenditures and outcomes, and that the effects of characteristics that change over time and are not measured in the available data, such as health behaviors, are inconsequential. Though the data sets we use are the richest available national data on cancer patients, we necessarily do not observe every clinical characteristic that may be important. For example, we do not have good observations on adherence to therapy, which plays an important role in determining survival and expenditure outcomes for cancer patients. Also, there may be important trends in unmeasured comorbid conditions, such as obesity. Trends in such characteristics could be responsible for the finding that survival actually worsened over time for women with breast or colorectal cancer; for example, an increasing percentage of women with breast cancer might have had significant comorbidities that influenced survival.

6.4.5   Younger Populations

Our findings cannot be presumed to apply to younger cancer patients or to the types of cancers that are more common among the young. However, cancer is primarily a disease of the elderly, and this is particularly true of the types of cancer that we studied. More than two-thirds of all cancer deaths occur among people aged sixty-five and older, and cancer is the second leading cause of death among the elderly, accounting for 113 deaths per year per 10,000 elderly people. Of all cancer patients alive in 2001, 61 percent were aged sixty-five or older.

6.4.6   Concluding Remarks

We find that trends in expenditures and outcomes among Medicare beneficiaries strongly suggest that changes in treatment during the periods we studied may have improved outcomes for some but not all cancers evaluated, and even under favorable assumptions would only be considered cost-effective for a subset of cancers. The years of analysis most corresponding to the recent treatment era did show generally cost-effective medical advances for cancer treatment, with the possible exception of men with lung cancer.

The American health care system simultaneously provides incentives for the use of cost-effective and cost-ineffective care. Only by evaluating each technology individually, and the clinical contexts in which it is used, will it be possible to determine whether it is a good investment. Such information is the foundation for rational choices about distributing limited health care resources.

References

Albertsen, P. C., J. A. Hanley, G. H. Barrows, D. F. Penson, P. D. Kowalczyk, M. M. Sanders, and J. Fine. 2005. "Prostate Cancer and the Will Rogers Phenomenon." *Journal of the National Cancer Institute* 97 (17): 1248–53.

Bailar, J. C., III, and H. L. Gornik. 1997. "Cancer Undefeated." *New England Journal of Medicine* 336 (22): 1569–74.

Breen, N., K. A. Cronin, H. I. Meissner, S. H. Taplin, F. K. Tangka, J. A. Tiro, and T. S. McNeel. 2007. "Reported Drop in Mammography: Is This Cause for Concern?" *Cancer* 109 (12): 2405–59.

Chambers, J. D., and P. J. Neumann. 2011. "Listening to Provenge—What a Costly Cancer Treatment Says about Future Medicare Policy." *New England Journal of Medicine* 364 (18): 1687–89.

Chee, K. G., D. V. Nguyen, M. Brown, D. R. Gandara, T. Wun, and P. N. Lara Jr. 2008. "Positron Emission Tomography and Improved Survival in Patients with Lung Cancer: The Will Rogers Phenomenon Revisited." *Archives of Internal Medicine* 168 (14): 1541–49.

Cooper, K. L., Y. Meng, S. Harnan, S. E. Ward, P. Fitzgerald, D. Papaioannou, L. Wyld, C. Ingram, I. D. Wilkinson, and E. Lorenz. 2011. "Positron Emission Tomography (PET) and Magnetic Resonance Imaging (MRI) for the Assessment of Axillary Lymph Node Metastases in Early Breast Cancer: Systematic Review and Economic Evaluation." *Health Technology Assessment* 15 (4): iii–iv, 1–134.

Cutler, D. 2004. *Your Money or Your Life: Strong Medicine for America's Health Care System.* New York: Oxford Press.

———. 2008. "Are We Finally Winning the War on Cancer?" *Journal of Economic Perspectives* 22 (4): 3–26.

Cutler, D. M., and M. McClellan. 2001. "Is Technological Change in Medicine Worth It?" *Health Affairs (Millwood)* 20 (5): 11–29.

D'Amico, A. V., J. W. Denham, J. Crook, M. H. Chen, S. Z. Goldhaber, D. S. Lamb, D. Joseph, et al. 2007. "Influence of Androgen Suppression Therapy for Prostate Cancer on the Frequency and Timing of Fatal Myocardial Infarctions." *Journal of Clinical Oncology* 25 (17): 2420–25.

Darling, G. E., D. E. Maziak, R. I. Inculet, K. Y. Gulenchyn, A. A. Driedger, Y. C. Ung, C. S. Gu, et al. "Positron Emission Tomography-Computed Tomography Compared with Invasive Mediastinal Staging in Non-Small Cell Lung Cancer:

Results of Mediastinal Staging in the Early Lung Positron Emission Tomography Trial." *Journal of Thoracic Oncology* 6 (8): 1367–72.

Draisma, G., R. Boer, S. J. Otto, I. W. van der Cruijsen, R. A. Damhuis, F. H. Schroder, and H. J. de Koning. 2003. "Lead Times and Overdetection Due to Prostate-specific Antigen Screening: Estimates from the European Randomized Study of Screening for Prostate Cancer." *Journal of the National Cancer Institute* 95 (12): 868–78.

Drazer, M. W., D. Huo, M. A. Schonberg, A. Razmaria, and S. E. Eggener. 2011 "Population-Based Patterns and Predictors of Prostate-Specific Antigen Screening among Older Men in the United States." *Journal of Clinical Oncology* 29 (13): 1736–43.

Duffy, S. W., I. D. Nagtegaal, M. Wallis, F. H. Cafferty, N. Houssami, J. Warwick, P. C. Allgood, et al. 2008. "Correcting for Lead Time and Length Bias in Estimating the Effect of Screen Detection on Cancer Survival." *American Journal of Epidemiology* 168 (1): 98–104.

Elkin, E. B., and P. B. Bach. 2010. "Cancer's Next Frontier: Addressing High and Increasing Costs." *Journal of the American Medical Association* 303 (11): 1086–87.

Feinstein, A. R., D. M. Sosin, and C. K. Wells. 1985. "The Will Rogers Phenomenon. Stage Migration and New Diagnostic Techniques as a Source of Misleading Statistics for Survival in Cancer." *New England Journal of Medicine* 312 (25): 1604–48.

Fischer, B., U. Lassen, J. Mortensen, S. Larsen, A. Loft, A. Bertelsen, J. Ravn, et al. 2009. "Preoperative Staging of Lung Cancer with Combined PET-CT." *New England Journal of Medicine* 361 (1): 32–39.

Fisher, E. S., J. E. Wennberg, T. A. Stukel, and S. M. Sharp. 1994. "Hospital Readmission Rates for Cohorts of Medicare Beneficiaries in Boston and New Haven." *New England Journal of Medicine* 331 (15): 989–95.

Fisher, E. S., F. S. Whaley, W. M. Krushat, D. J. Malenka, C. Fleming, J. A. Baron, and D.C. Hsia. 1992. "The Accuracy of Medicare's Hospital Claims Data: Progress Has Been Made, But Problems Remain." *American Journal of Public Health* 82 (2): 243–48.

Fleming, I. D. 2001. "AJCC/TNM Cancer Staging, Present and Future." *Journal of Surgical Oncology* 77 (4): 233–36.

Freeman, J. L., C. N. Klabunde, N. Schussler, J. L. Warren, B. A. Virnig, and G. S. Cooper. 2002. "Measuring Breast, Colorectal, and Prostate Cancer Screening with Medicare Claims Data." *Medical Care* 40 (8 Suppl): IV-36–42.

Fuchs, V. R., and A. M. Garber. 1990. "The New Technology Assessment." *New England Journal of Medicine* 323 (10): 673–77.

Fuchs, V. R., and A. M. Garber. 2003. "Medical Innovation: Promises and Pitfalls." *Brookings Review.* http://www.brookings.edu/articles/2003/winter_technology_fuchs.aspx.

Garber, A. M., and T. MaCurdy. 1993. "Nursing Home Discharges and Exhaustion of Medicare Benefits." *Journal of the American Statistical Association* 88: 727–36.

Garber, A. M., and C. E. Phelps. 1997. "Economic Foundations of Cost-Effectiveness Analysis." *Journal of Health Economics* 16 (1): 1–31.

Gofrit, O. N., K. C. Zorn, G. D. Steinberg, G. P. Zagaja, and A. L. Shalhav. 2008. "The Will Rogers Phenomenon in Urological Oncology." *Journal of Urology* 179 (1): 28–33.

Gould, M. K., W. G. Kuschner, C. E. Rydzak, C. C. Maclean, A. N. Demas, H. Shigemitsu, J. K. Chan, and D. K. Owens. 2003. "Test Performance of Positron

Emission Tomography and Computed Tomography for Mediastinal Staging in Patients with Non-Small-Cell Lung Cancer: A Meta-Analysis." *Annals of Internal Medicine* 139 (11): 879–92.

Hutter, R. L. 1984. "At Last-Worldwide Agreement on the Staging of Cancer." *AMA Archives of Surgery* 122: 1235–39.

Institute of Medicine. 1977. *Reliability of Medicare Hospital Discharge Records.* Washington, DC: National Academy of Sciences.

Keating, N. L., A. J. O'Malley, and M. R. Smith. 2006. "Diabetes and Cardiovascular Disease during Androgen Deprivation Therapy for Prostate Cancer." *Journal of Clinical Oncology* 24 (27): 4448–56.

Lenzer, J. 2006. "US Cancer Mortality Falls for the First Time." *British Medical Journal* 332 (7539): 444.

Lichtenberg, F. R. 2004. "Sources of U.S. Longevity Increase, 1960–2001." *Quarterly Review of Economics and Finance* 44:369–89.

Mark, D. H. 1994. "Mortality of Patients after Radical Prostatectomy: Analysis of Recent Medicare Claims." *Journal of Urology* 152 (3): 896–98.

McBean, A. M., J. L. Warren, and J. D. Babish. 1994. "Measuring the Incidence of Cancer in Elderly Americans Using Medicare Claims Data." *Cancer* 73 (9): 2417–25.

Medicare Trustees. 2008. *The 2008 Annual Report of the Boards of Trustees of the Federal Hospital Insurance and Federal Supplementary Medical Insurance Trust Funds.* Baltimore, MD: C. f. M. M. Services.

Meltzer, D. 2003. "Can Medical Cost Effectiveness Analysis Identify the Value of Medical Research?" In *Measuring the Gains from Medical Research: An Economic Approach,* edited by Kevin M. Murphy and Robert H. Topel, 206–247. Chicago: University of Chicago Press.

Murphy, K. M., and R. H. Topel. 2003. "The Economic Value of Medical Research." In *Measuring the Gains from Medical Research: An Economic Approach,* edited by Kevin M. Murphy and Robert H. Topel, 41–73. Chicago: University of Chicago Press.

———. 2005. "Black-White Differences in the Economic Value of Improving Health." *Perspect Biol Med* 48 (1 Suppl): S176–94.

National Cancer Institute. 2010. "Cancer Trends Progress Report—2009/2010 Update." Accessed on May 24, 2010. http://progressreport.cancer.gov.

Owens, D. K., A. Qaseem, R. Chou, and P. Shekelle. 2011. "High-Value, Cost-Conscious Health Care: Concepts for Clinicians to Evaluate the Benefits, Harms, and Costs of Medical Interventions." *Annals of Internal Medicine* 154 (3): 174–80.

Porter, M. E. 2010. "What Is Value in Health Care?" *New England Journal of Medicine* 363 (26): 2477–81.

Potetz, L., and L. F. DeWilde. 2009. *Cancer and Medicare: A Chartbook.* Cancer Action Network: American Cancer Society.

Rodriguez, T., M. Malvezzi, L. Chatenoud, C. Bosetti, F. Levi, E. Negri, and C. La Vecchia. 2006. "Trends in Mortality from Coronary Heart and Cerebrovascular Diseases in the Americas: 1970–2000." *Heart* 92 (4): 453–60.

Siegler, M., A. Weisfeld, and D. Cronin. 2003. "Is Medical Research Cost Effective? Response to Murphy and Topel." *Perspectives in Biology and Medicine* 46 (3 Suppl): S129–37.

Skinner, J. S., D. O. Staiger, and E. S. Fisher. 2006. "Is Technological Change in Medicine Always Worth It? The Case of Acute Myocardial Infarction." *Health Affairs (Millwood)* 25 (2): w34–47.

Yen, M. F., L. Tabar, B. Vitak, R. A. Smith, H. H. Chen, and S. W. Duffy. 2003.

"Quantifying the Potential Problem of Overdiagnosis of Ductal Carcinoma in situ in Breast Cancer Screening." *European Journal of Cancer* 39 (12): 1746–54.

Comment   Amitabh Chandra

It is always slightly terrifying to discuss a chapter by a team with so much intellectual firepower, and in this case doubly so, for Jay Bhattacharya and Alan Garber have taught me so much about health economics. My comments on their work will focus on the broader questions about assessing the productivity of medical spending, be it on cancer or other diseases.

In this chapter the authors demonstrate that the distribution of benefits from medical progress in cancer is not egalitarian. They find that spending on women with breast and colorectal cancer was not cost-effective until the mid-1990s, but started to look remarkably cost-effective after that; a finding that will excite cancer researchers and their advocates everywhere. The earlier period may even have been harmful as survival fell while expenditures increased. In contrast to the results for women, spending on prostate cancer is shown to confer immensely cost-effective benefits.

I have two comments. The first is one that Jonathan Skinner and I make in our paper "Technology Growth and Expenditure Growth in Healthcare" (Chandra and Skinner 2011). Studies of the aggregate productivity of health care spending collapse costs and benefits across technologies to measure the productivity of spending. The chapter by Bhattacharya and colleagues utilizes this framework, as does David Cutler and Murphy and Topel (2006), who estimate an increase in the value of health roughly three times accumulated health care costs during 1970 to 2000. Similarly, Lakdawalla et al. (2010) found high average cost-effectiveness for cancer treatments. A close cousin of this approach is found in the considerable work on geographic variations in spending, where health outcomes are regressed on spending. But in this research (which includes a lot of mine), the returns reflect the weighted means of survival gains and costs across different types of treatments. So it could easily be the case that one treatment is responsible for the bulk of the spending and another for the majority of the survival improvements. And while that does not change the overall conclusion about the cost-effectiveness of medical spending, it certainly changes how sanguine

Amitabh Chandra is economist and professor of public policy at the Harvard Kennedy School of Government, a research fellow at the IZA Institute in Bonn, Germany, and a research associate of the National Bureau of Economic Research.

For acknowledgments, sources of research support, and disclosure of the author's material financial relationships, if any, please see http://www.nber.org/chapters/c12440.ack.

(or upset) one should be when confronted with presence or absence of meeting aggregate cost-effective thresholds.

To see this better, imagine that there are two treatments, A and B. Treatment A is useful and costs a dollar, but treatment B is useless and costs $100,000. Over time we are using more of B. An aggregate productivity calculation that regresses survival on total spending may find that the extra spending "was worth it" and that "we should not cut spending." Such conclusions leave readers and policymakers thinking that all is right with the world, and that more spending is efficient, and perhaps even necessary. But in reality we could have slashed almost 100 percent of spending without harming patients.

What is the evidence for this concern?

There are two sources of evidence that support my view that aggregate productivity calculations may miss some important facts about mechanisms. Ford et al. (2007) note that 44 percent of the reduction in coronary deaths between 1980 and 2000 was the consequence of changing risk factors related to behaviors rather than health care per se. The implication of this is that aggregate productivity studies may overstate the overall improvement in life expectancy attributable to health care expenditures given that behavioral factors accounted for nearly half of the survival improvement. In terms of what caused the gains in coronary deaths, 35 percent of the decline in mortality was the consequence of inexpensive but highly effective treatments such as aspirin, beta-blockers, blood-thinning drugs, antihypertensives, diuretics, and pharmaceuticals such as ACE inhibitors, anticholesterol drugs (statins), and thrombolytics ("clot-busters"). The marginal cost of these inputs is modest. So almost 80 percent (44 percent + 35 percent) of the survival was caused by relatively inexpensive treatments. Innovations such as angioplasty (stents), bypass surgery, cardiac rehabilitation, and cardio-pulmonary resuscitation (such as automated defibrillators) explained less than 12 percent of the mortality decline, but are responsible for an enormous portion of the costs. And so, regressing outcomes on spending might find that the extra spending was worth it, but that would lose sight of the fact that virtually all the survival gains came from "home run" technologies such as beta-blockers and aspirin.

Another example that is more relevant to the present chapter comes from my work with Mary Beth Landrum and other collaborators (Landrum et al. 2008). We looked at the care of patients with colorectal cancer, and found that high-spending regions are more likely than other regions to use recommended care but are also more likely to use discretionary and nonrecommended care, the latter of which has adverse outcomes for patients. If the time-series variation in cancer treatment mimics the geographic variation in the use of recommended and nonrecommended care, then finding that spending more is cost-effective would miss this important nuance. It might result in our spending more on colorectal cancer when the appropriate policy response would be the opposite. The same can be said if we find that spending is "cost-ineffective"—the majority of the spending may have been effective but diluted by the presence of expensive but potentially harmful treatments. Absent knowing what is being purchased with the extra money, it is difficult to use aggregate productivity calculations to ascertain the allocative efficiency of what we are spending on cancer or coronary death. For this reason, we should try to ensure that measures of aggregate productivity can be reconciled with what clinical trials have found—so when we say that spending on prostate cancer was effective, are there interventions that diffused over this time that find support for this view?

My second point is about risk-adjustment. As a result of work by Song et al. (2010) and Welch et al. (2011), we now have fairly convincing evidence that claims-based risk-adjustment may be doing the opposite of what we want it to do. If more aggressive providers screen patients more often (not only for cancer, but also for diabetes and hypertension), they will look like they have "sicker" patients. In such a world, controlling for risk will reward exactly the wrong providers—the providers with the most upcoding will get the best risk-adjusted outcomes. What are we to do about this concern? On the one hand, concerns about lead-time bias encourage us to control for more and more (and in particular, to control for stage of diagnoses). I have done this in my own work, but I fear that it was not the right way forward because of concerns about the Will Rogers effect, which is discussed by the authors. Here, higher fidelity scans result in more patients being coded as being stage 3 and 4 patients. Controlling for stage (aka, looking within stage) will make survival look better, but that is entirely a consequence of a compositional change in who is at which stage. The Will Rogers effect would caution against controlling for stage, arguing instead that we should control for tumor size, which is probably the most important predictor of survival. Interestingly, this alternative control should also help with lead-time bias.

I enjoyed reading this chapter—the wealth of information in it is impressive and it forces us to grapple with core issues in measuring the productivity of health care spending.

References

Chandra, Amitabh, and J. S. Skinner. 2011. "Technology Growth and Expenditure Growth in Health Care." NBER Working Paper no. 16953. Cambridge, MA: National Bureau of Economic Research, April.

Ford, Earl S., Umed A. Ajani, Janet B. Croft, Julia A. Critchley, Darwin R. Labarthe, Thomas E. Kottke, Wayne H. Giles, and Simon Capewell. 2007. "Explaining the Decrease in U.S. Deaths from Coronary Disease, 1980–2000." *New England Journal of Medicine* 356:2388–98.

Lakdawalla, Darius N., Eric C. Sun, Anupam B. Jena, Carolina M. Reyes, Dana P. Goldman, and Tomas J. Philipson. 2010. "An Economic Evaluation of the War on Cancer." *Journal of Health Economics* 29 (3): 333–46.

Landrum, Mary Beth, Ellen Meara, Amitabh Chandra, Edward Guadagnoli, and Nancy Keating. 2008. "Is Spending More Always Wasteful? The Appropriateness of Care and Outcomes Among Colorectal Cancer Patients." *Health Affairs* 27:1159–68. doi:10.1377/hlthaff.27.1.159.

Murphy, Kevin M., and Robert H. Topel. 2006. "The Value of Health and Longevity." *Journal of Political Economy* 114 (5): 871–904.

Song, Y., J. Skinner, J. Bynum, J. Sutherland, J. E. Wennberg, and E. S. Fisher. 2010. "Regional Variations in Diagnostic Practices." *New England Journal of Medicine* 363:45–54.

Welch, Gilbert H., S. M. Sharp, D. J. Gottlieb, J. S. Skinner, and J. E. Wennberg. 2011. "Geographic Variation in Diagnosis Frequency and Risk of Death Among Medicare Beneficiaries." *Journal of the American Medical Association* 305 (11): 1113–38.

7

Self-Reported Disability
and Reference Groups

Arthur van Soest, Tatiana Andreyeva,
Arie Kapteyn, and James P. Smith

7.1 Introduction

In contrast to other social scientists, economists have long adhered to an individualistic notion of behavior, despite early contributions by, for example, Duesenberry (1949) and Veblen (1899). An important modern contribution to the modeling of social interactions is the seminal work of Becker (1974). Although of wider relevance, Becker's work emphasized the interactions among family members, caused by interdependent utilities as well as a common budget constraint. In more recent years, economists have increasingly recognized that individual actions are fundamentally influenced by the attributes and behaviors of those other individuals who form their social networks; see Topa (2001).

The span of behaviors that have been examined in this new research on social interactions has been expanding rapidly and even a very partial list now includes criminal activity (Glaeser, Sacerdote, and Scheinkman 1996, 2000), neighborhood effects on youth behavior (Case and Katz 1991), models of herd- or copycat-like behaviors (Banerjee 1992), peer effects in education (Hanushek et al. 2003; Ginther, Haveman, and Wolfe 2000), agglomeration economies (Audretsch and Feldman 1996), information

Arthur van Soest is professor in the Econometrics Department of Tilburg University, a research advisor at NETSPAR, and an economist at the RAND Corporation. Tatiana Andreyeva is director of economic initiatives at the Rudd Center for Food Policy and Obesity at Yale University. Arie Kapteyn is senior economist and program director of Labor and Population at the RAND Corporation. James P. Smith holds the Distinguished Chair in Labor Markets and Demographic Studies at the RAND Corporation.
This research was funded by the National Institute on Aging. We are grateful to David Cutler for useful comments. For acknowledgments, sources of research support, and disclosure of the authors' material financial relationships, if any, please see http://www.nber.org/chapters/c12441.ack.

exchanges in local labor markets (Topa 2001), labor supply (Woittiez and Kapteyn 1998), consumption (Kapteyn et al. 1997; Alessie and Kapteyn 1991), retirement plan choices (Duflo and Saez 2003), spillovers of cash transfers on noneligibles (Angelucci and Giorgi 2009), effects of lottery winnings on the consumption of neighbors (Kuhn et al. 2011), and social learning through neighbors (Bala and Goyal 1998). As these examples illustrate, the type of social interactions studied has moved well beyond the immediate family to much larger circles of friends, neighbors, and like-minded consumers and workers. Various reasons are given for why these types of social interactions matter, including information sharing, demonstration effects, and the formation of tastes and preferences.

Social interactions may also affect what individuals believe to constitute acceptable or normal behavior based on the standards of the subcommunities in which they live and work. In this chapter, we develop a direct test of this using data from a household survey representative of the Dutch population on how respondents evaluate work disability of hypothetical people with some work-related health problem (vignettes). Combining this with self-reports on the number of people receiving disability insurance (DI) benefits among one's friends and acquaintances, we estimate a model describing the influence of DI prevalence in one's reference group on the subjective scale used to report own and others' work disability.

Both the prevalence of DI benefit receipt and self-reported work disability vary substantially across countries; see Haveman and Wolfe (2000) and Bound and Burkhauser (1999). In particular, both are much higher in the Netherlands than in the United States. Bound and Burkhauser (1999) report that in 1995, the number of DI recipients per 1,000 workers in the age group forty-five to fifty-nine was 103 in the United States, compared to 271 in the Netherlands. Kapteyn, Smith, and van Soest (2007) report that in the age bracket fifty-one to sixty-four, self-reported work disability in The Netherlands is about 58 percent higher than in the United States (35.8 percent in the Netherlands against 22.7 percent in the United States). While the higher level of Dutch participation in DI programs is not surprising given higher DI benefits and easier eligibility compared to the United States,[1] greater Dutch prevalence of self-reported work disability is puzzling as the Dutch population appears to be healthier than the American population.[2]

Kapteyn, Smith, and van Soest (2007) investigated to what extent differences in self-reported work disability can be ascribed to differences in

1. See, for instance, Aarts, Burkhauser, and de Jong (1996). In 2004, DI recipients in the Netherlands made up 13 percent of the labor force (see Statistics Netherlands at http://statline .cbs.nl/StatWeb.), while in the United States, DI recipients constituted 4.8 percent of the civilian labor force (see U.S. Bureau of Labor Statistics at ftp://ftp.bls.gov/pub/news.release/ History/empsit.01072005.news).
2. This is suggested by the analysis of a broad set of health conditions by Banks et al. (2008).

reporting styles across countries. Exploiting the vignette methodology originally developed by King et al. (2004), Dutch and US respondents were given the same descriptions of work disability problems for hypothetical persons ("vignettes"). Dutch respondents appeared to be much more likely to describe the same work disability problem as constituting a work disability than American respondents. Kapteyn, Smith, and van Soest (2007) found that more than half of the observed difference in self-reported work disability between the two countries can be explained by this difference in response styles.

This result implies that US and Dutch respondents have different norms for evaluating work disability. Our chapter analyzes to what extent this is due to peer group effects: do respondents with many DI recipients in their peer group have social norms that make them more likely to evaluate given health problems as constituting a work disability?

We formalize this notion by introducing the concept of prevalence of DI benefit receipt in one's *reference group*, defined as one's circle of friends and acquaintances. In a Dutch survey that we designed and implemented, we asked respondents directly how many people among their friends and acquaintances receive DI benefits. In this chapter, we develop a model that jointly explains the categorical answer to this question and self-reported work disability. The main feature of the model is the notion that response scales for reporting no, mild, or severe work disability can be affected by a "peer group effect," that is, by the number of people in the reference group receiving disability benefits. To identify the determinants of response scales, we exploit anchoring vignettes as in Kapteyn, Smith, and van Soest (2007).

Using this additional information helps to solve the identification problem that is present in many models with peer group effects, known as the *reflection problem* (Manski 1993). Because our reference group variable refers to DI receipt in the reference group and not perceived disability, it seems reasonable to assume that this variable is uncorrelated to the unobservables driving the individuals' norms. This makes it possible to include reference group DI receipt as an exogenous variable in the vignette evaluations. Because the actual disability of the hypothetical vignette persons is by design independent of any respondent characteristic, the effect of reference group DI on vignette evaluations must be an effect on the respondent's norms used to evaluate (own or the vignette person's) work disability.

The remainder of the chapter is organized as follows. In the next section, we briefly describe the micro-data used in our analysis. Section 7.3 presents the model, which essentially consists of three equations. One equation explains the answers to the question about DI benefit receipt in the respondents' reference group. A second equation models self-reported work disability. The third equation (or rather set of equations) explains how individual response scales to questions on work disability (or anchoring vignettes) are affected by the prevalence of DI benefit receipt in the reference group. Throughout, we control for a large number of other variables, such as sociodemographic characteristics and health conditions.

Section 7.4 summarizes our main results. We find that DI benefit receipt in one's reference group has a significant effect on response scales in the expected direction. To gauge the size of this effect, we graph the relation between DI benefit receipt in the reference group against self-reported work disability. It turns out that to explain the complete difference in response scales between the United States and the Netherlands, the percentage of respondents in The Netherlands reporting to know at least some DI benefit recipients has to fall by about 25 percent. This is an order of magnitude that seems reasonable given the substantial difference in the number of Dutch and US people on DI benefits. The final section presents our conclusions.

7.2   The Data

In this research, we use information obtained from the Dutch CentER-panel. This is an Internet panel of about 2,250 households who have agreed to respond to a survey every weekend. Respondents are recruited by telephone. If they agree to participate and do not already have Internet access, they are provided with Internet access (and, if necessary, with a set-top box that can be used together with their television screen). Thus, the CentER-panel is not restricted to households with Internet access, but representative of the Dutch adult population except the institutionalized. Sample weights based upon data from Statistics Netherlands are used to correct for unit nonresponse. The sample that we use to estimate our model consists of about 2,000 respondents who participated in several interviews with questions on work disability in 2003.

From multiple waves of the data that have been collected in the past, the CentERpanel has a rich set of variables on background characteristics of the respondent and household, including their income and labor market status and several salient dimensions of health. In August 2003, we collected work disability self-reports and vignette evaluations (described in the following). In October 2003, we fielded a second wave of vignettes with slightly different wording of the questions and also included questions about reference groups. For our analysis, we will use the vignette and reference group data from this October wave. Appendix A lists the vignette questions. All vignettes are presented with either a female or a male name.[3]

For each of the vignettes, the respondent is asked the following question:

"Does . . . have a health problem that limits the amount or type of work he/she can do?"

with a five-point response scale:

---

3. Female or male names are assigned randomly. In appendix A, we only show one of the two names per vignette.

Table 7.1   Frequencies for vignette answers (CentERpanel, October 2003)

Affect vignettes	Affect 1	Affect 2	Affect 3	Affect 4	Affect 5
Not at all limited	41.2	96.2	11.1	18.7	2.2
Somewhat limited	49.7	2.8	44.3	44.8	8.4
Moderately limited	7.2	0.6	31.2	26.0	18.6
Severely limited	1.4	0.5	12.2	8.9	40.4
Extremely limited/cannot work	0.5	0.0	1.3	1.6	30.4
Pain vignettes	**Pain 1**	**Pain 2**	**Pain 3**	**Pain 4**	**Pain 5**
Not at all limited	22.5	8.2	0.6	0.3	0.8
Somewhat limited	61.8	47.1	6.6	6.2	12.9
Moderately limited	13.4	34.1	25.7	29.4	31.3
Severely limited	1.9	9.2	49.5	43.2	39.2
Extremely limited/cannot work	0.4	1.4	17.6	20.9	15.9
CVD vignettes	**CVD 1**	**CVD 2**	**CVD 3**	**CVD 4**	**CVD 5**
Not at all limited	91.2	10.6	1.8	20.7	6.7
Somewhat limited	7.8	46.2	18.2	44.9	34.1
Moderately limited	0.9	29.2	32.6	25.0	30.3
Severely limited	0.1	11.8	33.6	8.8	20.7
Extremely limited/cannot work	0.0	2.3	13.9	0.6	8.3

Notes: Data are weighted. $N = 1,980$ (complete sample). See appendix A for the wordings of the vignette questions. CVD = cardiovascular disease.

not at all; yes, mildly limited; yes moderately limited; yes, severely limited; yes, extremely limited/cannot work.

Table 7.1 presents the response frequencies for each of the fifteen vignette questions. The differences in distributions of answers correspond quite well with the variation in severity of the conditions described in the vignettes. For example, in all three domains of affect, pain, and CVD (cardiovascular disease), the condition described in the third vignette seems much more severe than that described in the first, and respondents ranked them accordingly. Moreover, there was also a great deal of consistency among respondents in how they ordered vignettes in terms of their severity, showing that respondents understood these experiments and took their responses seriously; see Banks et al. (2008) for details.[4]

Table 7.2 presents the distribution of the answers to the question on own work limitations by age group. These represent answers to the following question:

4. This does not imply that everyone ranks the vignettes in the same order. In some cases where average vignette rankings are quite similar (such as the vignettes Pain 3 and Pain 4 in table 7.1), order reversals frequently occur. The econometric model is able to capture this using idiosyncratic errors in the vignette evaluations; see section 7.3.

Table 7.2   Distribution of self-reported work disability by age (%)

	Age group						
	15–24	25–34	35–44	45–54	55–64	65+	Total
Not at all limited	86.8	74.1	69.2	55.9	52.8	48.4	63.1
Somewhat limited	5.4	20.7	17.5	24.2	28.5	34.3	22.8
Moderately limited	5.8	3.2	5.8	7.0	10.5	10.9	7.1
Severely limited	2.0	0	2.1	2.9	1.8	3.7	2.2
Extremely limited/cannot work	0	1.8	5.4	9.9	6.3	2.8	4.8
No. of observations	68	362	438	460	336	316	1,980

Notes: Data are weighted. $N = 1{,}980$ (complete sample).

"Do you have an impairment or health problem that limits you in the amount or kind of work you can do?".

The question allows respondents to reply on the five-point scale:

(1) No, not at all, (2) Yes, I am somewhat limited, (3) Yes, I am rather limited, (4) Yes, I am severely limited, (5) Yes, I am very severely limited—I am unable to work.

These response categories are identical to the ones used to gauge the severity of the vignette work limitations.

Table 7.2 implies that about 37 percent of the Dutch population reports to have at least a mild work limitation and about 14 percent have a work-limiting health problem or impairment that they gauge as moderately limiting or worse. Not surprisingly, work-related health deteriorates with age (although cohort effects may also play some role in this pattern).

The most interesting groups are probably people in the age groups forty-five to fifty-four and fifty-five to sixty-four. For them, the prevalence of work-limiting health problems is large, and this will often be an important reason not to participate in the labor market. For the sixty-five-plus, work-limiting health problems are even more prevalent, but these people are almost always retired anyhow because the Netherlands has mandatory retirement at age sixty-five for almost all employees.

Appendix B presents some of the questions about reference groups asked in the October wave and used in the empirical analysis. Our operationalization of a reference group is the circle of acquaintances mentioned in these questions. The first two reference group questions provide information on the modal age and modal education level in the respondent's reference group. In the analysis, we will combine the age and education categories into a smaller number of broader brackets. Table 7.3 presents descriptive statistics for our independent variables, including the responses to the first two reference group questions listed in appendix B. For example, 27 percent of

Table 7.3   **Sample statistics for independent variables**

	Mean or percent
Stroke	1.3
Cancer	3.8
Lung disease	6.0
Heart disease	7.1
High blood pressure	19.2
Diabetes	4.8
Emotional problems	11.0
Arthritis	10.4
Problems with vision	3.8
Often pain	25.4
Age in years	47.6
Low education level	39.1
Medium education level	38.7
High education level	22.1
Female	49.9
Northern provinces	14.3
Eastern provinces	21.6
Western provinces	38.7
Southern provinces	25.5
Age in reference group	
<25	8.7
25–35	20.2
36–45	27.0
46–55	19.7
56–65	14.7
66+	9.8
Low education level in reference group	24.9
Medium education level in reference group	47.9
High education level in reference group	27.2

Notes: Data are weighted. $N = 1,764$ (estimation sample). All variables other than "Age in years" are dummies. The table gives the percentage of observations for which the dummy has a value of 1. Northern provinces are Groningen, Friesland, and Drenthe; eastern provinces are Overijssel, Flevoland, and Gelderland; western provinces are Utrecht, Noord-Holland, and Zuid-Holland; southern provinces are Zeeland, Noord-Brabant & Limburg.

all respondents report that most of the people in their reference group are in the age group thirty-six to forty-five. About 48 percent say that most of their acquaintances have a medium education level (while almost 39 percent of the respondents has that level).

The other reference group questions refer to the number of acquaintances receiving disability benefits, separately for men and women. These are the crucial variables for our analysis as they measure DI benefit receipt in the reference group. For men, we will use the number of male acquaintances on disability benefits; for women, we will only consider the female acquaintances. We discuss the sensitivity of our results to this definition of the reference group variables in section 7.4.1.

Table 7.4   Distribution of disability in the reference group by age (%)

	Age group						
	15–24	25–34	35–44	45–54	55–64	65+	Total
Men							
None	82.9	65.6	52.5	55.1	39.4	53.8	56.7
Very few	17.1	31.5	41.5	36.6	44.1	34.7	35.5
A few/many	0	2.9	5.9	8.4	16.5	11.4	7.8
No. of observations	29	174	221	248	196	199	1,067
Women							
None	76.4	67.8	60.7	62.6	58.9	55.2	62.6
Very few	23.6	29.0	35.7	30.4	32.9	38.2	32.4
A few/many	0	3.2	3.6	7.1	8.2	6.5	5.0
No. of observations	39	188	217	212	140	117	913

Notes: Data are weighted. $N = 1,980$ (complete sample).

The distribution of reported DI receipt in the reference group by gender and age group is presented in table 7.4. Here, and in the rest of the chapter, we combine the categories of prevalence of DI receipt in the reference group to three: "Nobody," "Very Few," "A Few/Many," because the frequencies for "Few" and particularly "Many" are small. Young people typically know no one on disability benefits. The number of reference group members on disability benefits is highest for fifty-five to sixty-four-year-old respondents, who also most commonly receive disability benefits themselves. People older than sixty-five may often have a work disability (see table 7.2), but table 7.4 shows they hardly ever receive disability benefits—they receive a state pension and usually one or more additional occupational pensions. The number of women on disability benefits in women's reference groups is typically smaller than the number of men on disability benefits in men's reference groups, particularly at older ages. This may be because women in older cohorts often stopped working at an early age (usually to raise children) and never qualify for disability benefits after that.

Plausibly, these reference group variables are endogenous to the respondent's own work disability—respondents who have a work disability will often not work and will not only receive disability benefits, but will also more easily get acquainted with other people on disability benefits. Hence, we will treat the number of acquaintances on disability benefits as a dependent variable, modeled jointly with work limitations. Table 7.5 shows cross tabs of self-reported work limitations and self-reported prevalence of DI receipt in one's reference group. For simplicity of presentation, we combine categories for self-reported work disability to three: "Not Limited," "Mildly Limited," "Moderately Limited/Severely Limited/Extremely Limited." The table clearly illustrates a positive relation between self-reported work limita-

Table 7.5   **Self-reported work disability and reference group disability**

Self-reported work disability	Disability in the reference group (%)			
	None	Very few	A few/many	Total
Not limited	60.4	35.0	4.6	100.0
	70.6	66.2	41.5	66.9
Mildly limited	55.4	34.7	9.9	100.0
	21.7	22.0	30.0	22.4
Moderately, severely, and extremely limited	41.3	39.2	19.6	100.0
	7.7	11.9	28.5	10.7
Total	57.3	35.4	7.4	100.0
	100.0	100.0	100.0	100.0

Notes: Data are weighted. $N = 1,764$ (estimation sample). Row percentages (first line) and column percentages (second line).

tions and the number of people in one's reference group drawing disability benefits.

There are several competing explanations for this positive association. First of all, there may be a causal effect of the prevalence of DI receipt in one's reference group on the tendency to report work limitations. Second, as discussed in the preceding, it is possible that respondents with work limitations are more likely to associate with others who have a work disability (e.g., because of the existence of networks of people with work disabilities). Third, there may be other (observed or unobserved) factors that both increase the likelihood that respondents have a work limitation and the probability that they know others with work limitations. One such factor is age. Fourth, response scales used in answering the reference group questions might be correlated with response scales in self-reported work disability. Respondents may, for instance, exaggerate the number of friends or acquaintances on DI to "justify" their own report of a work limitation (Bound 1991). These explanations are not mutually exclusive. We think these explanations are the most plausible ones, but undoubtedly there are more. For example, knowing many people on disability benefits might increase genuine work disability. We are particularly interested in the role played by the first explanation, reflecting a social interaction effect. In the next section, we present a model that aims at isolating the importance of the first explanation; in the discussion of the results, we will also return to the competing explanations.

7.3   A Model with Reference Groups

Our econometric model explains the reported number of people receiving disability benefits in the reference group R (see table 7.4), self-reported work disability Y (see table 7.2), and reported work disability of the fifteen vignette persons $Y^1, \ldots, Y^{15}$ (see table 7.1).

7.3.1   Self-Reports of Own Work Disability

Individuals evaluate the extent of their work disability with a self-evaluation of whether their health problems and working conditions are sufficiently problematic to place them above their own subjective threshold of being somewhat limited or more than somewhat limited. The result of that evaluation depends on the extent of their true health problems as well as their subjective thresholds of what constitutes a disability, both of which vary across individuals.

More formally, self-reported work disability Y of respondent i is modeled on a three-point scale of "not at all limited," "somewhat limited," and "more than somewhat limited" (combining the three most serious categories "moderate," "severe," and "extreme," to one) as follows:

(1) $Y_i^* = X_i\beta + \varepsilon_i$

(2) $Y_i = j$ if $\tau_i^{j-1} < Y_i^* \le \tau_i^j, j = 1, 2, 3.$

For notational convenience, we define $\tau_i^0 = -\infty$ and $\tau_i^3 = \infty$. The remaining thresholds τ_i^1 and τ_i^2 will be modeled as functions of observable and unobservable respondent characteristics as described in section 7.4.1. The error term ε_i is assumed to be standard normally distributed. (Complete assumptions on error terms are given in section 7.3.5.)

Because thresholds depend on respondent characteristics, self-reported work disability alone is not enough to distinguish between variation in Y_i^* (that is, genuine variation in work-related health) and variation in the thresholds (that is, variation in what constitutes a disability in respondents' perceptions). Vignettes are used to identify this distinction.

7.3.2   Vignette Evaluations

The vignettes provide all respondents with the descriptions of the same set of work disability problems. As a consequence, variation in how respondents evaluate the given health problems informs us about variation in the subjective thresholds used by the respondents. More formally, the evaluations Y_i^l of vignettes $l, l = 1, \ldots, 15$, are given by

(3) $Y_i^{l*} = \theta^l + \delta F_i^l + \varepsilon_i^l$

(4) $Y_i^l = j$ if $\tau_i^{j-1} < Y_i^{l*} \le \tau_i^j, j = 1, 2, 3.$

Here F_i^l is a dummy variable indicating whether the person described in the vignette is female ($F_i^l = 1$) or male ($F_i^l = 0$). This specification follows earlier work by Kapteyn, Smith, and van Soest (2007), who find that respondents (both males and females) tend to be "harsher" on female than on male vignette persons, that is, $\delta < 0$. We assume that all ε_i^l are independent of each other and of the other error terms and follow a normal distribution with mean zero and variance σ_v^2. Thus, the ε_i^j are interpreted as idiosyncratic noise driving vignette evaluations; they reflect arbitrariness in each separate evaluation. If respondents have a persistent tendency to give low or high evaluations, this will not be captured by ε_i^j but by an unobserved heterogeneity term in the response scales; see section 7.3.3.

7.3.3   Response Scale Thresholds

The crucial assumption guaranteeing that vignettes help to identify response scale differences is that individuals use the same scales in evaluating themselves as they do with the vignette persons (*response consistency; see* King et al. 2004). The thresholds used in the vignette evaluation can vary across all types of individual attributes. In this study, we expand the set of attributes and include the number of persons among friends and acquaintances who are on disability benefits R_i^*. The thresholds τ_i^1 and τ_i^2 are modeled as follows:

(5) $$\tau_i^1 = X_i\gamma_1 + \gamma_1^R R_i^* + \xi_i$$

(6) $$\tau_i^2 = \tau_i^1 + e^{X_i\gamma_2 + \gamma_2^R R_i^*}.$$

We have included the vector X_i of respondent characteristics (independent of all error terms) to allow for a rather general way in which response scales vary with individual characteristics. The distance between the two thresholds is also allowed to depend on these characteristics. The exponential forces it to be positive, as in King et al. (2004). The key parameters of interest are γ_1^R and γ_2^R, the estimated impact of the number of people on DI in one's reference group on the threshold that is used to evaluate work disability. In particular, γ_1^R is expected to be negative: people who know many people on disability benefits will think of work disability as something common and will more often evaluate people (including themselves) as work disabled, thus using lower thresholds.[5]

The term ξ_i reflects unobserved heterogeneity in thresholds. For computational convenience, we do not allow for unobserved heterogeneity in the distance between the two thresholds. ξ_i is assumed to follow a normal distribution with variance σ_ξ^2, independent of X_i and all other unobservables in the model except one: the unobserved component of the thresholds driving the answer to the question how many people in the respondent's reference group receive disability benefits (ϕ_i^1 and ϕ_i^2; see section 7.3.4).

7.3.4   DI Receipt in the Reference Group

As explained in the preceding, we consider DI receipt in the respondent's reference group of the respondent's own sex and combine the outcomes

---

5. In the empirical work, we will allow the parameters γ_1^R and γ_2^R to depend on education level, age, and gender. For notational convenience, we do not make this explicit in the notation.

"few" and "many" because of the small number of observations with the latter outcome. Thus, we obtain an ordered response variable with three possible outcomes, $j = 1$ ("none"), $j = 2$ ("very few"), and $j = 3$ ("a few" or "many"). This will be modeled with an ordered probit equation:

(7) $$R_i^* = X_i \beta^R + \omega_i^R, \; \omega_i^R \sim N(0, \sigma_\omega^2)$$

(8) $$R_i = j \text{ if } \phi_i^{j-1} < R_i^* \le \phi_i^j, j = 1, 2, 3.$$

For notational convenience, we define $\phi_i^0 = -\infty$ and $\phi_i^3 = \infty$. In the following, we will further specify the thresholds ϕ_i^1 and ϕ_i^2. The vector X_i of respondent characteristics driving DI receipt in the reference group is assumed to be independent of all the errors in the model. Equation (7) has a "reduced form" nature in the sense that we do not explicitly model how work disability and labor force status affect disability in the reference group. The exogenous determinants of labor force status and disability are included among the regressors X_i to account for this.

Because it is likely that there are common unobserved factors affecting both the number of people one knows on disability benefits and one's own evaluation of work disability, we allow for a nonzero correlation coefficient ρ between ε_i and ω_i^R. This correlation also allows for the role of actual labor force status (which is not included explicitly in the model but "substituted out"): work disability drives labor force status, and labor force status drives the composition of the reference group.

We allow for a common unobserved heterogeneity component driving the thresholds $\tau_i^j, j = 1, 2$ and the thresholds in the reference group equation $\phi_i^k, k = 1, 2$ by specifying $\phi_i^1 = \phi_{0,1} + \mu\xi_i$ and $\phi_i^2 = \phi_{0,2} + \mu\xi_i$. We normalize $\phi_{0,1} = 0$. The parameter μ could be positive (respondents exaggerating their work disability also exaggerate the number of their acquaintances on DI) or negative (respondents who think of work disability as something exceptional will tend to interpret a given number of acquaintances on DI as large).[6] $\phi_{0,2}$ and μ are additional parameters to be estimated. Define $u_i^R = \omega_i^R - \mu\xi_i$. By way of normalization, we set $\text{Var}(u_i^R) = 1$. We can then rewrite equation (8) as

(9) $$R_i = j \text{ if } \phi_0^{j-1} < X_i\beta^R + u_i^R \le \phi_0^j, j = 1, 2, 3.$$

7.3.5   Error Terms and Identification

The error terms in the model, including unobserved heterogeneity components, are $\varepsilon_i, \varepsilon_i^l, l = 1, \ldots, 15, \omega_i^R$, and ξ_i. We assume they are all normally distributed and independent of the regressors X_i and F_i^l. The only correlation we allow for is between ε_i and ω_i^R. We assume $(\varepsilon_i, \omega_i^R)$ is bivariate normal with correlation coefficient ρ. The assumption that ξ_i is independent of ε_i implies

---

6. It seems natural to add another error term to the ϕ_i^j that is independent of everything else, but this will be subsumed in ω_i^R.

that people with higher thresholds do not tend to have larger or smaller genuine work disability (on a continuous scale), keeping observed characteristics X_i and V_i constant. The assumption seems quite plausible although one might argue that lower thresholds point at unobserved characteristics such as pessimistic views that can also genuinely reduce respondents' ability to work. As we shall see, the assumption is largely innocuous and does not affect identification of the structural parameters. To judge to what extent our assumptions impose restrictions and to investigate identification, it is useful to rewrite the model introduced so far somewhat.

Combine equations (1) and (2) to obtain

(10) $$Y_i = j \text{ if } \tau_i^{j-1} < X_i\beta + \varepsilon_i \le \tau_i^j, j = 1, 2, 3.$$

Similarly, combine equations (3) and (4):

(11) $$Y_i^l = j \text{ if } \tau_i^{j-1} < \theta^l + \delta F_i^l + \varepsilon_i^l \le \tau_i^j, j = 1, 2, 3.$$

Combining equation (10) with equations (5) and (6) leads to the following observational rule for observed work disability reports:

(12) $Y_i = 1$ if $X_i\beta + \varepsilon_i \le X_i\gamma_1 + \gamma_1^R R_i^* + \xi_i$

$Y_i = 2$ if $X_i\gamma_1 + \gamma_1^R R_i^* + \xi_i < X_i\beta + \varepsilon_i \le X_i\gamma_1 + \gamma_1^R R_i^* + \xi_i + e^{X_i\gamma_2 + \gamma_2^R R_i^*}$

$Y_i = 3$ if $X_i\beta + \varepsilon_i > X_i\gamma_1 + \gamma_1^R R_i^* + \xi_i + e^{X_i\gamma_2 + \gamma_2^R R_i^*}$

Inserting equation (7) into equation (12), this can be rewritten as

(13) $Y_i = 1$ if $X_i[\beta - \gamma_1 - \gamma_1^R\beta^R] \le \xi_i + \gamma_1^R\omega_i^R - \varepsilon_i$

$Y_i = 2$ if $\xi_i + \gamma_1^R\omega_i^R - \varepsilon_i < X_i[\beta - \gamma_1 - \gamma_1^R\beta^R]$
$$\le \xi_i + \gamma_1^R\omega_i^R - \varepsilon_i + e^{X_i[\gamma_2 + \gamma_2^R\beta^R] + \gamma_2^R\omega_i^R}$$

$Y_i = 3$ if $X_i[\beta - \gamma_1 - \gamma_1^R\beta^R] > \xi_i + \gamma_1^R\omega_i^R - \varepsilon_i + e^{X_i[\gamma_2 + \gamma_2^R\beta^R] + \gamma_2^R\omega_i^R}.$

Similarly, combining equation (11) with equations (5) and (6) and inserting equation (7) yields

(14) $Y_i^l = 1$ if $\theta^l + \delta F_i^l - X_i[\gamma_1 + \gamma_1^R\beta^R] \le \xi_i + \gamma_1^R\omega_i^R - \varepsilon_i^l$

$Y_i^l = 2$ if $\xi_i + \gamma_1^R\omega_i^R - \varepsilon_i^l < \theta^l + \delta F_i^l - X_i[\gamma_1 + \gamma_1^R\beta^R]$
$$\le \xi_i + \gamma_1^R\omega_i^R - \varepsilon_i^l + e^{X_i[\gamma_2 + \gamma_2^R\beta^R] + \gamma_2^R\omega_i^R}$$

$Y_i^l = 3$ if $\theta^l + \delta F_i^l - X_i[\gamma_1 + \gamma_1^R\beta^R] > \xi_i + \gamma_1^R\omega_i^R - \varepsilon_i^l$
$$+ e^{X_i[\gamma_2 + \gamma_2^R\beta^R] + \gamma_2^R\omega_i^R}.$$

For completeness, we repeat the equation for reference group disability (equation [8]):

(15) $$R_i = j \text{ if } \phi_0^{j-1} < X_i\beta^R + u_i^R \le \phi_0^j, j = 1, 2, 3.$$

We can see from equations (13), (14), and (15) that the stochastic behavior of the system is determined by the following composite error terms:

$\xi_i + \gamma_1^R \omega_i^R - \varepsilon_i$, $\xi_i + \gamma_1^R \omega_i^R - \varepsilon_i^l$, u_i^R ($= \omega_i^R - \mu \xi_i$), and ω_i^R (in the exponent). All of these error terms are allowed to be correlated with each other, the only restriction being that the covariance matrix of $\xi_i + \gamma_1^R \omega_i^R - \varepsilon_i^l$, ($l = 1, \ldots 15$) has a one-factor structure.

Next we turn to identification. First consider equation (15). Making the normalizing assumptions that $\phi_0^1 = 0$ and $\mathrm{Var}(u_i^R) = 1$, the vector β^R is identified. The vignette equations (equation [14]) next identify θ^l, δ, $\gamma_1 + \gamma_1^R \beta^R$ and $\gamma_2 + \gamma_2^R \beta^R$, where we normalize $\theta^1 = 0$. Because $\gamma_1 + \gamma_1^R \beta^R$ is identified, β is identified from equation (13). The remaining issue is how to identify γ_1^R and γ_2^R. Because $\gamma_1 + \gamma_1^R \beta^R$, and β^R are identified, we can identify γ_1^R if there is at least one exclusion restriction on γ_1. In other words, equation (15) needs to contain at least one X variable that is not present in equation (5). A similar exclusion restriction identifies γ_2^R. Once γ_1^R and γ_2^R are identified, γ_1 and γ_2 are identified as well.

Thus, identification of the reference group effect requires exclusion restrictions—variables that affect DI receipt in the reference group but do not have a direct effect on the evaluation threshold. For this, we use the directly elicited reference group variables on the typical age and education of respondents' acquaintances. These variables are allowed to affect response scales (represented by the thresholds τ_i^j) only through the reference group variable R_i^*. Because there are more reference group variables than needed for identification, we can perform a test exploiting overidentifying restrictions to investigate the plausibility of the exclusion restrictions. As we will see in the empirical results section, the restrictions are not rejected by the overidentification test.

As in all models with reference group effects, identifying the causal effect of the reference group variable requires model assumptions due to endogeneity issues and confounding effects (cf. Manski 1993). A crucial difference with the case discussed by Manski (1993) is that we have direct information on reference group disability receipt. As we have seen in the preceding, this identifies β^R and, hence, in combination with at least one exclusion restriction, we can identify γ_1^R and γ_2^R.

7.4   Results

We estimate the model using simulated maximum likelihood. Details of the likelihood function are presented in appendix C. The integrals in the likelihood contributions (equation [C6] in appendix C) are replaced by smooth simulation-based approximations, by drawing 200 times from the joint distribution of ξ and u^R and using Halton draws.[7] Experiments with a substantially larger number of draws did not lead to appreciable differences

---

7. We have used the program mdraws written by Lorenzo Cappellari and Stephen P. Jenkins. See Cappellari and Jenkins (2006).

in the results, implying that the number of draws is large enough to provide an accurate approximation of the integral.

7.4.1   Estimation Results

Table 7.6 presents the estimation results for the equation for own work disability (equation [1]) and for DI receipt in the reference group (equation [7]). The estimates for the threshold equations (5) and (6) are given in table 7.7. Estimates for the vignette equations (equation [3]) are not of primary interest; they are presented and briefly discussed in table 7A.1 in appendix D.

Table 7.6   **Estimation results for own work disability and receipt of DI benefits in the reference group**

	Self-reported disability		Reference group disability	
	Coefficient	Standard error	Coefficient	Standard error
Age	−0.189	0.224	0.423	0.138
Age squared	0.017	0.020	−0.031	0.013
Medium education level	0.043	0.091	0.089	0.074
Higher education level	−0.085	0.105	−0.046	0.075
Female	0.003	0.075	−0.334	0.062
Age in reference group				
25–35	0.339	0.233	0.058	0.057
36–45	0.383	0.266	0.107	0.077
46–55	0.859	0.296	0.124	0.087
56–65	0.599	0.319	0.058	0.079
>65	0.636	0.333	−0.010	0.084
Medium education level in reference group	−0.246	0.093	0.016	0.027
High education level in reference group	−0.383	0.113	0.009	0.032
Northern provinces	0.061	0.124	−0.081	0.101
Eastern provinces	−0.026	0.104	−0.083	0.089
Western provinces	0.078	0.090	−0.285	0.073
Stroke	1.250	0.337	−0.029	0.244
Cancer	0.357	0.144	−0.193	0.157
Lung disease	0.661	0.142	0.281	0.132
Heart disease	0.825	0.132	−0.004	0.118
High blood pressure	0.029	0.086	0.069	0.075
Diabetes	0.408	0.180	0.118	0.154
Emotional problems	0.639	0.103	0.285	0.099
Arthritis	0.425	0.120	0.197	0.108
Problems with vision	0.076	0.178	0.035	0.163
Often pain	1.260	0.083	0.258	0.077
Intercept	−1.077	0.510	−1.378	0.333
ρ	0.053	0.040		
φ_{02}			1.338	0.051

Table 7.7   Estimation results of threshold equations

| | Threshold shifts | | | |
| | γ_1 | | γ_2 | |
	Coefficient	Standard error	Coefficient	Standard error
Age	0.679	0.320	−0.104	0.037
Age squared	−0.055	0.027	0.009	0.003
Medium education level	0.157	0.102	−0.054	0.017
Higher education level	0.071	0.091	−0.040	0.016
Female	−0.373	0.187	0.024	0.016
Stroke	−0.110	0.320	−0.047	0.058
Cancer	−0.223	0.208	0.033	0.033
Lung disease	0.289	0.210	0.020	0.030
Heart disease	0.053	0.143	−0.065	0.029
High blood pressure	0.062	0.097	0.016	0.016
Diabetes	0.085	0.188	0.019	0.034
Emotional problems	0.238	0.186	−0.030	0.022
Arthritis	0.195	0.163	−0.021	0.022
Problems with vision	−0.038	0.198	0.031	0.036
Often pain	0.321	0.157	−0.025	0.017
Northern provinces	−0.128	0.128	0.022	0.021
Eastern provinces	−0.155	0.111	0.023	0.019
Western provinces	−0.347	0.167	0.046	0.017
Intercept	−2.068	0.898	0.259	0.108
μ	−0.968	0.023		
σ_ξ	0.733	0.072		

| | Interactions | | | |
| | γ_1^R | | γ_2^R | |
	Coefficient	Standard error	Coefficient	Standard error
Age 35–64	0.034	0.042	−0.085	0.029
Age 65+	0.173	0.051	−0.072	0.028
Medium education level	0.049	0.045	−0.079	0.031
Higher education level	0.021	0.072	−0.009	0.040
Female	0.106	0.043	−0.111	0.031
Intercept	−1.333	0.554	0.249	0.059

Work Disability Self-Reports

The equation for own work disability in table 7.6 shows that there is virtually no gender difference (keeping other variables constant). Own work disability decreases with age until age fifty-six (age is measured in decades) and increases afterward; it is lower for higher-educated individuals than for respondents with low education. These effects are not statistically significant, however. Regional differences are not significant either. As expected, work limitations are significantly more frequent among individuals with serious health conditions, such as strokes, heart problems, cancer, diabetes, emotional problems, pain, and lung problems. Having a reference group with more medium or high education significantly reduces work disability.

DI Receipt in the Reference Group

The reference group DI receipt equation shows that the reported prevalence of DI receipt in the reference group increases with age until about retirement age (the estimated quadratic age function reaches a maximum at sixty-seven years of age). This is consistent with the fact that in the Netherlands, individuals over sixty-five typically do not receive DI benefits but receive state and occupational pensions instead. There is virtually no relation between DI receipt in the reference group and education. On the other hand, DI receipt in the reference group increases significantly with several health conditions (lung disease, emotional problems, pain), in line with the argument that people with a health problem will more often be acquainted with other people in poor health. Also in line with the raw data (table 7.4) is that females are significantly less likely to report to have DI-benefit recipients in their (female) reference group. Respondents in the western provinces of the country (the most urbanized region) are less likely to know people on disability benefits than respondents in the rest of the country.

The variables affecting the number of people on DI in the reference group are of interest in part because, as we shall see in the following, the number of people in the reference group significantly affects the thresholds used in evaluating work disability. For example, women know fewer people on DI and because of that will less easily say that a given health problem constitutes a work disability. Similarly, having pain increases the number of people on DI in one's reference group, and this makes people with pain "softer" in evaluating disability. These indirect effects come on top of the direct effects that gender and health conditions may have on the thresholds (see the following).

Thresholds

The results for the threshold equations are presented in table 7.7. We note that the overidentifying restrictions stemming from the fact that the reference group variables are not included in these equations do not get rejected ($\chi^2(12) = 11.382$; $p = .503$). The top panel presents estimates for the coefficients on individual characteristics in equations (5) and (6), while the bottom part shows the estimates of the coefficients of peer group DI receipt R_i^* interacted with education, age, and gender in both threshold equations. The estimates for the first threshold imply that women use lower thresholds than men with the same other characteristics and, thus, more easily regard a given health problem as work limiting. People with higher education are less likely to evaluate a given health problem as work limiting than low-educated respondents, but the educational differences are not statistically significant.

The age pattern is significant, and the age function has a maximum at about sixty-two years, implying that until age sixty-two, older people are "tougher," that is, less likely to call a condition work disabling. The only significant health condition is pain—respondents who often suffer from pain less easily evaluate a given health problem as a (mild or worse) work limitation, possibly because they are more used to performing work or daily activities in spite of the handicap of their health problem.

For the distance between the first and second threshold (γ_2), results are quite different. The age function has a minimum at fifty-six years of age (if $R_i^* = 0$), while higher education leads to a smaller distance between thresholds. Heart problems do the same; these are the only type of health problems with a significant effect. The estimates are difficult to interpret individually due to the complexity of the model, where the same variables appear in several equations.

The model parameters of primary interest are the coefficients γ_1^R and γ_2^R on peer group DI receipt R_i^*. Both have been specified as a function of education level, age, and gender (see the bottom panel of table 7.7). Consider first the estimated main effect and the interactions with education. For males under thirty-five with lower education, γ_1^R is estimated at -1.33; for otherwise identical individuals with medium education, the estimate is -1.28 (not significantly different from the -1.33 estimate), while for the higher educated, the estimate is -1.31. Females are significantly less influenced by DI receipt in their reference group than males; for example, for a lower-educated woman younger than thirty-five, the peer group effect is -1.23 (versus -1.33 for males). The significantly positive interaction of DI receipt in the reference group with the age dummy for sixty-five-plus shows that the response scale of individuals over sixty-five is less influenced by the number of DI recipients in their reference group than the response scale of younger individuals: the peer group effects are -1.16 for men over age sixty-five and -1.05 for women over age sixty-five.

Because the estimated value of γ_1^R is negative in all cases, the fraction of people who are on DI benefits in the reference group will unambiguously shift the reporting threshold for at least a mild working disability downward. In this sense, γ_1^R is the more critical parameter of the two. The estimates for γ_2^R show that the distance between the two thresholds increases with the number of friends and acquaintances on disability benefits, particularly for young males with the lowest education level. In simulations using the estimates of both γ_1^R and γ_2^R, we find that if the number of people on DI in the reference group increases, this raises both the fraction of those reporting they are somewhat limited and the fraction of those reporting they are moderately limited or worse, showing that the effect of R^* on γ_1^R dominates the effect on γ_2^R.

As mentioned earlier, we defined reference groups separately for men and women in the sense that for women we took the number of women on DI amongst female acquaintances and for men the number of male DI recipients among male acquaintances. One question is how sensitive the results in table 7.7 are to this particular specification of reference groups. To test this, we reestimated the model using a common definition of reference groups for both sexes.[8] The estimated effects of the number of people on DI in the reference group are even larger using the common reference by gender than with the benchmark definition used for table 7.7. A likelihood ratio test, however, indicates that the model with separate reference groups by gender for which we present the results is significantly better than the alternative model.

Covariance Structure of the Errors

Table 7.6 shows that the parameter ρ, the correlation between the error terms in the equations for own work disability (equation [1]) and DI receipt in the reference group (equation [7]) is small and insignificant. This is surprising because we would expect that work disability (and thus the unobserved factors driving it) positively affects the number of acquaintances on DI receipt.

Unobserved heterogeneity in thresholds is significant—the estimated standard deviation of ξ is 0.73 and is very accurately determined (σ_ξ in table 7.7). To judge its size, it can be compared to the amount of idiosyncratic noise in self-reports and vignette evaluations. The former has standard deviation 1 (by normalization), the latter has standard deviation 0.51 (see table 7A.1). Thus, unobserved heterogeneity in the thresholds explains about 35 percent of the unsystematic variation in self-reports and about 60 percent of the unsystematic variation in vignette evaluations.

The parameter μ is estimated at -0.97. Because $u_i^R = \omega_i^R - \mu\xi_i$ and $\text{Var}(u_i^R) = 1$ by means of normalization, we have $\text{Var}(\omega_i^R) = 0.50$. The implied correlation between ξ_i and u_i^R is equal to 0.71. The sign of μ implies that respondents who use relatively high thresholds for answering questions about their own work limitations (given their observed characteristics) will tend to use relatively low thresholds when asked for DI prevalence in the reference group. Thus, someone who is unlikely to refer to a health problem as work limiting has a tendency to consider work limitations as more of an exception and will sooner consider a given number of people on DI in the reference group as "many."

8. All respondents were asked both the number of men and the number of women on DI in their reference group. To form a common definition for men and women, we used the maximum of the two. Thus, if for an individual respondent there were a lot of individuals of one gender who were more than somewhat limited, that is the value that applies.

Table 7.8   Model predictions of self-reported work disability and reference
                 group disability

Self-reported work disability	Disability in the reference group (%)			
	None	Very few	A few/many	Total
Not limited	61.3	32.7	6.0	100.0
	74.0	63.2	53.9	68.6
Mildly limited	50.6	39.7	9.7	100.0
	16.6	20.9	23.8	18.7
Moderately, severely, and extremely limited	42.1	44.6	13.3	100.0
	9.4	15.9	22.3	12.7
Total	57.1	35.2	7.7	100.0
	100.0	100.0	100.0	100.0

Notes: Data are weighted. $N = 1,764$ (estimation sample).

7.4.2   Model Performance

Table 7.8 provides a simple way of checking the fit of the model. Its structure is similar to that of table 7.5, but it reports simulated frequencies using the model instead of actual frequencies in the data. Comparing table 7.8 with table 7.5 suggests that the fit of the model is fairly good; judging from the marginal distributions, the model does a good job in replicating reported reference group DI receipt; it does a slightly worse job in reproducing the distribution of self-reported disability. The biggest deviation between the data and the model predictions occurs in the middle category (mildly limited). According to the data, 22.4 percent of the respondents classify themselves as mildly limited (table 7.5), whereas the model predicts 18.7 percent in that category (table 7.8).

7.4.3   Simulation of Reference Group Effects

One way to gauge the strength of the reference group effects is to artificially vary the number of people on DI in an individual's reference group and then to evaluate how this affects the prevalence of self-reported work limitations. We do this by varying the intercept in the equation for the number of people in the reference group on DI (equation [7]) and then simulate the reports of DI-benefit receipt in the reference group and the prevalence of self-reported work disability induced by that new level of reference group DI receipt.

Figure 7.1 shows the results for both the full sample and for the sample broken down by education. In each picture, the horizontal axis is the percentage of respondents who say that they know at least a few DI-benefit recipients, with the vertical lines representing the sample (or subsample) percentages (except the left vertical line in the first figure, see the following). The vertical axis represents the percentage who report that they suffer from

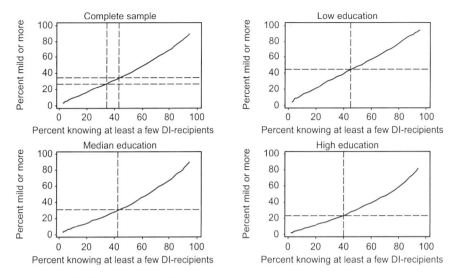

Fig. 7.1   Self-reported work disability and reference group DI

at least a mild work limitation; the horizontal line indicates the (sub)sample percentage (except the lower line in the first figure).

The graphs in the figures illustrate the sensitivity of reporting a work disability to DI receipt in the reference group. In line with the estimation results in table 7.6, the level of the curve is highest for the low educated and lowest for those with a high education level. This difference in levels implies that at the same level of perceived reference group DI benefit receipt, lower-educated respondents are more likely to report at least a mild work limitation than respondents with middle or higher education. In all cases, there is a notable peer group effect of DI receipt in the reference group on the probability to report a work disability: if the respondent knows more people on DI benefits, the chances of reporting a disability increase substantially.

To illustrate the size of the effect, in the picture for the full sample, additional horizontal and vertical lines have been drawn, both below the sample averages. The horizontal line is based on the finding of Kapteyn, Smith, and van Soest (2007) that if US scales are assigned to Dutch respondents, self-reported work limitations in the Netherlands would fall by 21 percent.[9] This second horizontal line can thus be interpreted as self-reported work limitations in the Netherlands if the Dutch respondents with the Dutch work limitations would use the American response scales. The second vertical line shows that if the percentage of individuals saying they know at least a few DI-benefit recipients in their reference group were to move from its

9. This is the finding in their benchmark model; the percentage varies somewhat depending on which model specification is chosen.

simulated sample mean of 42.9 percent to about 33.9 percent (the left most vertical line), this would move the scales used by the respondents enough to reach the US scales.

7.5   Concluding Remarks

Most people do not live in social isolation. Instead, they interact repeatedly with family, friends, and neighbors. As a consequence of those pervasive interactions, they allow themselves to be transformed in many ways, a transformation of which they may often be unaware. One type of transformation involves the formation of social norms about what normal or acceptable behavior might be. These social norms then fix the scales that they may be using in responding to questions about their own behaviors and current situations. If they had different neighbors and friends, their self-descriptions about their lives may well be quite different. While this may be true within a country where there exists a shared history and culture, it is especially likely to be the case when cross-national comparisons are made.

In this chapter, we test the importance of these types of social interactions using a specific application—the probability that people self-label themselves as work disabled. We estimated a model of self-reported disability with an emphasis on how the reporting of disability is affected by the prevalence of DI receipt in one's reference group. We find an effect in the hypothesized direction—larger reported numbers of people in one's reference group on DI increase the likelihood of seeing oneself as having a work disability.

An alternative interpretation of our main finding has been suggested. It is reasonable to expect that people with lenient standards also perceive more of their friends as disabled. This could invalidate our interpretation if our reference group variable was the number of friends perceived as disabled, but this is not the case—it refers to the number of friends receiving disability insurance benefits—an objective criterion.

These findings are suggestive of how policy programs affect social norms. If a policy makes receipt of DI benefits more attractive or easier (e.g., by loosening eligibility requirements) thus increasing the number of DI recipients, this changes social norms. Individuals are now more likely to label a given health condition as work limiting and the prevalence of self-reported work will rise.

There are of course alternative reasons why self-reported disability and reported DI-benefit receipt in one's reference group would be correlated. Our model is designed to capture many of these reasons. These include the possibility that individuals with a work disability are more likely to associate with others who suffer a similar fate. First, we allow for a considerable number of observable covariates in common, which by itself will generate correlation between self-reported disability and reported DI-benefit receipt in one's reference group. But we also allow for correlation between the errors in the reference group equation and the equation predicting the probability that someone is work disabled.

Even within this reasonably general model, we find a direct effect of the number of people in one's reference group on disability programs on the probability one considers oneself work disabled. The effects that we estimate are sufficiently strong to explain a good deal of the higher rates of self-reported work disability in the Netherlands compared to the United States. The Dutch population appears to have much more lenient thresholds about what constitutes a work disability (Kapteyn, Smith, and van Soest 2007). The results in this chapter suggest that this tendency stems from the fact that the Dutch are much more likely to know people on work disability programs, a direct consequence of the far more generous programs in the Netherlands as well as its more lenient rules for program eligibility at the time of the survey.

Appendix A
Vignette Questions

Vignettes for Affect

1. [Henriette] generally enjoys her work. She gets depressed every three weeks for a day or two and loses interest in what she usually enjoys but is able to carry on with her day-to-day activities on the job.

2. [Jim] enjoys work very much. He feels that he is doing a very good job and is optimistic about the future.

3. [Tamara] has mood swings on the job. When she gets depressed, everything she does at work is an effort for her, and she no longer enjoys her usual activities at work. These mood swings are not predictable and occur two or three times during a month.

4. [Eva] feels worried all the time. She gets depressed once a week at work for a couple of days in a row, thinking about what could go wrong and that her boss will disapprove of her condition. But she is able to come out of this mood if she concentrates on something else.

5. [Roberta] feels depressed most of the time. She weeps frequently at work and feels hopeless about the future. She feels that she has become a burden to her coworkers and that she would be better dead.

Vignettes for Pain

1. [Katie] occasionally feels back pain at work, but this has not happened for the last several months now. If she feels back pain, it typically lasts only for a few days.

2. [Catherine] suffers from back pain that causes stiffness in her back especially at work but is relieved with low doses of medication. She does not have any pains other than this generalized discomfort.

3. [Yvonne] has almost constant pain in her back, and this sometimes prevents her from doing her work.

4. [Jim] has back pain that makes changes in body position while he is working very uncomfortable. He is unable to stand or sit for more than half an hour. Medicines decrease the pain a little, but it is there all the time and interferes with his ability to carry out even day-to-day tasks at work.

5. [Mark] has pain in his back and legs, and the pain is present almost all the time. It gets worse while he is working. Although medication helps, he feels uncomfortable when moving around and when holding and lifting things at work.

Vignettes for CVD

1. [Trish] is very active and fit. She takes aerobic classes three times a week. Her job is not physically demanding, but sometimes a little stressful.

2. [Norbert] has had heart problems in the past, and he has been told to watch his cholesterol level. Sometimes if he feels stressed at work, he feels pain in his chest and occasionally in his arms.

3. [Paul]'s family has a history of heart problems. His father died of a heart attack when Paul was still very young. The doctors have told Paul that he is at severe risk of having a serious heart attack himself and that he should avoid strenuous physical activity or stress. His work is sedentary, but he frequently has to meet strict deadlines, which adds considerable pressure to his job. He sometimes feels severe pain in chest and arms and suffers from dizziness, fainting, sweating, nausea, or shortness of breath.

4. [Tom] has been diagnosed with high blood pressure. His blood pressure goes up quickly if he feels under stress. Tom does not exercise much and is overweight. His job is not physically demanding, but sometimes it can be hectic. He does not get along with his boss very well.

5. [Dan] has undergone triple bypass heart surgery. He is a heavy smoker and still experiences severe chest pain sometimes. His job does not involve heavy physical demands, but sometimes at work he experiences dizzy spells and chest pain.

Appendix B

Reference Group Questions

The questions are preceded by the following introduction: *The following questions concern your circle of acquaintances, that is, the people with whom you associate frequently, such as friends, neighbors, acquaintances, or maybe people at work.*

- If you think of your circle of acquaintances, into which age category do MOST of these people go? Please select the answer that is closest to reality.

   Age (in years) is mostly: 1. under 16; 2. 16–20; 3. 21–25; 4. 26–30; 5. 31–35; 6. 36–40; 7. 41–45; 8. 46–50; 9. 51–55; 10. 56–60; 11. 61–65; 12. 66–70; 13. 71 or over

- Which level of education do most of your acquaintances have?

   1. primary education; 2. junior vocational training; 3. lower secondary education; 4. secondary education/preuniversity education; 5. senior vocational training; 6. vocational colleges/first-year university education; 7. university education

- If you think of the men among your acquaintances, how many of them are on DI?

   1. Nobody; 2. Very few; 3. A few; 4. Many

- If you think of the women among your acquaintances, how many of them are on DI?

   1. Nobody; 2. Very few; 3. A few; 4. Many

Appendix C
Likelihood Contributions

Compared to the models in King et al. (2004) and Kapteyn et al. (2007), there are two complications: the thresholds now depend on an unobserved variable R^* and upon an unobserved heterogeneity term ξ. Replacing R^* using equation (7) and exploiting equations (5) and (6) gives:

(C1) $$\tau_1 = V\gamma_1 + \gamma_1^R X^R \beta^R + \xi + \gamma_1^R(u^R + \mu\xi),$$

(C2) $$\tau_2 = \tau_1 + e^{V\gamma_2 + \gamma_2^R X^R \beta^R + \gamma_2^R(u^R + \mu\xi)}.$$

Equations (1) and (2) imply

(C3) $$Y = j \text{ if } \tau_{j-1} - X\beta < \varepsilon < \tau_j - X\beta.$$

Similarly, for the vignette evaluations, we get:

(C4) $$Y^l = j \text{ if } \tau_{j-1} - \theta^l - \delta F^l < \varepsilon^l < \tau_j - \theta^l - \delta F^l.$$

The probability of observing a certain reference group category follows from equation (9):

(C5) $$R = j \text{ if } \phi_{0,j-1} - X^R \beta^R < u^R < \phi_{0j} - X^R \beta^R$$

Let the reported reference group variable be r, the observed work disability self-report y, and the observed vignette evaluations $y^1, \ldots, y^L$. Then the likelihood contribution of a given respondent can be written as a two-dimensional integral over the values of u^R that result in $R = r$ and all possible values of ξ:

(C6) $\displaystyle\int_{-\infty}^{\infty}\int_{\phi_{0,j-1}-X^R\beta^R}^{\phi_{0,j}-X^R\beta^R} P(Y = y\,|\,u^R,\xi)\prod_{l=1}^{L}P(Y^l = y^l\,|\,u^R,\xi)f(u^R\,|\,\xi)du^R\,\frac{1}{1\sigma_\xi}\phi\left(\frac{\xi}{\sigma_\xi}\right)d\xi,$

where ϕ is the standard normal density, and f is the conditional density of u^R given ξ, which is univariate normal. Of course, the crucial point here is that, conditional on u^R and η, all vignette evaluations and the self-report are mutually independent, allowing for the factorization in equation (C6). The conditional probabilities in equation (C6) follow from equations (C3) and (C4), together with the normality assumptions on the error terms, implying that the ε^l are independent of ε, ξ, and u^R but that $\varepsilon|(u^R, \xi) \sim N(\rho u^R, 1 - \rho^2)$:

$$P(Y = y\,|\,u^R,\xi) = \Phi\left(\frac{\tau_y - X\beta - \rho u^R}{\sqrt{1-\rho^2}}\right) - \Phi\left(\frac{\tau_{y-1} - X\beta - \rho u^R}{\sqrt{1-\rho^2}}\right)$$

$$P(Y^l = y^l\,|\,u^R,\xi) = \Phi\left(\frac{\tau_{y^l} - \theta^l - \delta F^l}{\sigma_\upsilon}\right) - \Phi\left(\frac{\tau_{y^l-1} - \theta^l - \delta F^l}{\sigma_\upsilon}\right),$$

where the $\tau_{...}$ are given by equations (C1) and (C2) and depend on ξ and u^R.

Appendix D
Estimates of the Vignette Equation (Equation [3])

The dummy coefficients in table 7A.1 reflect the average severity of the work limitations described in the vignettes. One can relate the dummy coefficients θ^l, $l = 1, \ldots, 15$ to the relative frequencies in table 7.1—vignettes that are evaluated as more severely on average have higher coefficients. The estimate of δ, the coefficient of the dummy for a female vignette name, is small and insignificant. The estimated idiosyncratic variation in vignette evaluations σ_υ (independent across vignettes) is smaller than the unsystematic variation in self-assessments ($\sigma_\varepsilon = 1$, by means of normalization). Still, the idiosyncratic terms ε_υ are large enough in comparison to the differences in the estimated coefficients on the vignette dummies θ^l to explain that the same vignettes are often ranked in different ways by different respondents—in line with what is seen in the data.

Table 7A.1	Estimates of vignette equations	
Vignette	Coef.	s.e.
1	—	
2	–1.295	0.067
3	0.716	0.041
4	0.541	0.032
5	1.246	0.066
6	0.302	0.025
7	0.758	0.039
8	1.589	0.079
9	1.549	0.077
10	1.360	0.069
11	–0.962	0.050
12	0.685	0.037
13	1.149	0.060
14	0.487	0.030
15	0.795	0.044
σ_v	0.515	0.024
δ	–0.006	0.019

References

Aarts, L., R. Burkhauser, and P. de Jong. 1996. *Curing the Dutch Disease: An International Perspective on Disability Policy Reform.* Advanced Textbooks in Economics. Avebury, UK: Aldershot.

Alessie, R., and A. Kapteyn. 1991. "Habit Formation, Interdependent Preferences and Demographic Effects in the Almost Ideal Demand System." *Economic Journal* 101:404–19.

Angelucci, M., and G. D. Giorgi. 2009. "Indirect Effects of an Aid Program: How Do Cash Transfers Affect Ineligibles' Consumption?" *American Economic Review* 99 (1): 468–508.

Audretsch, D., and M. Feldman. 1996. "R&D Spillovers and the Geography of Innovation and Production." *American Economic Review* 86:630–40.

Bala, V., and S. Goyal. 1998. "Learning from Neighbours." *Review of Economic Studies* 65:595–622.

Banerjee, A. V. 1992. "A Simple Model of Herd Behavior." *Quarterly Journal of Economics* 107:797–817.

Banks, J., A. Kapteyn, J. P. Smith, and A. van Soest. 2008. "Work Disability is a Pain in the *****, Especially in England, the Netherlands, and the United States." In *Health at Older Ages: The Causes and Consequences of Declining Disability Among the Elderly,* edited by D. Cutler and D. Wise, 251–94. Chicago: University of Chicago Press.

Becker, G. S. 1974. "A Theory of Social Interactions." *Journal of Political Economy* 83 (6): 1063–93.

Bound, J. 1991. "Self-Reported versus Objective Measures of Health in Retirement Models." *Journal of Human Resources* 26 (1): 106–38.

Bound, J., and R. Burkhauser. 1999. "Economic Analysis of Transfer Programs Targeted on People with Disabilities." In *Handbook of Labor Economics*. Vol. 3C, edited by O. Ashenfelter and D. Card, 3417–3528. Amsterdam: Elsevier.

Cappellari, L., and S. Jenkins. 2006. "Calculation of Multivariate Normal Probabilities by Simulation, with Applications to Maximum Simulated Likelihood Estimation." IZA Discussion Paper no. 2112. Bonn, Germany: Institute for the Study of Labor.

Case, A., and L. Katz. 1991. "The Company You Keep: The Effects of Family and Neighborhood on Disadvantaged Youth." NBER Working Paper no. 3705. Cambridge, MA: National Bureau of Economic Research.

Duesenberry, J. 1949. *Income, Saving and the Theory of Consumer Behavior.* Cambridge, MA: Harvard University Press.

Duflo, E., and E. Saez. 2003. "The Role of Information and Social Interactions in Retirement Plan Decisions: Evidence from a Randomized Experiment." *Quarterly Journal of Economics* 118 (3): 815–42.

Ginther, D., R. Haveman, and B. Wolfe. 2000. "Neighborhood Attributes as Determinants of Children's Outcomes: How Robust are the Relationships?" *Journal of Human Resources* 35 (4): 603–42.

Glaeser, E. L., B. Sacerdote, and J. A. Scheinkman. 1996. "Crime and Social Interactions." *Quarterly Journal of Economics* 111 (2): 507–48.

———. 2000. "The Social Multiplier." *Journal of the European Economic Association* 1 (2–3): 345–53.

Hanushek, E., J. Kain, J. Markman, and S. Rivkin. 2003. "Does Peer Ability Affect Student Achievement?" *Journal of Applied Econometrics* 18 (5): 527–44.

Haveman, R., and B. Wolfe. 2000. "The Economics of Disability and Disability Policy." In *Handbook of Health Economics*. Vol. 1B, edited by J. Newhouse and A. Culyer, 995–1051. Amsterdam: Elsevier.

Kapteyn, A., J. P. Smith, and A. H. van Soest. 2007. "Vignettes and Self-Reports of Work Disability in the U.S. and the Netherlands." *American Economic Review* 97 (1): 461–73.

Kapteyn, A., S. van de Geer, H. van de Stadt, and T. Wansbeek. 1997. "Interdependent Preferences: An Econometric Analysis." *Journal of Applied Econometrics* 12 (6): 665–86.

King, G., C. Murray, J. Salomon, and A. Tandon. 2004. "Enhancing the Validity and Crosscultural Comparability of Measurement in Survey Research." *American Political Science Review* 98 (1): 567–83.

Kuhn, P., P. Kooreman, A. R. Soetevent, and A. Kapteyn. 2011. "The Effects of Lottery Prizes on Winners and Their Neighbors. Evidence from the Dutch Postcode Lottery." *American Economic Review* 101 (5): 2226–47.

Manski, C. F. 1993. "Identification of Endogenous Social Effects." *Review of Economic Studies* 60 (3): 531–42.

Topa, G. 2001. "Social Interactions, Local Spillovers and Unemployment." *Review of Economic Studies* 68 (2): 261–95.

Veblen, T. 1899. *The Theory of the Leisure Class.* New York: Dover.

Woittiez, I., and A. Kapteyn. 1998. "Social Interactions and Habit Formation in a Model of Female Labour Supply." *Journal of Public Economics* 70:185–205.

Comment   David M. Cutler

Arthur van Soest and colleagues have written a very interesting paper on reference groups and self-reported health. The basis of their paper is a simple correlation. People with more "disabled" friends are more likely to be "disabled." The quotation marks around disability refer to the fact that the entire notion of what it means to be disabled is up in the air, given that it is not a perfectly measurable term. The magnitude of this correlation is large: 20 percent of those who are moderately, severely, or extremely limited report that their reference group has a few or many disabled people, compared to only 5 percent of those who are not limited.

The question is why this is the case. Van Soest and colleagues put forward two explanations. The first explanation is that it is a reporting effect. People who know more disabled people are more aware of what disability means and, hence, view their own health as worse. The second theory is sorting of friends: disabled people find it more pleasurable to be with other disabled people, and nondisabled people prefer the company of other nondisabled people.

One cannot tell these two theories apart without some objective evidence. In this case, the objective evidence consists of assessments of disability for hypothetical individuals who are asked of all people—that is, vignettes. If the issue is perception of health status, then having more friends who are disabled will lower the trigger point for calling a person disabled. This will show up as greater reports of disability among the vignettes. If the issue is selection of friends, in contrast, that will not be the case. Rather, there will be a correlation between the error term in the self-assessment of disability and the error term in the share of friends who are on disability. That is, people who happen to have more friends who are disabled will themselves be more disabled. But this will not affect the vignette answers.

Somewhat surprisingly, van Soest et al. conclude that the reporting effect is the dominant explanation. People report vignette individuals as more likely to be disabled when they have more friends who are disabled. And conditional on Xs (most importantly age), people who self-report disability are no more likely to have friends who are disabled.

The lack of evidence for sorting of friendships is intriguing and puzzling. How can it not be that disabled people know more disabled people? One institutional detail that would help flesh out these findings is to know more about who people consider their friends in the Netherlands. If friends are largely work-related, one would be hard-pressed to imagine this correlation

David M. Cutler is the Otto Eckstein Professor of Applied Economics at Harvard University and a research associate of the National Bureau of Economic Research.

For acknowledgments, sources of research support, and disclosure of the author's material financial relationships, if any, please see http://www.nber.org/chapters/c12442.ack.

not existing. After all, work is not a place where disabled people gather. If friendships were formed around neighborhoods, churches, soccer teams, or other leisure pastimes, in contrast, the idea is more plausible. Thus, it would be nice to see a bit more about how the Dutch social structure influences these findings.

The use of vignettes in this setting is novel and important. The authors have done an excellent job of framing and analyzing the vignette data. They talk about vignettes in other papers, but it would be nice to know a bit more about how plausible the responses to them are. The authors note that, on average, people judge vignettes with greater problems to be more disabled. But the outliers are curious. For example, consider the question: [*Jim*] *enjoys work very much. He feels that he is doing a very good job and is optimistic about the future. "Does Jim have a health problem that limits the amount or type of work he can do?"* The vast bulk of people rate Jim as not at all limited. But .5 percent of the sample—about ten people—report that Jim is extremely limited or cannot work. Do these people simply misunderstand the question? Are they playing games with the interviewers? Do the same people report strange answers to other questions? It would be good to explore the unusual responses in more detail. For example, are people consistent, in the sense that everyone ranks the vignettes that are objectively in worse health as more limited than the ones in objectively better health?

There is one other theory that the authors do not explore but that would be good to consider. It may be that having disabled friends makes one feel worse. For example, disabled people may complain about their health, and this may lead a person to notice their own health limitations more. In terms of the model in the chapter, having disabled friends may translate the same physical health impairment into a greater degree of self-perceived limitation.

There are a couple of ways the authors can test this. First, they could use an objective standard. For example, if it is known that two people can each walk one mile in about the same time, does the person with more friends who are disabled report themselves as more limited? Alternatively, it may be that the authors can look at self-assessments along the scales likely to reflect self-perceived limitations the most, given the objective conditions of their life. For example, do people with more disabled friends report more pain, even given a set of health impairments? Is emotional status worse for people with more disabled friends, even given their relationships and job characteristics? It may be that the translation from objective health status into true self-perceived health differs across individuals.

In sum, this is an excellent chapter that makes a good deal of progress on a very difficult question.

"Healthy, Wealthy, and Wise?" Revisited
An Analysis of the Causal Pathways from Socioeconomic Status to Health

Till Stowasser, Florian Heiss, Daniel McFadden, and Joachim Winter

8.1 Introduction

In health economics, there is little dispute that the socioeconomic status (SES) of individuals is positively correlated with their health status. The size of the body of literature documenting that wealthy and well-educated people generally enjoy better health and longer life is impressive.[1] The robustness of this association is underscored by the fact that the so-called health-wealth gradient has been detected in different times, countries, populations, age structures, and for both men and women. Moreover, the results are largely insensitive to the choice of SES measures (such as wealth, income, education, occupation, or social class) and health outcomes.

While the existence of the gradient may be uncontroversial, the same cannot be said about its explanation. Medical researchers, economists, and other social scientists have developed a large number of competing theories that can broadly be categorized as follows: there may be causal effects from SES

Till Stowasser is a PhD student at the Ludwig Maximilian University of Munich. Florian Heiss is chair of the Statistics and Econometrics Department at the Johannes Gutenberg University of Mainz. Daniel McFadden is the E. Morris Cox Professor of Economics at the University of California, Berkeley, the Presidential Professor of Health Economics at the University of Southern California, and a research associate of the National Bureau of Economic Research. Joachim Winter is chair for empirical research in economics at the Ludwig Maximilian University of Munich.

We are grateful to Bob Willis and participants of the 2011 National Bureau of Economic Research (NBER) Economics of Aging conference for helpful comments. Financial support was provided by the National Institute on Aging (NIA) grant no. P01-AG005842. For acknowledgments, sources of research support, and disclosure of the authors' material financial relationships, if any, please see http://www.nber.org/chapters/c12443.ack.

1. Smith (1999) and Goldsmith (2001) provide extensive surveys of the earlier literature. A brief summary of more recent contributions to this field can be found in Michaud and van Soest (2008).

to health, causal effects that work in the opposite direction, and unobserved common factors that influence both variables in the same direction without a causal link between the two. Distinguishing among these explanations is important because they have different implications for public policy aimed at improving overall well-being. For instance, if causal links between wealth and health were confirmed, society would likely benefit from more universal access to health care and redistributive economic policy. Yet, if such causal links were rebutted, resources would be better spent on influencing health knowledge, preferences, and, ultimately, the behavior of individuals.

Besides its importance, the discrimination between these alternative hypotheses also poses a great methodological challenge because the variation found in observational data is typically endogenous. This is especially true for cross-sectional data, which only offers a snapshot of the association between health and wealth. Without further information on the history of both variables, the researcher faces a fundamental simultaneity problem, which makes the identification of causal paths a hopeless venture. A possible remedy consists of finding some sort of exogenous variation in SES or health to infer causality and the direction of its flow. This search, however, is typically quite difficult because convincing instrumental variables are very hard to come by. As a consequence, researchers often face the unattractive choice between the easy path of ignoring the endogeneity problem, which casts serious doubts on any drawn conclusions, and the more involved use of instrumental variable (IV) strategies that critically rely on the untestable quality of the instruments.

The nexus of health, wealth, and wisdom is also the subject of the study by Adams et. al. (2003; HWW henceforth). The authors propose an innovative approach that attempts to solve the preceding trade-off, on the premise that causal inference may be possible without having to isolate exogenous variation in SES. Their identification strategy consists of two main ingredients: first, they exploit the dynamic nature of panel data, focusing on health *innovations* rather than the prevalence of medical conditions. Second, they make use of the so-called Granger causality framework, which represents a purely statistical approach to the theory of causation. The great advantage of working with this alternative concept is that the detection of potential Granger causality is a rather easy task. While knowledge on the existence of Granger causality may not be useful in its own right, it allows for tests on the *absence* of "true" causality in a structural sense.

Applying this framework to the first three waves of the Asset and Health Dynamics among the Oldest Old (AHEAD) survey study, HWW find that in an elderly US population, causal channels that operate from wealth to health are an exception rather than the rule: while causality cannot be ruled out for some chronic and mental conditions for which health insurance coverage is not universal, SES is unlikely to be causal for mortality and most other illnesses. Considering these strong results, as well as the methodological novelty of HWW's approach, it is not surprising that their work has subsequently been the subject of vivid debate within the literature.[2] So far, the focus has clearly been on the validity of HWW's identification strategy in general, with some calling into question the ability to truly infer causality with a concept that arguably is a rather sparse characterization of causal properties.

We certainly agree that HWW's model would benefit from certain methodological refinements and plan to implement these in future research. For the present project, however, we deliberately leave the econometrics unchanged, to study a different aspect that also merits attention: the stability of HWW's results when confronted with new data that allows for hypothesis tests of greater statistical power. Special interest lies in assessing whether the somewhat surprising absence of direct causal links from SES to most medical conditions is a robust finding or perhaps the artifact of a particular data sample. Since the publication of HWW's original article, the AHEAD survey has been incorporated into the more-encompassing Health and Retirement Study (HRS). This permits deviations from HWW's data benchmark along the following dimensions: the same individuals can be tracked for a longer period of time, the analysis can be extended to new cohorts of respondents, and the working sample can be widened by including younger individuals aged fifty and older. The last point is of special interest as it offers variation in health insurance status that is not available in a Medicare-eligible population. To understand which of these data changes contribute to any deviating conclusions, we do not apply the whole bundle of modifications at once. Instead, we estimate the model multiple times, by applying it to several different data samples, which are gradually augmented along the dimensions just outlined.

We lay out the theoretical background of our analysis in section 8.2, where we review the potential explanations for the association between SES and health and specify the econometric challenges that arise when trying to discriminate among them. This is followed by a discussion of how to address these challenges. Section 8.3 describes the approach proposed by HWW. A reanalysis of HWW with new data is presented in section 8.4. Section 8.5 concludes and outlines topics for future research.

8.2   The Difficulty of Causal Inference

8.2.1   The Issue: Potential Channels between SES and Health

Correlation does not necessarily imply causation. This insight is one of the main lessons every empiricist needs to internalize. At times, however, it can be tempting to neglect this admonition, especially when a causal

---

2. As an example, consider the comments to HWW by Adda, Chandola, and Marmot (2003), Florens (2003), Geweke (2003), Granger (2003), Hausman (2003), Heckman (2003), Hoover (2003), Poterba (2003), Robins (2003), and Rubin and Mealli (2003) published in the same issue as the original article.

Table 8.1   Median wealth by self-rated health status by year

Self-rated health	1992	1996	2000	2004	2008
Excellent	155.6	192.0	256.0	331.4	363.0
Very good	122.1	159.0	202.6	240.0	304.0
Good	82.5	106.2	130.6	160.0	194.0
Poor	46.7	62.2	69.0	75.1	86.1
Fair	19.5	35.0	36.5	39.7	48.1

Notes: Calculations by authors based on HRS data. Numbers reported in thousands of US$.

interpretation of a joint motion of two variables is very intuitive. The relationship between SES and health is a prime example for such a situation. As an illustration, consider table 8.1, which lists household median wealth of HRS respondents arrayed against self-reported health status. Here, the wealth-health gradient is prominently on display as median wealth monotonically decreases with impairing health self-reports—an observation that is remarkably stable over time.

What could be more natural than to interpret this strong correlation as a causal influence of wealth on health? After all, it is the explanation best in line with conventional wisdom: money can buy (almost) anything—even better health. Yet the most intuitive conclusion may not necessarily be the only valid one. In fact, there are two additional hypotheses for the association of SES and medical conditions: the causation could flow from the latter to the former, and the correlation may actually be spurious, with third factors affecting health and wealth in a similar way. This section describes these rivaling theories and gives an overview of the most commonly cited potential pathways between SES and health (see Adler and Ostrove 1999; Smith 1999; Goldsmith 2001; and Cutler, Lleras-Muney, and Vogl 2011) for more extensive reviews).

Hypothesis A: SES Has a Causal Influence on Health Outcomes

This is the hypothesis most energetically advocated within the epidemiological literature. While it is true that the main contribution from economists consists of formulating alternative interpretations of the SES health gradient (see hypothesis B in the following), it should be emphasized that they are not on record of categorically challenging hypothesis A, either. In the following, we list the most prominent theories of channels through which SES may have a causal effect on health.

Channel A1: Affordability of Health Care. This potential channel is arguably one of the most intuitive explanations and may be active both before and after an individual is diagnosed with an illness. For one, varying SES may be responsible for differentials in the onset of health conditions as poorer people may be overly sensitive to the costs of preventive health care. In addition, wealth could play a crucial role in determining the quality or even the plain affordability of medical treatments once they become necessary.

Channel A2: The Psychological Burden of Being Poor. Medical scientists increasingly emphasize the importance of psychological consequences of low SES. They argue that low-wage employment is typically associated with a high degree of work monotonicity and low job control, leading to psychosocial stress. Similarly, economically disadvantaged individuals are believed to be repeatedly exposed to episodes of high emotional discomfort, either due to long phases of unemployment or a general feeling of social injustice. When accumulated, these stressful experiences may well have strong adverse effects on physical health as well. Furthermore, adverse wealth shocks—such as the loss of life savings in a stock market crash—are likely to cause anxiety and depression, representing a more immediate avenue through which SES may impact health.

Channel A3: Environmental Hazards. Another line of argument is that the exposure to perilous environments is considerably higher for the poor. This may concern job-related risks because it can be argued that workplace safety is lower and physical strain higher for poorly paid occupations. The reasoning also extends to people's living environments as neighborhood safety, dwelling condition, air and water quality, and so on are usually much better in exclusive residential areas.

Channel A4: Health Knowledge. Considering that education is an integral component of SES, it is conceivable that part of the correlation between SES and health is attributable to differences in health knowledge. According to this argument, information on medical risk factors or the importance of preventative care may be more widespread among the highly educated and wealthy, leading to healthier lifestyles and lower morbidity rates among this group.

Channel A5: Risk Behaviors. An often-cited pathway through which SES may influence health is the asymmetric distribution of unhealthy lifestyles such as smoking, drinking, and poor diet. To the extent that all of these vices are less common among the rich, health differentials may in fact be driven by SES variables. Note that the question of why smoking, excess alcohol consumption, and obesity are especially prevalent in lower social classes is interesting in its own right, with channels A2 and A4 potentially accounting for part of this relationship.

Hypothesis B: Health Has a Causal Influence on SES Outcomes

Economists and other social scientists were among the first to challenge the conception that causal mechanisms would work their way exclusively from SES to health. Much of this research is inspired by Grossman's (1972) health production framework, which models the impact of health capital on savings, labor market participation, and retirement decisions. We believe the following three channels to be the most important in describing causal effects from health to SES outcomes.

Channel B1: Productivity and Labor Supply. Arguably, the most relevant reason why health may be causal for SES outcomes can be found on the labor market. The productivity of an individual in poor health is generally lower than that of someone whose physical robustness allows for longer working hours, less absenteeism, and better career options. As a consequence, frail people will tend to earn lower wages and accumulate less assets throughout their life course. Adverse health shocks may even be so severe that people are forced to leave the labor market altogether, depriving them from any realistic chance to improve their SES.

Channel B2: Life Expectancy and Time Preferences. To the extent that severe illnesses increase mortality risks, there may be an impact of poor health on time preferences. Life-cycle models predict that the optimal response to a perceived reduction in life expectancy is to move consumption from an uncertain future toward the present. Thus, a history of dire medical events may induce individuals to dissave faster, establishing a causal link from health to SES.

Channel B3: Medical Care Expenditures. The most immediate form of impact health events can have on financial endowments are out-of-pocket costs of medical care. While it can be argued that the influence of this pathway should only be modest in size, this is certainly untrue for people without health insurance. In many cases, not even the insured are completely shielded from medical bills: the existence of deductibles and lifetime coverage limits poses great financial threats especially for the chronically ill.

Hypothesis C: SES and Health Are Jointly Caused by an Unobserved Third Factor

This hypothesis makes the case that the association between health and wealth could have other reasons than causal mechanisms between the two: there may be hidden third factors with a common influence on both SES and health, rendering the correlation among the latter spurious. This distinction is vital because policies that aim at improving health outcomes by, say, redistributing wealth are bound to be ineffective, as long as the true common cause remains unaffected.

Channel C1: Unobserved Genetic Heterogeneity. A good candidate for an unobserved common cause is genetic disposition. For instance, genetic frailty may reduce the physical resistance as well as the intellectual and professional skills of an individual. In such cases, health will be poorer and SES will be lower despite the absence of causal links among the two.

Channel C2: Unobserved Family Background. Genetic endowment is not the only determinant of people's physical and personal traits. Similarly influential are matters of parentage and upbringing. Especially, prenatal and early childhood nutrition as well as stress are believed to have lasting negative effects on well-being and functional abilities, establishing an association between health and SES that is similar to that of channel C1.

Channel C3: Unobserved Preferences. Irrespective of whether they are inherited or learned, preferences that influence certain behavior and lifestyles are another often-cited source of common effects. The prime example are descendants of dysfunctional families, who adopt both the unhealthy lifestyles (such as poor diet or smoking) and the unambitious attitudes toward education and work by which they are surrounded. Another example are time preferences: overly myopic people will underinvest in preventative medical care and in education because in both cases pay-offs will materialize in a distant future, to which only little importance is attached.

8.2.2   The Challenges: Simultaneity and Omitted Variables

The fact that all of the aforementioned hypotheses are generally plausible makes the inference on causation a methodologically challenging task. Suppose—as is the case for the remainder of this chapter—we were interested in testing the validity of hypothesis A, that is, whether SES has a causal effect on health outcomes. Ideally, we would want our analysis to rely on truly exogenous variation in SES variables, similar to that attained in controlled experiments. The reality for economists, however, is far from being ideal because the sources of variation we find in observational data is unknown to us. As a consequence, causal variables are potentially endogenous themselves.

The possible sources of endogeneity in the wealth-health case have been described in section 8.2.1. Ultimately, they generate two fundamental econometric challenges: we have to distinguish hypothesis A from hypothesis B and hypothesis A from hypothesis C. As we discuss in the following, the first consists of dealing with a simultaneity problem and the second of finding a solution to the problem of omitted variables.

Challenge 1: The Simultaneity Problem
(Hypothesis A versus Hypothesis B)

Imagine for a moment that hypothesis C could be dismissed so that any association between SES and health had to be due to either hypothesis A or B. Even with this kind of simplification in place, the identification of

SES causality for health is still difficult. Of course, we could regress our health variable of interest (H_i) on SES (S_i) and a vector of exogenous control variables $(\mathbf{X}_i)$, estimating the following equation with OLS:

$$(1) \qquad H_i = \theta_0 + \theta_s S_i + \mathbf{X}'_i \theta_x + \eta_i,$$

where i denotes the unit of observation, and η_i is the residual. Yet the crucial question is if we could interpret the parameter estimate $\hat{\theta}_s$ as the causal effect of SES on health. The answer would be affirmative if the structural model were to look like

$$E(H_i | S_i, \mathbf{X}_i) = \alpha + \beta S_i + \mathbf{X}'_i \gamma,$$

$$E(S_i | H_i, \mathbf{X}_i) = E(S_i | \mathbf{X}_i).$$

This model describes a world in which causality only flows from SES to health, with β capturing the true causal effect. In this world, $\hat{\theta}_s$ would indeed have a causal interpretation, with plim $\hat{\theta}_s = \beta$. However, the existence of hypothesis B indicates that the preceding model may not be a realistic description of reality. In fact, the true structural model is likelier to look like

$$(2) \qquad E(H_i | S_i, \mathbf{X}_i) = \alpha + \beta S_i + \mathbf{X}'_i \gamma,$$

$$(3) \qquad E(S_i | H_i, \mathbf{X}_i) = a + b H_i + \mathbf{X}'_i c,$$

with β again measuring the true causal effect of SES on health and b capturing any causation working its way in the opposite direction. Equations (2) and (3) describe a standard simultaneous-equation model (SEM) as both dependent variables are jointly determined with each being a function of the other. When trying to estimate this SEM by simply running regression equation (1), $\hat{\theta}_s$ will be subject to simultaneous-equation bias, picking up the information conveyed in b as well. As a result, the parameter of interest, β, is not identified, making a test for causation of SES to health all but impossible.

Challenge 2: The Omitted-Variable Problem
(Hypothesis A versus Hypothesis C)

Even in the absence of challenge 1, we would still face the problem of having to discriminate between hypotheses A and C. Presume we were able to plausibly exclude causal paths from health to SES. In this case, the identification problem no longer consists of confounding the causal effect of wealth on health with reverse causality. Instead, the question arises if an association between both variables is attributable to causality at all because it could also stem from a joint reaction to a third factor. As the review of hypothesis C has shown, all of these potential common causes (such as genetics or preferences) are inherently unobservable, rendering challenge 2 an omitted-variable problem.

Suppose the true structural model is best described by

(4) $$E(H_i | S_i, \mathbf{X}_i, C_i) = \alpha + \beta S_i + \mathbf{X}'_i \gamma + \delta C_i,$$

with C_i standing for an individual-specific variable that influences both SES and health. If this common cause were observable, we could simply include it in our regression function, and the causal effect, β, would be readily identified. However, given its omitted-variable nature, C_i will be swamped into the error term, as the comparison of the structural model in error form (equation [5]) with the estimable model (equation [6]) demonstrates:

(5) $$H_i = \alpha + \beta S_i + \mathbf{X}'_i \gamma + \delta C_i + \varepsilon_i,$$

(6) $$H_i = \alpha + \beta S_i + \mathbf{X}'_i \gamma + u_i.$$

Here, the well-behaved structural error is denoted by ε_i, whereas the composite residual is $u_i = \delta C_i + \varepsilon_i$. Given that C_i has an impact on our explanatory variable of interest, S_i, the latter will be endogenous because $\mathrm{cov}(S_i, u_i) \neq 0$. As a consequence, the estimation of this model by means of regression equation (1) will yield a parameter estimate $\hat{\theta}_s$ that suffers from omitted-variable bias, with plim $\hat{\theta}_s \neq \beta$. Importantly, $\hat{\theta}_s$ will absorb any causal impact that C_i may have on H_i. As a result, the presence of common effects could easily lead to erroneous conclusions of active causal links between wealth and health in cases where β actually equals zero.

Causal Inference in the Face of Both Challenges

Naturally, there is no reason to believe that both econometric problems are mutually exclusive. As a rule, they will be present at the same time, aggravating causal inference even more. Ultimately, we have to estimate a structural model that takes the following form:

(7) $$H_i = \alpha + \beta S_i + \mathbf{X}'_i \gamma + \underbrace{\delta C_i + \epsilon_i}_{=u_i},$$

(8) $$S_i = a + b H_i + \mathbf{X}'_i c + \underbrace{d C_i + e_i}_{=v_i},$$

with e_i denoting a structural error and v_i representing the composite unobservable. Given this multitude of potential confounders, we truly cannot expect the simple regression function 1 to uncover β, the structural parameter of interest. While this assessment is certainly sobering, it also sets a clearly defined bar for any alternative identification strategy: in order to be convincing, it has to live up to the challenges of simultaneity and omitted variables.

A common way of dealing with the potential endogeneity of SES is the use of instrumental variable (IV) estimators. The virtue of this approach is that—at least in theory—it solves both of these challenges at once. A good instrument is, however, hard to find in practice. In the context of SES-health causality, exogenous wealth shocks have been used as instrumental variables. For instance, Meer, Miller, and Rosen (2003) as well as Michaud and van Soest (2008) use inheritances. In a similar vein, Smith (2005) interprets the strong stock market surge in the 1990s as a positive wealth shock, and it is probably just a matter of time until we will see the first papers that make use of the exogenous variation in wealth caused by the recent global financial crisis.

We do not discuss IV approaches in detail, but we would like to point out one problem that arises in the analysis of the SES-health gradient. While the preceding instruments may well be exogenous and certainly have an impact on wealth, it is not entirely clear if the SES variation they induce is really that relevant for *health*. According to Grossman's (1972) standard economic model of health, an individual's general health status can be viewed as a latent capital stock that reflects the entire history of medically relevant events and behaviors. As a result, the human body will certainly react to current influences, but it will not forget how it was treated in the past either. This "memory effect" likely extends to any influence SES may have had during one's lifetime. In light of this, it is questionable whether sudden changes in wealth are really that informative when testing for causal links between SES and health. In fact, because an IV estimator makes use of exogenous variation in wealth *at one point in time* to identify β, there is a great chance that causal links from SES to health are statistically rejected even though they have been operating in the past.[3] Admittedly, an IV estimator will still capture any *instantaneous* impact a wealth shock would have on health outcomes. As a renewed look at the potential causal pathways for hypothesis A suggests, immediate effects are most likely to arise through channel A2 if wealth shocks are severe enough to have direct psychological consequences.

8.3   The Approach of the HWW Study

The previous section demonstrates that the identification of causal paths between health and wealth with IV approaches is not always feasible. Especially, the isolation of truly exogenous and yet meaningful variation in SES poses considerable problems. On this account, HWW propose an alternative identification strategy that avoids this critical step altogether. In fact, they make use of the entire observed variation in SES variables, tacitly accepting that some of it may well be of endogenous nature. The authors argue that, in spite of this methodological simplification, their approach still allows for at least indirect inference of causal links from SES to health.[4]

---

3. In this light, it is not too surprising that none of the aforementioned studies using wealth shocks as an instrument for SES was able to find evidence supportive of hypothesis A.

4. In their article, HWW also formulate tests on causality working in the opposite direction. However, the authors themselves are quite skeptical about this part of their analysis, admitting that it is likely subject to model misspecification. As they stop short of endorsing their own results, we follow their lead and concentrate on the more promising test of hypothesis A.

Naturally, HWW need to find convincing answers to the two econometric challenges described in section 8.2.2. When testing hypothesis A, they face challenge 1 of excluding the possibility that any observed comovement of wealth and health is in reality due to reverse causality. In addition, they have to tackle challenge 2 of ruling out that the association is driven by unobserved common effects.

8.3.1   Challenge 1: Ruling Out Hypothesis B

Distinguishing hypotheses A and B without the aid of IVs is a difficult task. We may observe that the poor are less healthy, but we have no information on which happened first: were people already poor before they got sick, or were they already sick before they became poor? With cross-sectional data that only offers a snapshot of this association, there is no way of finding out. Panel data, on the other hand, provide valuable information on transitions in health and wealth, making it possible to analyze the dynamics of their relationship and to identify the direction of the causality flow. Imagine we were to analyze the dependence of health *innovations* on past levels of SES. As long as one agrees that a cause must precede its effect, we can be sure that the (unanticipated) onset of an illness at time t cannot have caused the amount of wealth or education at time $t - 1$. Given there is any causation at work, it must flow from the past to the present, or—as in this case—from SES to health innovations.

HWW take this insight to heart by applying their framework to the first three panel waves of the aforementioned AHEAD survey study, which spans the years between 1993 and 1998 and is representative of the US population aged seventy and older. They propose a dynamic model of health incidence that takes the following form:

$$(9) \qquad f(HI_{it}^j | \mathbf{HI}_{it}^{k<j}, \mathbf{H}_{it-1}, \mathbf{S}_{it-1}, \mathbf{X}_{it-1}),$$

where i once again stands for the unit of observation (in this case: household) and the newly introduced t denotes time. The index j stands for the respective health condition as the authors apply their model to twenty different medical outcomes.[5] The dependent variable, HI_{it}^j, measures a new incidence of a given health condition.[6] According to this model, a health innovation is potentially influenced by the following explanatory variables:

---

5. These include acute illnesses (cancer, heart disease, stroke), mortality, chronic conditions (lung disease, diabetes, high blood pressure, arthritis), accident-related events (incontinence, severe fall, hip fracture), mental problems (cognitive impairment, psychiatric disease, depression), as well as information on interview status (self versus by proxy), BMI, smoking behavior, ADL/IADL impairments, and self-rated health.

6. Note that this measure of health innovation *cannot* be interpreted as a simple change in health status ($\Delta H_{it}^j = H_{it}^j - H_{it-1}^j$) because HI_{it}^j generally captures deteriorations in health only. For chronic illnesses, such as diabetes, it measures when the condition was first diagnosed. For acute health events, such as stroke, HI_{it}^j indicates every new occurrence.

Past Level of SES

The vector S_{it-1} includes five SES variables, namely wealth, income, years of education, dwelling condition, and neighborhood safety. These are the variables of main interest. Conceptually, if SES had any direct causal impact on health, we would expect to observe that rich individuals are less likely to develop a new medical condition compared with poor individuals. While this finding alone would not yet prove the existence of a causal link from SES to health, confounding with reverse causality could be ruled out because S_{it-1} precedes HI_{it}^j.

Past Health Status

New medical events are likely influenced by a respondent's health history as well. This may take the form of state dependence (e.g., past cancer influences the onset of new cancer) and comorbidities (e.g., past cancer influences the onset of depression). For this reason, HWW control for vector H_{it-1}, containing the past levels of all twenty health conditions.

Current Health Incidences with Immediate Impact

In theory, health innovations could also be influenced by contemporaneous shocks in SES or other health conditions. This constitutes a problem for HWW's concept of dealing with simultaneity as it critically relies on the ability to observe the timing of innovations in both variables. HWW solve this problem by imposing further structure: On the one hand, they make the assumption of no instantaneous causation of SES to health shocks, arguing that any causal action as described by channels A1 to A5 takes time.[7] On the other hand, they impose a chain structure on contemporaneous health innovations, grouping them in the order in which instantaneous causality is most likely to flow.[8] Thus, they include the vector $HI_{it}^{k<j}$, containing the incidence variables for all health conditions $(1, \ldots, k)$ that are causally arranged upstream of condition j.

Demographic Control Variables

Finally, the authors control for a number of demographic factors that could have an impact on health events, too. The corresponding vector, X_{it-1}, includes the respondent's age, marital status, as well as information on the parent's mortality and age at death.

7. The authors themselves make the point that this assumption loses its innocuousness if the time intervals between panel waves become too large because even the more inertial causal links will then have enough time to unfold. Given that the AHEAD study is conducted biennially, the time aggregation to observation intervals may indeed reintroduce some degree of simultaneity.

8. HWW list cancer, heart disease, and stroke first because they can have an immediate impact on mortality. The other medical conditions are grouped such that degenerative illnesses can cause chronic diseases, which, in turn, may influence accidents and finally mental health. Importantly, instantaneous causality is not designed to flow in the opposite direction.

Building on model 9, HWW design a test for noncausality of SES in the spirit of Granger (1969) and Sims (1972). This so-called Granger causality (or G-causality) approach is a purely statistical take on the concept of causation, having its origin in the time series literature. Formally, SES is not Granger causal for health condition j if

(10) $f(HI_{it}^j | \mathbf{HI}_{it}^{k<j}, \mathbf{H}_{it-1}, \mathbf{S}_{it-1}, \mathbf{X}_{it-1}) = f(HI_{it}^j | \mathbf{HI}_{it}^{k<j}, \mathbf{H}_{it-1}, \mathbf{X}_{it-1})$,

that is, HI_{it}^j is conditionally independent of $\mathbf{S}_{it-1}$, given $\mathbf{HI}_{it}^{k<j}$, $\mathbf{H}_{it-1}$, and $\mathbf{X}_{it-1}$. Intuitively, given health history, knowledge of SES history must not contribute to the predictability of health innovations. The test is implemented by estimating the model by maximum likelihood (ML) both unconstrained (with $\mathbf{S}_{it-1}$ as regressors) and constrained (without $\mathbf{S}_{it-1}$) and by subsequently comparing the log likelihoods of both versions. The motivation for this likelihood ratio test is that the two values should be the same if the null hypothesis of noncausality is true.

The detection of Granger causality, however, does not guarantee the presence of "true" causality in a structural sense, which is the concept we are ultimately interested in.[9] Admittedly, information on the presence of G-causality is helpful when predicting health innovations for an individual with *given* health and SES history. However, the reduced-form nature of G-causality renders it unsuitable to predict the effects of (economic) policy interventions. If SES is Granger causal for health innovations, we only know that, for instance, the onset of an illness is likelier for a person with low SES. Yet we do not know if this statistical dependence is due to a real causal link from wealth to health (hypothesis A) or due to unobserved common effects (hypothesis C). Given the diverging policy conclusions both interpretations would trigger, HWW also need to address the second methodological challenge of dealing with the omitted-variable problem.

8.3.2   Challenge 2: Ruling Out Hypothesis C

Most of the omitted variables identified in section 8.2.1 to potentially have a common influence on health and SES are unobservable by definition. As a result, challenge 2 cannot simply be resolved by improvements in data quality and the addition of missing variables to the vector of covariates. HWW also refrain from making use of fixed-effects estimation, which represents another common strategy to heal omitted-variable bias in cases where

9. There are three major "schools" of causal analysis: the structural approach (S-causality) described by Hoover (2001) and Hausman (2003) that is grounded in econometric simultaneous equations models, the potential-outcomes approach (P-causality) characterized by Rubin (1974) and Heckman (2000) that is based on the analysis of experimental treatments and the time series prediction approach (G-causality) employed here. The conventional interpretation of "true" causality is arguably best described by S- and P-causality treatments. In fact, Pearl (2000) demonstrates a formal equivalence between the two concepts. Both of these schools are critical of G-causality, arguing that its purely positivistic approach does not realistically characterize causal properties.

panel data is available. In fact, the efforts made by the authors to distinguish between structural causality and common effects are limited to using a rich set of covariates in the hope that this will mitigate the importance of unobservables. They argue that:

> [F]or example, genetic frailty that is causal to both health problems and low wages, leading to low wealth, may be expressed through a health condition such as diabetes. Then, onset of new health conditions that are also linked to genetic frailty may be only weakly associated with low wealth, once diabetic condition has been entered as a covariate. (6)

Despite this conciliating argument, HWW acknowledge that the failure to cleanly identify causal structures questions their approach's ability to gauge the effects of "out-of-sample" policy changes. To address this issue, they scrutinize the generality of their results by adding invariance tests to the analysis. Intuitively, a model is only suitable for the sort of predictions HWW have in mind if it remains valid under different scenarios than those covered by the data, or—as the authors put it—if it has the invariance property of being valid for each possible history. For instance, if the application of the model to different populations, time periods, and policy regimes had a negligible impact on estimation results, there would be reasonable hope that the Granger noncausality tests are indeed informative. The invariance tests as implemented by HWW mainly inspect the stability of findings across time. Model 9 is estimated by stacking the data for the two available panel wave transitions (i.e., W1 → W2 and W2 → W3) above another. The same model is also estimated for both wave transitions individually, and a test statistic is constructed that compares the log-likelihoods of these three estimations. The motivation for this likelihood ratio test is similar to that of a Chow test. If the null hypothesis of model invariance is true, estimated parameters of the stacked model should not differ from those of the two single-transition models.

All told, HWW apply the following system of noncausality and invariance tests to the estimations of all twenty health conditions: First, they test for Granger noncausality of SES for health innovations in the stacked version of the model under the maintained assumption of invariance (S|I). Then, they employ an unconditional invariance test, as described in the preceding (I), followed by an invariance test with noncausality imposed (I|noS). Finally, they implement a joint test of invariance and noncausality (S&I). Conceptually, HWW condition the validity of their noncausality tests on the outcome of the corresponding invariance test: only if invariance is confirmed will they put faith in the model's results. The authors are optimistic that with these refinements in place, their model is well placed to make meaningful predictions even if it fails to identify true causal links, stating that:

> [I]t is unnecessary for this policy purpose to answer the question of whether the analysis has uncovered a causal structure in any deeper

sense. Econometric analysis is better matched to the modest task of testing invariance and non-causality in limited domains than to the grander enterprise of discovering universal causal laws. However, our emphasis on invariance properties of the model, and on tests for Granger causality within invariant families, is consistent with the view of philosophers of science that causality is embedded in "laws" whose validity as a description of the true data generation process is characterized by their invariance properties. (10)

They even go a step further and suggest that their approach—while not powerful enough to distinguish between causation and common effects—permits at least the one-sided test for the *absence* of true causal links. Essentially, they view Granger causality as a necessary but insufficient condition for a structural causal pathway from SES to health. Their decision criteria when interpreting results are as follows: if the invariance test fails, one should question the validity of the model for this particular health variable and refrain from drawing any conclusions. If invariance holds and Granger causality is present, one cannot distinguish between a direct causal link and a common factor. Yet, if invariance holds and Granger causality is ruled out, it should be safe to deduce that SES does not have a causal impact on the health condition under consideration.

8.3.3   Summary of HWW's Findings

Contrary to conventional wisdom, the evidence from applying HWW's approach to the elderly US population is not *universally* supportive of hypothesis A. In fact, they find that SES is unlikely to be causal for mortality, most acute health conditions, accidents, and a large number of degenerative diseases. Medical conditions, for which direct causal links cannot be ruled out, include self-rated health status, most mental illnesses, and some chronic conditions such as diabetes, lung disease, and arthritis. This pattern loses some of its mysteriousness when viewed in the context of US health-policy characteristics. The population under examination is of advanced age and eligible for Medicare, which will likely weaken any causal impact wealth could have on well-being via the affordability of health care. Yet even Medicare coverage is not fully comprehensive and tends to focus on acute care procedures, while generally failing to limit out-of-pocket costs for treatments of chronic and psychological conditions.[10] This lends indirect evidence for the importance of channel A1 because the socioeconomic gradient emerges exactly for those health conditions, for which the ability to pay is most likely to be an issue.

Reflecting the substantial degree of ambiguity in these results, the policy

---

10. Note that the study was conducted well before the introduction of Medicare Part D in 2006 that especially benefited the chronically ill by improving the coverage of prescription drugs.

conclusions formulated by HWW are rather contained in both phrasing and substance. On the one hand, they cannot overcome the methodological challenge of inferring true causality when G-causality is detected. This leaves open whether SES-linked preventive care induces onset of chronic and mental illnesses or whether persistent unobserved factors are to blame for the observed health-wealth association. On the other hand, even convincing evidence for the absence of direct causal links might not necessarily warrant the bluntest form of policy recommendation. Sure enough, SES-linked therapies for acute diseases do not appear to induce health and mortality differentials, which—to quote HWW—should *theoretically* permit the strong conclusion that "policy interventions in the Medicare system to increase access or reduce out-of-pocket medical expenses will not alter the conditional probabilities of new health events" (10). However, the authors stop short of actually drawing this conclusion, which reflects their reluctance to base overly aggressive policy proposals on a concept whose ability to simulate the effect of system shocks is not indisputible.

8.3.4   Discussion of HWW's Approach

All things considered, what should we make of HWW's approach of inferring causality and yet avoiding the cumbersome search for exogenous variation in SES? Does their reliance on Granger causality and their decision to focus on health innovations really do the trick of solving the endogeneity problem, or have they entered a methodological dead-end street? Overall, the response within the literature has been fairly critical, albeit not excoriating, pointing out a number of issues briefly discussed in the following.

Existence versus Activation of Channels

It is important to understand the limitations of an approach that focusses on *innovations* in health, rather than health status itself. HWW detect a strong and ubiquitous association of SES and prevalence of health conditions in the initial wave of their sample. This suggests that the elderly population under consideration has potentially been affected by some of the causal channels between health and wealth in the past. This history, however, remains a blind spot for HWW's model: by concentrating on future health events, they are unable to explain what factors lead to the preexisting SES gradient. By contrast, they study the question whether SES has an impact on the onset of *additional* medical conditions, given an individual is already old, still alive, and has gone through a long and unexplained health-wealth history. While the analysis of an elderly population is not illegitimate and certainly interesting in its own right, one should entertain some doubts about its external validity. In theory, HWW's findings could—if extrapolated backward—also provide a retrospective explanation for the early relation between SES and health. However, as pointed out by Adda, Chandola, and Marmot (2003), Heckman (2003), Poterba (2003), and HWW themselves, this extreme form of time invariance over the entire life cycle is unlikely to hold as certain causal channels are probably relevant at different stages in one's life.[11] In light of this, an accepted noncausality test should perhaps not be taken as evidence against the plain existence of a causal link but rather against its *activation* within the class of invariances under consideration.

Unobserved Common Effects

As argued in the preceding, the major weakness of HWW's approach is that it cannot separate true causality from hidden common effects. Yet, according to the authors, this will only constitute a problem if Granger causality is detected. In the absence of G-causality, causation in a structural sense should be ruled out as well. This interpretation implies that the detection of conditional dependence is a prerequisite for an active causal link—an assumption that is questioned by Heckman (2003), who argues that persistent hidden factors may also work in the opposite direction of causal pathways and offset them. If this were the case, information on G-causality might actually not tell us anything about true causal mechanisms, rendering HWW's strategy ineffective. However, the likelihood of direct causal effects being *exactly* offset by unobserved common factors should be practically zero, making this argument irrelevant for identification. Then again, there are obvious limits to this defence in finite samples so that statistical inference of causation could indeed be seriously jeopardized by the failure to account for hidden common causes.

Invariance Tests

Anticipating that their framework might fall short of inferring deep causal structures, HWW subject their model to the aforementioned invariance tests. On a conceptual level, model invariance would arguably justify predictions of policy effects, but there are legitimate concerns whether the actual tests implemented in their paper are statistically powerful enough. Granger (2003), Hausman (2003), Heckman (2003), and, once more, HWW themselves point out that invariance under historical interventions is of little use when the panel is as short as AHEAD, offering hardly any in-sample variation in populations, age structures, and—most important—policy regimes. As a consequence, an accepted invariance test as implemented by HWW is unlikely to be a sufficient condition for the sort of model validity necessary to make out-of-sample predictions. On top of that, Poterba (2003) even questions whether one should view the acceptance of HWW's invariance tests as a *necessary* condition for meaningful analysis. Instead of discarding results when invariance tests are rejected, one could follow up on the

11. For retirees, pension income is not affected by (contemporary) ability to work, occupational hazards vanished on the day of retirement, and Medicare provides basic health insurance, rendering channels B1, A3, and A1, respectively, of little importance when late in the life cycle. At younger ages, however, all of these pathways may well have played an important role.

reasons for time invariance failures as they may be informative of structural breaks in causal relationships. For instance, certain causal pathways may switch on or off in the course of policy changes or as the observed cohort grows older. In such cases, failed invariance tests would actually shed light on the circumstances under which causal links will be active or unexpressed, allowing for sharper, channel-specific causality tests.

Health Dynamics

Another reason for concern is the fact that HWW model health dynamics as a first-order Markov process, which cannot be expected to properly capture the medium and long-run evolution of health. Intuitively, this is because the Markov model assumes that all relevant information about the whole past is captured in the observed variables one period ago. This is unrealistic because knowledge of longer histories would better capture the stock characteristics of health capital as envisioned by Grossman (1972). Taking functional limitations as an example, a respondent who reported difficulties with walking one year ago and no limitations previously has a different outlook than a respondent who consistently reported difficulties with walking for the last ten years.

Instantaneous Causality

Finally, Florens (2003), Geweke (2003), and Heckman (2003) express their skepticism about HWW's handling of instantaneous causality. The hierarchy imposed on health conditions (with the assumption that incidence of each condition is conditioned on upstream incidences but not on downstream ones) may be acceptable as a reduced-form assumption and is etiologically fairly reasonable. Yet it likely falls short of the structural stability explored by invariance tests and is a potential source of serious model misspecification, making it a prime target for methodological improvements in the course of future research.

8.4   Reanalysis of HWW with New Data

The preceding discussion indicates that HWW's approach of disentangling the association between health and wealth while avoiding the often futile struggle of finding exogenous variation in SES comes at the price of limited methodological persuasiveness. However, because the generic alternative—instrumental variables—is not exempt from substantial criticism either, we certainly feel that this identification concept merits methodological refinement rather than being dismissed altogether. Some weaknesses, such as the treatment of common effects, health dynamics, or instantaneous causality, require significant modifications to the original model, and we plan to implement these in future research.

Yet one of the major downsides of HWW's study—the lack of invariance test power—can be addressed without the need for complex changes but instead by applying the largely unaltered model to a more apposite set of data. Recall that the root of this problem is that the invariance tests are based on rather limited variation in "histories" of states relative to the universe of potential histories. Increasing the N as well as the T dimension of the panel data will arguably raise the number of histories and enhance the power of these tests. Of course, we can also expect larger sample sizes to boost the statistical power of noncausality tests, effectively reducing the risk of committing type-II errors. But sample size is not everything. We believe that the analysis will also greatly benefit from larger sample "diversity," with data covering different kinds of populations that are subject to varying institutional setups. For instance, the inclusion of younger respondents could shed light on the question if the activation of causal links is stable throughout the life cycle or if reaching the retirement age induces some sort of structural break.

Given that the HRS survey study provides panel data that meets all of the preceding requirements, the present analysis keeps methodological changes to an absolute minimum and assesses the stability of HWW's results when applying their model to new and more encompassing data.[12] Of particular interest is the question whether HWW's somewhat surprising result of SES not having any direct causal impact on most health conditions is confirmed as test power increases.

8.4.1   The HRS Panel Data

Sample Characteristics

Our data—which are representative of the noninstitutionalized US population over the age of fifty—come from the Health and Retirement Study (HRS), a large-scale longitudinal survey project that studies the labor force participation and health transitions of individuals toward the end of their work lives and in the years that follow. While the data is collected by the University of Michigan Survey Research Center for the National Institute of Aging, we use the public-release file from the RAND Corporation that merged records from the nine panel waves available to date. The wave 1 interviews were conducted in 1992 and then repeated every two years so that HRS incorporates data from 1992 to 2008. Due to significant changes to the survey design between waves 1 and 2, the first cross-section cannot be directly compared to subsequent observations and is, therefore, not used in our analysis. To ensure that HRS stays representative of the population as

---

12. In fact, this study exactly replicates HWW's model of health incidence with one notable exception. For simplicity, we skip their treatment of interview delay, which accounts for the fact that interview timing appears to depend on health status. While this potentially calls into question the comparability of responses from healthy and severely ill individuals, we find that results are virtually unaffected by this nonrandom distribution of time at risk.

time goes by, the panel is periodically refreshed with new cohorts of respondents. Up to now, the sample consists of five different entry cohorts: the original 1992 HRS cohort (born 1931 to 1941), the 1993 AHEAD cohort (born 1923 or earlier), the CODA (Children of Depression, born 1924 to 1930) and WB (War Baby, born 1942 to 1947) cohorts entering in 1998, and the EBB cohort (Early Baby Boomer, born 1948 to 1953) added in 2004.

At baseline in wave 2 (covering interviews conducted between 1993 to 1994), the data set contains 18,694 individuals with usable records. The panel is subject to considerable attrition, which reduces sample sizes from wave to wave—a trend that is only temporarily disrupted when a refreshment cohort is added to the sample (see figure 8.1). The two sources for attrition are mortality (especially for the elderly AHEAD cohort) and "sample fatigue." Death-related attritors are kept in the working sample because mortality is one of the key outcomes of interest. With respect to all others attritors, we apply two alternative sampling schemes. The first exactly mirrors HWW's benchmark in that it categorically excludes nonrespondents from the working sample, irrespective of when their drop-off occurs or whether they rejoin the survey in later waves. As detailed in the following, the second sampling procedure assures that the information of these households is used for as long as they are part of the sample.

Much like in HWW's original study, we exclude all individuals with missing information on critical variables. This includes item nonresponse for key demographic variables as well as cases where information on health conditions is generally unavailable. If respondents merely fail to answer isolated health queries, these gaps are filled by means of simulation-based imputation. Certain health questions on cognitive ability, severe falls, and

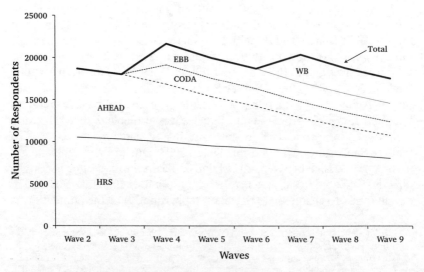

Fig. 8.1   Sample sizes, decomposed by entry cohorts

hip fractures are not asked to participants below the age of sixty-five, which is why these variables are excluded from all estimations that include younger subpopulations. While HWW went to great lengths to impute a large number of wealth and income observations with first-order Markov cross-wave hot deck imputation methods, we are in the more convenient position to rely on the imputations that are now readily available within the RAND/HRS data. We should note that, in spite of this data cleaning, the self-reported wealth and income measures are still suspect of considerable measurement error. The summary statistics for all variables used in our analysis is given in table 8A.1.

Comparison with HWW's Data Benchmark

HWW's original data sample consists of the AHEAD cohort of US Americans aged seventy and older who are tracked through panel waves 2 to 4. Using the HRS data that are available to date, allows for deviations from this benchmark along several dimensions. Naturally, we can follow the same individuals for *more time periods* because the AHEAD cohort is now biennially observed between 1993 and 1994 and 2008. Given the introduction of the four additional entry cohorts, the analysis can also be extended to *different individuals* with potentially diverging histories compared to those in the original study. In addition, it is now possible and certainly interesting to also widen the working sample by incorporating *younger individuals,* aged fifty and older. Finally, it should be noted that there is an additional, albeit minor, deviation from HWW's data benchmark even for the same observations as in the original study. One reason for this is that the early AHEAD data have subsequently been subject to data updates and revisions within the HRS project. Similarly, there may be differences between the SES imputations carried out by HWW and those conducted by RAND/HRS.

8.4.2   Results

Following the strategy described in section 8.3, we fit model 9 as binomial probits except for body mass index (BMI) and Activities of Daily Living/Instrumental Activities of Daily Living (ADL/IADL) impairments, which are estimated with ordinary least squares (OLS) and ordered probit, respectively. Appendix tables 8A.2 and 8A.3 contain the empirical significance values for the system of noncausality and invariance tests specified in the preceding. For a more concise overview of results, refer to tables 8.2 and 8.3. In a nutshell, the reanalysis with fresher and more encompassing data suggests that direct causal links from SES to health can be ruled out for much fewer health conditions than in the original study. This casts some doubt on the stability of HWW's findings. In order to understand which of the data changes contribute to these deviating conclusions, we estimate the model multiple times, using several different data sets by augmenting them stepwise along the dimensions outlined in the preceding. In the first step,

Table 8.2   Tests for noncausality (steps 2–4)

Test results for Granger noncausality

Health condition	HWW (70+) W2–4 F	HWW (70+) W2–4 M	Step 2 (70+) W2–4 F	Step 2 W2–4 M	Step 2 W4–6 F	Step 2 W4–6 M	Step 2 W7–9 F	Step 2 W7–9 M	Step 3 (70+) W2–9 F	Step 3 W2–9 M	Step 4 (50+) W2–9 F	Step 4 W2–9 M
Cancer									*	*		**
Heart									*		**	**
Stroke		**			*					**	***	◆◆ **
Mortality				*							◆◆	◆◆ **
Lung		**		*							***	
Diabetes		**										
High blood pressure			*								*	
Arthritis							**		***		***	***
Incontinence			*		*		*	*	*	*	n/a	n/a
Fall					**	◆◆			*		n/a	n/a
Hip fracture				◆◆		◆◆ *				*	***	***
Proxy				◆◆		◆◆ *	**	***	**	***	n/a	n/a
Cognition	◆◆ **	*	**		*				***	***	n/a	*
Psychiatric	*							***		*		*
Depression				**	**	**	***		***	**	***	***
BMI					*				◆		◆◆◆	◆◆◆
Smoke now												
ADL	◆	◆◆	◆	◆◆	◆				◆◆	***		
IADL	◆◆	◆ *	◆◆	*			***	***	◆◆ ***	***	◆◆◆ ***	◆◆
Self-reported health	**		◆◆		◆				◆◆		◆	◆◆

Notes: Results are for white females (F) and males (M). HWW = Healthy, Wealthy, and Wise (Adams et al. 2003); W = waves (e.g., W2–4 = waves 2–4); n/a = not applicable; blank cells = indicate that Granger noncausality cannot be rejected. Black diamonds indicate that the corresponding invariance test is rejected at the 5% level.

*Granger noncausality rejected at 5 percent level.
**Granger noncausality rejected at 1 percent level.
***Granger noncausality rejected at 0.1 percent level.

Table 8.3   **Tests for noncausality (pre- versus postretirement population)**

	Test results for Granger noncausality			
	Waves 2–9			
	Step 4 (0–64)		Step 4 (65+)	
Health condition	Female	Male	Female	Male
Cancer				
Heart			*	
Stroke			*	
Mortality		♦ ♦	♦	**
Lung				*
Diabetes	***		**	♦
High blood pressure			♦	
Arthritis			***	***
Incontinence	***		***	***
Fall	n/a	n/a	*	*
Hip fracture	n/a	n/a		
Proxy		♦ ♦ ♦	***	♦ ♦ ♦
Cognition	n/a	n/a	***	***
Psychiatric	***			♦
Depression	***	***	***	***
BMI	♦		♦ ♦	
Smoke now	♦ ♦ ♦	♦ ♦ ♦		
ADL	***	***	♦ ♦ ♦	***
IADL	***	♦ ♦ ♦	*	♦ ♦ ♦
Self-reported health	♦ ♦ ♦	♦ ♦ ♦	♦ ♦ ♦	♦ ♦ ♦

Note: See table 8.2 notes.

we rerun HWW's benchmark study for the same cohort and time periods, yet reverting to the current version of HRS data instead.[13] This will detect any impact arising from data revisions and differences in imputations. The second step consists of extending the analysis to the other three cohorts in the sample, hence testing whether HWW's conclusions are also valid for different individuals. The third step addresses the question of how results are affected by increasing the number of time periods under consideration.

13. To ensure that none of the observed changes is confoundedly rooted in the way certain variables are constructed and program codes are implemented, we also reran HWW's study verbatim using their original data. While the goal to exactly reproduce HWW was ultimately achieved, it should be noted that results are identical to those published as log files within the appendix of the original 2003 paper but not to those in the article itself. This difference is attributable to data revisions that HWW accounted for shortly after the paper was published, which means that the outcome from the appendix should be preferred as the ultimate benchmark. As is evident from comparing columns (1) and (2) of table 8A.2, said differences are not always trivial in size. Most strikingly, invariance tests tend to fail less frequently when applied to HWW's postpublication data set. Yet the impact on causality tests is negligible, thus not challenging the author's main conclusions from the article.

Because in HWW's model there is no self-evident way to aggregate the information from multiple time intervals, we compare two different sampling approaches: one that refills the sample after each wave with applicable observations and one that does not. In the fourth and final step, we evaluate the impact on estimation results when younger individuals are included in the analysis as well. This stepwise decomposition of all data and sampling changes appears to be more informative than applying the whole bundle of modifications at once.

Step One: Reestimating HWW with Revised Data

In order to gauge the result's sensitivity to data revisions and imputations, the model is reestimated with fresh HRS data for the exact same cohort (AHEAD) and time periods (waves 2 to 4) as in the original study. The differences between the new results and HWW's benchmark are quite modest, and outcomes of causality test are mostly unchanged. The most notable exception is diabetes for which the noncausality test had to be previously rejected among male respondents. With revised data, however, a direct causal link from SES to diabetes seems unlikely to exist. For further details, compare columns (2) and (3) of table 8A.2.

Step Two: Adding New Cohorts

While the relative stability of results in face of data revisions is certainly encouraging, a much stricter test is posed by extending the analysis to all available cohorts. To achieve this, we run three separate estimations on the following samples: first, we revisit waves 2 to 4 but allow members of cohorts other than AHEAD to be part of the working sample. This barely changes the sample composition because the only other cohort that is part of the survey in this early stage is HRS, which hardly contains any individuals aged seventy+. For the other two estimations, HWW's data benchmark is additionally changed inasmuch as later waves are used. The second estimation starts at wave 4, when the new cohorts CODA and EB are interviewed for the first time. Note that we do not restrict analysis to these two cohorts. Rather, all respondents who are at least seventy years old at wave 4 and who are not subject to subsequent sample attrition are followed until wave 7. This closely mirrors HWW's approach of analyzing a three-period panel, hence still keeping the deviations from the benchmark to a minimum. The third estimation repeats the second for waves 7 to 9, coinciding with the entry of the most recent cohort, namely WB.

Not surprisingly, the first estimation (table 8A.2, column [4]) yields results that are almost identical to those of HWW's benchmark with revised data (table 8A.2, column [3]). The hypothesis tests associated with the other two estimations, however, prove to be rather different. As far as noncausality tests are concerned, the differences seem to be unsystematic. For some medical conditions, such as depression and ADL impairments for females and incontinence for males, causality from SES can no longer be ruled out as noncausality tests are now consistently rejected. For other health conditions, namely diabetes and lung disease for males as well as psychiatric disease for females, the opposite holds true, as noncausality tests can no longer be rejected. In addition, there are a number of diseases for which the benchmark causality test results are not confirmed for only one of the subsamples. For further details, compare columns (4), (5), and (6), respectively, with column (3) of table 8A.2. Invariance tests, on the other hand, tend to be accepted more often than those under the benchmark scenario. At first glance, this may seem contradictory because causality tests have yielded fairly different results depending on which panel waves are under consideration. One should, however, not forget that the invariance tests merely check whether the model is time invariant within each of the three estimations but not among them. This is changed in the third step when the information from more than just three waves is incorporated.

Step Three: Increasing the Number of Time Periods

Step two has indicated that results depend on which panel waves are chosen to form the working sample. In order to reduce this arbitrary element and to maximize the use of available information in the data, it makes sense to increase the number of panel waves. Because there is no unequivocal way to implement this in practice, we propose two different sampling approaches. The first approach is a simple extrapolation of HWW's sampling method. The working sample consists of all individuals who participated in the survey in wave 2 and who were not subject to sample-fatigue-related attrition in later waves. This cohort is then followed for as many waves as possible. This sampling scheme has two major disadvantages. First, by restricting the sample to individuals who were part of the survey from the very start, we exclude refreshment cohorts CODA, EB, and WB, basically discarding useful information. The second drawback is of a more practical nature: death-related attritors cause the sample to dramatically thin out over time so that sample sizes eventually become too small to conduct any meaningful analysis. Moreover, as time moves on, the sample arguably becomes less representative of the true population because the ongoing attrition will select against the most frail. Nevertheless, and for the sake of maximum comparability with HWW, we estimate two versions of this first approach: one that follows individuals from wave 2 until wave 6 (covering cohorts HRS and AHEAD) and another that follows individuals from wave 4 until wave 9 (covering HRS, AHEAD, CODA, and EB). The number of waves is chosen so that sample sizes in the last respective wave are still reasonably large.

The alternative sampling scheme directly addresses the downsides of the preceding approach. Instead of limiting the sample to respondents who are part of the survey from the beginning, it is now refilled in each wave with all available respondents who meet the respective age criterion (i.e., seventy+)

and who answer all relevant questions for two consecutive waves. That way, all cohorts are used for analysis, sample sizes never diminish to levels too low for efficient estimation, and, consequently, all 8 waves can be used simultaneously. As a positive side effect, attrition bias is reduced as well, as the mortality-induced loss of observations is offset by filling up the sample with new respondents, once they become age eligible. One might object that this approach reduces the power of panel analysis as it does not make much use of its potential time series length. For the purpose of reproducing HWW, however, we deem it suitable because the original model does not use the theoretical length of the panel either, assuming that health and wealth trajectories are sufficiently described by single lags. Given that the models are estimated by simply stacking the data of all two-waves transitions above another, it is irrelevant how long an individual is part of the survey. The information conveyed in the responses of a person who only participates in, say, waves 4 and 5 is no less valuable than that of a respondent who participates from the very beginning to the end and should, therefore, not be excluded.[14]

It is noteworthy that the invariance tests of both sampling schemes have slightly different interpretations. In both cases, they test whether parameter estimates stay constant over time by comparing the log likelihood when all single wave transitions are pooled together with those when estimated separately. For a sample with refilling, an accepted invariance test indicates that the uncovered (non)causal relationships hold for different populations at different times, underlining the generality of results. Invariance tests for samples without refilling, however, cannot answer the question whether causal links hold for different populations because only one cohort is being followed. They rather check whether these links remain constant as a steadily diminishing cohort becomes older over time, ultimately comparing the frail (who exit the sample early) with the medically more robust.

The main change in results from using a larger number of sample waves is that causality from SES to health can no longer be ruled out for a large array of conditions, even for an elderly population aged seventy and older. This observation holds, no matter which of the two preceding approaches is used, even though there are some differences. As columns (7), (8), and (9) of table 8A.2 reveal, there are seven health conditions for which the samples without refilling yield a rejection of noncausality tests, even though this was not the case for shorter samples. This number even increases to ten conditions if the sample with refilling is used instead. The most unambiguous evidence exists for six conditions (mortality and falls for males, proxy and BMI for females, and cancer irrespective of gender) for which both approaches suggest that,

---

14. Of course, the validity of this argument relies on HWW's conceptualization of health trajectories as a first-order Markov process. The future development of more realistic models of health dynamics will require a more sophisticated sampling procedure as well.

contrary to earlier evidence, causality may well play a role. The reversed case of causality becoming less likely to exist as panel length grows is as good as nonexistent. The influence of analyzing more time periods at once on invariance tests is about the same for both approaches and not very strong. If anything, invariance failures tend to be somewhat likelier—a result that makes sense because it is more demanding for a model to be valid for eight waves than a mere three.

Step Four: Adding Younger Individuals

So far, the consequence of applying HWW's model to data that include more individuals and time periods is that the number of medical conditions for which SES causality may play a role has considerably increased. However, for a population aged seventy and older, there remains a large number of diseases for which causal links are not detected, despite the fact that high SES is associated with a lower prevalence of these conditions. While this cross-sectional correlation cannot be interpreted causally, it indicates that causal channels may have been at work earlier in life, before the individual even entered the sample. In light of that, it is interesting to also include younger individuals to test if the data will pick up additional causal links that are already mute in an elderly population.

First, the sample is opened up to people who are at least sixty-five years old so that it represents (with some exceptions) the whole Medicare-eligible subpopulation. This yields a net increase of three to six health conditions (depending on whether samples with or without refilling are used) for which causality can no longer be rejected, affirming the preceding speculation. See columns (2), (6), and (10) of table 8A.3 for details. A similar effect can be observed when the sample is opened up even further to include individuals aged fifty+, exploiting the entire age range available within HRS. This time, the net increase amounts to another three to nine conditions, rendering cases for which causal links can be ruled out the exception rather than the rule. Among the latter are illnesses such as strokes and high blood pressure for males, lung disease for females, and cancer for both men and women. For all other health conditions, the existence of causal links cannot be refuted. For further details, consider columns (3), (7), and (11) of table 8A.3.

It is also worthwhile to split up the sample into older (sixty-five+) and younger (fifty to sixty-four) individuals to study how the activation of causal channels differs between a mostly retired, Medicare-eligible population and people who are typically still on the labor market and not quasi-universally health insured. As table 8.3 shows, there is quite a number of medical conditions for which SES may be a causal driving force irrespective of age. These include depression for both genders, IADL impairments, incontinence, and diabetes for women as well as ADL impairments for men. For other conditions like arthritis, heart disease, strokes for females, or incontinence for males, SES is only a good predictor of new medical incidences at a higher age. On the other hand, smoking behavior as well as psychiatric problems for women are among the conditions for which a causal link may only be active at a preretirement age. Intriguingly, when young and old people are studied separately, results appear to be sensitive to whether samples with or without refilling are chosen (see table 8A.3). For older individuals, the sample with refilling suggests more cases of Granger causality than its counterparts without refreshment do. The exact opposite, however, is true for younger individuals, because for them rejected causality is a less frequent outcome in samples without refilling. The latter observation is likely an artifactual side effect of the way the sampling methods are defined: Sampling with refilling effectively excludes people from the fifty to sixty-four sample once they become older than sixty-five, whereas sampling without refilling follows all individuals until they die, even if they grow much older. As a consequence, unrefilled "young" samples may arguably pick up some of the causal effects that are exclusively active for the older subjects of the cohort.

Model invariance is not systematically influenced by adding younger individuals to the data set. The fact that the seeming structural breaks in the relation of SES and health as people grow older are not detected by HWW's invariance tests, should, however, not be surprising. Recall that the test design does not pit the young against the old but the past against the future. The idea is to check parameter invariance as time progresses. Because the age structure within the sample varies only little from wave to wave (especially when it is regularly refreshed), the invariance test will not permit a direct comparison of, say, pre- and postretirement populations. In light of this, the results in table 8A.3 merely suggest that the *time* stability of the model is rather insensitive to changes in the age composition of the sample.

Changes in Results of the Underlying Prediction Models

Given the strong dependence of noncausality test results on both the size and age coverage of the estimation sample, it seems natural to investigate how these changes are related to the size and the precision of coefficients of the underlying prediction models.[15] As table 8.4 exemplifies, precision of SES coefficient estimates does generally increase with the size of the respective sample, even though this relation is not perfect. While standard errors remain fairly constant across estimations based on similarly sized three-waves samples (step 2), they surprisingly spike upwards once all waves are pooled together in step 3. This observation may well be rooted in the aforementioned switch from a sampling procedure without (steps 1 and 2) to one with refilling (steps 3 and 4). Precision follows a more predictable pattern within step 4, as standard errors are invariably smaller the larger the respective sample (note that $N_{50+} > N_{65+} > N_{70+} > N_{0-64}$). The same pattern

---

15. HWW did not report the coefficients of the prediction models, but these estimates are also available in their online appendix.

Table 8.4   **Prediction model: Average standard errors of socioeconomic status (SES) coefficients: average of all health conditions and SES regressors**

| | | Step 2 (70+) | | | Step 3 (70+) | Step 4 (W2–9) | | |
| | HWW | | | | | | | |
	W2–4	W2–4	W4–6	W7–9	W2–9	65+	50+	0–64
Female	0.081	0.083	0.087	0.091	0.126	0.107	0.085	0.172
Male	0.108	0.105	0.111	0.110	0.167	0.135	0.098	0.185

Notes: Reported are average standard errors of SES coefficients obtained from estimating model 9. Each entry is an average of 160 single standard errors (twenty health variables and eight SES regressors). Individual standard errors follow the depicted pattern quite uniformly. HWW = Healthy, Wealthy, and Wise (Adams et al. 2003); W = waves (e.g., W2–4 = waves 2–4).

emerges when comparing results by gender, as the number of women exceeds that of men in each of the subsamples.

Despite increased precision, table 8.5 suggests that the number of statistically significant SES coefficients does not seem to be systematically affected as samples become more encompassing. In HWW's benchmark sample, there is a total of twenty-nine SES regression coefficients that are significant at the 5 percent level. This number stays rather constant across the performed steps. Yet note that in the benchmark case, there is a fair amount of cases for which coefficients have an unintuitive sign, suggesting that respondents with high SES are likelier to develop a new health condition. The share of these cases stays rather high for three-waves samples and drops significantly once all waves are used at once. This means that, while the overall number of significant SES coefficients does not increase, the direction of effects is now more in line with theory. This is an additional insight because noncausality tests as implemented here do merely check whether health innovations are conditionally independent of SES variables, whereas the quality of this dependence is not under consideration.

8.5   Conclusion and Future Research

All in all, reestimating HWW's model of health incidence with new HRS data alters conclusions about SES causation quite significantly. While the impact of data revisions within HRS is encouragingly small, the addition of new cohorts shows that causal inference critically depends on which time periods are used for estimation. Using the information of many—ideally all—waves at once has the greatest effect on results, with many health conditions moving to the column of illnesses for which SES causality may well play a role. Adding younger individuals to the sample has a very similar effect, reducing the number of medical conditions for which the existence of causal links can be statistically rejected even further. As a consequence,

Table 8.5 Prediction model: Significant socioeconomic status coefficients (significant at 5 percent level)

| | HWW (70+) | | Step 2 (70+) | | | | | | Step 3 (70+) | | Step 4 (50+) | |
| | W2–4 | | W2–4 | | W4–6 | | W7–9 | | W2–9 | | W2–9 | |
Health condition	F	M	F	M	F	M	F	M	F	M	F	M
Cancer		*E*		*E*			*H*		*W*			N
Heart	**I**		**I**	*I*			**E**			**NH**		
Stroke	*I*		*E*	*I*	*E*	*H*	**W**	*H*		**I**	**W**	**W**
Mortality	*E*	**W**	**W**				**W**		**W**	**W**	**W**	
Lung	**W**			**W**	**H**		*E*		**WH**			
Diabetes		**E**		**E**	**W**			**W**	**E**		**WE**	
High blood pressure	**E**			**E**	**W**			**E**				
Arthritis	**E**		**E**				**I**		**W**		*E*	
Incontinence	**N**				*E*	**N**	*I*	*E*	*I*		*W*	*H*
Fall							*E*	*E*			n/a	n/a
Hip fracture	**W**	**I**	**W**	**I**	**E**	**W**	**W**		*I*		n/a	n/a
Proxy	*I*	**E**	*I*	**E**		**E**	**E**	**E**	**E**		*E*	
Cognition	*WIN*	**W**	*WIN*	*I*							n/a	n/a
Psychiatric	**I**	**N**	**I**	**W**								
Depression				**N**	**E**	**IH**	**EH**		**E**	**E**	**WE**	
BMI					**H**	*N*	*IH*		**E**	**E**		**H**
Smoke now	**W**	**W**		**W**	*E*	*E*	*W*	**E**	**W**	**E**	**W**	**I**
ADL	**WI**		**WIH**	**WE**	*IE*	*N*	*IE*		**H**	**W**	**WI**	**W**
IADL	**WE**		**WE**		*N*	*E*			**IEH**	*NH*	*N*	**W**
Self-reported health	**EH**	**WE**	**EH**	**WE**	**N**	**EH**	**INH**	**IEH**	**IEH**	*NH*	**WIENH**	**IEH**

Notes: Results are for white females (F) and males (M). Significant coefficients at 5 percent level for wealth (W), income (I), education (E), neighborhood (N), or housing quality (H). Bold symbols indicate that signs are in line with theory. Italic symbols denote the opposite case. HWW = Healthy, Wealthy, and Wise (Adams et al. 2003); W = waves (e.g., W2–4 = waves 2–4); BMI = body mass index; ADL = activities of daily living; IADL = instrumental activities of daily living; n/a = not applicable; blank cells = none of the SES variables have a statistically significant impact on the respective health outcome.

the only health conditions for which SES causation can be ruled out when estimation is based on the most encompassing data set with refilling are cancer (irrespective of gender), lung disease for females, and high blood pressure for males. For all other health incidences, SES is either G-causal or the failure of invariance tests does not permit reliable conclusions. This represents a stark contrast to HWW's original findings, where the rejection of structural causality was the most frequent outcome.

Given that the greatest changes are triggered by the addition of panel waves (step 3), the main driving force behind this reversal in results is most likely an increase in test power as sample sizes soar. After all, in HWW's stacking model, a longer panel is equivalent to a larger sample (with respect to N) because all waves are pooled together and treated as if they formed one cross-section. This interpretation is corroborated by the fact that test results from long panels do not always reflect the average outcome of the respective three-wave panels they consist of. As the example of cancer in table 8A.2 illustrates, noncausality tests are often rejected in the long samples, even though they are consistently accepted in each of the short panels. Similar observations can be made when comparing test results by age group. In some cases, a noncausality test is only rejected for the largest, most-encompassing sample of all individuals aged fifty and older. However, in all smaller subsamples (fifty to sixty-four, sixty-five+, and seventy+) the same null hypothesis cannot be rejected. As an example for the latter case, see heart disease for females in table 8A.3. All of this evidence permits the emergence of a clear picture: the larger the sample under consideration, the likelier the rejection of noncausality.

We also find that causal inference depends on the age structure of the underlying population, with certain conditions being Granger caused by SES at younger or older ages only. This yields at least indirect evidence that the activation of causal links may indeed change over the life cycle. However, we recommend to take these results with a grain of salt because their lack of robustness is far from comforting, as evidenced by the sensitivity to the choice of sampling schemes. In addition, we should note that the data set for the sixty-five+ population is about three times as large as that of the preretirement group. As a consequence, we face the risk of confounding the true effect of age structures with the impact of varying sample sizes identified in the preceding. This may well provide an alternative explanation for the failure to detect many cases of G-causality among the fifty- to sixty-four-year-olds if estimation is based on a refilling sample—a result that is not confirmed if samples without refilling are used instead.

From a methodological point of view, the results of this study pose bad news for a model whose identification strategy relies on Granger causality. Recall that the reduced-form nature of G-causality cannot discriminate between structural causation and ecological association due to common unobserved effects if G-causality is detected. Ultimately, HWW's framework allows only the one-sided test for the absence of direct causal links, which is confirmed if G-causality is rejected as well. While HWW's original data set provided us with a large number of such cases, the more-encompassing data samples analyzed here do not do us this favor. As a result, we find ourselves in the unfortunate situation that little can be learned about the true links between SES and health, making it impossible to draw meaningful policy conclusions.[16]

In light of this, the need to improve the empirical model within future research so as to account for the confounding influence of hidden common factors becomes even more pressing. In our view, there are two alternative ways to achieve this. The first mirrors the identification strategy of IV approaches: instead of using endogeneity-stricken SES histories as regressors, one could concentrate on the impact of clearly exogenous *changes* in these variables. If these SES innovations meet the standard IV assumptions, we would be able to formulate two-sided tests that permit the clean identification of causality in a structural sense. Among the natural experiments one could exploit are the major negative shock to housing and financial wealth that many people experienced during the ongoing financial market crisis of 2008 to 2009, the positive shock Medicare households received as a result of the introduction of the heavily subsidized Medicare Part D program in 2006, and the shocks some employed individuals received from changes in employer-provided health insurance.[17] Particular attention could be given to the differential exposure to wealth shocks in the presence of health care delivery systems that vary in the financial impact of copayments, premiums, and coverage, particularly for chronic conditions and preventative and palliative therapies. Provided that the causal link in questions even exists, wealth shocks will take some time to affect health outcomes. Therefore, we expect any effects of the 2008 to 2009 financial crisis or Medicare Part D to leave their marks only in future waves of the HRS data set.

However, the use of such natural experiments is not immune to objection, which leads to a fundamental trade-off. On the one hand, we can try to infer causality by relying on wealth shocks like the ones just described,

---

16. While invariance tests have arguably gained power by the inclusion of different time spans, cohorts, and age structures, we are still doubtful that their acceptance would attest the model the kind of stability necessary to make out-of-sample predictions of policy effects. The reason for this is that—with the notable exception of the introduction of Medicare Part D in 2006—the observed variation in relevant policies remains rather low.

17. When it comes to the recent financial crisis, we acknowledge that the equity shock might not be large enough to provide strong identification. Using HRS data, Gustman, Steinmeier, and Tabatabai (2010) report that equity accounted only for about 15 percent of assets prior to the 2008 to 2009 crisis. Whether this is sufficient exogenous variation would have to be scrutinized as part of future research. Alternatively, one could explore negative shocks to housing wealth, which represent another aspect of the financial market crunch. Exogenous variation in these shocks is provided by regional differences in house prices and the severity of declines in real estate value during the crisis.

which has the advantage of not having to worry about endogeneity issues. Yet, as argued in section 3, there is a risk that these shocks may not be all that *relevant* for health, especially when occurring late in life. On the other hand, the information contained in past levels of SES—the regressor used in HWW's G-causality framework—is certainly of great relevance as it reflects the entire history between SES and health status. The disadvantage is that this pool of information may also include confounding elements, such as the impact of hidden common causes, calling into question the exogeneity of such explanatory variables.

The other alternative we deem feasible of discriminating among hypotheses A and C seeks to solve this trade-off by exploiting the relevant information contained in SES histories, while eliminating the misleading influence of common effects. As extensively argued in the fixed and random effects literature, this may be achieved by interpreting the problem of common effects as an issue of unobserved individual heterogeneity, whose effect is controlled by fully exploiting the panel structure of HRS. This being said, the choice of a suitable estimator is not trivial because it needs to combine three important features that often tend to be mutually exclusive. First and foremost, the estimation strategy must allow heterogeneity to be correlated with SES, which makes fixed effects (FE) estimators a logical candidate. However, FE estimation is generally ridden by matters of inconsistency, once confronted with the other two features, namely a dependent variable that is both binary (requiring a non-linear specification) and state-dependent (reflecting the dynamic nature of the model). A feasible way of tackling these three issues at once, promises to be a dynamic correlated random effects (RE) probit approach as implemented by Contoyannis, Jones, and Rice (2004). It solves the usual trade-offs between FE and RE setups by allowing for correlated heterogeneity and the estimation of time-invariant regressors even when confronted with nonlinear data structures and lagged dependent variables.[18] We acknowledge that this alternative strategy of coping with common effects is not devoid of criticism either, which is why we consider it reasonable to independently explore both routes in what lies ahead. This is especially true inasmuch as both approaches are expected to uncover different causal channels: while the latter strategy of modelling individual heterogeneity may allow the detection of average causal effects as manifest in SES histories, the exploitation of natural experiments will predominantly shed light on the most immediate (mental) health consequences of wealth shocks.

---

18. Michaud and van Soest (2008) adopt a similar strategy by eliminating the effect of individual heterogeneity with GMM estimators in the spirit of Arellano and Bond (1991). In analyzing the HRS population aged fifty-one to sixty-one, they find that causal effects of wealth on health can be ruled out if unobserved heterogeneity and a more realistic lag structure are accounted for. However, given that their approach is incompatible with nonlinear models, it is not directly applicable to our research question.

A second opportunity for future research lies in improving the limited microfoundation of causal pathways, which is inherent in the reduced-form nature of Granger causality. Even if we were able to univocally confirm the presence of causal effects from wealth to health, we still would not know the channels through which they operate. Yet the latter information is absolutely critical from a policy perspective: interventions to increase the affordability of health insurance would be warranted if channel A1 were to be active, but would prove ineffective if the causal link were to work through, say, channel A3 instead. To address this issue, we intend to specify and test more differentiated hypotheses that may facilitate the discrimination among these channels. For instance, if channel A1 is truly relevant, we should observe a certain sensitivity of results to the availability and generosity of health care systems. Possible comparisons include the time before and after Medicare Part D, individuals with and without health insurance, or cross-country differences in health care regimes.[19] Another way of gauging the importance of health care affordability is to compare individuals with and without health insurance. Of particular interest will be the preretirement population not yet eligible for Medicare as their insurance status will be endogenous unless they are covered by employer-provided health care. Even if health insurance proves to be of little importance for the *onset* of a health condition, it may well be decisive in determining whether and how it is treated, given that the individual has already gotten sick. On this account, we intend to follow the health trajectories as well medical care use of respondents that share the characteristic of having developed a certain medical condition.

Finally, the model would certainly benefit from addressing another of the methodological shortcomings identified in section 8.3: the treatment of health dynamics. In our view, there are several ways to accommodate the long memory effects that prove to be so critical for a realistic description of health trajectories. The simplest fix consists of adding higher-order lags of health condition prevalences to the list of explanatory variables. A better, albeit more demanding, alternative is a hidden Markov structure in which health is controlled by a latent random process that drives the onset of health conditions, self-rated health, and mortality. According to Heiss (2010), such models are parsimonious and capture the observed dynamics better than commonly applied random effects or conditional Markov chain models.

---

19. In fact, Hurd and Kapteyn (2003) find that causal effects from SES to health status are less pronounced in the Netherlands than in the United States. Given that the Dutch health care system is basically universal, they see this result as an indication of the general importance of differential access to health care: SES gradients in health are strongest in institutional environments in which affordability should a priori matter most.

Appendix

Table 8A.1   Variables used for analysis: Summary statistics

Variable	Wave 2 (N = 18,694)		Wave 3 (N = 18,022)		Wave 4 (N = 21,645)		Wave 5 (N = 19,961)		Wave 6 (N = 18,703)		Wave 7 (N = 20,365)		Wave 8 (N = 18,806)		Wave 9 (N = 17,588)	
	Mean	SD	Mean	SD	Mean	SD	Mean	SD	Mean	SD	Mean	SD	Mean	SD	Mean	SD
					Health prevalence											
Cancer (ever)	0.097	0.296	0.127	0.333	0.127	0.333	0.140	0.347	0.155	0.362	0.152	0.359	0.168	0.373	0.179	0.384
Heart disease (ever)	0.225	0.418	0.265	0.442	0.256	0.436	0.270	0.444	0.287	0.452	0.275	0.447	0.296	0.456	0.306	0.461
Stroke (ever)	0.066	0.248	0.090	0.286	0.090	0.287	0.098	0.297	0.105	0.306	0.099	0.298	0.107	0.309	0.113	0.316
Lung disease (ever)	0.107	0.309	0.115	0.319	0.102	0.302	0.103	0.304	0.106	0.308	0.105	0.307	0.112	0.316	0.120	0.325
Diabetes (ever)	0.133	0.340	0.150	0.357	0.140	0.357	0.161	0.368	0.183	0.387	0.187	0.390	0.211	0.408	0.229	0.420
High blood pressure (ever)	0.464	0.499	0.500	0.500	0.488	0.500	0.517	0.500	0.556	0.497	0.553	0.497	0.597	0.491	0.629	0.483
Arthritis (last 2 years)	0.190	0.392	0.227	0.419	0.220	0.414	0.223	0.416	0.237	0.425	0.228	0.420	0.231	0.421	0.240	0.427
Incontinence (ever)	0.146	0.353	0.214	0.410	0.237	0.425	0.290	0.454	0.331	0.471	0.324	0.468	0.364	0.481	0.398	0.490
Fall (ever)	0.075	0.263	0.148	0.355	0.169	0.374	0.203	0.402	0.225	0.418	0.247	0.431	0.262	0.440	0.288	0.453
Hip fracture (ever)	0.024	0.152	0.025	0.157	0.027	0.162	0.029	0.167	0.031	0.173	0.035	0.183	0.038	0.192	0.040	0.195
Proxy interview (now)	0.077	0.267	0.138	0.345	0.145	0.352	0.164	0.370	0.182	0.386	0.143	0.350	0.131	0.337	0.134	0.341
Cognitive impairment (ever)	0.221	0.415	0.151	0.358	0.208	0.406	0.257	0.437	0.254	0.435	0.198	0.398	0.234	0.424	0.230	0.421
Psychiatric disease (ever)	0.128	0.334	0.158	0.365	0.151	0.358	0.159	0.365	0.170	0.375	0.177	0.381	0.191	0.393	0.199	0.400
Depression (last 2 years)	0.130	0.337	0.096	0.295	0.110	0.313	0.111	0.314	0.112	0.315	0.111	0.314	0.114	0.318	0.104	0.305
BMI (now)	26.5	5.0	26.5	5.1	26.8	5.2	27.0	5.4	27.2	5.4	27.4	5.7	27.8	5.8	28.0	5.9
Smoker (now)	0.182	0.386	0.169	0.375	0.164	0.371	0.149	0.356	0.137	0.343	0.148	0.355	0.136	0.343	0.133	0.339
No. of ADL impairments (now)	0.239	0.751	0.378	0.990	0.376	0.998	0.384	1.003	0.393	1.020	0.364	0.984	0.399	1.022	0.403	1.035
No. of IADL impairments (now)	0.288	0.847	0.344	0.967	0.336	0.966	0.345	0.990	0.370	1.027	0.340	0.964	0.369	1.014	0.377	1.027
Poor/fair self-rated health (now)	0.291	0.454	0.282	0.450	0.319	0.466	0.286	0.452	0.294	0.456	0.300	0.458	0.301	0.459	0.307	0.461

(continued)

Table 8A.1   (continued)

Variable	Wave 2 (N = 18,694)		Wave 3 (N = 18,022)		Wave 4 (N = 21,645)		Wave 5 (N = 19,961)		Wave 6 (N = 18,703)		Wave 7 (N = 20,365)		Wave 8 (N = 18,806)		Wave 9 (N = 17,588)	
	Mean	SD	Mean	SD	Mean	SD	Mean	SD	Mean	SD	Mean	SD	Mean	SD	Mean	SD
Health incidence																
Cancer (first/new)			0.040	0.197	0.046	0.209	0.039	0.194	0.044	0.206	0.041	0.198	0.042	0.201	0.046	0.209
Heart disease (first/new)			0.092	0.289	0.125	0.331	0.099	0.299	0.110	0.313	0.117	0.322	0.107	0.309	0.110	0.313
Stroke (first/new)			0.038	0.191	0.047	0.213	0.038	0.190	0.042	0.201	0.039	0.194	0.036	0.186	0.039	0.193
Died since last wave			0.054	0.225	0.055	0.229	0.065	0.246	0.076	0.264	0.058	0.234	0.066	0.249	0.071	0.257
Lung disease (first)			0.017	0.127	0.020	0.139	0.017	0.130	0.020	0.141	0.023	0.149	0.018	0.133	0.021	0.142
Diabetes (first)			0.023	0.151	0.023	0.150	0.023	0.150	0.032	0.176	0.028	0.166	0.032	0.176	0.030	0.171
High blood pressure (first)			0.043	0.204	0.045	0.207	0.050	0.218	0.059	0.235	0.054	0.227	0.055	0.227	0.052	0.221
Arthritis (first/new)			0.105	0.307	0.099	0.298	0.098	0.298	0.110	0.313	0.109	0.312	0.099	0.298	0.106	0.308
Incontinence (first/new)			0.159	0.365	0.166	0.372	0.183	0.387	0.201	0.401	0.201	0.401	0.220	0.414	0.252	0.440
Fall (first/new)			0.110	0.313	0.109	0.312	0.101	0.302	0.104	0.306	0.109	0.312	0.112	0.316	0.126	0.332
Hip fracture (first/new)			0.008	0.089	0.013	0.112	0.009	0.094	0.013	0.111	0.014	0.119	0.015	0.121	0.016	0.124
Proxy interview (now)			0.138	0.345	0.145	0.352	0.164	0.370	0.182	0.386	0.143	0.350	0.131	0.337	0.134	0.341
Cognitive impairment (first)			0.096	0.295	0.074	0.261	0.058	0.233	0.062	0.240	0.047	0.212	0.047	0.212	0.482	0.214
Psychiatric disease (first)			0.032	0.175	0.027	0.162	0.024	0.152	0.027	0.162	0.025	0.157	0.028	0.165	0.022	0.147
Depression (first/new)			0.050	0.218	0.072	0.258	0.061	0.240	0.062	0.242	0.059	0.236	0.060	0.238	0.053	0.223
BMI (now)			26.5	5.1	26.8	5.2	27.0	5.4	27.2	5.4	27.4	5.7	27.8	5.8	28.0	5.9
Smoker (now)			0.169	0.375	0.164	0.371	0.149	0.356	0.137	0.343	0.148	0.355	0.136	0.343	0.133	0.339
No. of ADL impairments (now)			0.378	0.990	0.376	0.998	0.384	1.003	0.393	1.020	0.364	0.984	0.399	1.022	0.403	1.035
No. of IADL impairments (now)			0.344	0.967	0.336	0.966	0.345	0.990	0.370	1.027	0.340	0.964	0.369	1.014	0.377	1.027
Poor/fair self-rated health (now)			0.282	0.450	0.319	0.466	0.286	0.452	0.294	0.456	0.300	0.458	0.301	0.459	0.307	0.461

SES variables

Wealth in 1997 US$ (000)	225.9	469.6	273.8	704.3	288.2	1,057	853.1	310.0	789.0	348.6	1,226	418.8	1,877	360.6	1,034
1st quartile wealth indicator	0.264	0.441	0.246	0.431	0.253	0.435	0.427	0.229	0.421	0.246	0.430	0.239	0.426	0.240	0.427
4th quartile wealth indicator	0.190	0.393	0.215	0.411	0.236	0.425	0.439	0.275	0.447	0.283	0.451	0.311	0.463	0.304	0.450
Income in 1997 US$ (000)	44.1	79.5	45.2	65.9	47.2	90.2	93.1	45.0	80.8	50.1	85.3	50.6	255.4	49.0	359.1
1st quartile income indicator	0.289	0.453	0.268	0.443	0.251	0.434	0.435	0.250	0.433	0.240	0.427	0.242	0.428	0.251	0.434
4th quartile income indicator	0.213	0.410	0.230	0.421	0.247	0.432	0.432	0.236	0.425	0.263	0.441	0.249	0.432	0.253	0.435
Poor/fair housing condition	0.108	0.310	0.119	0.324	0.113	0.317	0.307	0.095	0.294	0.124	0.330	0.114	0.318	0.109	0.311
Poor/fair neighborhood safety	0.146	0.353	0.122	0.327	0.101	0.301	0.282	0.078	0.268	0.097	0.296	0.101	0.301	0.096	0.295
Education (in years)	11.5	3.5	11.6	3.5	11.8	3.4	3.4	12.0	3.4	12.3	3.3	12.3	3.3	12.4	3.3
High school (educ. > 10 yr)	0.701	0.458	0.706	0.456	0.737	0.440	0.435	0.758	0.429	0.787	0.410	0.795	0.404	0.801	0.400
College (educ. > 14 yr)	0.181	0.385	0.184	0.387	0.204	0.403	0.408	0.218	0.413	0.242	0.428	0.244	0.429	0.251	0.434

Demographic variables

Widowed	0.200	0.400	0.209	0.407	0.203	0.402	0.412	0.230	0.421	0.201	0.401	0.213	0.410	0.221	0.415
Divorced/separated	0.087	0.282	0.087	0.281	0.095	0.293	0.294	0.097	0.296	0.109	0.311	0.109	0.312	0.114	0.318
Never married	0.031	0.174	0.029	0.168	0.033	0.177	0.174	0.030	0.170	0.037	0.188	0.034	0.182	0.034	0.180
Current age	65.9	11.0	67.2	10.7	66.5	10.9	10.6	69.0	10.3	67.0	11.5	68.4	11.1	69.6	10.8
Mother's current/death age	73.7	15.3	74.4	15.3	75.0	15.0	15.1	75.8	15.2	75.6	14.7	76.1	14.8	76.5	14.8
Father's current/death age	70.8	14.4	71.2	14.6	71.4	14.4	14.5	71.9	14.5	71.9	14.2	71.1	14.3	71.4	14.4
Ever smoked	0.588	0.492	0.587	0.492	0.590	0.492	0.493	0.583	0.493	0.579	0.494	0.579	0.494	0.577	0.494

Notes: SD = standard deviation; BMI = body mass index; ADL = activities of daily living; IADL = instrumental activities of daily living; SES = socioeconomic status.

Table 8A.2 Tests for invariance and noncausality (ages 70+)

			Significance levels of tests								
			Benchmark: HWW (70+)			3-waves samples (70+)			Longer samples (70+)		
			Article	Appendix	New data	No refilling			No refilling		Refilling
Health condition	Test	Sex	W2–4 (AHEAD) (1)	W2–4 (AHEAD) (2)	W2–4 (AHEAD) (3)	W2–4 (all cohorts) (4)	W4–6 (all cohorts) (5)	W7–9 (all cohorts) (6)	W2–6 (all cohorts) (7)	W4–9 (all cohorts) (8)	W2–9 (all cohorts) (9)
Cancer	I	F	0.056	0.528	0.933	0.930	0.870	0.605	0.683	0.777	0.591
	I|noS	F	0.023	0.309	0.895	0.896	0.845	0.543	0.628	0.788	0.489
	S|I	F	0.311	0.613	0.271	0.264	0.483	0.280	0.350	0.020	0.048
	I&S	F	0.057	0.600	0.855	0.846	0.854	0.515	0.653	0.546	0.441
	I	M	0.000	0.016	0.119	0.172	0.355	0.179	0.349	0.585	0.156
	I|noS	M	0.000	0.007	0.095	0.134	0.158	0.450	0.187	0.419	0.263
	S|I	M	0.225	0.198	0.203	0.178	0.806	0.302	0.047	0.294	0.030
	I&S	M	0.000	0.012	0.088	0.117	0.516	0.163	0.194	0.545	0.081
Heart disease	I	F	0.000	0.085	0.000	0.000	0.849	0.392	0.017	0.874	0.051
	I|noS	F	0.000	0.052	0.000	0.000	0.903	0.440	0.010	0.946	0.084
	S|I	F	0.812	0.398	0.068	0.059	0.701	0.010	0.301	0.406	0.020
	I&S	F	0.000	0.099	0.000	0.000	0.891	0.080	0.016	0.863	0.021
	I	M	0.017	0.690	0.505	0.603	0.248	0.635	0.484	0.262	0.185
	I|noS	M	0.020	0.619	0.458	0.566	0.197	0.856	0.384	0.702	0.343
	S|I	M	0.290	0.243	0.162	0.224	0.468	0.533	0.216	0.077	0.098
	I&S	M	0.018	0.571	0.349	0.478	0.279	0.662	0.413	0.168	0.130
Stroke	I	F	0.068	0.384	0.016	0.015	0.814	0.690	0.023	0.710	0.206
	I|noS	F	0.034	0.266	0.030	0.028	0.817	0.578	0.035	0.791	0.313
	S|I	F	0.056	0.657	0.193	0.147	0.044	0.197	0.062	0.311	0.065
	I&S	F	0.023	0.481	0.012	0.009	0.461	0.540	0.010	0.675	0.135
	I	M	0.086	0.204	0.030	0.017	0.403	0.446	0.036	0.745	0.015
	I|noS	M	0.042	0.135	0.006	0.003	0.276	0.334	0.004	0.437	0.014
	S|I	M	0.290	0.059	0.213	0.195	0.750	0.664	0.215	0.529	0.682
	I&S	M	0.080	0.080	0.024	0.013	0.535	0.543	0.029	0.757	0.020

Mortality	I	F	0.010	0.221	0.092	0.085	0.169	0.517	0.165	0.491	0.011
	I|noS	F	0.006	0.315	0.161	0.162	0.220	0.403	0.321	0.355	0.010
	S|I	F	0.812	0.652	0.331	0.309	0.453	0.108	0.248	0.092	0.029
	I&S	F	0.030	0.308	0.093	0.083	0.195	0.312	0.140	0.368	0.005
	I	M	0.021	0.378	0.306	0.262	0.846	0.370	0.491	0.156	0.077
	I|noS	M	0.032	0.492	0.236	0.227	0.594	0.395	0.318	0.064	0.072
	S|I	M	0.228	0.364	0.274	0.247	0.371	0.154	0.331	0.002	0.009
	I&S	M	0.018	0.360	0.259	0.212	0.796	0.244	0.462	0.033	0.027
Lung disease	I	F	0.493	0.552	0.386	0.403	0.154	0.526	0.421	0.253	0.496
	I|noS	F	0.479	0.483	0.486	0.487	0.154	0.324	0.435	0.273	0.732
	S|I	F	0.381	0.343	0.218	0.190	0.669	0.057	0.185	0.219	0.329
	I&S	F	0.470	0.504	0.295	0.291	0.235	0.250	0.343	0.213	0.474
	I	M	0.603	0.689	0.210	0.273	0.059	0.493	0.102	0.069	0.241
	I|noS	M	0.620	0.502	0.064	0.094	0.119	0.428	0.082	0.074	0.192
	S|I	M	0.013	0.010	0.023	0.026	0.084	0.617	0.161	0.584	0.255
	I&S	M	0.174	0.203	0.052	0.076	0.026	0.569	0.073	0.085	0.215
Diabetes	I	F	0.110	0.189	0.344	0.379	0.572	0.667	0.158	0.282	0.384
	I|noS	F	0.177	0.281	0.407	0.403	0.477	0.655	0.098	0.143	0.593
	S|I	F	0.246	0.110	0.657	0.601	0.086	0.672	0.483	0.134	0.071
	I&S	F	0.091	0.101	0.439	0.454	0.329	0.740	0.174	0.211	0.280
	I	M	0.243	0.234	0.377	0.269	0.603	0.393	0.029	0.103	0.063
	I|noS	M	0.199	0.128	0.284	0.179	0.585	0.403	0.021	0.061	0.068
	S|I	M	0.043	0.025	0.188	0.149	0.609	0.304	0.794	0.419	0.115
	I&S	M	0.085	0.062	0.271	0.171	0.663	0.345	0.049	0.107	0.044
High blood pressure	I	F	0.004	0.007	0.008	0.010	0.154	0.217	0.006	0.683	0.099
	I|noS	F	0.009	0.024	0.043	0.047	0.051	0.138	0.018	0.416	0.074
	S|I	F	0.777	0.534	0.488	0.516	0.018	0.465	0.835	0.084	0.228
	I&S	F	0.012	0.013	0.014	0.018	0.032	0.246	0.012	0.550	0.084
	I	M	0.220	0.393	0.074	0.083	0.053	0.759	0.049	0.111	0.186
	I noS	M	0.121	0.172	0.014	0.017	0.029	0.579	0.029	0.041	0.052
	S|I	M	0.668	0.990	0.697	0.633	0.474	0.283	0.327	0.035	0.091
	I&S	M	0.310	0.666	0.132	0.133	0.072	0.667	0.047	0.052	0.130

(continued)

Table 8A.2 (continued)

			Benchmark: HWW (70+)			3-waves samples (70+)			Longer samples (70+)		
						No refilling			No refilling		Refilling
Health condition	Test	Sex	Article	Appendix	New data						
			W2–4 (AHEAD)	W2–4 (AHEAD)	W2–4 (AHEAD)	W2–4 (all cohorts)	W4–6 (all cohorts)	W7–9 (all cohorts)	W2–6 (all cohorts)	W4–9 (all cohorts)	W2–9 (all cohorts)
			(1)	(2)	(3)	(4)	(5)	(6)	(7)	(8)	(9)
Arthritis	I	F	0.041	0.046	0.093	0.087	0.270	0.928	0.363	0.399	0.053
	I|noS	F	0.017	0.032	0.104	0.109	0.156	0.663	0.234	0.352	0.015
	S|I	F	0.042	0.085	0.034	0.055	0.622	0.003	0.011	0.035	0.000
	I&S	F	0.012	0.020	0.025	0.031	0.349	0.342	0.145	0.240	0.005
	I	M	0.187	0.071	0.081	0.102	0.259	0.960	0.125	0.581	0.884
	I|noS	M	0.276	0.167	0.110	0.151	0.246	0.963	0.112	0.325	0.690
	S|I	M	0.145	0.395	0.382	0.313	0.472	0.409	0.404	0.276	0.009
	I&S	M	0.116	0.082	0.090	0.098	0.289	0.935	0.128	0.538	0.718
Incontinence	I	F	0.357	0.781	0.285	0.271	0.494	0.798	0.195	0.540	0.185
	I|noS	F	0.329	0.597	0.235	0.238	0.646	0.793	0.199	0.727	0.402
	S|I	F	0.080	0.163	0.082	0.077	0.010	0.015	0.004	0.000	0.000
	I&S	F	0.183	0.615	0.142	0.130	0.126	0.351	0.048	0.134	0.000
	I	M	0.161	0.351	0.681	0.614	0.257	0.236	0.553	0.022	0.393
	I|noS	M	0.486	0.682	0.924	0.903	0.396	0.337	0.730	0.312	0.616
	S|I	M	0.237	0.463	0.296	0.374	0.316	0.010	0.175	0.048	0.002
	I&S	M	0.129	0.373	0.602	0.578	0.234	0.043	0.464	0.010	0.169
Fall	I	F	0.864	0.904	0.616	0.626	0.100	0.955	0.089	0.444	0.359
	I|noS	F	0.763	0.790	0.372	0.384	0.193	0.997	0.037	0.525	0.478
	S|I	F	0.515	0.600	0.494	0.482	0.507	0.064	0.296	0.261	0.015
	I&S	F	0.861	0.913	0.630	0.634	0.131	0.764	0.081	0.402	0.205
	I	M	0.402	0.263	0.126	0.248	0.044	0.549	0.013	0.275	0.301
	I|noS	M	0.383	0.207	0.092	0.159	0.028	0.481	0.005	0.111	0.073
	S|I	M	0.507	0.592	0.347	0.474	0.338	0.103	0.009	0.079	0.015
	I&S	M	0.438	0.329	0.126	0.278	0.047	0.342	0.003	0.185	0.164

Significance levels of tests

Hip fracture	I	F	0.604	0.492	0.260	0.256	0.711	0.790	0.083	0.569	0.143
	I|noS	F	0.470	0.280	0.283	0.284	0.646	0.907	0.086	0.302	0.043
	S|I	F	0.275	0.159	0.275	0.259	0.597	0.983	0.195	0.821	0.689
	I&S	F	0.520	0.348	0.222	0.213	0.750	0.925	0.064	0.643	0.170
	I	M	0.056	0.126	0.010	0.017	0.359	0.104	0.000	0.097	0.006
	I|noS	M	0.051	0.053	0.105	0.111	0.203	0.094	0.036	0.155	0.006
	S|I	M	0.305	0.430	0.069	0.078	0.003	0.686	0.011	0.048	0.203
	I&S	M	0.055	0.143	0.004	0.007	0.048	0.167	0.000	0.051	0.005
Proxy interview	I	F	0.345	0.301	0.597	0.582	0.283	0.764	0.953	0.482	0.444
	I|noS	F	0.442	0.465	0.922	0.922	0.506	0.663	0.998	0.782	0.652
	S|I	F	0.250	0.254	0.130	0.144	0.236	0.134	0.009	0.182	0.001
	I&S	F	0.283	0.248	0.413	0.412	0.226	0.577	0.784	0.414	0.185
	I	M	0.424	0.591	0.013	0.018	0.040	0.642	0.000	0.001	0.001
	I|noS	M	0.326	0.378	0.009	0.013	0.017	0.884	0.000	0.001	0.010
	S|I	M	0.019	0.032	0.000	0.000	0.002	0.925	0.000	0.004	0.000
	I&S	M	0.131	0.261	0.000	0.000	0.001	0.803	0.000	0.000	0.000
Cognitive impairment	I	F	0.020	0.005	0.278	0.287	0.417	0.057	0.445	0.053	0.090
	I|noS	F	0.007	0.008	0.436	0.435	0.239	0.108	0.430	0.013	0.127
	S|I	F	0.001	0.002	0.002	0.002	0.034	0.007	0.052	0.000	0.000
	I&S	F	0.000	0.000	0.027	0.026	0.160	0.006	0.285	0.004	0.001
	I	M	0.429	0.288	0.129	0.167	0.357	0.772	0.219	0.034	0.157
	I|noS	M	0.245	0.143	0.068	0.113	0.408	0.705	0.166	0.052	0.228
	S|I	M	0.022	0.026	0.049	0.060	0.031	0.010	0.036	0.001	0.000
	I&S	M	0.140	0.089	0.046	0.068	0.126	0.291	0.109	0.005	0.003
Psychiatric disease	I	F	0.075	0.127	0.164	0.154	0.711	0.075	0.074	0.945	0.175
	I|noS	F	0.031	0.052	0.147	0.150	0.491	0.296	0.063	0.950	0.269
	S|I	F	0.012	0.004	0.012	0.011	0.270	0.522	0.041	0.737	0.299
	I&S	F	0.012	0.012	0.031	0.028	0.622	0.102	0.033	0.958	0.162
	I	M	0.194	0.295	0.036	0.037	0.009	0.099	0.066	0.006	0.088
	I|noS	M	0.546	0.365	0.106	0.115	0.028	0.174	0.212	0.021	0.143
	S|I	M	0.110	0.065	0.110	0.080	0.674	0.004	0.428	0.076	0.035
	I&S	M	0.108	0.137	0.019	0.016	0.019	0.009	0.071	0.003	0.048

(continued)

Table 8A.2 (continued)

| Health condition | Test | Sex | Benchmark: HWW (70+) | | | 3-waves samples (70+) | | | Longer samples (70+) | | |
| | | | Article | Appendix | New data | No refilling | | | No refilling | | Refilling |
			W2–4 (AHEAD) (1)	W2–4 (AHEAD) (2)	W2–4 (AHEAD) (3)	W2–4 (all cohorts) (4)	W4–6 (all cohorts) (5)	W7–9 (all cohorts) (6)	W2–6 (all cohorts) (7)	W4–9 (all cohorts) (8)	W2–9 (all cohorts) (9)
Depression	I	F	0.299	0.211	0.196	0.197	0.236	0.125	0.199	0.732	0.068
	I|noS	F	0.347	0.299	0.503	0.505	0.182	0.133	0.177	0.748	0.095
	S|I	F	0.078	0.011	0.086	0.107	0.001	0.000	0.000	0.000	0.000
	I&S	F	0.151	0.042	0.098	0.109	0.019	0.002	0.023	0.062	0.000
	I	M	0.767	0.944	0.578	0.694	0.185	0.252	0.007	0.452	0.093
	I|noS	M	0.856	0.934	0.478	0.581	0.209	0.125	0.007	0.414	0.041
	S|I	M	0.302	0.065	0.003	0.002	0.005	0.016	0.000	0.007	0.000
	I&S	M	0.695	0.753	0.112	0.148	0.023	0.062	0.000	0.222	0.002
Body mass index	I	F	0.419	0.260	0.192	0.192	0.113	0.008	0.039	0.038	0.001
	I|noS	F	0.330	0.251	0.096	0.104	0.127	0.025	0.018	0.027	0.000
	S|I	F	0.738	0.673	0.932	0.953	0.352	0.083	0.503	0.001	0.011
	I&S	F	0.531	0.345	0.356	0.368	0.115	0.003	0.046	0.006	0.000
	I	M	0.010	0.009	0.011	0.015	0.000	0.353	0.000	0.000	0.000
	I|noS	M	0.002	0.002	0.014	0.017	0.001	0.618	0.000	0.000	0.000
	S|I	M	0.249	0.664	0.664	0.623	0.642	0.248	0.931	0.316	0.487
	I&S	M	0.009	0.019	0.022	0.028	0.000	0.290	0.000	0.000	0.000
Smoke now	I	F	0.509	0.420	0.151	0.158	0.267	0.760	0.085	0.421	0.031
	I|noS	F	0.242	0.214	0.063	0.063	0.382	0.763	0.062	0.655	0.046
	S|I	F	0.838	0.625	0.637	0.635	0.034	0.082	0.140	0.309	0.172
	I&S	F	0.650	0.492	0.210	0.219	0.097	0.525	0.060	0.396	0.024
	I	M	0.366	0.710	0.598	0.579	0.001	0.128	0.000	0.577	0.221
	I|noS	M	0.146	0.504	0.390	0.420	0.068	0.196	0.679	0.016	0.374
	S|I	M	0.064	0.129	0.217	0.424	0.539	0.721	0.459	0.400	0.305
	I&S	M	0.182	0.528	0.488	0.570	0.001	0.200	0.000	0.569	0.208

ADL impairment	I	F	0.010	0.004	0.020	0.019	0.518	0.133	0.046	0.193	0.000
	I|noS	F	0.018	0.022	0.047	0.048	0.343	0.156	0.031	0.181	0.000
	S|I	F	0.818	0.831	0.859	0.850	0.011	0.049	0.238	0.000	0.000
	I&S	F	0.027	0.011	0.049	0.046	0.170	0.052	0.039	0.042	0.000
	I	M	0.004	0.067	0.016	0.020	0.339	0.229	0.026	0.397	0.018
	I|noS	M	0.044	0.114	0.018	0.026	0.692	0.640	0.305	0.468	0.264
	S|I	M	0.370	0.352	0.093	0.131	0.232	0.068	0.453	0.639	0.081
	I&S	M	0.005	0.069	0.008	0.012	0.275	0.111	0.029	0.433	0.011
IADL impairment	I	F	0.673	0.724	0.615	0.598	0.207	0.276	0.467	0.108	0.442
	I|noS	F	0.514	0.525	0.555	0.544	0.150	0.296	0.312	0.106	0.337
	S|I	F	0.368	0.230	0.303	0.281	0.021	0.668	0.114	0.110	0.053
	I&S	F	0.636	0.625	0.555	0.529	0.061	0.353	0.364	0.075	0.335
	I	M	0.016	0.024	0.038	0.022	0.658	0.202	0.009	0.137	0.053
	I|noS	M	0.003	0.011	0.024	0.014	0.633	0.069	0.003	0.084	0.010
	S|I	M	0.006	0.009	0.006	0.004	0.127	0.009	0.023	0.001	0.000
	I&S	M	0.002	0.003	0.004	0.002	0.486	0.041	0.003	0.031	0.002
Self-rated health	I	F	0.151	0.376	0.006	0.008	0.021	0.493	0.004	0.000	0.000
	I|noS	F	0.111	0.341	0.018	0.019	0.078	0.358	0.024	0.000	0.000
	S|I	F	0.001	0.001	0.000	0.000	0.004	0.000	0.000	0.000	0.000
	I&S	F	0.009	0.044	0.000	0.000	0.004	0.001	0.000	0.000	0.000
	I	M	0.581	0.634	0.733	0.650	0.033	0.062	0.052	0.039	0.004
	I|noS	M	0.570	0.607	0.610	0.574	0.008	0.033	0.019	0.009	0.006
	S|I	M	0.034	0.020	0.004	0.003	0.002	0.000	0.000	0.000	0.000
	I&S	M	0.282	0.278	0.226	0.169	0.002	0.000	0.001	0.000	0.000

Notes: Results are for white females (F) and males (M). HWW = Healthy, Wealthy, and Wise (Adams et al. 2003); AHEAD = Asset and Health Dynamics among the Oldest Old survey study; W = waves (e.g., wave 2–4 = W234); I = unconditional invariance; I|noS = invariance, conditional on noncausality; S|I = noncausality, conditional on invariance; I&S = joint invariance and noncausality; ADL = activities of daily living; IADL = instrumental activities of daily living.

Table 8A.3 Tests for invariance and noncausality (all ages)

Health condition	Test	Sex	Significance levels of tests											
			No refilling								Refilling			
			Waves 2–6				Waves 4–9				Waves 2–9			
			70+ (1)	65+ (2)	50+ (3)	50–64 (4)	70+ (5)	65+ (6)	50+ (7)	50–64 (8)	70+ (9)	65+ (10)	50+ (11)	50–64 (12)
Cancer	I	F	0.683	0.666	0.889	0.126	0.777	0.506	0.265	0.388	0.591	0.250	0.497	0.410
	I|noS	F	0.628	0.454	0.720	0.125	0.788	0.513	0.238	0.306	0.489	0.078	0.281	0.318
	S|I	F	0.350	0.367	0.659	0.552	0.020	0.007	0.064	0.349	0.048	0.151	0.077	0.301
	I&S	F	0.653	0.642	0.909	0.151	0.546	0.229	0.159	0.370	0.441	0.198	0.375	0.383
	I	M	0.349	0.269	0.160	0.021	0.585	0.623	0.136	0.108	0.156	0.024	0.116	0.068
	I|noS	M	0.187	0.096	0.245	0.056	0.419	0.647	0.119	0.142	0.263	0.034	0.112	0.055
	S|I	M	0.047	0.082	0.179	0.993	0.294	0.438	0.315	0.689	0.030	0.109	0.110	0.917
	I&S	M	0.194	0.166	0.120	0.058	0.545	0.620	0.127	0.143	0.081	0.015	0.080	0.106
Heart disease	I	F	0.017	0.012	0.043	0.113	0.874	0.867	0.853	0.397	0.051	0.057	0.211	0.546
	I|noS	F	0.010	0.007	0.028	0.144	0.946	0.864	0.912	0.749	0.084	0.039	0.112	0.520
	S|I	F	0.301	0.192	0.035	0.679	0.406	0.053	0.041	0.709	0.020	0.020	0.001	0.115
	I&S	F	0.016	0.009	0.016	0.153	0.863	0.733	0.689	0.460	0.021	0.023	0.053	0.448
	I	M	0.484	0.380	0.405	0.601	0.262	0.336	0.558	0.523	0.185	0.109	0.480	0.117
	I|noS	M	0.384	0.241	0.149	0.376	0.702	0.569	0.485	0.474	0.343	0.200	0.343	0.056
	S|I	M	0.216	0.316	0.071	0.045	0.077	0.092	0.025	0.043	0.098	0.084	0.007	0.119
	I&S	M	0.413	0.352	0.255	0.384	0.168	0.234	0.333	0.336	0.130	0.070	0.245	0.083
Stroke	I	F	0.023	0.008	0.018	0.073	0.710	0.690	0.319	0.199	0.206	0.152	0.201	0.008
	I|noS	F	0.035	0.043	0.052	0.046	0.791	0.730	0.377	0.138	0.313	0.248	0.286	0.037
	S|I	F	0.062	0.167	0.007	0.038	0.311	0.195	0.051	0.252	0.065	0.027	0.007	0.332
	I&S	F	0.010	0.005	0.003	0.029	0.675	0.616	0.189	0.172	0.135	0.078	0.078	0.008
	I	M	0.036	0.042	0.001	0.063	0.745	0.398	0.025	0.011	0.015	0.010	0.005	0.096
	I|noS	M	0.004	0.006	0.000	0.046	0.437	0.151	0.012	0.010	0.014	0.008	0.001	0.113
	S|I	M	0.215	0.181	0.426	0.775	0.529	0.673	0.486	0.958	0.682	0.570	0.082	0.630
	I&S	M	0.029	0.031	0.001	0.099	0.757	0.450	0.030	0.025	0.020	0.013	0.003	0.115

Mortality	I	F	0.165	0.044	0.111	0.079	0.491	0.317	0.305	0.280	0.011	0.002	0.051	0.019
	I|noS	F	0.321	0.096	0.324	0.105	0.355	0.288	0.221	0.199	0.010	0.005	0.130	0.033
	S|I	F	0.248	0.423	0.033	0.029	0.092	0.111	0.005	0.269	0.029	0.030	0.000	0.060
	I&S	F	0.140	0.048	0.045	0.029	0.368	0.231	0.100	0.249	0.005	0.001	0.006	0.010
	I	M	0.491	0.218	0.071	0.049	0.156	0.400	0.424	0.022	0.077	0.118	0.037	0.008
	I|noS	M	0.318	0.138	0.093	0.045	0.064	0.254	0.178	0.005	0.072	0.081	0.007	0.001
	S|I	M	0.331	0.372	0.338	0.279	0.002	0.001	0.000	0.013	0.009	0.006	0.000	0.002
	I&S	M	0.462	0.213	0.069	0.044	0.033	0.096	0.078	0.006	0.027	0.041	0.003	0.001
Lung disease	I	F	0.421	0.511	0.267	0.537	0.253	0.159	0.153	0.216	0.496	0.516	0.347	0.606
	I|noS	F	0.435	0.455	0.175	0.298	0.273	0.556	0.220	0.118	0.732	0.600	0.351	0.564
	S|I	F	0.185	0.283	0.291	0.331	0.219	0.262	0.189	0.616	0.329	0.412	0.432	0.442
	I&S	F	0.343	0.465	0.240	0.504	0.213	0.140	0.120	0.253	0.474	0.512	0.349	0.605
	I	M	0.102	0.040	0.017	0.254	0.069	0.102	0.591	0.361	0.241	0.346	0.574	0.952
	I|noS	M	0.082	0.053	0.020	0.361	0.074	0.082	0.601	0.311	0.192	0.321	0.643	0.903
	S|I	M	0.161	0.210	0.166	0.893	0.584	0.464	0.014	0.021	0.255	0.026	0.004	0.096
	I&S	M	0.073	0.031	0.012	0.363	0.085	0.111	0.330	0.179	0.215	0.207	0.303	0.909
Diabetes	I	F	0.158	0.305	0.032	0.027	0.282	0.700	0.427	0.248	0.384	0.241	0.115	0.220
	I|noS	F	0.098	0.232	0.037	0.020	0.143	0.529	0.387	0.679	0.593	0.295	0.110	0.218
	S|I	F	0.483	0.434	0.000	0.000	0.134	0.116	0.000	0.000	0.071	0.004	0.000	0.000
	I&S	F	0.174	0.311	0.001	0.001	0.211	0.590	0.036	0.018	0.280	0.091	0.001	0.018
	I	M	0.029	0.092	0.391	0.729	0.103	0.242	0.067	0.338	0.063	0.047	0.029	0.021
	I|noS	M	0.021	0.067	0.266	0.684	0.061	0.135	0.110	0.569	0.068	0.016	0.016	0.115
	S|I	M	0.794	0.723	0.009	0.029	0.419	0.506	0.185	0.621	0.115	0.039	0.329	0.061
	I&S	M	0.049	0.129	0.145	0.481	0.107	0.259	0.051	0.381	0.044	0.023	0.027	0.011
High blood pressure	I	F	0.006	0.003	0.249	0.568	0.683	0.450	0.167	0.037	0.099	0.003	0.028	0.116
	I|noS	F	0.018	0.008	0.215	0.547	0.416	0.255	0.236	0.080	0.074	0.012	0.079	0.202
	S|I	F	0.835	0.690	0.440	0.708	0.084	0.111	0.134	0.232	0.228	0.202	0.025	0.061
	I&S	F	0.012	0.006	0.258	0.633	0.550	0.345	0.120	0.031	0.084	0.377	0.011	0.069
	I	M	0.049	0.077	0.115	0.297	0.111	0.686	0.506	0.264	0.186	0.633	0.111	0.401
	I|noS	M	0.029	0.048	0.103	0.456	0.041	0.427	0.591	0.338	0.052	0.235	0.167	0.709
	S|I	M	0.327	0.257	0.201	0.085	0.035	0.168	0.260	0.082	0.091	0.041	0.335	0.253
	I&S	M	0.047	0.066	0.090	0.188	0.052	0.604	0.458	0.173	0.130	0.001	0.106	0.364

(continued)

Table 8A.3 (continued)

Health condition	Test	Sex	Significance levels of tests											
			No refilling								Refilling			
			Waves 2–6				Waves 4–9				Waves 2–9			
			70+ (1)	65+ (2)	50+ (3)	50–64 (4)	70+ (5)	65+ (6)	50+ (7)	50–64 (8)	70+ (9)	65+ (10)	50+ (11)	50–64 (12)
Arthritis	I	F	0.363	0.198	0.895	0.656	0.399	0.592	0.629	0.271	0.053	0.153	0.502	0.565
	I|noS	F	0.234	0.107	0.974	0.697	0.352	0.388	0.459	0.676	0.015	0.040	0.199	0.668
	S|I	F	0.011	0.001	0.110	0.489	0.035	0.016	0.434	0.161	0.000	0.000	0.027	0.671
	I&S	F	0.145	0.032	0.800	0.664	0.240	0.356	0.626	0.211	0.005	0.029	0.333	0.605
	I	M	0.125	0.470	0.857	0.705	0.581	0.912	0.790	0.168	0.884	0.979	0.833	0.022
	I|noS	M	0.112	0.399	0.869	0.764	0.325	0.806	0.706	0.129	0.690	0.945	0.695	0.001
	S|I	M	0.404	0.168	0.020	0.040	0.276	0.058	0.017	0.269	0.009	0.001	0.000	0.053
	I&S	M	0.128	0.382	0.622	0.488	0.538	0.814	0.560	0.149	0.718	0.850	0.432	0.011
Incontinence	I	F	0.195	0.256	0.186	0.231	0.540	0.758	0.241	0.824	0.185	0.321	0.081	0.109
	I|noS	F	0.199	0.294	0.096	0.071	0.727	0.918	0.394	0.596	0.402	0.651	0.079	0.010
	S|I	F	0.004	0.002	0.000	0.040	0.000	0.000	0.000	0.000	0.000	0.000	0.000	0.001
	I&S	F	0.048	0.059	0.006	0.116	0.134	0.066	0.000	0.320	0.000	0.001	0.000	0.014
	I	M	0.553	0.465	0.644	0.093	0.022	0.257	0.067	0.390	0.393	0.235	0.051	0.027
	I|noS	M	0.730	0.650	0.579	0.043	0.312	0.523	0.171	0.228	0.616	0.391	0.112	0.005
	S|I	M	0.175	0.023	0.013	0.190	0.048	0.018	0.002	0.028	0.002	0.000	0.000	0.055
	I&S	M	0.464	0.249	0.356	0.071	0.010	0.121	0.012	0.220	0.169	0.055	0.004	0.014
Fall	I	F	0.089	0.066	n/a	n/a	0.444	0.544	n/a	n/a	0.359	0.071	n/a	n/a
	I|noS	F	0.037	0.040	n/a	n/a	0.525	0.654	n/a	n/a	0.478	0.194	n/a	n/a
	S|I	F	0.296	0.347	n/a	n/a	0.261	0.063	n/a	n/a	0.015	0.039	n/a	n/a
	I&S	F	0.081	0.064	n/a	n/a	0.402	0.399	n/a	n/a	0.205	0.038	n/a	n/a
	I	M	0.013	0.004	n/a	n/a	0.275	0.399	n/a	n/a	0.301	0.156	n/a	n/a
	I|noS	M	0.005	0.001	n/a	n/a	0.111	0.159	n/a	n/a	0.073	0.030	n/a	n/a
	S|I	M	0.009	0.049	n/a	n/a	0.079	0.013	n/a	n/a	0.015	0.047	n/a	n/a
	I&S	M	0.003	0.002	n/a	n/a	0.185	0.203	n/a	n/a	0.164	0.094	n/a	n/a

Hip fracture												
I	F	0.083	0.134	n/a	n/a	0.569	0.392	n/a	0.143	0.116	n/a	n/a
I|noS	F	0.086	0.097	n/a	n/a	0.302	0.241	n/a	0.043	0.040	n/a	n/a
S|I	F	0.195	0.206	n/a	n/a	0.821	0.713	n/a	0.689	0.325	n/a	n/a
I&S	F	0.064	0.108	n/a	n/a	0.643	0.447	n/a	0.170	0.110	n/a	n/a
I	M	0.000	0.155	n/a	n/a	0.097	0.175	n/a	0.006	0.026	n/a	n/a
I|noS	M	0.036	0.384	n/a	n/a	0.155	0.202	n/a	0.006	0.034	n/a	n/a
S|I	M	0.011	0.032	n/a	n/a	0.048	0.028	n/a	0.203	0.382	n/a	n/a
I&S	M	0.000	0.070	n/a	n/a	0.051	0.087	n/a	0.005	0.026	n/a	n/a
Proxy interview												
I	F	0.953	0.792	0.820	0.519	0.482	0.512	0.059	0.444	0.202	0.130	0.093
I|noS	F	0.998	0.975	0.964	0.480	0.782	0.745	0.094	0.652	0.376	0.145	0.021
S|I	F	0.009	0.007	0.000	0.577	0.182	0.317	0.000	0.001	0.001	0.000	0.073
I&S	F	0.784	0.490	0.278	0.553	0.414	0.484	0.001	0.185	0.054	0.001	0.059
I	M	0.000	0.000	0.003	0.071	0.001	0.005	0.001	0.001	0.000	0.000	0.018
I|noS	M	0.000	0.000	0.001	0.184	0.001	0.020	0.005	0.010	0.007	0.000	0.018
S|I	M	0.000	0.000	0.000	0.000	0.004	0.001	0.000	0.000	0.221	0.000	0.000
I&S	M	0.000	0.000	0.000	0.000	0.000	0.000	0.000	0.000	0.000	0.000	0.000
Cognitive impairment												
I	F	0.445	0.356	n/a	n/a	0.053	0.353	n/a	0.090	0.092	n/a	n/a
I|noS	F	0.430	0.395	n/a	n/a	0.013	0.234	n/a	0.127	0.154	n/a	n/a
S|I	F	0.052	0.018	n/a	n/a	0.000	0.000	n/a	0.000	0.000	n/a	n/a
I&S	F	0.285	0.168	n/a	n/a	0.004	0.004	n/a	0.001	0.000	n/a	n/a
I	M	0.219	0.218	n/a	n/a	0.034	0.244	n/a	0.157	0.225	n/a	n/a
I|noS	M	0.166	0.344	n/a	n/a	0.052	0.347	n/a	0.228	0.217	n/a	n/a
S|I	M	0.036	0.010	n/a	n/a	0.001	0.000	n/a	0.000	0.000	n/a	n/a
I&S	M	0.109	0.076	n/a	n/a	0.005	0.022	n/a	0.003	0.000	n/a	n/a
Psychiatric disease												
I	F	0.074	0.034	0.858	0.756	0.945	0.757	0.615	0.175	0.024	0.488	0.823
I|noS	F	0.063	0.029	0.748	0.741	0.950	0.794	0.531	0.269	0.033	0.340	0.885
S|I	F	0.041	0.004	0.000	0.000	0.737	0.208	0.028	0.299	0.196	0.000	0.000
I&S	F	0.033	0.006	0.260	0.397	0.958	0.701	0.410	0.162	0.019	0.044	0.362
I	M	0.066	0.204	0.506	0.790	0.006	0.038	0.357	0.088	0.013	0.260	0.747
I|noS	M	0.212	0.174	0.496	0.851	0.021	0.056	0.541	0.143	0.020	0.276	0.798
S|I	M	0.428	0.280	0.248	0.870	0.076	0.018	0.049	0.035	0.036	0.022	0.354
I&S	M	0.071	0.183	0.450	0.856	0.003	0.013	0.224	0.048	0.006	0.144	0.730

(continued)

Table 8A.3 (continued)

Significance levels of tests

Health condition	Test	Sex	No refilling — Waves 2–6				No refilling — Waves 4–9				Refilling — Waves 2–9			
			70+ (1)	65+ (2)	50+ (3)	50–64 (4)	70+ (5)	65+ (6)	50+ (7)	50–64 (8)	70+ (9)	65+ (10)	50+ (11)	50–64 (12)
Depression	I	F	0.199	0.224	0.224	0.438	0.732	0.207	0.292	0.708	0.068	0.175	0.293	0.827
	I|noS	F	0.177	0.196	0.457	0.547	0.748	0.217	0.222	0.802	0.095	0.167	0.456	0.746
	S|I	F	0.000	0.000	0.000	0.000	0.007	0.000	0.000	0.000	0.000	0.000	0.000	0.000
	I&S	F	0.023	0.018	0.000	0.001	0.062	0.001	0.000	0.004	0.000	0.000	0.000	0.000
	I	M	0.007	0.069	0.207	0.158	0.452	0.052	0.285	0.233	0.093	0.138	0.529	0.065
	I|noS	M	0.007	0.039	0.064	0.078	0.414	0.045	0.109	0.143	0.041	0.045	0.133	0.029
	S|I	M	0.000	0.000	0.000	0.000	0.007	0.000	0.000	0.000	0.000	0.000	0.000	0.000
	I&S	M	0.000	0.001	0.000	0.000	0.222	0.004	0.000	0.003	0.002	0.001	0.000	0.000
Body mass index	I	F	0.039	0.010	0.019	0.002	0.038	0.000	0.000	0.000	0.001	0.000	0.000	0.000
	I|noS	F	0.018	0.005	0.008	0.004	0.027	0.000	0.000	0.000	0.000	0.000	0.000	0.000
	S|I	F	0.503	0.328	0.221	0.437	0.001	0.004	0.004	0.116	0.011	0.008	0.002	0.042
	I&S	F	0.046	0.010	0.015	0.002	0.006	0.000	0.000	0.000	0.000	0.000	0.000	0.000
	I	M	0.000	0.000	0.000	0.000	0.000	0.000	0.000	0.000	0.000	0.000	0.000	0.000
	I|noS	M	0.931	0.828	0.260	0.388	0.316	0.182	0.006	0.102	0.487	0.007	0.004	0.147
	S|I	M	0.000	0.000	0.000	0.000	0.000	0.000	0.000	0.000	0.000	0.000	0.000	0.000
	I&S	M	0.000	0.000	0.000	0.000	0.000	0.000	0.000	0.000	0.000	0.000	0.000	0.000
Smoke now	I	F	0.085	0.039	0.065	0.171	0.421	0.231	0.073	0.004	0.031	0.049	0.015	0.038
	I|noS	F	0.062	0.061	0.031	0.161	0.655	0.343	0.228	0.113	0.046	0.031	0.007	0.261
	S|I	F	0.140	0.046	0.000	0.000	0.309	0.084	0.000	0.000	0.172	0.166	0.000	0.000
	I&S	F	0.060	0.018	0.010	0.006	0.396	0.159	0.005	0.000	0.024	0.038	0.000	0.000
	I	M	0.000	0.904	0.103	0.351	0.577	0.087	0.700	0.170	0.221	0.415	0.087	0.003
	I|noS	M	0.679	0.000	0.173	0.564	0.016	0.076	0.543	0.315	0.374	0.382	0.055	0.001
	S|I	M	0.459	0.053	0.002	0.016	0.400	0.302	0.000	0.003	0.305	0.079	0.000	0.000
	I&S	M	0.000	0.794	0.019	0.162	0.569	0.081	0.287	0.046	0.208	0.325	0.002	0.000

Measure	Test	Sex												
ADL impairment	I	F	0.046	0.101	0.066	0.058	0.193	0.210	0.024	0.068	0.000	0.000	0.000	0.051
	I|noS	F	0.031	0.072	0.079	0.020	0.181	0.244	0.036	0.030	0.000	0.000	0.000	0.028
	S|I	F	0.238	0.295	0.000	0.000	0.000	0.000	0.000	0.000	0.000	0.000	0.000	0.000
	I&S	F	0.039	0.093	0.002	0.004	0.042	0.012	0.000	0.000	0.000	0.000	0.000	0.000
	I	M	0.026	0.011	0.003	0.059	0.397	0.414	0.675	0.254	0.018	0.180	0.324	0.423
	I|noS	M	0.305	0.264	0.038	0.019	0.468	0.688	0.850	0.443	0.264	0.386	0.381	0.208
	S|I	M	0.453	0.197	0.000	0.000	0.639	0.034	0.000	0.000	0.081	0.000	0.000	0.000
	I&S	M	0.029	0.009	0.000	0.003	0.433	0.273	0.003	0.001	0.011	0.036	0.000	0.004
IADL impairment	I	F	0.467	0.602	0.577	0.546	0.108	0.008	0.006	0.344	0.442	0.243	0.131	0.052
	I|noS	F	0.312	0.395	0.507	0.600	0.106	0.021	0.004	0.154	0.337	0.103	0.080	0.074
	S|I	F	0.114	0.056	0.001	0.007	0.110	0.030	0.000	0.003	0.053	0.011	0.000	0.003
	I&S	F	0.364	0.443	0.199	0.261	0.075	0.003	0.000	0.081	0.335	0.129	0.003	0.014
	I	M	0.009	0.166	0.097	0.201	0.137	0.105	0.005	0.004	0.053	0.007	0.014	0.010
	I|noS	M	0.003	0.092	0.071	0.251	0.084	0.082	0.021	0.015	0.010	0.008	0.005	0.014
	S|I	M	0.023	0.027	0.000	0.000	0.001	0.000	0.000	0.000	0.000	0.000	0.000	0.000
	I&S	M	0.003	0.078	0.000	0.006	0.031	0.007	0.000	0.000	0.002	0.000	0.000	0.000
Self-rated health	I	F	0.004	0.001	0.003	0.084	0.000	0.004	0.004	0.011	0.000	0.000	0.000	0.034
	I|noS	F	0.024	0.003	0.014	0.056	0.000	0.003	0.005	0.005	0.000	0.000	0.000	0.009
	S|I	F	0.000	0.000	0.000	0.000	0.000	0.000	0.000	0.000	0.000	0.000	0.000	0.000
	I&S	F	0.000	0.000	0.000	0.000	0.000	0.000	0.000	0.000	0.000	0.000	0.000	0.000
	I	M	0.052	0.017	0.020	0.216	0.039	0.016	0.021	0.063	0.004	0.001	0.001	0.011
	I|noS	M	0.019	0.009	0.016	0.468	0.009	0.010	0.004	0.037	0.006	0.003	0.001	0.018
	S|I	M	0.000	0.000	0.000	0.000	0.000	0.000	0.000	0.000	0.000	0.000	0.000	0.000
	I&S	M	0.000	0.000	0.000	0.000	0.000	0.000	0.000	0.000	0.000	0.000	0.000	0.000

Notes: Results are for white females (F) and males (M). I = unconditional invariance; I|noS = invariance, conditional on noncausality; S|I = noncausality, conditional on invariance; I&S = joint invariance and noncausality; ADL = activities of daily living; IADL = instrumental activities of daily living; n/a = not applicable.

References

Adams, Peter, Michael D. Hurd, Daniel McFadden, Angela Merrill, and Tiago Ribeiro. 2003. "Healthy, Wealthy, and Wise? Tests for Direct Causal Paths between Health and Socioeconomic Status." *Journal of Econometrics* 112:3–56.

Adda, Jerome, Tarani Chandola, and Michael Marmot. 2003. "Socioeconomic Status and Health: Causality and Pathways." *Journal of Econometrics* 112:57–63.

Adler, Nancy E., and Joan M. Ostrove. 1999. "Socioeconomic Status and Health: What We Know and What We Don't." In *Socioeconomic Status and Health in Industrialized Nations,* edited by Nancy E. Adler et al., 3–15. Bethesda, MD: Annals of the New York Academy of Sciences.

Arellano, Manuel, and Stephen R. Bond. 1991. "Some Tests of Specification for Panel Data: Monte Carlo Evidence and an Application to Employment Equations." *Review of Economic Studies* 58 (2): 277–97.

Contoyannis, Paul, Andrew M. Jones, and Nigel Rice. 2004. "The Dynamics of Health in the British Household Panel Survey." *Journal of Applied Econometrics* 19 (4): 473–503.

Cutler, David M., Adriana Lleras-Muney, and Tom Vogl. 2011. "Socioeconomic Status and Health: Dimensions and Mechanisms." In *The Oxford Handbook of Health Economics,* edited by Sherry Glied and Peter C. Smith. Oxford: Oxford University Press, forthcoming.

Florens, Jean-Pierre. 2003. "Some Technical Issues in Defining Causality." *Journal of Econometrics* 112:127–28.

Geweke, John. 2003. "Econometric Issues in Using the AHEAD panel." *Journal of Econometrics* 112:115–20.

Goldsmith, Noreen. 2001. "Social Inequalities in Health: Disentangling the Underlying Mechanisms." In *Strengthening the Dialogue between Epidemiology and Demography.* Vol. 954, edited by M. Weinstein and A. Hermalin, 118–39. Bethesda, MD: Annals of the New York Academy of Sciences.

Granger, Clive W. J. 1969. "Investigating Causal Relations by Econometric Models and Cross-Spectral Methods." *Econometrica* 37 (3): 424–38.

———. 2003. "Some Aspects of Causal Relationships." *Journal of Econometrics* 112:69–71.

Grossman, Michael. 1972. "On the Concept of Health Capital and the Demand for Health." *Journal of Political Economy* 80 (2): 223–55.

Gustman, Alan L., Thomas L. Steinmeier, and Nahid Tabatabai. 2010. "What the Stock Market Decline Means for the Financial Security and Retirement Choices of the Near-Retirement Population." *Journal of Economic Perspectives* 24 (1): 161–82.

Hausman, Jerry A. 2003. "Triangular Structural Model Specification and Estimation with Application to Causality." *Journal of Econometrics* 112:107–13.

Heckman, James J. 2000. "Causal Parameters and Policy Analysis in Economics: A Twentieth Century Perspective." *Quarterly Journal of Economics* 114 (1): 45–97.

———. 2003. "Conditioning, Causality and Policy Analysis." *Journal of Econometrics* 112:73–78.

Heiss, Florian. 2010. "Dynamics of Self-Rated Health and Selective Mortality." *Empirical Economics* 40 (1): 119–40.

Hoover, Kevin D. 2001. *Causality in Macroeconomics.* Cambridge: Cambridge University Press.

———. 2003. "Some Causal Lessons from Macroeconomics." *Journal of Econometrics* 112:121–25.

Hurd, Michael, and Arie Kapteyn. 2003. "Health, Wealth, and the Role of Institutions." *Journal of Human Resources* 38 (2): 386–415.

Meer, Jonathan, Douglas L. Miller, and Harvey S. Rosen. 2003. "Exploring the Health–Wealth Nexus." *Journal of Health Economics* 22 (5): 713–30.

Michaud, Pierre-Carl, and Arthur van Soest. 2008. "Health and Wealth of Elderly Couples: Causality Tests Using Dynamic Panel Data Models." *Journal of Health Economics* 27:1312–25.

Pearl, Judea. 2000. *Causality: Models, Reasoning, and Inference.* Cambridge: Cambridge University Press.

Poterba, James M. 2003. "Some Observations on Health Status and Economic Status." *Journal of Econometrics* 112:65–67.

Robins, James M. 2003. "General Methodological Considerations." *Journal of Econometrics* 112:89–106.

Rubin, Donald B. 1974. "Estimating Causal Effects of Treatments in Randomized and Nonrandomized Studies." *Journal of Educational Psychology* 66 (5): 668–701.

Rubin, Donald B., and Fabrizia Mealli. 2003. "Assumptions Allowing the Estimation of Direct Causal Effects." *Journal of Econometrics* 112:79–87.

Sims, Christopher A. 1972. "Money, Income, and Causality." *American Economic Review* 62 (4): 540–52.

Smith, James P. 1999. "Healthy Bodies and Thick Wallets: The Dual Relationship between Health and Economic Status." *Journal of Economic Perspectives* 13 (2): 145–66.

———. 2005. "Consequences and Predictors of New Health Events." In *Analyses in the Economics of Aging,* edited by David A. Wise, 213–40. Chicago: University of Chicago Press.

Comment   Robert J. Willis

This paper revisits the important and controversial paper of Adams et al. (2004)—denoted HWWA—which sought to uncover the causal direction of the correlation between health and economic status using longitudinal data from the Asset and Health Dynamics among the Oldest Old (AHEAD) cohort of the Health and Retirement Study (HRS). Their methodology and their finding that they could not reject the hypothesis that economic status has no causal effect on health, a test of Granger noncausality together with tests of invariance, stimulated much controversy. Indeed, an entire issue of the *Journal of Econometrics* was devoted to the HWWA paper and to a set of detailed comments on its methodology and findings by an exceptionally distinguished group of scholars from economics, epidemiology, philosophy, and statistics.

Much of the importance of the earlier paper stems from the importance of the basic questions it addresses. Do economic resources determine health?

Robert J. Willis is professor of economics and research professor at the Institute for Social Research and the Population Studies Center at the University of Michigan and a research associate of the National Bureau of Economic Research.

For acknowledgments, sources of research support, and disclosure of the author's material financial relationships, if any, please see http://www.nber.org/chapters/c12444.ack.

Does health determine economic success? Or are both health and wealth dependent on some third factor? In a country that devotes nearly a fifth of its gross national product (GNP) to health expenditures and has growing disparities in income and wealth, the answers to these questions obviously have enormous implications for health policy and economic policy. HWWA proposed a novel approach for testing the direction of causality. Their approach and results are important and controversial from a scientific point of view both because the literatures in public health and economics have long had opposite views about the direction of causality between health and economic status and because conventional econometric reasoning strongly suggests that it is exceedingly difficult to disentangle the many plausible sources of endogeneity underlying the health-wealth correlation in order to estimate credible causal effects in population data.

The current chapter—denoted SHMW—is billed as the first step of a longer project to address the methodological and substantive issues raised by the HWWA paper and its critics. SHMW have chosen in this chapter to employ the same methodology that HWWA used in order to test the hypothesis that economic status has no effect on health in a broader sample that includes younger people and more waves of the HRS.

Their argument for this strategy has two main elements. First, many of the doubts about the validity of the earlier finding of Granger noncausality of economic resources on health center on the idea that people over the age of seventy in the AHEAD sample are much less resource-constrained in terms of access to medical care than younger Americans because of Medicare. More generally, it may be noted that socioeconomic health differentials experience seem to expand until people reach age fifty to seventy and then become more compressed in very old age (Smith 2004). These considerations suggest that it should be harder to reject a Granger noncausality test in the expanded sample and that a failure to reject would yield a more convincing conclusion than HWWA.

The second reason for their strategy is that it is straightforward to test for Granger noncausality and invariance while it is very difficult to identify a structural model in which the causal impact of a particular policy change or economic event such as a change in the age of eligibility for Medicare or a negative wealth shock from the Great Recession. SHMW acknowledge that Granger causality is a purely statistical concept that fails to answer the kinds of causal questions that are of interest to scientists who seek to understand the mechanisms that link economic resources and health outcomes or to policymakers who are trying to find economic policy levers that can improve health. Still, finding that SES is not G-causal and that the relationship is invariant across SES and health histories of different length, covering samples of varying age would be informative. Indeed, such a finding would undermine the credibility of epidemiological research that assumes that inequality in SES is a major cause of health disparities, and it would also call into question the value of policies to increase access to health care by expanding health insurance coverage.

In the course of discussing their strategy, SHMW provide an excellent extended discussion of the alternative meanings of causality, of alternative mechanisms that might underlie health-wealth correlations, and of the econometric issues that must be addressed before it is possible to test specific causal hypotheses or estimate the effect of a policy on health outcomes. This discussion will be useful to any researcher or consumer of research in this area. It should also serve as a warning that research on causal linkages between health and wealth needs to pass a high bar to be credible.

The empirical work presented in the current chapter provides an important intermediate step in the long-term project, but ultimately demonstrates that the original HWWA strategy is unlikely to achieve its aim of narrowing the search for structural models of the health-wealth connection that are relevant for policymakers by ruling out, for example, all possible models that involve causal impacts of economic variables on health outcomes. The chapter examines a very wide range of health outcomes in a series of samples carefully chosen to isolate if and when the HWWA findings supporting Granger noncausality of wealth and health break down as younger individuals and longer histories are considered. The results indicate that tests of noncausality are rejected fairly often and that it is not easy to find an informative pattern in the samples or outcomes for which rejection or nonrejection occur.

To me, the broad conclusion to be drawn from this chapter is, unsurprisingly, that it is quite likely that economic resources matter for some but not all health outcomes. This conclusion is supported by recent research on findings from natural experiments on the health effects of mass layoffs (Sullivan and von Wachter 2009) and access to health insurance (Finkelstein, et al. 2011). Moreover, as SHMW suggest, the new health care legislation in combination with the large shocks to employment and wealth generated by the Great Recession will generate more evidence from natural experiments whose outcomes will be recorded in the HRS and administrative data. I would hope that future researchers, including SHMW, will make use of this exogenous variation—purchased at such high cost!—to go beyond broad causality tests and investigate more narrowly focused questions about the mechanisms that connect specific health outcomes to specific changes in prices, income, and wealth. Ultimately, both science and policy require more specific information about what connects means to ends.

References

Adams, Peter, Michael D. Hurd, Daniel McFadden, Angela Merrill, and Tiago Ribeiro. 2003. "Healthy, Wealthy, and Wise? Tests for Direct Causal Paths between Health and Socioeconomic Status." *Journal of Econometrics* 112:3–56.

Finkelstein, Amy, Sarah Taubman, Bill Wright, Mira Bernstein, Jonathan Gruber, Joseph P. Newhouse, Heidi Allen, Katherine Baicker, and the Oregon Health Study Group. 2011. "The Oregon Health Insurance Experiment: Evidence from the First Year." NBER Working Paper no. 17910. Cambridge, MA: National Bureau of Economic Research.

Smith, James P. 2004. "Unraveling the SES-Health Connection." In *Aging, Health and Public Policy: Demographic and Economic Perspectives, Population and Development Review*, supplement to vol. 30, edited by Linda J. Waite, 108–32. New York: The Population Council.

Sullivan, Daniel, and Til von Wachter. 2009. "Job Displacement and Mortality: An Analysis using Administrative Data." *Quarterly Journal of Economics* 124 (3): 1265–1306.

Childhood Health and Differences in Late-Life Health Outcomes between England and the United States

James Banks, Zoë Oldfield, and James P. Smith

9.1 Introduction

International comparisons of health have risen in importance as a method of gaining insight into social and economic determinants of health status. Partly, this is due to the recent discovery and documentation of large unexplained differences in morbidity health outcomes that suggest that Americans are much sicker than their Western European counterparts (Banks et al. 2006; Avendano et al. 2009). In a set of recent papers, we compared disease prevalence among middle age adults fifty-five to sixty-four and at older ages in England and in the United States (Banks et al. 2006, 2009; Banks, Muriel, and Smith 2010; Banks, Berkman, and Smith 2011). Based on self-reported prevalence of seven important illnesses (diabetes, heart attack, hypertension, heart disease, cancer, diseases of the lung, and stroke), Americans were much less healthy than their English counterparts. These differences were large at all points of the socioeconomic status (SES) distribution.

Biological markers of disease showed similar health disparities between Americans and the English, suggesting that these large health differences were not a result of differential reporting of illness. We also found that these health differences existed with equal force among both men and women

James Banks is professor of economics at the University of Manchester and deputy research director at the Institute for Fiscal Studies. Zoë Oldfield is senior research economist at the Institute of Fiscal Studies. James P. Smith is senior economist at the RAND Corporation.

We are grateful for comments by participants at the conference and our discussant Amitabh Chandra. The research was supported by grants from the National Institute on Aging (NIA). Banks and Oldfield are grateful to the Economic and Social Research Council for cofunding through the Centre for Microeconomic Analysis of Public Policy at the Institute of Fiscal Studies (IFS). For acknowledgments, sources of research support, and disclosure of the authors' material financial relationships, if any, please see http://www.nber.org/chapters/c12445.ack.

(Banks et al. 2009). Because we purposely excluded minorities (African Americans and Latinos in America and nonwhites in England), these differences were not solely due to health issues in the minority or immigrant population. Moreover, these disparities in prevalence of chronic illness were also not the consequence of differences between the two countries in conventional risk factors such as smoking, obesity, and drinking—estimates of health disparities were essentially unchanged when we controlled for different levels of these risk factors in America and in England. Models of diabetes prevalence that controlled for both body mass index (BMI) and waist circumference displayed much reduced country differences (Banks et al. 2011). However, the extent to which this can be interpreted as an explanation of cross-country diabetes differences is somewhat limited if one views raised waist circumference for a given BMI as part of the fundamental etiology of diabetes. We still have to be able to explain why—for given levels of obesity—Americans have larger waists than the English. All in all, therefore, it remains the case that much of the US-English difference in later life adult health remains unexplained.

In this chapter, we investigate another hypothesis to help us understand underlying reasons for the large American health disadvantage. This hypothesis is that differential prevalence and differential impacts of early life conditions, and particularly childhood health, between England and the United States may have led to differences in subsequent later-life health outcomes. Considerable evidence has emerged that variation in health outcomes at middle and older ages may be traced in part to health and other conditions during childhood (Barker 1997; Case, Lubotsky, and Paxson 2005; Case, Fertig, and Paxson 2005; Currie and Stabile 2003; Smith 2009a, Smith and Smith 2010). In this chapter, we will test whether such variation accounts for important parts of country differences in adult health.

This remainder of this chapter is divided into four sections. The next section describes the data that we will use in this analysis, while the section that follows compares prevalence of childhood illnesses for birth cohorts in the two countries. Section 9.4 summarizes the main results obtained from analytical models relating these childhood illnesses to measures of adult health. The purpose of this analysis is to assess how much of the large differences in illness at middle and older ages in America compared to England can be explained by any differences that prevailed when these people were children and adolescents. The final section of the paper highlights our main conclusions.

9.2   Childhood Health Data in the HRS and ELSA

This research uses data from two surveys—the English Longitudinal Survey of Aging (ELSA) and the US Health and Retirement Survey (HRS).

Both surveys collect longitudinal data on health, disability, economic circumstances, work, and well-being from a representative sample of the English and American populations aged fifty and older. Both ELSA and HRS are widely viewed as strong in the measurement of socioeconomic variables (education, employment, income, wealth) and health (self-reported subjective general health status, prevalence and incidence of physical and mental disease during the post-age fifty adult years, such as hypertension, heart disease, diabetes, stroke, chronic lung diseases, asthma, arthritis and cancer, and emotional and mental illness including depression), disability and functioning status, and several salient health behaviors (smoking, alcohol consumption, and physical activity). The HRS and ELSA have both been widely used in stand-alone studies as well as comparative studies of adult health.

One limitation of ELSA and HRS, along with the various other new international aging data sets, is that data collection only begins at age fifty (and even later for those cohorts who were older at the time of the initial baseline interview). Fortunately, this limitation was recognized, and many of these data sets subsequently fielded questionnaires or questionnaire modules that aimed to fill in, through retrospective recall, the more salient episodes in respondents' prebaseline life histories. Childhood events including childhood health were an important part of these life history interviews.

Both the HRS and ELSA included very similar retrospectively reported childhood health histories. The ELSA fielded their childhood health history between its wave 3 and wave 4 core interviews between February and August 2007. The ELSA used a stand-alone life-history computer assisted personal interview (CAPI) covering a variety of childhood circumstances and events as well as the prebaseline adult years. All ELSA respondents were eligible, and there was an 80 percent response rate ($N = 7,855$). For the purposes of our analysis, the data from the life history questionnaire were combined with the data from the third wave the main interview, which was fielded between June 2006 and March 2007. The HRS childhood health history was initially placed into an Internet survey in 2007 for those respondents who had Internet access and who agreed to be interviewed in that mode ($N = 3,641$). The remainder of HRS respondents ($N = 12,337$) received the same childhood health history as part of the 2008 core interview.[1]

In addition to a subjective question rating their childhood health before age sixteen on the standard five-point scale from excellent to poor, respondents in both surveys were asked about the occurrence of a set of common childhood illnesses. If the condition did exist, they were asked the age of first onset. The list of childhood illnesses that were asked was very similar in the two surveys but not identical—some diseases were asked in one sur-

---

1. See Smith (2009a) for details.

vey but not the other.[2] Thus, we confine our analysis in this chapter only to childhood illnesses and conditions that were asked in both surveys. Even within this set of childhood conditions, there are differences in wording or inclusion that must be taken into account. The following childhood diseases have basically the same wording in both surveys—asthma, diabetes, heart trouble, chronic ear problems, severe headaches or migraines, and epilepsy or seizures. For the common childhood infectious diseases, HRS respondents were asked about mumps, measles, and chicken pox separately, while ELSA respondents were asked a single question about all infectious disease with the question wording mentioning these three diseases but also including polio and tuberculosis.

The biggest difference between the two surveys involves allergies and respiratory problems. In the HRS, respondents were asked about respiratory disorders, which included bronchitis, wheezing, hay fever, shortness of breath, and sinus infections, and were separately asked about any allergic conditions. The ELSA respondents were asked about allergies including hay fever and then separately about respiratory problems. Thus, hay fever shows up in a different category in the two surveys. The other difference of possible significance concerns the category of emotional and psychological problems, which included two questions about depression and other emotional problems in the HRS and one question about emotional, nervous, or psychiatric problems in the ELSA.

In addition to any impact of these wording differences, the form in which the questions were asked also differed between the two surveys. The HRS respondents were asked separate questions about each condition, while the ELSA respondents were shown a showcard that contained a list of conditions and then asked to identify any that they may have had before age sixteen. The showcard format could lead to lower reported prevalence if respondents that had multiple conditions only identify a subset from showcards, while they would have answered in the affirmative to each of the questions individually had they been asked.

9.3   Comparing Childhood Health in England and the United States

Our first descriptive analysis compares prevalences of childhood conditions that are more or less comparably defined in England and the United States using these two surveys. In addition to presenting overall prevalence in the two samples, we also stratified the data by four broadly defined birth

2. For example, the following childhood conditions and diseases were asked in the ELSA but not in the HRS—broken bones and fractures; appendicitis; leukemia or lymphoma; cancer or malignant tumor. The following conditions were asked in the HRS but not in the ELSA—difficulty seeing even with glasses or prescription lenses; a speech impairment; stomach problems; high blood pressure; a blow to the head, head injury, or trauma severe enough to cause loss of consciousness or memory loss for a period of time.

cohorts—those born pre-1930, those born between 1930 and 1939, those born between 1940 and 1949, and those born in 1950 or after. Given the age selection of the HRS and ELSA respondents and the fact that both samples were refreshed with younger cohorts prior to the retrospective data collection (in 2006 for the ELSA and 2004 for the HRS), the youngest cohort of our sample contains only those born between 1950 and 1956.

Such age stratification may reveal the nature of any secular trends in the prevalence of childhood diseases in the two countries. Given the reliance on recall for this data, however, considerable caution in interpreting any age patterns is advisable. One problem involves mortality selection if those with healthier childhoods live longer as they undoubtedly do. This is a selection effect that should become stronger at older ages.

Because these prevalence measures are based on recall, a second problem is that memory biases may be playing a role in these trends as well, and these may also be stronger at older ages. It is well established that memory typically declines with time from the event (Sudman and Bradburn 1974). Salient events may suffer less from this type of memory decay, and memory of childhood happenings appear to be superior than for other times of life. Smith (2009a) shows that data from these recall histories on childhood health show similar age-cohort patterns to those collected from contemporaneous sources, for example.

The third and final problem is the difficulty in separating cohort or time trends in true prevalence and incidence from improved detection or changing diagnostic thresholds. For most childhood diseases, there is very likely improved diagnosis and detection of childhood diseases over time, and, for some diseases, including mental illness, there may be some effect of a lowering of the threshold for diagnosis.

With these caveats in mind, table 9.1 presents the patterns revealed in the data on the prevalence of early life health conditions in England and the United States. The first pattern of note is that across all ages in all nine childhood diseases, reported prevalence is actually higher in the United States than in England. In some cases, the prevalence rates are rather close (epilepsy, migraines, and asthma), but, in most cases, the rates in the United States are much higher, especially if we use relative risk as the metric for comparison. For example, there is a 45 percent higher risk of childhood allergies in the United States and a 29 percent higher risk of respiratory problems in the United States compared to England. Because England includes hay fever in allergies and the United States in respiratory, the relative risk difference between the two countries is even higher for allergies. Similarly, even though overall prevalence is low in both countries, relative risk of childhood heart disease and diabetes is much higher in the United States. Supporting evidence for an American excess of childhood disease compared to the English comes from Martinson, Teitler, and Reichman (2011), who demonstrate using biomarker data from the National Health and Nutrition Examina-

Table 9.1   Childhood disease prevalence (%) in the US Health and Retirement Survey (HRS) and English Longitudinal Survey of Aging (ELSA)

	Heart disease		Emotional problems		Diabetes		Epilepsy		Ear problems	
	ELSA	HRS	ELSA	HRS	ELSA	HRS	ELSA	HRS	ELSA	HRS
Pre-1930	0.49	2.06	1.33	2.63	0.00	0.11	0.24	0.34	5.06	8.56
1930–39	0.64	1.87	1.55	2.98	0.05	0.11	0.54	0.47	7.62	8.99
1940–49	0.93	2.32	2.38	3.75	0.00	0.08	0.59	0.67	7.28	9.39
1950–56	0.70	1.74	1.75	4.52	0.06	0.47	0.91	0.89	6.42	10.06
All	0.73	2.05	1.85	3.53	0.02	0.18	0.59	0.61	6.80	9.29

	Migraines		Asthma		Respiratory problems		Allergies	
	ELSA	HRS	ELSA	HRS	ELSA	HRS	ELSA	HRS
Pre-1930	2.90	4.47	2.48	2.33	7.61	7.12	3.29	4.50
1930–39	4.14	4.41	2.80	3.10	8.61	10.77	4.36	6.54
1940–49	5.64	5.03	3.38	4.54	9.65	12.41	6.19	9.76
1950–56	6.30	6.28	3.97	4.02	8.32	13.33	8.76	11.49
All	4.94	5.04	3.21	3.69	8.75	11.27	5.80	8.42

tion Survey (NHANES) and the Health Survey for England that in more contempory times there is also an American excess of childhood disease. It is important to note that their comparisons do not rely on recall.

The second salient pattern in these data is country differences in across-cohort trends. While for most childhood diseases in both countries secular trends indicate growing prevalence over time, these secular trends appear to be much sharper in the United States than in England. For example, take respiratory diseases as the first example—childhood prevalence is almost twice as high in the youngest birth cohorts compared to the oldest birth cohorts in table 9.1. The comparable figure for England is 9 percent higher.

We have discussed three potential difficulties in interpreting the cross-cohort trends in table 9.1, namely mortality selection, imperfect recall, and secular trends in diagnosis. In principal, each of these effects could also be operating differentially in England and the United States and, hence, affecting our cross-country comparisons as well. Of the three, the one that is most amenable to investigation is mortality selection, and particularly the concern that cohort trends in mortality selection may be rather different in the two countries.

What would be most worrying would be higher rates of mortality prior to older ages in England. This might lead one to suppose that those who had the specific childhood conditions identified in this table would be more likely to have died in England than in the United States, hence leading us to measure lower prevalence in England when we interview survivors of these cohorts many years later. In previous research, we have already documented lower mortality rates in England between ages fifty and sixty-five (Banks, Muriel, and Smith 2010) so to further our evidence on this issue we analyzed the Human Mortality Database data on survival to various ages for the two countries for all cohorts born between 1934 and 1958 (data on earlier cohorts are not available for the United States).[3] The analysis (presented in figure 9B.1 in appendix B) demonstrates that English cohorts were, in fact, more likely to survive to age fifty than their US counterparts. If childhood disease is predictive of mortality prior to age fifty, we may, if anything, be understating the true prevalence differences between the two countries at the time these cohorts were young.

Interestingly, cohort trends in these survival probabilities are somewhat different across countries. For cohorts born from 1948 onward, the differences between countries in the likelihood of living to age fifty becomes rather more substantial than for the earlier cohorts. Once again, this cohort-specific country divergence may be worrying for our analysis. But further investigation of this feature indicates that it is due to a sharp increase in the probability of living to age one in England after the Second World War for these later cohorts so that their survival rates were comparable to similar cohorts in the United States, while their predecessors had rather lower survival probabilities.[4] When we look at cohort trends in survival to age fifty conditional on survival to age one, the pattern of cohort trends in the two countries is much more comparable with, in fact, an even greater advantage in favor of the English. Given that much of the diagnosis and onset of our childhood conditions will occur after age one, it is this last evidence that we think is most relevant for our purposes here.

Turning back to the ELSA and HRS childhood data that form the core of our analysis, table 9.2 compares later-life health outcomes in England and the United States, with the outcomes measured at or near to the time the retrospective data were collected (i.e., 2007 in England and 2007 to 2008 in the United States). We divide health outcomes into three groups—illnesses that we label major, those labeled minor, and those labeled "Barker." Major illness includes cancer, lung disease, stroke, angina, heart attack, and heart failure. Minor illness includes hypertension, diabetes, and arthritis. Barker illnesses include those related to heart disease and diabetes (angina, heart attack, heart failure, hypertension, and diabetes)—the diseases that are at the core of the Barker hypothesis linking early life and particularly in utero factors to later life health. For both countries, prevalence rates are stratified by age and gender in table 9.2.

There are several salient patterns revealed in table 9.2. Not surprisingly,

3. See http://www.mortality.org/.
4. One hypothesis is that this improvement in infant mortality in England in this period was due to better nutrition (Deaton 1976).

Table 9.2   Patterns of types of adult illness in England and the United States

Age	Male		Female		Total	
	ELSA	HRS	ELSA	HRS	ELSA	HRS
Major adult illness						
50–54	0.09	0.18	0.10	0.20	0.10	0.19
55–59	0.15	0.25	0.12	0.25	0.13	0.25
60–64	0.25	0.34	0.24	0.34	0.25	0.34
65–69	0.30	0.44	0.28	0.37	0.29	0.40
70–74	0.38	0.55	0.29	0.42	0.33	0.48
75–79	0.49	0.64	0.36	0.50	0.42	0.56
80–84	0.48	0.70	0.37	0.55	0.42	0.61
85+	0.45	0.68	0.43	0.58	0.43	0.61
Total	0.27	0.40	0.24	0.37	0.26	0.38
Minor adult illness						
50–54	0.41	0.53	0.38	0.60	0.39	0.56
55–59	0.55	0.65	0.56	0.66	0.56	0.65
60–64	0.63	0.70	0.64	0.78	0.63	0.74
65–69	0.64	0.80	0.73	0.83	0.69	0.82
70–74	0.71	0.82	0.78	0.86	0.75	0.84
75–79	0.73	0.87	0.79	0.88	0.76	0.88
80–84	0.74	0.85	0.85	0.91	0.81	0.88
85+	0.74	0.85	0.82	0.90	0.79	0.89
Total	0.61	0.72	0.66	0.78	0.64	0.75
Barker illness						
50–54	0.33	0.43	0.25	0.42	0.29	0.43
55–59	0.45	0.53	0.38	0.45	0.42	0.49
60–64	0.51	0.59	0.43	0.55	0.47	0.57
65–69	0.55	0.70	0.52	0.64	0.54	0.67
70–74	0.61	0.71	0.61	0.68	0.61	0.69
75–79	0.69	0.77	0.66	0.73	0.67	0.74
80–84	0.67	0.78	0.69	0.78	0.68	0.78
85+	0.67	0.77	0.72	0.77	0.70	0.77
Total	0.52	0.62	0.49	0.59	0.51	0.60

Note: ELSA = English Longitudinal Survey of Aging; HRS = US Health and Retirement Survey.

for all three disease categories, disease prevalence rises rapidly with age in both countries, with ages in the fifties and sixties witnessing the most rapid rate of increase. Most important, across all three categories of illness used in table 9.2, Americans have much higher rates of disease than the English do. This pattern of excess illness in America compared to England when defined using these aggregated disease groupings appears to be true for men and women and accords with the various findings on the more specific conditions and diseases that we have documented in our other research (Banks et al. 2006; Banks et al. 2010).

Table 9.3   **Modeling country differences in adult health outcomes—baseline model**

	Major	Minor	Major or minor	Barker
Age	0.177***	0.259***	0.274***	0.224***
Age^2	−0.018***	−0.039***	−0.042***	−0.028***
Male	0.037***	−0.044***	−0.032***	0.042***
US	0.072***	0.145***	0.159***	0.111***
Age*US	0.030	−0.023	−0.045**	0.001
Age^2*US	−0.002	0.001	0.005	−0.003
Male*US	0.025	0.002	0.011	−0.001
Constant	0.027	0.390***	0.423***	0.233***
N	19,583	19,583	19,583	19,583

Notes: See text for more detailed descriptions of major, minor, and Barker illness categories.
***Significant at the 1 percent level.
**Significant at the 5 percent level.

9.4   Analytical Models Comparing Effects of Childhood Health on Adult Health in England and the United States

Table 9.3 presents our baseline ordinary least squares (OLS) models that attempt to isolate the salient country level differences in adult disease prevalence. These models contain only a quadratic in age (normalized so that age fifty is zero and defined for expositional convenience as [(age–50)/10]), a gender dummy (male = 1), a country dummy (US = 1) and interactions of the US indicator variable with the age quadratic and gender. Not surprisingly, given the patterns revealed in table 9.2, we find that all three disease groups increase with age at a decreasing rate, there is a small but statistically significant male disease excess for major and Barker disease categories and a small (but again statistically significant) female excess for minor diseases in England.[5] In terms of our main interest in country differences, we find a statistically significant common excess of disease in the United States. On average, and for the base case individuals (fifty-year-old females), disease excess in the United States over England is 7.2 percentage points for major diseases, 14.5 percentage points for minor diseases, and 11.1 percentage points for Barker diseases. There is no strong evidence that this American disease excess differs across age and gender because the US interactions with these variables are not generally statistically significant.

In the tables that follow, we expand the models in table 9.3 with additional groups of covariates with an eye toward examining the marginal impact of these additions on the country-level main effect differences in adult health status. The added covariates in table 9.4 include our few available common measures of childhood circumstances, parental background, and SES. These

5. As always, these age patterns could partially reflect cohort effects as well.

Table 9.4   Modeling country differences in adult health outcomes—adding
                  childhood socioeconomic status (SES) controls

	Major	Minor	Major or minor	Barker
Age	0.178***	0.245***	0.259***	0.200***
Age^2	−0.019***	−0.038***	−0.040***	−0.026***
Male	0.047***	−0.022	−0.021	0.090***
Mother died	0.120***	0.118***	0.107***	0.156***
Mother age died	−0.001***	−0.001***	−0.001**	−0.001***
Father died	0.078**	0.101***	0.123***	0.183***
Father age died	−0.001	−0.001***	−0.002***	−0.002***
SES_low	0.014	0.040***	0.038***	0.037***
Height	−0.002	−0.004**	−0.002	−0.009***
US	0.069**	0.120***	0.150***	0.098***
Age*US	−0.002	−0.042	−0.074***	−0.011
Age^2*US	0.004	0.005	0.010**	0.001
Male*US	0.024	−0.004	0.013	−0.023
Mother died*US	0.021	−0.045	−0.017	−0.007
Mother age died*US	0.000	0.001	0.000	0.000
Father died*US	0.077	0.012	−0.012	0.018
Father age died*US	−0.001	0.001	0.001**	0.000
SES_low*US	0.013	−0.020	−0.017	−0.004
Height*US	0.001	0.002	0.000	0.005
Constant	−0.019	0.359***	0.380***	0.166***
N	19,583	19,583	19,583	19,583

Notes: Base group is a 50-year-old female with mother and father alive, average height, and
high childhood SES. See text for more detailed descriptions of major, minor, and Barker illness categories.
***Significant at the 1 percent level.
**Significant at the 5 percent level.

measures are (a) whether the mother or father of the respondent was dead
at the time of the collection of the retrospective data and, if so, their age
of death, which could be seen as measures of shared familial environment
during the childhood years and/or genetic factors; (b) whether your SES
was low during the childhood years based on father's occupation when you
were sixteen years old; (c) adult height measured in centimeters (normalized
to mean height—sixty-five inches), an often used summary statistic to capture elements of the Barker hypothesis related to childhood nutrition. Once
again, all variables in these models are interacted with a country dummy
(US = 1). These new variables in (a) and (c) could equally well be thought
of as alternative indicators of childhood health. Parents and children shared
genes forever and environment for at least decades so that parental deaths
and/or date of death may pick up elements of health transmitted from parents to their children. Even more so, adult height is often used as a summary
statistic for childhood health, or at least the nutritional components of childhood health and as a marker for Barker-related diseases.

Examining the effects of new variables included in these models, all forms of adult disease are higher if either the mother or father of the respondent was dead at the time of the HRS or ELSA survey interview—an effect that is larger the younger the age at which parent died. The effect of these variables is not generally statistically significantly different in the two countries though. Through either shared family environment or genetics, having a parent die at a younger age may indicate greater shared familial proneness to illness. Particularly for minor and Barker diseases, adult levels of disease are higher among those who were a member of a low-SES family during their childhood years. Finally, consistent with Barker's hypothesis, taller adults are also healthier adults. This association is especially strong for the Barker category of disease.

Once again and somewhat remarkably, very few of the interactions of variables with the US country indicator are statistically significant with the exception of the US main effect, which still signals statistically significantly higher levels of disease in America compared to England, on average. This US-level effect is only slightly smaller in table 9.4 compared to that obtained in the baseline models in table 9.3 indicating that this set of childhood SES or parental health measures do not contribute very much to "explaining" the country difference in adult health.

Our first attempt to evaluate the contributory role of childhood health toward country level adult disease differences is contained in table 9.5, which adds to the set of variables in models in table 9.4 the summary childhood measure of subjective health status, that is, whether the respondents report that they had excellent or very good health as a child. The other covariates are not appreciably altered by this addition of childhood subjective health, so we will confine our discussion to the subjective childhood health measures. The estimated effect of being in excellent or very good health during one's childhood years is to lower the probability of all forms of adult disease. This association also appears to be statistically significantly larger in the United States compared to England, but only for the major disease category.

However, the estimated overall average adult health differences between America and England in table 9.5 has remained essentially unchanged compared to those in table 9.4 and in the case of major illnesses has actually increased from 0.069 to 0.102. If childhood health problems raise the probability of adult health problems and if, as the data in table 9.1 indicate, there are more such problems in America than in England, how is it possible that these problems fail to explain the between-country health difference or even more perversely make them even larger?

Table 9.6 provides the answer by displaying country differences in excellent or very good subjective childhood health as a child by birth cohort in both England and the United States. In spite of the fact that the data in table 9.1 show that in almost all childhood diseases for all birth cohorts that Americans were sicker as children than their English counterparts, table 9.6

Table 9.5   Modeling country differences in adult health outcomes—adding childhood subjective health

	Major coef.	Minor coef.	Major or minor coef.	Barker coef.
Age	0.174***	0.241***	0.255***	0.199***
Age^2	–0.018***	–0.037***	–0.039***	–0.026***
Male	0.047***	–0.023	–0.021	0.090***
Mother died	0.117***	0.115***	0.103***	0.154***
Mother age died	–0.001***	–0.001**	–0.001**	–0.001***
Father died	0.075**	0.097***	0.119***	0.181***
Father age died	–0.001	–0.001***	–0.002***	–0.002***
SES_low	0.013	0.039***	0.037***	0.036***
Height	–0.002	–0.004	–0.002	–0.009***
Exc health as child	–0.047***	–0.053***	–0.057***	–0.024**
US	0.102***	0.121***	0.145***	0.117***
Age*US	0.001	–0.040	–0.072***	–0.010
Age^2*US	0.004	0.005	0.010**	0.000
Male*US	0.023	–0.005	0.012	–0.024
Mother died*US	0.018	–0.044	–0.016	–0.008
Mother age died*US	0.000	0.001	0.000	0.000
Father died*US	0.074	0.013	–0.011	0.017
Father age died*US	–0.001	0.001	0.001**	0.000
SES_low*US	0.013	–0.019	–0.016	–0.004
Height*US	0.001	0.002	0.000	0.005
Exc health as child*US	–0.031**	0.006	0.014	–0.019
Constant	0.018	0.401***	0.426***	0.185***
N	19,583	19,583	19,583	19,583

Notes: Base group is a 50-year-old female with mother and father alive, average height, high childhood SES, and good/fair/poor self-reported childhood health. See text for more detailed descriptions of major, minor, and Barker illness categories.

***Significant at the 1 percent level.

**Significant at the 5 percent level.

Table 9.6   Fraction in excellent or very good health during childhood in the US Health and Retirement Survey (HRS) and English Longitudinal Survey of Aging (ELSA)

	Male		Female		Total	
	ELSA	HRS	ELSA	HRS	ELSA	HRS
Pre-1930	0.62	0.70	0.64	0.70	0.63	0.70
1930–39	0.68	0.76	0.61	0.78	0.64	0.77
1940–49	0.68	0.79	0.68	0.82	0.68	0.88
1950–56	0.77	0.81	0.71	0.79	0.74	0.80
All	0.69	0.77	0.66	0.78	0.68	0.78

indicates that when asked to evaluate their childhood health on a subjective scale that Americans respond that their childhoods were healthier than the responses of the English would indicate about their own English childhood. The problem with using the childhood subjective health scale is actually the same as the problem with using the adult variant of these scales—given the same objective level of health on subjective scales, Americans will report themselves as healthier than the English (Banks et al. 2009; Kapteyn, Smith, and van Soest 2007). For example, the fraction of ELSA respondents who report excellent or very good childhood health is 0.68, while in the HRS, it is 0.78—a ten-point differential in favor of the Americans. Because of this, and because being in excellent or very good health as a child is associated with better adult health in both countries, this will make the unexplained country adult health difference even larger.

Putting aside for a moment this problem of country differences in subjective scales, the within-country patterns revealed in table 9.6 are also of interest. The within-country gender differences in subjective childhood health are not large. However, there is a clear and very pronounced trend across cohort in both countries where subjective childhood health is reported to be better among the more recent cohorts. If we compare most recent cohorts in table 9.6 to the oldest cohorts, the increase in the fraction in excellent or very good health as a child is about 10 percentage points in both England and America. While it is possible that childhood health improved across these cohorts (contrary to the evidence on chronic diseases presented in table 9.1 above, and subject to the various caveats and especially to the role of improved diagnosis we identified in the discussion of that table), the magnitude of this increase seems rather implausible, particularly in the presence of health survivor effects, which would tend to work across cohorts in the opposite direction. This points to another major puzzle in the reconciliation of secular trends in subjective and objective childhood health measures.

Table 9.7 extends our modeling of adult health in table 9.6 by adding the set of childhood disease indicators to the model as well as interactions of this set of childhood diseases with the US country indicator variable. Because the prevalence rates of some of these childhood diseases are low, we aggregated them into six groups. The six groups are ear problems, respiratory, allergies, asthma, rare diseases (childhood diabetes, epilepsy, emotional), and all others. Main effects and interactions with the US country indicator are included in the model. Because of the across-country scale comparability issue mentioned previously, the model estimated in table 9.7 does not include the subjective childhood health variable.

Once again, coefficients of other variables in the model are not significantly affected by adding childhood disease indicators. The diseases that appear to have most consistently statistically significant main effects are ear problems, respiratory diseases, and rare diseases. Especially for major illness,

Table 9.7   Modeling country differences in adult health outcomes—adding childhood disease indicators

	Major	Minor	Major or minor	Barker
Age	0.175***	0.244***	0.258***	0.201***
Age^2	−0.018***	−0.037***	−0.039***	−0.026***
Male	0.052***	−0.019	−0.016	0.090***
Mother died	0.120***	0.115***	0.104***	0.153***
Mother age died	−0.001***	−0.001**	−0.001**	−0.001***
Father died	0.080**	0.101***	0.123***	0.182***
Father age died	−0.001	−0.002***	−0.002***	−0.002***
SES_low	0.016	0.040***	0.039***	0.036***
Height	−0.002	−0.004**	−0.002	−0.009***
Ear problems	0.045**	0.011	0.017	−0.014
Respiratory	0.092***	0.044**	0.073***	0.017
Allergies	−0.022	−0.036	−0.036	−0.027
Asthma	0.039	0.006	0.003	0.015
Rare	0.027	0.058***	0.063***	0.027
All other	−0.004	−0.000	−0.009	−0.018
US	0.041	0.110***	0.142***	0.080**
Age*US	0.005	−0.041	−0.072***	−0.010
Age^2*US	0.004	0.005	0.011**	0.001
Male*_US	0.027	−0.004	0.011**	−0.020
Mother died*US	0.019	−0.041	−0.013	−0.005
Mother age died*US	0.000	0.001	0.000	0.000
Father died*US	0.071	0.010	−0.014	0.017
Father age died*US	−0.001	0.001	0.001**	0.000
SES_low*US	0.013	−0.019	−0.017	−0.003
Height*US	0.001	0.002	0.001	0.005
Ear problems*US	0.002	0.027	0.015	0.045
Respiratory*US	−0.030	−0.018	−0.042**	−0.008
Allergies*US	0.030	0.042	0.039	0.030
Asthma*US	0.055	−0.005	0.020	0.015
Rare*US	0.101***	−0.015	−0.022	0.035
All other*US	0.024	0.021	0.030	0.023
Constant	−0.034	0.350***	0.370***	0.167***
N	19,583	19,583	19,583	19,583

Notes: Base group is a 50-year-old female with mother and father alive, average height, high childhood SES, good/fair/poor self-reported childhood health, and no specific childhood health conditions. See text for more detailed descriptions of major, minor, and Barker illness categories.

***Significant at the 1 percent level.
**Significant at the 5 percent level.

transmission into poorer adult health appears to be stronger in the United States for rare diseases and for asthma.

Table 9.8 provides a summary of the estimated main effect American excess of disease from our models in tables 9.3 to 9.7. If we compare the estimates from table 9.7 with the age-adjusted "raw" country differences

Table 9.8   **Summary table of estimated US excess adult illness**

Model	Major	Minor	Barker
Baseline (table 9.3)	0.072***	0.145***	0.111***
+ childhood SES (table 9.4)	0.069**	0.120***	0.098***
+ childhood subjective health (table 9.5)	0.102***	0.121***	0.117***
+ childhood diseases (table 9.7)	0.041	0.110***	0.080**
+ childhood diseases but without US interaction with disease (table 9A.1)	0.082**	0.113**	0.113***

***Significant at the 1 percent level.
**Significant at the 5 percent level.

from table 9.3, the combination of SES or parental health transmission variables and the childhood diseases does "explain" a significant part of the country differences. For example, for major diseases, the raw difference in table 9.3 was 7.2 percentage points of excess disease in America. The adjusted difference in table 9.4 is 4.1 percentage points (and not statistically significant) so that using this metric, 43 percent of the American excess major disease is explained compared to the base case model.

The comparable numbers for minor diseases is a 14.5 percentage point "raw" disease excess in America and an 11.1 percentage point adjusted excess so that 23 percent of the excess is explained. Finally, for the Barker diseases, the comparable numbers are 11.1 "raw" and 8.0 "adjusted" so that 28 percent of the American excess is explained.

As a final note, it is instructive to consider the degree to which this explanation of the excess disease in the United States arises from the inclusion in the model of the indicators of prevalence of the specific childhood illnesses themselves as opposed to the interactions of these prevalence indicators with the US country dummy. To investigate this we ran a similar model to that presented in table 9.7 but with the childhood health country interaction terms excluded (full estimates presented in table 9A.1 in the appendix and estimates of the US intercept term presented in the final row of table 9.8). On comparison of these results with those in the earlier tables, it is apparent that the main contribution to the reduction in both the size and statistical significance of the US country effect arises from the inclusion of the interaction terms—while there is some role for the greater prevalence of childhood conditions in the United States, it is the differential impacts of these childhood conditions on later-life health outcomes in the United States that has the main effect on changing the coefficient on the US dummy variable. While these interaction terms are, of course, just another form of country effect, this does suggest that investigation of the mechanisms by which early-life health is transmitted to late-life disease outcomes in the two countries would be a promising avenue for future research.

9.5   Conclusions

The analysis in this chapter uses comparable retrospective modules placed in the HRS and the ELSA—nationally representative surveys of the age fifty-plus population in America and England, respectively—to show that the poorer adult health of older Americans in comparison to their English counterparts is also apparent right back in the childhood years of these cohorts. Furthermore, the transmission rates of childhood illnesses into poor health in midlife and older ages are also higher in America compared to England. However, these differences in childhood health conditions and the transmission rates of childhood health to adult health between the two countries only partially explain the poor health of older Americans compared to the English.

Of course, every partial answer raises yet another question. In this case, conditions in America appear to make people of all ages sicker than the English. This conclusion highlights a caution that age-specific answers to the question of why Americans are sicker may not serve as a useful guide to uncovering the more fundamental causes of this important question. Our research shows that the primary sources of the American excess in disease are not unique to midadulthood or old age but are more common throughout the age distribution of the two populations. Finally, it is worth noting that we are dealing in this research with the onset of disease rather than the treatment of disease so that the medical system and availability of health insurance are not likely to be the primary actors in this puzzle. This is particularly true given our use of a non-Hispanic white sample, so 95 percent of our American sample have access to health insurance.

Appendix A

Table 9A.1   **Modeling country differences in adult health outcomes—adding childhood disease indicators without interaction terms**

	Major coef.	Minor coef.	Major or minor coef.	Barker coef.
Age	0.175**	0.240**	0.255**	0.199**
Age^2	−0.018**	−0.036**	−0.039**	−0.026**
Male	0.055**	−0.019	−0.017	0.093**
Mother died	0.117**	0.114**	0.103**	0.153**
Mother age died	−0.001**	−0.001*	−0.001*	−0.001**
Father died	0.077*	0.099**	0.121**	0.182**
Father age died	−0.001	−0.001**	−0.002**	−0.002**
SES_low	0.016	0.040**	0.038**	0.037**
Height	−0.002	−0.004*	−0.002	−0.009**
Exc health as child	−0.023*	−0.045**	−0.047**	−0.018
Ear problems	0.044*	0.025*	0.023*	0.015
Respiratory	0.069**	0.026*	0.040**	0.009
Allergies	−0.003	−0.009	−0.012	−0.007
Asthma	0.064**	−0.008	0.005	0.018
Rare	0.090**	0.042**	0.042**	0.047**
All other	0.007	0.007	0.005	−0.006
US	0.082*	0.113*	0.136**	0.113**
Age*US	0.003	−0.039	−0.070**	−0.010
Age^2*US	0.004	0.005	0.010*	0.000
Male*US	0.023	−0.005	0.013	−0.024
Mother died*US	0.019	−0.044	−0.015	−0.007
Mother age died*US	0.000	0.001	0.000	0.000
Father died*US	0.071	0.010	−0.011	0.017
Father age died*US	−0.001	0.001	0.001*	0.000
SES_low*US	0.012	−0.019	−0.016	−0.004
Height*US	0.001	0.002	0.000	0.005*
Exc health as child*US	−0.020	0.011	0.019	−0.015
Constant	−0.027	0.385**	0.407**	0.173**
N	19,583	19,583	19,583	19,583

Notes: See text for more detailed descriptions of major, minor, and Barker illness categories.
**Significant at the 5 percent level.
*Significant at the 10 percent level.

Appendix B

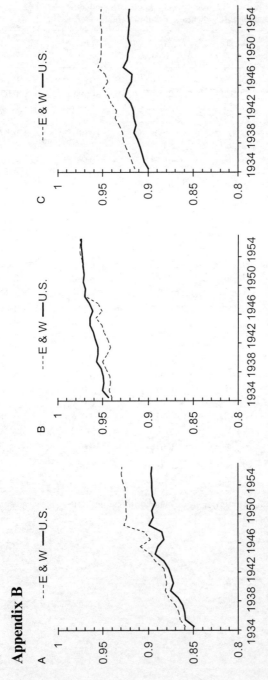

Fig. 9B.1 Survival probabilities in England and Wales compared to the United States by date of birth cohort: *A,* **Probability of surviving to age 1;** *B,* **Probability of surviving to age 50;** *C,* **Probability of surviving to age 50, conditional on surviving to age 1**

Source: Authors' calculations from Human Mortality Database.

References

Avendano, M., M. Glymour, J. Banks, and J. Mackenbach. 2009. "Health Disadvantage in US Adults Aged 50–74: Are Poor Europeans Healthier Than Americans?" *American Journal of Public Health* 99:540–48.

Banks, J., L. Berkman, and J. P. Smith. 2011. "Do Cross-Country Variations in Social Integration and Social Interactions Explain Differences in Life Expectancy in Industrialized Countries?" In *International Differences in Mortality in Older Ages: Dimensions and Sources,* edited by E. Crimmins, S. Preston, and B. Cohen, 210–67. Washington, DC: National Academies Press.

Banks, J., M. Kurmari, J. P. Smith, and P. Zaninotto. 2011. "What Explains the American Disadvantage in Health Compared to the English? The Case of Diabetes." *Journal of Epidemiology and Community Health,* forthcoming.

Banks, J., M. Marmot, Z. Oldfield, and J. P. Smith. 2006. "Disease and Disadvantage in the United States and in England." *Journal of the American Medical Association* 295 (17): 2037–45.

———. 2009. "SES and Health on Both Sides of the Atlantic." In *Developments in the Economics of Aging,* edited by D. Wise, 359–406. Chicago: University of Chicago Press.

Banks, J., A. Muriel, and J. P. Smith. 2010. "Disease Prevalence, Disease Incidence, and Mortality in the United States and in England." *Demography* 47 (Supplement): S211–S231.

Barker, D. J. P. 1997. "Maternal Nutrition, Fetal Nutrition and Diseases in Later Life." *Nutrition* 13 (9): 807–13.

Case, A., A. Fertig, and C. Paxson. 2005. "The Lasting Impact of Childhood Health and Circumstance." *Journal of Health Economics* 24 (2): 365–89.

Case, A., D. Lubotsky, and C. Paxson. 2002. "Economic Status and Health in Childhood: The Origins of the Gradient." *American Economic Review* 92 (5): 1308–34.

Currie, J., and M. Stabile. 2003. "Socioeconomic Status and Child Health—Why Is The Relationship Stronger for Older Children?" *American Economic Review* 93 (5): 1813–23.

Deaton, Angus S. 1976. "The Structure of Demand in Europe 1920–1970." In *The Fontana Economic History of Europe.* Vol. 5, edited by Carlo M. Cippola, 89–131. London: Collins/Fontana.

Kapteyn, A., J. P. Smith, and A. van Soest. 2007. "Vignettes and Self-Reported Work Disability in the US and the Netherlands." *American Economic Review* 97 (1): 461–73.

Martinson, M. L., J. L. Teitler, and N. E. Reichman. 2011. "Health across the Life Span in the United States and England." *American Journal of Epidemiology,* advance access published March 9.

Smith, J. P. 2009a. "Reconstructing Childhood Health Histories." *Demography* 46 (2): 387–403.

———. 2009b. "The Impact of Childhood Health on Adult Labor Market Outcomes." *The Review of Economics and Statistics* 91 (3): 478–89.

Smith, J. P., and G. Smith. 2010. "Long-Term Economic Costs of Psychological Problems during Childhood." *Social Science and Medicine* 71 (1): 110–15.

Sudman, S., and N. Bradburn. 1974. *Response Effect in Surveys: A Review and Synthesis.* Chicago: Aldine.

Comment   Amitabh Chandra

In a series of penetrating papers, Jim Smith and collaborators have demonstrated that Americans are sicker than their British counterparts and that these differences are not the consequence of better diagnosis in the United States. Nor are they the consequence of the United States having larger minority or immigrant populations, for these groups were excluded from their analysis. What we do not know is why are Americans at a health disadvantage? Simple explanations such as diet, drinking, and smoking are insufficient explanations. Americans are not always lagging in these behaviors, and the implied health effects of these behaviors are not large enough to explain the puzzle that Banks, Oldfield, and Smith have confronted us with. And so, we wonder—what explains these cross-national health gradients? And how much of the higher medical spending in the United States is a consequence of greater disease burden?

This chapter suggests that the answer might be the differential impact of conditions early in life and in childhood. There is now a well-developed literature on the importance of the "fetal origins" hypothesis and the long reach of childhood insults on adult health outcomes. This chapter invokes these mechanisms to demonstrate that they may be also explain cross-national differences in adult health outcomes.

My summary of the chapter is this: there is a 7 percentage point difference in the prevalence of major diseases (with the United States being the disadvantaged country); these are diseases such as cancer, lung disease, stroke, angina, heart attack, and heart failure, and 40 percent of this difference is explained by childhood socioeconomic status and disease. For diseases such as angina, heart attack, heart failure, hypertension, and diabetes, the difference in prevalence is 11 percentage points, 30 percent of which is explained by these factors. The chapter does not separate the role of in utero factors from those that emphasize the role of childhood factors, so we should think of it as assessing the fullness of both these influences and the role of early circumstance more generally.

Explanations for worse early childhood probably lie in three categories—policy differences, environmental influences, and genetic differences. While differences in gene expression have been shown to predict health outcomes, my reading of the genetics literature is that these characteristics are sufficiently diffuse and their effects too small and too fragile to account for

Amitabh Chandra is economist and professor of public policy at the Harvard Kennedy School of Government, a research fellow at the Institute for the Study of Labor (IZA) in Bonn, Germany, and a research associate of the National Bureau of Economic Research.

For acknowledgments, sources of research support, and disclosure of the author's material financial relationships, if any, please see http://www.nber.org/chapters/c12446.ack.

cross-national differences in health outcomes. More likely is the role of policy and the environment, and I explore these channels next.

One reason for England's superior performance during childhood may be the presence of better health care, especially for the most vulnerable children. The National Health Service (NHS) was created after World War II in England. It offered universal coverage for hospital services and primary care. Most relevant for child health were that its provisions included maternity and child welfare clinics, vaccination, and immunization programs. There were "health visitors," community health nurses who provided families with information on infant caring and feeding, and evaluations of development. In contrast, the United States created the Medicaid program almost twenty years after the United Kingdom (in 1965). Medicaid is a needs-based program whose generosity is substantially less than what the NHS offers, and so while it is targeted, it targets children and not their parents. Despite these limitations, Janet Currie and Jonathan Gruber have found large effects of Medicaid expansions on the dimension of infant mortality. Infant mortality is only one (rather extreme) dimension of childhood health, so it's possible that the protective effects of these expansions are larger than what has been measured. It may also be the case that it is not the health insurance per se that improves child health, but the preventative care and surveillance that came with the NHS but rarely accompany health insurance contracts in the United States. So one explanation for United States-England differences in health are consistent with the interpretation that England offered more comprehensive health care than the United States and that these investments pay off in later life.

One implication of my suggestion that health care and health insurance affect childhood well-being is that the English advantage in health should not be the consequence of selective survival, where vulnerable infants die early. Thankfully, the authors earlier work rules out this channel. But what is troubling for my explanation is table 9.1. If the NHS and associated interventions were responsible for the English advantage, we should see reduced prevalence of childhood illnesses for cohorts born after the introduction of the NHS. That evidence is not there in my reading of this table. Either the channel that I have posited is not at work, or we're asking too much of the data in being able to discern cohort level differences in the prevalence of self-reported medical conditions (an exercise where idiosyncratic variation in reporting may swamp the signal that we're chasing). Perhaps someone will examine the effect of the NHS on child health more directly.

Alternatively, there is the role of the physical and social environment. Janet Currie, Ken Chay, and Michael Greenstone have been chipping away at this problem, and their work proves that reductions in air pollution, even from a very low base, can exert large effects on infant mortality. Are there other such environmental stressors that harm American children? Relatedly, the social environment can matter for adults, and through this channel, their children. I'm thinking here of issues concerning work-life balance that affect adult stress, depression, and anger, as well as aggravators such as financial security and job insecurity that affect parents' ability to concentrate on children's health needs, allergies, and well-being. Is it possible that Americans are materially better off, but on these margins of performance, we lag the English? Clearly, we have much work to do in sorting out these channels.

As you can tell, I've enjoyed this chapter very much. There is much to like about this work and research program, and I look forward to the next installation from this wonderful team.

The Financial Crisis and the Well-Being of America

Angus Deaton

10.1 Introduction

The financial crisis that began in the summer of 2008 saw a rise in the unemployment rate from 4.8 percent in April 2008 to 10.6 percent at its peak in January 2010, a 4.4 percent drop in employee compensation over five months in 2009 to 2010, large stimulus-associated tax credits and rebates, 4.7 percent of personal disposable income in May 2008 and 1.7 percent in May 2009, as well as a collapse and subsequent recovery of the stock market—the S&P 500 Index on March 6, 2009 had fallen to 40 percent of its all time high of October 2007 and then more than doubled again by end 2010. Through the fall in the market and the fall in the prices of housing and other assets, 60 percent of households saw their wealth decline between 2007 and 2009, and 25 percent lost more than half of their wealth (Bricker et al. 2011); these declines were widespread, affecting large shares of households

Angus Deaton is the Dwight D. Eisenhower Professor of Economics and International Affairs at the Woodrow Wilson School of Public and International Affairs and the Economics Department at Princeton University and a research associate of the National Bureau of Economic Research.

I am grateful to the Gallup Organization for access to their data; to Jim Harter of Gallup for his extensive help in understanding the design of the Gallup Healthways Wellbeing Index survey; and to Daniel Kahneman, Daniel McFadden, and Norbert Schwarz for extensive help and comments. I also thank David Cutler, Paul Dolan, Ori Heffetz, David Laibson, Richard Layard, Matthew Rabin, and Arthur Stone for comments on an earlier version of the chapter. This work was supported by the Gallup Organization and by the National Institute on Aging through grants AG024928–06 and P30 AG024361 to Princeton and P01 AG05842-14 to the National Bureau of Economic Research. For acknowledgments, sources of research support, and disclosure of the author's material financial relationships, if any, please see http://www .nber.org/chapters/c12447.ack. Paper also published as Angus Deaton (2012), "The Financial Crisis and the Well-Being of Americans," *Oxford Economic Papers* 64 (1): 1–26, by permission of Oxford University Press.

across all age, income, and education groups (Chakrabarti et al. 2011; Hurd and Rohwedder 2010). Financial losses were associated with reductions in consumption, and many households reduced consumption even without experiencing financial losses (Christelis, Georgarakos, and Jappelli 2011; Shapiro 2010).

These are large fluctuations in magnitudes that matter to people. Income, wealth, and joblessness are among the measures on which economists have traditionally focused. In the well-being literature, too, a host of studies identify income and unemployment as two of the most important and reliable determinants of self-reported well-being (SWB). Unemployment, in particular, typically exerts a larger negative influence than can be accounted for by the associated reduction in income. Although there is less literature on the effects of wealth on well-being, a 60 percent drop in the market has dramatic effects on expected future incomes, especially for those who are nearing a retirement to be funded out of accumulated saving or defined-contribution pension funds. These events had different economic implications for people of different ages; the elderly are not much affected by unemployment or employee compensation, but some are susceptible to stock market fluctuations. Young people may shrug off falls in wealth when they have not yet accumulated much and have many years before they need it, while their parents, nearing retirement, may see an imminent threat to their future.

The crisis brought harm to many, but it is a boon to researchers on self-reported well-being, for whom it provided an unparalleled opportunity to examine how these events affected the standards of living, the emotional experiences, and life evaluations of those who lived through it. Our ability to make this evaluation is made possible by the data from the Gallup Healthways Well-Being Index (henceforward GHWBI). Starting on January 2, 2008, Gallup has run a daily (landline and cell phone) telephone poll of 1,000 randomly sampled adult Americans each day who are asked about how their lives are going, whether they are satisfied with their standard of living, and whether they experienced a range of feelings on the previous day. Over the three-year period examined here, from 2 January 2008 to 29 December 2010, there are around a million observations on self-reported well-being, as well as on demographics, income, occupation, employment status, and numerous health measures. These data allow daily tracking, not only of national averages, but of the outcomes of different groups.

In addition to investigating reports of well-being over the crisis, I look at a range of methodological issues. One is the long-standing question of whether variations in self-reported well-being (SWB) over time correspond to what might be expected from cross-section analysis. A three-year period is too short to address the Easterlin paradox, that long-term growth appears not to generate the increase in SWB that would be predicted from the positive effects of income in the cross-section, but I can examine whether the large fluctuations in income and unemployment generate fluctuations in

SWB that match the findings from the cross-section. The literature on well-being over the business cycle (Di Tella, MacCulloch, and Oswald 2001, 2003; Wolfers 2003; Di Tella and MacCulloch 2007) has relied on data pooled over several countries, rather than on tracking well-being over time within a single country as here, although Stevenson and Wolfers (2008) argue that the output gap in the United States predicts well-being. This literature also argues that people dislike inflation and unemployment, even controlling for their own experience, which would drive a wedge between the cross-sectional and time series effects of macroeconomic outcomes; see also Clark, Knabe, and Rätzel (2011) for discussion and reinterpretation.

I also ask whether the temporal tracking of self-reported well-being measures is useful for economic policy beyond the standard dashboard of measures such as employment, income, and financial market indicators. Many happiness researchers argue that SWB provides a deeper and more comprehensive measure than standard economic indicators and should take priority over them. That SWB should be routinely collected by national statistical agencies, at least as a supplementary measure, was given impetus by the positive recommendations in Stiglitz, Sen, and Fitoussi (2009), and many statistical offices in Europe are currently moving in this direction. Yet questions remain. Although SWB measures have led to many important insights in the cross-section—for example, about the relative importance of income and unemployment, or of marriage and marital dissolution, or of nonpriced amenities—the usefulness of average SWB for macroeconomic monitoring over time is far from established, and investigating that is one of my main concerns in this chapter.

The chapter is constructed as follows. I start in section 10.2 with a brief discussion of concepts of well-being, including reminders of long-standing concerns about happiness measures in general and, within SWB measures, the differences between hedonic and evaluative measures of well-being; this distinction is important in what follows. Section 10.3 discusses the behavior of life evaluation over the crisis and documents the sensitivity of the measure to questionnaire order effects. It also presents an attempt to repair the series to permit substantive analysis. Section 10.4 shows what happened to life evaluation and hedonic experience over the crisis, and section 10.5 relates that experience to macroeconomic magnitudes such as income, unemployment, and the stock market. Section 10.6 concludes.

10.2   Preliminaries: Concepts and Measures of Well Being

Self-reported well-being is my main topic in this chapter, but I do not wish to approach it uncritically, but rather to keep in mind long-standing objections to these measures. Sir John Hicks played a central role in banishing cardinal utility from economics, replacing it with "choice" utility, an ordinal representation of preferences, together with a welfare economics that eschewed interpersonal comparisons and, at the individual level, emphasized the income required to attain a given standard of living. This long-standing skepticism has been eroded in recent years by a literature in economics and psychology that has demonstrated the usefulness of self-reported well-being measures in a number of contexts. Nor has choice utility gone unscathed. Experimental work has also found biases in recollections of events that will sometimes cause choices to deviate from people's own preferences (Kahneman, Wakker, and Sarin 1997), suggesting that direct measures of momentary feelings, integrated over time, might be more reliable guides to decisions that remembered utility.

Yet many of the original concerns remain important. One of the most important is associated with adaptation to circumstances. If people become accustomed to economic misery so that the response of SWB to such pain is only temporary, the continuing harm is no less real nor demanding of policy attention just because people say that they are used to it. Sen (1985, 14) notes that "a person who is ill-fed, undernourished, unsheltered, and ill can still be high up in the scale of happiness or desire fulfillment if he or she has learned to have 'realistic' desires and to take pleasures in small mercies." By accepting people's own assessment in such circumstances, "the metric of happiness may, therefore, distort the extent of deprivation in a specific, and biased way," and "it would be ethically deeply mistaken to attach a correspondingly small value to the loss of well-being because of this survival strategy" Sen (1987, 45–46). I accept these arguments and believe that we should not base policy on a measure that is subject to hedonic adaptation. Yet the extent to which any particular measure of SWB is actually subject to the adaptation critique is a question that can be investigated empirically so that it is possible that Sen's concern is hypothetical, or is hypothetical for some measures but real for others. Note also that Sen does not deny the goodness of happiness in and of itself, only that it is an unreliable indicator of overall well-being.

A second concern, documented in the psychology literature, is about measurement of SWB, particularly in response to questions about the evaluation of life as a whole. The answers to these questions are often treated as if "global feelings of well-being . . . remain relatively constant over extended periods, and that people can describe them with candor and accuracy," Campbell 1981, quoted in Schwarz and Strack 1999). But as Schwarz and Strack's review makes clear, actual reports "do not reflect a stable inner state of well-being" that is always available, but rather judgments that are formed in response to the question, which makes them subject to context effects (Schwarz and Strack 1999, 61). That these warnings must be taken seriously will be amply documented in the results presented in the following.

One key distinction is between "living life" and "thinking about life," Kahneman and Riis (2005). On the one hand, there is a range of feelings that comprise emotional well-being (or hedonic well-being or experienced happiness); these feelings, such as enjoyment, sadness, happiness, anger, stress, or worry, are mostly evanescent and rapidly forgotten but make up the hedonic texture of life as we live it. On the other hand, there is the assessment or evaluation of life as a whole that is prompted by questions about life satisfaction or about how life is going overall.

The gold standard for measuring emotional well-being is experience sampling, by which people are randomly prompted to record their current activities and feelings; a less demanding alternative is the Day Reconstruction Method (DRM; Kahneman et al. 2004), by which people are asked to reconstruct their activities over the previous day and to associate feelings experienced during each episode. Experience sampling and the DRM both allow the construction of hedonic well-being measures by summing over episodes. The American Time Use Survey contains a DRM module. In the Gallup data, a DRM is not feasible, but respondents are presented with a list of emotions, such as stress, worry, and happiness, and are asked to say yes or no to questions about whether they experienced a lot of each on the previous day. In this chapter, I shall look at a range of these feelings, including happiness, smiling, enjoyment, sadness, worry, stress, and anger, as well as a similar question about physical pain.

Life evaluation is most often measured by a question that asks people to report on a several-point scale how satisfied they are with their life as a whole. In the Gallup surveys, the question is Cantril's (1965) Self-Anchoring Scale, a ladder question that asks respondents on which rung they stand on an eleven-rung ladder where zero is the "worst possible life for you" and ten is the "best possible life for you." It is possible that this ladder question, analyzed here, is a purer question of life evaluation than is life satisfaction, where the use of the word "satisfaction" invites contamination by the respondent's current hedonic state.

That hedonic and evaluative well-being behave differently has been reported in a number of studies. Kahneman et al. (2004) find, contrary to their initial hypothesis, that measures of affect are more subject to adaptation and less tightly linked to long-term life circumstances than are measures of life evaluation. Kahneman and Deaton (2010) find that reports of life evaluation (Cantril's ladder), positive affect, negative affect, and stress are all better at higher incomes. However, while the effects of income on affect and stress satiate at an annual income of around $75,000, higher incomes continue to be associated with higher life evaluation throughout beyond $75,000, with the average ladder approximately linear in the logarithm of household income. In a similar vein, life evaluation, but not affect, is better among more-educated people.

Figure 10.1 explores the distinction in another way and shows the average reports for life evaluation and for affect for each day of the week. The average reported ladder, in the top left panel, shows essentially no variation over the week, while positive affect, negative affect, and stress (here coded so

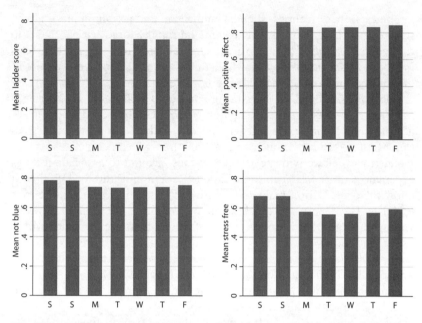

Fig. 10.1   Ladder scores, positive affect, not blue, and stress free by days of week
Notes: Averages are taken over all respondents from January 2, 2008 to December 29, 2010. Positive affect is the average of the fractions of respondents who said that they experienced a lot of smiling, enjoyment, and happiness in the previous day. Not blue is one minus the average of respondents who reported a lot of worry or sadness in the previous day. Stress free is the fraction of respondents who did not report a lot of stress on the previous day.

that higher is better) all show superior hedonic outcomes at weekends than in the week, with Fridays intermediate between week and weekend. At this daily frequency, affect responds to circumstance, while life evaluation does not. (Note that people generally evaluate their lives very highly, around 7 on a scale of 0 to 10, and that most people experience a great deal of positive emotion, little negative emotion, and no stress.) There are also marked differences in patterns of life evaluation and of affect over the life cycle. Stone et al. (2010) replicate the now familiar finding that life evaluation falls with age until middle age, rising mildly thereafter, but also a remarkably large decline in reported stress, worry, and anger with age. This is consistent with socioemotional selectivity theory (Carstensen, Isaacowitz, and Charles 1999), according to which people, as they age, acquire emotional capital, a set of skills that allows the ever more successful avoidance of negative emotional experiences. These benefits of age, together with more modest increases in positive emotional experience, perhaps offset the increase in physical pain and may help account for the increase in overall well-being with age in spite of deteriorating health.

That the ladder responds to long-term circumstances and emotions to short-term circumstances is further supported by international evidence from Gallup's World Poll, which asks similar questions in more than 150 countries around the world. In Deaton (2008), I show that, across countries, average ladder scores are linearly related to the logarithm of per capita gross domestic product (GDP). There are large differences across countries, from Togo, Benin, and Chad, with average ladder scores between 3 and 4, to Denmark, with an average ladder score around 8. An Increase of 1 in the log of per capita GDP by 1 is associated with an increase in the average ladder score of 0.84, and the simple correlation is 0.83 (Deaton 2008, table 1, figure 1.) For future reference, it is important to note that international differences in income are very large compared to what is seen in time series; a difference in log GDP of 1 corresponds to a GDP that is 2.7 times as large or about twenty years of rapid economic growth, while Togo's per capita income is barely 2 percent of that of the United States, a difference that took a quarter of a millennium to develop.

In contrast to life evaluation, the average hedonic experiences of countries are only weakly related to per capita GDP. The fraction of the population that reports a lot of happiness yesterday is only mildly related to national income, essentially because of a few outliers such as, at the bottom, Togo, which is notably unhappy and, at the top, the United States, where the pursuit of happiness is constitutionally guaranteed. Otherwise, there are happy and unhappy countries at all levels of GDP per capita. Hence, as far as self-reported *happiness* (the affect) is concerned, the data support Sen's argument that even the poorest people in the world are often happy, although when we look at *life evaluation,* poor people generally recognize that their lives are going badly. That the hedonic and evaluative components of well-being have such different correlates implies not only that they are different concepts that reflect different parts of human experience, but that we must also consider each separately in assessing what happened over the financial crisis. A single broad measure of "happiness" will not do. From now on, I shall use the term "happiness" for happiness proper, referring to the hedonic experience of being happy, and I shall keep life evaluation for the judgment of life as a whole, as in the Cantril ladder. The evidence cited in this section shows that the emotional measures adapt to life circumstances, at least over the long term, and that this is not true, or at least less true, for measures of life evaluation.

10.3   Life Evaluation in the Crisis

Figure 10.2 shows the daily average of the ladder from the beginning of 2008 to the end of 2010; I have shown it as a twenty-one-day (triangularly weighted) moving average in order to remove the day to day sampling variance that otherwise obscures the trends. The broken line is for those aged sixty and over, the solid line for the whole population; as has often been

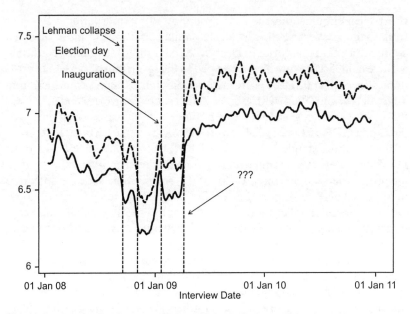

Fig. 10.2   Average ladder scores for general population and for those sixty and over

Notes: The broken line is for the population aged sixty and above, the solid line for the whole population. The underlying data are daily averages, and the figure shows twenty-one-day triangularly weighted moving averages.

found in the literature, see Stone et al. (2010) for these data, the elderly generally do better on life evaluation measures. Although there are features of these plots that make sense—for example, the sharp drop in well-being around the time of the collapse of Lehman Brothers—they are mostly very hard to explain. The oddest feature is that the ladder should be higher at the end of the period than at the beginning; indeed, according to this figure, the general population had more than recovered from the crisis by the spring of 2009, even though unemployment was still rising and even though the stock market, although past its low in March, was still far below its value before the crash. The graphs also show a sharp drop in well-being on Election Day and a somewhat more credible spike on the day that President Obama was inaugurated. The huge increase on April 6, 2009, is substantively inexplicable. The boost to the ladder would require a more than doubling of per capita GDP, and the main events of the day—the earthquake in L'Aquila in Italy, Robert Gates's unveiling of the US defense budget, or even the winning of a country music award by American Idol winner Carrie Underwood—are surely insufficient to explain an increase in well-being that is the single largest change over this otherwise very eventful period.

In fact, the largest changes in the ladder are driven, not by real events, but by changes in question order in the GHWBI survey, the context effects discussed in section 10.2. A full account and analysis will be presented elsewhere, and I confine myself here to a summary of the main points and an outline of the methods used to correct the data.

Gallup uses its daily poll to collect information on political preferences, including whether the respondent plans to vote, if so for whom, who is preferred in a primary, whether the respondent approves of the president's performance, or whether the country is headed in the right direction. Because 2008 was an election year and because these polling questions are important to Gallup whose statisticians are well aware of context effects, they were placed first in the survey, immediately prior to the ladder question. The precise questions were changed frequently depending on the election calendar so that, for example, voter preference questions were dropped on the eve of the presidential election, and the Bush approval question was dropped when he left office. Changes in ladder scores at the time of these events prompted Gallup to randomly split the sample, with half the respondents being asked the political questions as usual and half the respondents being asked none so that the first question they were asked was the ladder of life evaluation. This randomized controlled trial enables us to assess the effect of asking the political questions as opposed to not asking them, and it turns out that these questions cause a large *negative* effect on reported well-being. People appear to dislike politics and politicians so much that prompting them to think about them has a *very* large downward effect on their assessment of their own lives; over the 111th Congress (2009 to 2010), only 25 percent of the population approved of Congress, then one of the lowest numbers in history. Indeed, as we shall see, the effect of asking the political questions on well-being is only a little less than the effect of someone becoming unemployed so that to get the same effect on average well-being, three-quarters of the population would have to lose their jobs. Not everyone becomes unemployed, but either half or all of the respondents are asked the political questions.

Figure 10.3 shows the twenty-one-day moving averages of mean ladder scores, split by the two randomized forms of the survey. The two forms were identical until January 5, 2009, after which the political questions were dropped from form 2; this is shown as the beginning of the shaded area in the figure. During the shaded period, which ends on April 5, form 1 respondents were asked political questions (which changed occasionally), while form 2 respondents were asked none. The difference between the solid and the broken line, about 0.6 of a rung on the ladder, is the negative effect of the political questions on life evaluation; it is about the same size as the decline in the ladder from the beginning to the end of 2008. The form 1 spike is on inauguration day; on this day and this day only, there were no political questions on either form; the difference between the two means on that day was 0.15 and appears much larger in the figure because of the moving average.

After the end of the shaded period, on April 6, 2009, Gallup added a

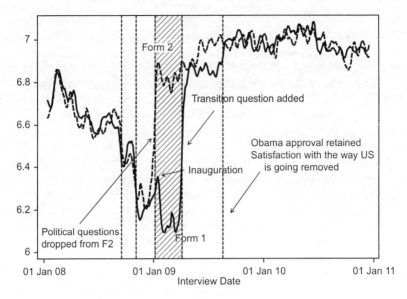

Fig. 10.3   Average ladder score by questionnaire type

Notes: Twenty-one-day triangular weighted averages of averaged daily data for the population as a whole. Forms 1 and 2 are two versions of the questionnaire, identical until the beginning of the shaded area, after which the political questions at the beginning of the questionnaire were removed from form 2. The end of the shaded period shows the date on which a "transition" question about life satisfaction was added to the questionnaire after the political forms and before the ladder question.

"transition question" between the political questions and the ladder question. After asking the political question to form 1 respondents, the interviewer asked, "Now thinking about your personal life, are you satisfied with your personal life today?" This is intended to remove the effects of the political questions by refocusing the respondent's attention, and the figure shows that it is remarkably, if not totally, successful in doing so; see Schwarz and Schuman (1997) for discussion of such buffer questions to offset order effects. From April 6 on, the difference falls from 0.6 of a rung to less than 0.1 of a rung. Starting August 18, the political questions were reduced from two to one; the question about satisfaction with the way that things are going in the United States was dropped, retaining only a question about approval of President Obama. Once that is done, the form 1 and form 2 means are indistinguishable.

For the period from January 6, 2009, we have available a "clean" measure of the ladder from the half of the sample who were asked no prior political questions. This is useful but leaves unanswered the main question, which is the evolution of well-being through 2008, for which it is necessary to make some corrections. There is no assumption-free or nonparametric way of doing this, but there is a very strong correlation between the ladder and the responses to questions about the respondent's standard of living, questions that are asked later in the survey. There are two relevant questions: "Are you satisfied with your standard of living, all the things you can buy and do?" with a Yes/No answer, and "Right now, do you feel your standard of living is getting better or getting worse?" with answers "Getting better, staying the same, or getting worse." The answers to both of these questions predict the ladder with high significance. When I use the "clean" data, from form 2 for 2009 on or after January 6, to regress the ladder on the standard of living answers and collapse the predictions to get a daily time series, the correlation between this prediction and the actual ladder is 0.54. When I do the same for the period before January 6, and during which there are much larger fluctuations in the series, the correlation is 0.80.

My corrections are as follows. Using the "clean" data, I fit an ordered probit to the eleven ladder values (0 to 10) using the standard of living questions as predictors and then use the results to predict the probabilities of each rung for each household in the period up to January 5, 2009. These predicted probabilities are then used to give an expected ladder value for each household. Figure 10.4 shows the daily mean of these predicted values as the lower (light broken) of the two upper lines; for the period after January 6, I use the actual ladder from form 2, dropping form 1. The bottom line is the original, contaminated, ladder score, and even this first correction

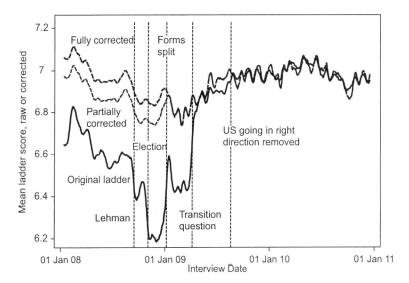

Fig. 10.4   Correcting the ladder for context effects

Notes: The bottom line is the original, uncorrected ladder. The middle line uses only form 2 after the political questions were removed and imputes the ladder prior to the split from the answers to two standard of living questions. The top line makes a further correction for bias in the answers to the standard of living questions. See text for details. All plots are twenty-one-day triangularly weighted moving averages of population means.

makes a dramatic difference to the behavior of well-being over the crisis. Most important, and in contradiction to the original graph, the corrected series estimates that, on average, well-being had not recovered to its January 2008 level by the end of 2010.

This correction likely still understates well-being at the beginning of the period. The reason is that the values used for the adjustment, the answers to the standard of living question, are themselves biased downward by the political questions, even though there are sixteen or so—depending on skip patterns—(mostly health-related) questions between the ladder and the standard of living question; see Bishop (1987) for an example of an order effect that persists in spite of the insertion of up to 101 intervening questions. That this happens here can be established from an analysis of the period from January (when the political questions were removed from form 2 respondents) to April 5, 2009, when the "transition" question was added to form 1. From January 21, after the inauguration, the political questions (approval of Obama, satisfaction with way things are going in the United States) did not change, so there is a clean randomized treatment and control design. Respondents who were given the political questions over this period were 3.6 percentage points less likely to report satisfaction with their standard of living than those who were not asked; the t-value on this is greater than 10. For the future standard of living, where there are three answers, an ordered probit shows a similarly significant downward shift. Because political questions in one form or another were asked throughout 2008, it seems likely that the standard of living answers were biased downward throughout that period, which means that my first correction is probably insufficient.

The political questions changed several times over the election period so that I cannot immediately apply the results from the randomization period to the earlier period. However, the political questions had only a small effect compared with the effect of there being political questions at all; with 1,000 observations every day, regression discontinuity methods can be used to investigate what happens as the questions change. So it seems that *any* political question will depress the answers to the ladder and that the effects persist through the questionnaire into the standard of living and some other questions.

I have, therefore, made a second adjustment to all of the data prior to January 6, 2009, based on the use of the pure randomization period. The method is as follows. From the ordered probit calculated for the first adjustment and estimated on the full "clean" period, I calculate the predicted $x'b$, and then compare the values of this index between experimentals and controls over the randomization period. This gives me an estimate of the downward bias from the political questions, which I add back in, to give $x'b + \delta$, say, which I then use in place of $x'b$ with the originally estimated cut points, to calculate a predicted set of probabilities for each rung for each household. From these, I calculate a predicted ladder for each household.

The moving average of the daily mean of this series is the top line in figure 10.4. This second adjustment is modest compared with the first—the standard of living responses are not nearly as badly affected as is the ladder by the political questions—but it further shifts up the early well-being measures, suggesting more strongly still that Americans are indeed still some way from recovering from the crisis.

10.4   Riding the Waves: Life Evaluation and Hedonics over the Crisis

Stock market fluctuations have a direct effect on those who own assets and are, thus, important for linking the financial crisis to the well-being of individuals. Ideally, the data would allow us to separate people with direct, indirect, or no involvement in the market, but this information was not collected. One way to look at this issue imperfectly is to look at effects across the age and income distributions. Rather than use the corrected ladder itself, I look directly at the fraction of people who report that they are satisfied with their standard of living. This series tracks the ladder closely, which is why it works for the correction, and although it is also contaminated by the political questions, it is much less so than is the case for the ladder. Judgments about standard of living are of interest in their own right and can readily be decomposed by age or income. Figure 10.5 shows the results disaggregated by age group, showing the working age population, fifteen to fifty-nine, as well as sixty to sixty-nine, seventy to seventy-nine, and eighty and over. As

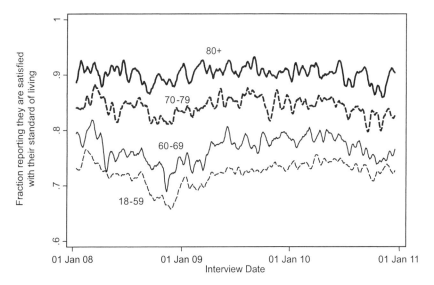

Fig. 10.5   Fractions satisfied with their standard of living, by age group

Notes: Twenty-one-day moving averages of daily averages by age group.

is the case for the ladder itself, the fraction of people satisfied with their standard of living rises with age, even though the level of income itself falls with age; among other things, this result demonstrates that neither the ladder nor the standard of living question is a recode of income. All groups showed some decline in their standard of living from spring 2008 until late in the year, and there was some recovery through 2009. But the severity of the effects diminishes with age, and the crisis had a barely perceptible effect on those aged eighty and above. Interestingly, the sixty to sixty-nine age group was affected as severely as those under sixty, possibly because of their greater dependence on the market through defined-contribution pensions. The oldest group, whose pension income is unlikely to depend on the market, are the least affected by the crisis.

Figure 10.6 shows the corresponding information by household income group; this is somewhat less satisfactory because about a quarter of respondents either refuse to answer the question or report that they don't know and are, therefore, dropped from the analysis. That people who live in higher-income households are more likely to be satisfied with their standard of living is no surprise. More difficult to explain, at least through the wealth channel, is that the impact of the financial crisis on perceived standards of living is much larger—about twice as large—for those whose incomes are below $4,000 a month than for those whose incomes are more than $4,000 a month. An obvious hypothesis is that the rich were affected by the wealth shock and the poor by unemployment but, as we shall see, the decline in standard of living perceptions happened before unemployment began to rise.

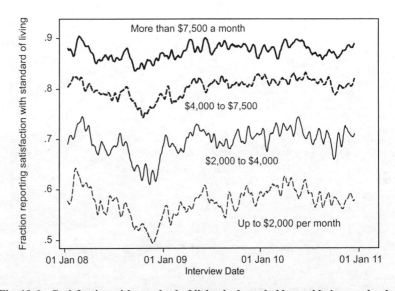

Fig. 10.6   Satisfaction with standard of living by household monthly income level

Notes: Question is about whether you are satisfied with your standard of living plotted as twenty-one-day moving averages by household income groups.

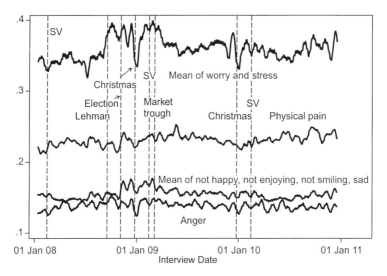

Fig. 10.7   Negative hedonic experience, 2008 to 2010

Notes: Twenty-one-day moving averages of underlying daily averages over the whole population. The top line is the averages of the fractions reporting worry or stress on the previous day. The second line is the fraction reporting physical pain on the previous day. The third line is the average of the fractions who reported sadness or did not report happiness, enjoyment, or smiling on the previous day. The bottom line is the fraction of those reporting anger on the previous day. The vertical broken lines represent, from left to right, Saint Valentine's Day 2008, Lehman collapse, Election Day 2008, Christmas 2008, Saint Valentine's Day 2009, the market trough, Christmas 2009, and Saint Valentine's Day 2009.

The effects of the financial crisis can also be seen in the reports of hedonic well-being. In figure 10.7, I have grouped together the various experiences, averaging and changing signs as necessary, so that higher numbers always mean worse outcomes. The underlying positive emotions (smiling, enjoyment, happiness) appear to be unaffected by the presence or absence of the political questions at the beginning of the survey; there is no significant difference in outcomes by form over the randomization period. These questions are deeper in the questionnaire than even the standard of living questions. However, people are somewhat more likely to express negative emotions when they have been asked the political questions at the beginning of the survey. Over the randomization period, asking the political questions increases reported anger by 0.006, stress by 0.017, and worry by 0.006; the effect on worry is barely significant, that on anger has a t-value of 2.5 and that on stress a value of 5.0. These results mean that the top and bottom lines in figure 10.7 overstates worry, stress, and anger at the beginning of the period, and although even the largest effect, for stress, is not very large, it is enough to suggest that the average of stress and worry is still somewhat higher at the end of 2010 than it was in early 2008.

The results in figure 10.7 are an important part of the overall story. Hedonic experience, particularly worry and stress, but also physical pain, deteriorated during the crisis, becoming rapidly worse during the summer and fall of 2008, recovering briefly during the holidays, only to reach their worst values around the time that the stock market was at its lowest. There is a (small) increase in hedonic affect in all of these measures on Saint Valentine's Day and a much larger one around the Christmas holidays. As the stock market revived, negative affect fell. By mid-2010, there is very little trace of the crisis in these measures—though admittedly it is hard to detect small trends among the variability—even though the crisis continued in terms of lower incomes, employment, and home and stock prices. These results are consistent with hedonic adaptation, especially in the positive measures (happiness, enjoyment, smiling, not being sad). Worry and stress (which behave similarly to one another) are particularly sensitive to the crisis, at least in terms of the increase in the fraction of the population reporting them. Hedonic adaptation is somewhat less clear for worry and stress than for the positive emotions. Although these series came close to full recovery by mid-2010, they never quite reached their original values, especially if we recognize that there is some upward bias in the series at the start of the period.

10.5   Correlates of Changes in Well-Being over the Crisis

The literature on the correlates of SWB has identified many factors that consistently show up as important for one or more measure. Some of these factors, like health, education, marital status, or religiosity, are also important in the GHWBI data, but they do not change quickly enough at the population level to be candidates for explaining the fluctuations that I am considering here. This is obviously not true of income and of employment, both of which saw rapid changes over the crisis; the literature finds that both contribute to well-being and that becoming unemployed has a very large negative effect on well-being. Two early studies are Clark and Oswald (1994), who find that being unemployed is worse than being divorced or separated, and Winkelman and Winkelman (1998), who use the German panel data to show that the effect of unemployment operates in addition to the effects of lost income. The relationship between stock market prices and well-being seems to have been less researched, perhaps because it is not easily addressed in cross-sectional data; while it is true that individuals are differentially affected according to their exposure to a market shock, the effects of the shock are identified from whatever determines stock holding, not from the shock itself. Exploring the link between stock prices and well-being requires relatively high frequency time series data.

To tie the well-being outcomes in the GHWBI to the crisis-related behavior of income and unemployment requires, as a preliminary, matching of the Gallup data to official series on income and unemployment. This is not straightforward, given that one is daily, seasonally unadjusted, while the other is typically monthly and seasonally adjusted. Beyond that, the GHWBI asks a single question on monthly household income, and the respondent is asked to choose from a set of income intervals; we have no way of knowing how the respondent interprets this question, nor whether the respondent is well-informed about his or her household's income. Gallup has also experimented with several sets of questions about work status, so the data do not contain a consistent unemployment measure over the whole three-year period.

I have calculated an estimate of log income for each respondent by filling in midpoints assuming that income is log-normally distributed; this is available for the three-quarters of all respondents who answered the income question. This is clearly at best a rough and ready measure of income, but averaged over congressional districts, there is a correlation of 0.96 with log median income from the American Community Survey (Kahneman and Deaton 2010). For the current comparison, I have averaged log income over all respondents for each day, and over each day in each month, and compared the results with Bureau of Economic Analysis (BEA) data on per capita disposable income and on total employee compensation, both of which are available only on a seasonally adjusted basis.

Figure 10.8 shows the means of the logarithms of reported income by age group. For the typically working-age group, eighteen to fifty-nine, there is a sharp reduction in reported incomes from late 2008 through to the middle of 2009. This roughly corresponds to a drop in employee compensation in

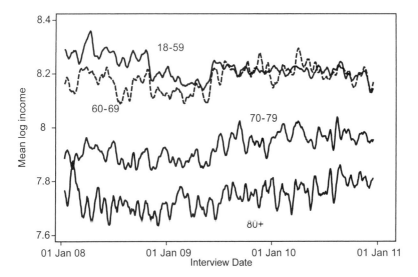

Fig. 10.8   Mean log income by age group
Notes: Twenty-one-day weighted moving averages of raw means of reported log incomes. Note that 25 percent of the sample either refused to answer or said they did not know.

the BEA statistics. However, this reduction in income is either much less or altogether absent among the other age groups. From the summer of 2009 onward, the reported incomes of the working-age group are not distinguishable from those of the age group sixty to sixty-nine, who are typically retired. The incomes of the two older groups, although lower, actually increased after early 2009. It is notable that the two stimulus-related payments, one in April to June 2008 (tax rebates) and May and June 2009 (one-time $250 transfers sent to those receiving Social Security, Supplemental Security Income (SSI), railroad retirement benefits, and veteran benefits) make no appearance in this figure although a graph of the official series is dominated by those two spikes. This is an interesting finding in its own right. Either people did not recall these transfers or, more likely, did not think of them as income.

Unemployment series are shown in figure 10.9. For the periods where they overlap, the two series are quite close, reflecting the considerable amount of work that Gallup has done to match the data from the Bureau of Labor Statistics (BLS). The timing of unemployment is important and is quite different from the timing of the stock market. Although unemployment inched up during the events of the fall of 2008, the big rise was between November 2008 and March 2009—a period when the market was also falling—but it then continued to rise, albeit more slowly, reaching a (seasonally unadjusted) peak of 10.6 percent in January 2010. The unemployment consequences of the financial crisis came much later than the financial crisis itself.

Table 10.1 shows that, in the cross-section, unemployment and income

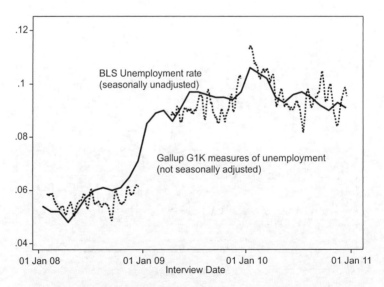

Fig. 10.9   Unemployment rates from Bureau of Labor Statistics (BLS) and Gallup Healthways Well-Being Index Poll

Notes: Both series are seasonally unadjusted.

Table 10.1   Regression coefficients of unemployment and of log income

	Unemployed	Log income
Ladder	–0.803	0.425
	(51.2)	(95.8)
Smile	–0.061	0.029
	(18.9)	(32.0)
Enjoy	–0.038	0.039
	(12.4)	(45.8)
Happy	–0.048	0.034
	(17.6)	(44.4)
Anger	0.060	–0.025
	(20.3)	(30.2)
Worry	0.175	–0.052
	(44.9)	(47.1)
Stress	0.096	–0.032
	(23.4)	(27.9)
Sad	0.116	–0.049
	(37.0)	(55.2)
Pain	0.051	–0.060
	(14.6)	(61.1)

Notes: Numbers in parentheses are *t*-values. Estimated using approximately 255,000 observations from January 2, 2010 to December 29, 2010 for which there are data on both unemployment and income using the final definitions of the former. For the ladder, the left-hand-side variable runs from 0 to 10; for the other experienced emotions, the left-hand-side variable is dichotomous. Also included in the regressions were dummies for other kinds of employment status, marital status, age group, sex, Hispanic status, and race. The comparison group for unemployment is full-time employees.

play the expected roles in conditioning both life evaluation and hedonic experience. People who report themselves unemployed are 0.80 of a ladder rung below those who are in full-time employment. Compensating for this would require an increase of 1.89 in log income, or more than a six-fold increase in income itself; this compensation is close to but somewhat smaller than that calculated by Winkelman and Winkelman (1998) using German panel data. Income is also good and unemployment bad for both positive and negative emotions as well as for physical pain. (Note that these estimates are likely inflated by reverse causality; disabilities cause pain and make people less likely to be in the labor force, and people with more positive emotion and less negative emotions may have better outcomes as a result; see also Graham, Eggers, and Sukhtankar 2004.) Unemployed people are particularly more likely to be worried and sad, and these are also the two cases (along with stress) where the ratio of the unemployment coefficient to the log income coefficient is the highest. As repeatedly found in the literature, unemployment is associated with poor life evaluation and poor hedonic outcomes and is so independently of (and in addition to) the effects of (current) lost earnings.

Based on these cross-sectional results, we might expect variations in income and unemployment to be the main drivers of well-being over the financial crisis, with the role of the stock market an open question. But it should be already clear from the timing in the figures that unemployment cannot provide a good account of the time series, at least on its own. To look at the correlates more formally, I start with the daily averages and with the relation between income and the ladder.

The correlation between mean log income (from the Gallup data) and the mean corrected ladder is 0.32 and the regression coefficient 0.71 ($t = 11.0$), which is substantially larger than the cross-sectional coefficient in table 10.1. This difference is in the opposite direction to what is predicted by the Easterlin paradox. Both the correlation and the regression coefficients are biased down by the fact that both the daily ladder and daily mean log income contain substantial day-to-day sampling error. The daily corrected ladder is correlated with the S&P 500 at 0.46, and the regression of the corrected daily ladder on mean log income and the log of the S&P 500 index reduces the coefficient on the latter to 0.33 ($t = 4.2$), while the coefficient on the log of the stock index is 0.31 ($t = 11.4$). The high correlation between the corrected ladder and the market is shown in figure 10.10; although it is clear that most of the correlation comes at the (low) frequency of the crisis itself, some higher frequency correlation is visible, too.

Moving to monthly data, so as to use the unemployment data from the BLS at the price of reducing the number of observations to 36, the ladder remains correlated (0.43) with the S&P 500, and in a regression of the cor-

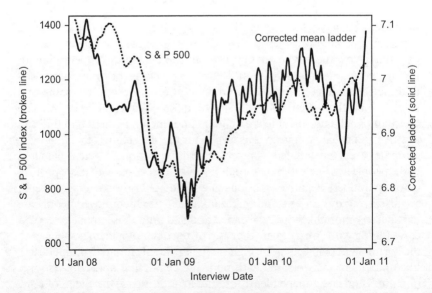

Fig. 10.10   Corrected mean ladder and S&P 500 index

rected ladder on the log of the S&P 500, unemployment, and the log of employee compensation, unemployment is significantly *positively* related to the ladder, the log S&P 500 has a t-value of 7.2, and employee compensation is insignificant.

Averages of emotions and physical pain are also significantly correlated with average log income on a daily basis; as is the case for the ladder and once again contrary to the Easterlin paradox, the coefficients are all (absolutely) larger than the cross-section coefficients in table 10.1. On monthly data, with only thirty-six monthly data points, fluctuations in the S&P 500 are correlated with all of the hedonics except physical pain; neither the unemployment rate nor employee compensation have any effect conditional on the market. For physical pain, only the unemployment rate has predictive power in the monthly data. That the market is more closely related to hedonic outcomes and to the ladder in monthly than in daily data is consistent with figure 10.10 (and similar figures for hedonics) in which there is little high frequency correlation.

In addition to these regression results, it is informative to check whether the changes in SWB over the whole three-year period are what might be expected from the cross-sectional results. We know that unemployment is twice as high at the end of the period and that some measures of income also fell, and we need to know if these changes—which are very large in business-cycle terms—show up in the well-being data. For the ladder, the corrected average value in January 2008 was 7.07, which had fallen to an average of 6.99 in December 2010. To make the point, I take the largest possible changes in income and unemployment that are consistent with the data, a decline of 5 percent in the former and an increase of 5 percent in the latter. From the cross-section regressions in table 10.1, these changes should cause the ladder to fall by 0.06, somewhat less than calculated, but surely within any reasonable margin of error given the corrections for the order effects. Similar calculations for the hedonic experiences show that the positive emotions do not respond as they should. Predicted from unemployment and income, the fractions reporting smiling, enjoyment, and happiness should all decrease by 0.004. In fact, enjoyment is actually *higher* (by 0.014) at the end of the period, and happiness and smiling are exactly the same at the end of 2010 as they were at the beginning of 2008. By contrast, the negative emotions are all higher at the end of the period, and the increases are larger than predicted from the cross-section regressions and the changes in income and unemployment by twice or more, especially if we allow for some elevation at the beginning of the period from the presence of the political questions.

We might conjecture that the positive emotions are more subject to hedonic adaptation than are the negative emotions or that the negative emotions respond, not only to personal circumstances, but also to the macroeconomic environment in general. But there is a more important point. Even in the face of some of the largest macroeconomic disruptions since the Great

Depression, both the actual and predicted changes in these well-being measures are very small, possibly smaller than our ability to detect given the difficulties of measuring well-being. Even with 30,000 observations each month as here, the standard errors of the monthly averages for the hedonics range from 0.002 to 0.003, which would mean that we would *just* be able to detect the predicted effects of a major macroeconomic upheaval with a 5 percentage point increase in the rate of unemployment and a 5 percent fall in average income.

It is true that, for an individual, unemployment is associated with very large declines in reported well-being. It is also true that the increase in unemployment after the financial crisis was very large by business-cycle standards. Yet that very large increase affects only one-twentieth of the population. In consequence, even major changes in unemployment predict only small changes in average well-being. Detecting such changes presents both statistical and conceptual challenges. A decline in the ladder of 0.06 is (a little) smaller than the standard error in the ladder on the daily sample of 1,000 respondents and is only three times larger than the standard error from a monthly sample of 30,000 respondents. But 0.06 is an *order of magnitude* smaller than the mean effect on the ladder of adding political questions to the beginning of the survey. In a sense, cross-sections of individuals are much more like cross-sections of countries than they are like a time series for a single country. The differences in incomes across countries are many times larger than the differences in income to be expected over a few years or even over a few decades; the differences in income between the United States and China or the United States and Togo took hundreds of years to come about. So the fact that the ladder is highly correlated with incomes across countries, or with income and unemployment across individuals, tells us very little about what will happen if we use the measure to track national well-being over time.

10.6   Conclusions

Perhaps my most surprising substantive finding is how closely well-being tracked the stock market over the 1,000 days of 2008, 2009, and 2010. Yet it is surely wrong that we can abandon income, unemployment, and well-being measures in favor of a stock market index. Most Americans have no direct or indirect financial interest in the stock market, so whatever is the mechanism it cannot work through personal portfolios or at least not entirely so. My guess is that for much of the financial crisis, the stock market became the most watched indicator, not only of the present, but also of the future. As suggested by Dan McFadden in comments on this chapter, both SWB and the stock market were likely responding to the same underlying stream of news, assessing its implications for the future. During the early spring of 2009, with a newly installed administration and a stock market that was falling even beyond the already precipitous drop at the end of 2008, it was reasonable enough to have dire fears about the future—indeed, the stock market itself was reflecting that fear—and those fears were heavily reinforced by media coverage, sending highly correlated interpretations of the events to a large segment of the population. From mid-2008 to mid-2009, the stock market was *the* indicator of the state of the economy, something that would not necessarily be true in more normal times. The pattern in figure 10.10 may simply reflect the peculiarities of this particular recession. In any case, the correlation with the market reinforces that even at best, the well-being measures are not measuring *current* well-being, in the sense of today's level of real income, but also picking up the fear of the future associated with evolving economic news. For those who own assets to support future consumption, the effect is immediate. For lower-income households, who are less likely to own market assets and whose well-being was, if anything, *more* affected by the market, market movements may generate changes in expectations about unemployment. In standard intertemporal models, today's utility reflects not only what is happening today, but also the expected utility of future outcomes, predictions of which are changed by today's news. Such effects would be amplified if "news" utility is important in and of itself, as in Kőzsegi and Rabin (2009) or Kimball and Willis (2006).

How do measures of self-reported well-being survive the stress testing provided by the financial crisis? They perform well in that they respond to income, unemployment, and the stock market in the directions that we would expect. Yet they are more successful as gauges of short-term fear or hope for the future than of the current state of well-being in terms of income or employment. The worry and stress (see figure 10.7) that came with these events is surely real enough and worth measuring and taking into account in policy.

Even so, there are serious problems in using well-being measures for tracking the performance of the economy over time. They cannot be expected to change much in response to even historically large changes in macroeconomic activity—the predicted (and actual) effects are just too small. Detecting these changes in real time will require very large standing samples, and, even then, risk being swamped by the much larger short-term effects of day-to-day events that are sometimes clearly important—a major stock market crash or events such as 9/11 (Metcalfe, Powdthavee, and Dolan 2011)—but sometimes have only dubious implications for well-being. We also know from the effects of the political questions in the Gallup surveys that the measures are sensitive to the context in which they are asked. In one sense, this is a technical issue that could be dealt with by suitable positioning of the questions or by the use of buffer questions, though we do not currently know how to do so in a way that would ensure comparability over time or over countries. But the sensitivity induced by question context extends to sensitivity to news and events widely portrayed in the media—for example, the large one-day effect of the fall of Lehman Brothers. While it is conceivable that, as is sometimes argued for the stock market, the SWB measures are giving an accurate take on expected future well-being, it seems more plausible that, like the stock market, they have actually very little to do with well-being. As McFadden suggests in comments on this chapter, we may be looking at "cognitive bubbles" that are essentially irrelevant for any concept of well-being that we care about. It is an important future task to explore whether or not SWB is excessively sensitive to changes in the market and to other news.

It is possible that the ladder question used in the Gallup surveys is more sensitive to context effects than are other evaluative questions such as questions about satisfaction with life or with one's standard of living. But this seems most unlikely; questions about the standard of living and about emotion are also affected in the Gallup data, even though they are asked long after the political questions that make people feel worse about their lives.

There are many unresolved challenges before well-being measures become a standard part of macroeconomic monitoring, however useful such measures are in and of themselves. The measures have proved themselves in the cross-section across different groups, for example, for looking at the effects of life circumstances, such as ill-health, divorce, or unemployment. They still have a long way to go in establishing themselves as good time series monitors for the aggregate economy. In a world of bread and circuses, measures like happiness that are sensitive to short-term ephemera and that are affected more by the arrival of Saint Valentine's Day than by a doubling of unemployment are measures that pick up the circuses but miss the bread.

References

Bishop, George F. 1987. "Context Effects on Self-Perceptions of Interest in Government and Public Affairs." In *Social Information Processing and Survey Methodology,* edited by Hans-J. Hippler, Norbert Schwarz, and Seymour Sudman, 179–99. New York: Springer-Verlag.

Bricker, Jesse, Brian K. Bucks, Arthur Kennickell, Traci L. Mach, and Kevin Moore. 2011. "Drowning or Weathering the Storm? Changes in Family Finances from 2007 to 2009." NBER Working Paper no. 16985. Cambridge, MA: National Bureau of Economic Research.

Campbell, Angus. 1981. *The Sense of Well-Being in America.* New York: McGraw Hill.

Cantril, Harvey. 1965. *The Pattern of Human Concern.* New Brunswick, NJ: Rutgers University Press.

Carstensen, Laura, Derek M. Isaacowitz, and Susan T. Charles. 1999. "Taking Time Seriously: A Theory of Socioemotional Selectivity." *American Psychologist* 54 (3): 165–81.

Chakrabarti, Rajashri, Donghoon Lee, Wilbert van der Klaauw, and Basit Zafar. 2011. "Household Debt and Saving during the 2007 Recession." NBER Working Paper no. 16999. Cambridge, MA: National Bureau of Economic Research.

Christelis, Dimitris, Dimitris Georgarakos, and Tullio Jappelli. 2011. "Wealth Shocks, Unemployment Shocks and Consumption in the Wake of the Great Recession." http://ssrn.com/abstract=17929881.

Clark, Andrew E., Andreas Knabe, and Steffen Rätzel. 2011. "Boon or Bane? Others Unemployment, Well-Being and Job Insecurity." Paris School of Economics Working Paper, April.

Clark, Andrew E., and Andrew J. Oswald. 1994. "Unhappiness and Unemployment." *Economic Journal* 104 (424): 648–59.

Deaton, Angus. 2008. "Income, Health, and Well-Being around the World: Evidence from the Gallup World Poll." *Journal of Economic Perspectives* 22 (2): 53–72.

Di Tella, Rafael, and Robert MacCulloch. 2007. "Happiness, Contentment, and Other Emotions for Central Banks." In *Policymaking Insights from Behavioral Economics,* edited by Christopher L. Foote, Lorenz Goette, and Stephan Meier, 311–66. Boston: Federal Reserve Bank of Boston.

Di Tella, Rafael, Robert J. MacCulloch, and Andrew J. Oswald. 2001. "Preferences over Inflation and Unemployment: Evidence from Surveys of Happiness." *American Economic Review* 91 (1): 335–41.

———. 2003. "The Macroeconomics of Happiness." *Review of Economics and Statistics* 85 (4): 809–27.

Graham, Carol, Andrew Eggers, and Sandip Sukhtankar. 2004. "Does Happiness Pay? An Exploration Based on Panel Data from Russia." *Journal of Economic Behavior and Organization* 55 (3): 319–42.

Hurd, Michael D., and Susan Rohwedder. 2010. "Effects of the Financial Crisis and Great Recession on American Households." NBER Working Paper no. 16407. Cambridge, MA: National Bureau of Economic Research.

Kahneman, Daniel, and Angus Deaton. 2010. "High Income Improves Evaluation of Life But Not Emotional Well-being." *Proceedings of the National Academy of Sciences* 107 (38): 16489–93.

Kahneman, Daniel, Alan Krueger, David A. Schkade, Norbert Schwarz, and Arthur A. Stone. 2004. "A Survey Method for Characterizing Daily Life Experience: A Day Reconstruction Method." *Science* 306:1776–80.

Kahneman, Daniel, and Jason Riis. 2005. "Living and Thinking about It: Two Perspectives on Life." In *The Science of Well-Being,* edited by Felicia A. Huppert, N. Baylis, and B. Keverne, 285–304. Oxford: Oxford University Press.

Kahneman, Daniel, Peter P. Wakker, and Rakesh Sarin. 1997. "Back to Bentham? Explorations of Experienced Utility." *Quarterly Journal of Economics* 112 (2): 376–405.

Kimball, Miles, and Robert Willis. 2006. "Utility and Happiness." University of Michigan, Department of Economics, Working Paper, March 3.

Kőszegi, Botond, and Matthew Rabin. 2009. "Reference Dependent Consumption Plans." American Economic Review 99 (3): 909–36.

Metcalfe, David, Nattavudh Powdthavee, and Paul Dolan. 2011. "Destruction and Distress: Using a Quasi-Experiment to Show the Effects of the September 11 Attacks on Mental Well-Being in the United Kingdom." *Economic Journal* 121:F81–F103.

Schwarz, Norbert, and Howard Schuman. 1997. "Political Knowledge, Attribution, and Inferred Interest in Politics: The Operation of Buffer Items." *International Journal of Public Opinion Research* 9 (2): 191–95.

Schwarz, Norbert, and Frtiz Strack. 1999. "Reports of Subjective Well-Being: Judgmental Processes and Their Methodological Implications." In *Well-Being: The Foundations of Hedonic Psychology,* edited by Daniel Kahneman, Ed Diener, and Norbert Schwarz, 61–84. New York: Russell Sage.

Sen, Amartya K. 1985. *Commodities and Capabilities.* Amsterdam: Elsevier.

———. 1987. *On Ethics and Economics.* Oxford, UK: Blackwell.

Shapiro, Matthew. 2010. "The Effects of the Financial Crisis on the Well-Being of Older Americans: Evidence from the Cognitive Economics Study." University of Michigan. http://www-personal.umich.edu/~shapiro/papers/CogFinCrisis.pdf.

Stevenson, Betsey, and Justin Wolfers. 2008. "Economic Growth and Subjective Well-Being: Reassessing the Easterlin Paradox." *Brookings Papers on Economic Activity* Spring:1–87.

Stiglitz, Joseph, Amartya Sen, and Jean-Paul Fitoussi. 2009. *Report of the Commission on the Measurement of Economic Performance and Social Progress.* http://www.stiglitz-sen-fitoussi.fr/en/index.htm.

Stone, Arthur A., Joseph E. Schwartz, Joan E. Broderick, and Angus Deaton. 2010. "A Snapshot of the Age Distribution of Psychological Well-Being in the United States." *Proceedings of the National Academy of Sciences* 107 (22): 9985–90.

Winkelman, Liliana, and Rainer Winkelman. 1998. "Why Are the Unemployed So Unhappy? Evidence from Panel Data." *Economica* 65 (257): 1–15.

Wolfers, Justin. 2003. "Is Business Cycle Volatility Costly? Evidence from Surveys of Subjective Well-Being." *International Finance* 6 (1): 1–26.

Comment   Daniel McFadden

Let there be granted to the science of pleasure what is granted to the science of energy, to imagine an ideally perfect instrument, a psychophysical machine, continually registering the height of pleasure experienced by an individual, exactly according to the verdict of consciousness, or rather diverging therefrom according to a law of errors. From moment to moment the hedonimeter varies; the delicate index now flickering with the flutter of the passions, now steadied by intellectual activity, low sunk whole hours in the neighbourhood of zero, or momentarily springing up toward infinity.

—Francis Y. Edgeworth, *Mathematical Psychics,* 1881

Angus Deaton studies the time series properties and sensitivity to economic events and context of subjective measures of hedonic experience and well-being that have been promoted by Danny Kahneman and others and adopted in popular surveys. Some interpreters of these measures have used them as proxies for or alternatives to traditional economic indices of well-

Daniel McFadden is the E. Morris Cox Professor of Economics at the University of California, Berkeley, the Presidential Professor of Health Economics at the University of Southern California, and a research associate of the National Bureau of Economic Research.

For acknowledgments, sources of research support, and disclosure of the author's material financial relationships, if any, please see http://www.nber.org/chapters/c12448.ack.

being such as expected present value of a life-cycle stream of felicities. Do these subjective measures approximate Edgeworth's hedonimeter or replace it with psychologically more fundamental indicators of the human condition? Can and should they be adopted as tools of economic policy analysis, used to monitor economic progress and assess policy alternatives? There are reasons to be skeptical, on two levels. The first is that these subjective measures are demonstrably sensitive to context, making it difficult to separate a well-being signal from the noise of measurement. The second is that neither the revealed well-being of economists nor subjective well-being of psychologists are entirely convincing scientific concepts, apart from difficulties of reliable measurement. Economists and psychologists have been critical of their own measures and even more critical of each other's. In the words of Danny Kahneman, "economists have preferences, psychologists have attitudes." While behavioral economics has taken on some of the attitudes of psychology, to the substantial benefit of economic science, economists have traditionally been and continue to be suspicious of subjective rather than revealed information on economic state. A little history may be instructive.

Fifty years ago, Angus Deaton's chapter could not have been published. The economics profession at that time derided Edgeworth's wistful call for a hedinometer and was wholly unreceptive to the proposition that stated preferences of consumers could be used in economic analysis. A famous encounter a few decades earlier characterized this economic thinking. In 1932, the iconic psychologist Leon Thurstone gave a paper at the second meeting of the newly formed Econometric Society that proposed direct recovery of preferences from elicited indifference points. Ragnar Frisch, Harold Hotelling, and Milton Friedman were all in the audience, and it is reported that they excoriated Thurstone, labeling his method totally unsuitable for recovering preferences that determined real economic behavior. This rejection of subjective data also pervaded other social sciences. For example, behavioral psychologists in the 1950s rejected subjective reports as unscientific and pursued a self-consciously observationalist path.

Since then, economists have grudgingly come to accept the proposition that subjective beliefs, perceptions, and intentions, carefully elicited, can reflect and predict economic behavior. Now, surveys routinely elicit subjective probabilities of future events, ratings of product attributes, and purchase intentions, and these are used by applied economists and market researchers to predict consumer response to news and to product innovations. Preference elicitation is more problematic. Market researchers have made wide use of conjoint analysis, an elicitation methodology that comes out of psychometrics, and contingent valuation, a version developed by resource economists, and have found these methods reasonably reliable for forecasting demand for new variants of familiar products. In transportation, quite a few studies have combined revealed and subjective preference data in applications where market outcomes of policy interventions allow assessment of the usefulness of subjective data. Broadly, the findings are that stated preferences are substantially predictive, but not identical to revealed preferences, with differences that seem to be explained by context, salience, prominence, and social interaction effects; see Morakawa, Ben-Akiva, and McFadden (2002), Louviere, Hensher, and Swait (2000), and Louviere et al. (1999). Neuroeconomic studies provide some support for Bentham's notion of a utilitarian calculus of pain and pleasure that might be tracked by cognitive science. However, subjective preferences for unfamiliar alternatives with no direct market counterparts, such as protection of remote endangered species, are found to be extremely sensitive to elicitation format and context, and their use remains intensely controversial; see Green et al. (1998) and McFadden (2005).

Angus considers two conceptually distinct subjective reports. The first are self-reported hedonic states, measures of experienced feelings such as joy, sadness, happiness, anger, stress, or worry. These could be collected contemporaneously by experience sampling, but in this study, they are obtained retrospectively by an approximation to the Day Reconstruction Method of Kahneman et al. (2004). The second is self-reported well-being (SWB), where respondents are asked to evaluate their life as a whole. These measures were proposed by Kahneman, Diener, and Schwarz (1999) and advanced by Kahneman et al. (2006), Kahneman and Krueger (2006), and others. The spirit of their approach is that these measures are predictive for behavior and revealing for human thinking, not that they mimic classical welfare measures. In fact, there is ample experimental evidence, much of it due to Kahneman, Schwartz, and other psychologists, showing that these are not measures of stable preferences. This has been taken as evidence that the economic concepts of preferences and life-cycle well-being are themselves flawed. Nevertheless, as the subjective measures have gained attention, it has been tempting for policymakers to treat them as empirical approximations to Edgeworth's hedinometer and use them for evaluation of economic events and policy. It would be a boon to economic analysis if these measures proved to be broadly reliable. However, there are many conceptual, behavioral, and psychometric issues in their use, and they deserve careful, critical assessment. In this comment, I will focus on dynamic transients in SWB, *cognitive bubbles* that are analogs of the bubbles that appear in asset markets. The presence of such bubbles does not invalidate SWB or stock prices as measures of the reality of evaluations, but they do complicate considerably the use of these measures as indicators of fundamentals.

For classical economic consumers with instantaneous utilities or felicities and life satisfaction characterized by expected present value of the stream of felicities, one could think of self-reported hedonic states as indicators for felicity and SWB as an indicator for expected present value of life-cycle utility. Suppose for the moment that these associations are valid. It is then instructive to work out for the neoclassical consumer what the relationship between hedonic experience and changes in well-being should be. For the moment, put aside the issues of intertemporal separability and additivity of felicities that enter life-cycle utility and of intertemporal and interpersonal cardinality/comparability of the expected present value of a stream of felicities at various points in the life cycle. Consider the well-being at time T of a neoclassical consumer born at time zero. Let u_t denote instantaneous utility or felicity at time t, equal ideally to the experience that would be measured by Edgeworth's hedonimeter or the Day Reconstruction Method, and assume that felicity is scaled so that $0 \leq u_t \leq 1$. Felicity may depend on consumption of goods and services, and other variables such as health, and may be limited by budgets and other constraints, but for current purposes none of this needs to be made explicit. Let r denote a real discount rate, assumed constant for simplicity. Let S_t denote the probability of survival to time t, and $m_t = -d(\ln S_t)/dt$ denote the mortality hazard rate. Let $\mathbf{E}_T$ denote the expectation operator at time T, which incorporates subjective beliefs regarding the future, given all the information available at time T. The present value of the past stream of felicities up to T is $P_T = \int_0^T u_t \cdot e^{-r(t-T)}dt$. This expression is conditioned on realized felicities and survival to T and so does not involve survival probabilities or expectations. The present value of the future stream of felicities is $F_T = \int_T^\infty u_t \cdot (S_t/S_T) \cdot e^{-r(t-T)}dt$; this incorporates the probability of survival and further is random due to unrealized future economic events. Define neoclassical well-being as $W_T = (1 - \delta) P_T + \delta \mathbf{E}_T F_T$, with a weight δ to allow for the possibility that the past and future are treated differently, and $\delta = 1/2$ corresponding to the case of full expected present value of the life-cycle felicity stream. An important component of this formula, and potential source of volatility in neoclassical well-being, is the subjective expectation operator $\mathbf{E}_T$, which will react to news. While the most orthodox economists will insist that $\mathbf{E}_T$ mimics objective probabilities of future events, the market mechanisms that would force this outcome are notably incomplete, and the case for variable psychological influences on beliefs is strong. The rate of change in neoclassical well-being is

$$\frac{dW_T}{dT} = (1 - 2\delta)u_T + rW_T + m_T \cdot \delta \mathbf{E}_T F_T + [\mathbf{E}_T F_T - P_T]\frac{d\delta}{dT} + \delta\frac{d\mathbf{E}_T}{dT}FT.$$

Notable features of this derivative are (a) that it will depend on current felicity only to the extent that δ differs from 1/2, (b) the effect of the discount rate r and mortality rate m_T is to increase W_T with age, and (c) changes in attention to the future, influencing δ, and news, influencing $\mathbf{E}_t$, are potentially strong sources in volatility of W_T. As in Hall (1978), the effect of news entering $\mathbf{E}_T$ may give W_T the properties of a random walk.

If subjective measures of hedonic experience and well-being did proxy the parallel economic concepts of felicity and life-cycle expected present value of the felicity stream, then SWB would be an integral of hedonic experience over time, weighted for time discounting and adjusted for beliefs regarding future events. Then, the rate of change in SWB would follow a formula analogous to the one in the preceding and would be correspondingly sensitive to changes in the weight δ given to the future rather than the past and changes in beliefs as the result of news. Then, one might expect self-reported hedonic states to reflect current experience and be largely independent of subjective probabilities of future events and changes in SWB to have some of the properties of a random walk. Subjective probabilities may loom large in this calculus, turning on the manner in which low-probability, large-impact, ambiguous future events are processed by the consumer. In this respect, the stock/flow relationship between hedonic experience and SWB should be similar to the stock/flow relationship between the current profits of a firm and its stock price, where beliefs about uncertain future events may react strongly to current information on cash flows. It is possible that one of the reasons that the Dow Jones Industrial Average (DJIA) and the measure studied by Angus, Gallop's SWB are so closely associated through the Great Recession is that both are reacting strongly to changing subjective probabilities of the same dreaded events.

Now the psychologists have convincing experimental evidence that SWB is not a simple integral of hedonic experience. For example, retrospective evaluation of a hedonic episode, which is similar to SWB, depends more on peak and last experience than integrated experience. Nevertheless, it seems likely that SWB will be as sensitive as its neoclassical counterpart to changes in orientation to the future versus the past and to news that changes beliefs regarding future events. An additional issue for both neoclassical consumers and for SWB is that subjective probabilities of future events may shadow current hedonic experience, for example, the claimed phenomenon that your sensory experience is amplified when you know you are to be hanged tomorrow.

A consistently-elicited self-reported well-being measure may exhibit transients that are primarily due to changes in subjective probabilities for the future, rather than discounted experience. Psychological experiments find that humans have difficulty forming consistent subjective probabilities and behavioral responses for remote, rare, highly consequential events, in some cases overestimating the probability and reacting strongly and in other cases through denial or fatalism ignoring the possibility of these events. Thus, SWB is likely to be unevenly sensitive to the prospect of events viewed with dread, such as the accidental death of oneself or a family member, a financial catastrophe that wipes out assets, or a natural or man-made disaster. A little news may lead to an exaggerated change in SWB that is not just the accumulation of current hedonic experience, particularly when an event such as a bank failure, a terrorist attack, a tornado, or a plane crash leads the consumer to dread events that had previously been denied. The behavior of humans as social animals, using information networks for news and behavioral exemplars, can introduce further instabilities, the panic responses of herds. As a result, SWB may exhibit dynamic transients that can be interpreted as cognitive bubbles, responding to and feeding the perceptions of others regarding future events.

In this view of the evolution of SWB, an event such as the failure of Lehman Brothers can have a large impact, even on individuals who have no assets or income at immediate risk, because of dread of the possibility of a depression. Suddenly, a range of outcomes previously denied becomes possible. If, subsequently, the worst case outcomes are not realized, there may be a sense of relief and a rationalization that because the worst did not happen, it is fated to not happen in the future. As a result, SWB may rebound in the other direction.

At least some of the evidence that Angus has collected on the behavior of the Gallup measure of self-reported well-being through the Great Recession seems to be consistent with the development of cognitive bubbles induced by changing levels of dread about worst case outcomes. This, in turn, suggests considerable caution in attributing changes in SWB over the course of the recession to real changes in economic circumstances of individual consumers. Aside from the events of losing one's job or house, the economic effects of the recession are mostly on future prospects rather than current circumstances. Nevertheless, SWB may react strongly due to increased dread. Then, SWB may provide valuable information on beliefs and how they evolve. However, it is unlikely to be a reliable indicator of objective life-cycle economic status.

There are substantial conceptual, behavioral, and psychometric issues in measurement of hedonic state and life-cycle well-being, some related to the possibility of cognitive bubbles, others to the sensitivity of self-reports to the framing and context of the elicitation. Angus has discussed some of these. Many of these issues were originally documented in the research of Kahneman and of Norbert Schwarz, both occasional coauthors of Angus. One is the "hedonic treadmill," the finding that humans adapt quickly and achieve homeostasis under widely varying objective conditions. For example, studies by Norbert Schwarz find that people rate their home community highly, even after forced migration to places they rate lowly before the fact, and find that paraplegics and nonparaplegics are equally happy after the fact of injury. Applied to SWB, one can expect this to trend to similar equilibrium levels even under substantially different economic circumstances. As Angus notes, this drives a wedge between ex ante and ex post subjective evaluation of policy changes, even if reported satisfaction is exactly accurate. Another important psychometric effect is sensitivity to context. A study, again by Norbert Schwarz, finds that college students give very different satisfaction ratings to college life depending on whether they had previously been asked about the quality of their sex life. Angus notes that this is an important issue in the Gallup measures of SWB, finding that they are quite sensitive to the presence of earlier questions that focus on politics. This appears to be the explanation for the strong April 6 effect he observes. It would not be surprising if external political information effects, such as media coverage, also have an influence. My preceding discussion of cognitive bubbles suggests that news that has modest implications for individual economic status, such as an election outcome, could through social networks and key pundits nevertheless have a large effect on SWB. Context operates by forming a frame of reference in which elicitations are interpreted and also by altering the salience of various factors and ease of reconstruction and retrieval of experience and memory. Thus, hedonic evaluations obtained by the Day Reconstruction Method can be influenced by first asking the subject to recall the best or worst thing that happened to them yesterday. It is worth noting that many of the effects at issue here also appear, in muted form, in objective questions. For example, if a respondent is asked to list household assets, frames that mention and prioritize asset categories can change reports, a phenomenon observed in the Health and Retirement Study (HRS). Similarly, one should expect that order and context will matter in the collection of data on self-reported health conditions and overall health state and expect variations in self-reported health status (SRHS) that are sensitive to news that influences beliefs.

In summary, economists should give Angus's chapter careful attention. Directly elicited measures of well-being have the potential to tell us a lot about the formation of beliefs and the evaluation of hedonic experience. As to whether they are sufficiently reliable to be used to evaluate economic events and policies, I am skeptical—I suspect cognitive bubbles will introduce too much volatility. However, more analysis is needed. Finally, economists should take seriously the position of psychologists like Kahneman and Schwarz that there are no stable underlying economic preferences or perceptions, and psychological moods, affect, and attitudes are all there is. If this is so, the deep conceptual question is where economic policy analysis can find an anchor.

References

Green, D., K. Jacowitz, D. Kahneman, and D. McFadden. 1998. "Referendum Contingent Valuation, Anchoring, and Willingness to Pay for Public Goods." *Resource and Energy Economics* 20:85–116.
Hall, R. 1978. "Stochastic Implications of the Life Cycle-Permanent Income Hypothesis: Theory and Evidence." *Journal of Political Economy* 86 (6): 971–87.
Kahneman, D., E. Diener, and N. Schwarz, eds. 1999. *Well-Being: The Foundations of Hedonic Psychology.* New York: Russell Sage Foundation.
Kahneman, D., and A. B. Krueger. 2006. "Developments in the Measurement of Subjective Well-Being." *Journal of Economic Perspectives* 20 (1): 3–24.
Kahneman, D., and A. B. Krueger, D. A. Schkade, N. Schwarz, and A. A. Stone. 2004. "A Survey Method for Characterizing Daily Life Experience: The Day Reconstruction Method." *Science, New Series* 306 (5702): 1776–80.

————. 2006. "Would You Be Happier If You Were Richer? A Focusing Illusion." *Science* 312:5782.

Louviere, J. J., D. A. Hensher, and J. Swait. 2000. *Stated Choice Methods: Analysis and Applications in Marketing, Transportation and Environmental Valuation.* Cambridge: Cambridge University Press.

Louviere, J. J., R. J. Meyer, D. A. Hensher, R. Carson, M. Hanemann, and D. Bunch. 1999. "Combining Sources of Preference Data." *Marketing Letters* 10 (3): 205–18.

McFadden, D. 2005. "The New Science of Pleasure: Consumer Behavior and the Measurement of Well-Being." Frisch Lecture, Econometric Society World Congress (ESWC), London, 2005.

Morakawa, T., M. Ben-Akiva, and D. McFadden. 2002. "Discrete Choice Models Incorporating Revealed Preferences and Psychometric Data." In *Econometric Models in Marketing,* edited by P. Franses and A. Montgomery, 29–55. Amsterdam: Elsevier Science.

Contributors

Tatiana Andreyeva
Rudd Center for Food Policy and
  Obesity
Yale University
PO Box 208369
New Haven, CT 06520-8369

James Banks
School of Social Sciences
The University of Manchester
Oxford Road
Manchester M13 9PL, United Kingdom

John Beshears
Stanford Graduate School of Business
Stanford University
655 Knight Way
Stanford, CA 94305-7298

Jay Bhattacharya
Center for Primary Care and Outcomes
  Research
Stanford University
117 Encina Commons
Stanford, CA 94305-6019

Amitabh Chandra
John F. Kennedy School of
  Government
Harvard University
79 JFK Street
Cambridge, MA 02138

James J. Choi
Yale School of Management
135 Prospect Street
P.O. Box 208200
New Haven, CT 06520-8200

David M. Cutler
Department of Economics
Harvard University
1805 Cambridge Street
Cambridge, MA 02138

Angus Deaton
Woodrow Wilson School
328 Wallace Hall
Princeton University
Princeton, NJ 08544-1013

Alan M. Garber
Provost, Harvard University
Massachusetts Hall
Cambridge, MA 02138

Gopi Shah Goda
SIEPR
Stanford University
366 Galvez Street
Stanford, CA 94305

Florian Heiss
Department of Statistics and
    Econometrics
Johannes Gutenberg University of
    Mainz
Haus Recht und Wirtschaft II
D-55099 Mainz, Germany

Michael D. Hurd
RAND Corporation
1776 Main Street
Santa Monica, CA 90407

Arie Kapteyn
RAND Corporation
1776 Main Street
Santa Monica, CA 90407

David Laibson
Department of Economics
Littauer M-12
Harvard University
Cambridge, MA 02138

Mary Beth Landrum
Department of Health Care Policy
Harvard Medical School
180 Longwood Avenue
Boston, MA 02115

Brigitte C. Madrian
John F. Kennedy School of
    Government
Harvard University
79 JFK Street
Cambridge, MA 02138

Daniel McFadden
Department of Economics
549 Evans Hall #3880
University of California, Berkeley
Berkeley, CA 94720-3880

Matthew Miller
c/o McKinsey & Company
2000 Avenue of the Stars, Suite 800N
Los Angeles, CA 90067

Zoë Oldfield
Institute for Fiscal Studies
7 Ridgmount Street
London WC1E 7AE, England

Daniella Perlroth
CHP/PCOR
Stanford University
117 Encina Commons
Stanford, CA 94305-6019

James M. Poterba
Department of Economics E52-350
Massachusetts Institute of Technology
50 Memorial Drive
Cambridge, MA 02142-1347

Susann Rohwedder
RAND Corporation
1776 Main Street
Santa Monica, CA 90407

John B. Shoven
Department of Economics
Stanford University
579 Serra Mall at Galvez Street
Stanford, CA 94305-6015

Sita Nataraj Slavov
Department of Economics
Occidental College
1600 Campus Road
Los Angeles, CA 90041

James P. Smith
RAND Corporation
1776 Main Street
Santa Monica, CA 90407

Till Stowasser
Ludwig Maximilian University of
    Munich
Munich Graduate School of
    Economics
Kaulbachstr. 45
D-80539 Munich, Germany

Arthur van Soest
Department of Econometrics and OR
Tilburg University
P.O. Box 90153
5000 LE Tilburg, The Netherlands

Steven F. Venti
Department of Economics
Dartmouth College
6106 Rockefeller Center
Hanover, NH 03755

David R. Weir
3053 ISR
University of Michigan
426 Thompson Street
Ann Arbor, MI 48106

Robert J. Willis
ISR
University of Michigan
P. O. Box 1248, 426 Thompson Street
Ann Arbor, MI 48106

Joachim Winter
Department of Economics
Ludwig Maximilian University of
    Munich
Ludwigstraße 28/ Rgb.
80539 Munich, Germany

David A. Wise
Kennedy School of Government
Harvard University
79 John F. Kennedy Street
Cambridge, MA 02138

Richard Woodbury
National Bureau of Economic
    Research
1050 Massachusetts Avenue
Cambridge, MA 02138

Author Index

Page numbers followed by the letter *f* or *t* refer to figures or tables, respectively.

Aarts, L., 238n1
Adams, P. M., 32, 86, 268, 295t, 317
Adda, J., 269n2, 282
Adler, N. E., 270
Albertsen, P. C., 227
Alessie, R., 238
Alonso, L., 147, 147n3, 149, 150f, 151f, 152f, 159f, 162f, 163f
Angelucci, M., 238
Arellano, M., 299n18
Audretsch, D., 237
Avendano, M., 321

Babish, J. D., 206
Bach, P. B., 204
Bailar, J. C., III, 204
Bala, V., 238
Banerjee, A. V., 237
Banks, J., 238n1, 241, 321, 322, 327, 328, 333
Barker, D. J. P., 188, 322
Becker, G. S., 237
Ben-Akiva, M., 370
Bernheim, B. D., 21
Bishop, G. F., 354
Bond, S. R., 299n18
Börsch-Supan, A., 141
Boskin, M. J., 120, 140
Bound, J., 238, 245
Bradburn, N., 325
Breen, N., 211

Bricker, J., 343
Burdick, C., 120, 122n2
Burkhauser, R., 238, 238n1

Campbell, A., 346
Cantril, H., 347
Cappellari, L., 250n7
Carstensen, L., 348
Case, A., 32, 237, 322
Chakrabarti, R., 344
Chambers, J. D., 204
Chandola, T., 269n2, 282
Chandra, A., 233
Charles, S. T., 348
Chee, K. G., 227
Christelis, D., 344
Clark, A. E., 345, 358
Clive, J., 180, 186
Contoyannis, P., 299
Cooper, K. L., 227
Copeland, C., 21
Corder, L. S., 180, 186
Coutts, E., 111
Cristia, J. P., 126
Cronin, D., 204
Currie, J., 322
Cutler, D. M., 203, 204, 205, 208, 229, 233, 270

D'Amico, A. V., 229
Darling, G. E., 228

Deaton, A., 32, 327n4, 343, 347, 349, 359
de Jong, P., 238n1
Delorme, L., 114
DeWilde, L. F., 205
Diener, E., 370
Di Nardi, M., 131
Di Tella, R., 345
Dolan, P., 365
Drazer, M. W., 226
Duffy, S. W., 226
Duflo, E., 238
Dusenberry, J., 237

Edgeworth, F. Y., 368
Eggers, A., 361
Elkin, E. B., 204
Engen, E., 21

Feenberg, D. R., 111
Feinstein, A. R., 227
Feldman, M., 237
Fertig, A., 322
Finkelstein, A., 319
Fisher, E. S., 205, 206, 229
Fisher, L., 120, 122n2
Fitoussi, J.-P., 345
Fleming, I. D., 209
Florens, J.-P., 269n2, 284
Ford, E. S., 234
Freedman, V. A., 180, 182
Freeman, J. L., 211
French, E., 123n4, 131, 132
Fuchs, V. R., 204

Gale, W., 21
Garber, A. M., 204, 207
Garson, A., 180, 186
Georgarakos, D., 344
Geweke, J., 269n2, 284
Ginther, D., 237
Giorgi, G. D., 238
Glaeser, E. L., 237
Gofrit, O. N., 227
Goldsmith, N., 270
Goldwyn, J., 36
Golub-Sass, F., 21, 105
Gornik, H. L., 204
Gould, M. K., 228
Goyal, S., 238
Graham, C., 361
Granger, C. W., 269n2, 279, 283
Green, D., 370

Grossman, M., 276, 284
Gu, X., 180
Gustman, A. L., 298n17

Haider, S. J., 28
Hanuschek, E., 237
Hauser, P., 86
Hausman, J. A., 269n2, 279n9, 283
Haveman, R., 21, 237, 238
Heckman, J. J., 269n2, 279n9, 282, 283, 284
Hensher, D. A., 370
Hobijn, B., 120
Holden, S., 147, 147n3, 149, 150, 150f, 151f, 152f, 159f, 162f, 163f
Hoover, K. D., 269n2, 279n9
Hurd, M. D., 21, 28, 36, 79, 90, 92, 93n9, 105n13, 120, 140, 300n19, 344
Hutter, R. L., 209

Isaacowitz, D. M., 348

Jappelli, T., 344
Jenkins, S. P., 250n7
Jette, A. M., 186
Johnson, R., 36
Jones, A. M., 299
Jones, J. B., 123n4, 131, 132
Juster, F. T., 79

Kahneman, D., 346, 347, 359, 370
Kapteyn, A., 238, 239, 246, 257, 261, 300n19, 333
Katz, L., 237
Keating, N. L., 229
Khitatrakun, S., 21, 105, 114
Kimball, M., 365
King, G., 239, 247, 261
Kitagawa, E., 86
Knabe, A., 345
Kotlikoff, L. J., 116
Kozsegi, B., 365
Krueger, A. B., 370
Kuhn, P., 238

Lagakos, D., 120
Lakdawalla, D. N., 233
Lamb, V. L., 180, 186
Landrum, M. B., 234
Lenzer, J., 203
Li, G., 169n26, 170n27, 175
Lichtenberg, F. R., 229

List, M. P., 120
Lleras-Muney, A., 270
Louviere, J. J., 370
Love, D., 21
Lu, T. J., 168, 168n25
Lubotsky, D., 322

MacCulloch, R., 345
MaCurdy, T., 207
Manski, C. F., 239, 250
Manton, K. G., 180, 186
Mark, D. H., 206
Marmot, M. G., 86, 269n2, 282
Martin, L. G., 182
Martinson, M. L., 325
McBean, A. M., 206
McClellan, M., 204, 205, 208, 229
McFadden, D., 370
McNair, L., 21
Mealli, F., 269n2
Meer, J., 276
Meltzer, D., 204
Metcalfe, D., 365
Michaud, P.-C., 32, 276, 299n18
Miller, D. L., 276
Mitchell, O., 21, 168, 168n25
Moore, J., 21
Morakawa, T., 370
Munnell, A., 21, 105, 114
Muriel, A., 321, 327
Murphy, K. M., 204, 233

Neumann, P. J., 204

O'Malley, A. J., 229
Ostrove, J. M., 270
Oswald, A. J., 345, 358
Owens, D. K., 204

Pardes, H., 179
Paxon, C., 322
Pearl, J., 279n9
Phelps, C. E., 204, 207
Porter, M. E., 204
Poterba, J. M., 23, 38, 269n2, 282, 283
Potetz, L., 205
Powdthavee, N., 365

Rabin, M., 365
Rätzel, S., 345
Reichman, N. E., 325
Rice, N., 299

Riis, J., 346
Robins, J. M., 269n2
Rodriguez, T., 204, 229
Rohwedder, S., 21, 28, 79, 92, 93n9, 105n13, 344
Rosen, H. S., 276
Rubin, D. B., 269n2, 279n9

Sacerdote, B., 237
Saez, E., 238
Sarin, R., 346
Scheinkman, J. A., 237
Schoeni, R. F., 180, 182
Scholz, J. K., 21, 105, 114
Schuman, H., 352
Schwarz, N., 346, 352, 370
Sen, A. K., 345, 346
Seshadri, A., 21, 105, 114
Sevak, P., 36
Shapiro, M., 344
Siegler, M. A., 204
Sims, C. A., 279
Skinner, J. S., 205, 229, 233
Smith, G., 322
Smith, J. P., 32, 238, 239, 246, 257, 270, 318, 321, 322, 323n1, 325, 327, 333
Smith, M. R., 229
Smith, P. A., 21, 169n26, 170, 175
Song, Y., 235
Sosin, D. M., 227
Spivak, A., 116
Stabile, M., 322
Stahl, K., 141
Staiger, D. O., 205, 229
Stallard, E., 180, 186
Steinmeier, T. L., 298n17
Stevenson, B., 345
Stewart, K. J., 120, 122n2, 140n1
Stiglitz, J., 345
Stone, A. A., 348, 350
Strack, F., 346
Sudman, S., 325
Sukhtankar, S., 361
Sullivan, D., 319
Suzman, R., 79
Swait, J., 370

Tabatabai, N., 298n17
Teitler, J. L., 325
Tolley, D., 180, 186
Topa, G., 237, 238
Topel, R. H., 204, 233

Uccello, C., 21, 36
Utkus, S. P., 168n25, 170

VanDerhei, J., 21, 147, 147n3, 149, 150,
    150f, 151f, 152f, 159f, 162f, 163f
van Soest, A., 32, 238, 239, 246, 257, 276,
    299n18, 333
Veblen, T., 237
Venti, S. F., 23, 33, 38, 46, 92
Verbrugge, L. M., 186
Vogl, T., 270
von Wachter, T., 319

Wakker, P. P., 346
Waldron, H., 126
Wallace, R. B., 180
Warren, J. L., 206
Webb, A., 21, 105, 114

Weir, D., 36
Weisfeld, A., 204
Welch, G. H., 235
Wells, C. K., 227
Wennberg, J. E., 206
Whaley, F. S., 206
Willis, R., 36, 365
Winkelman, L., 358, 361
Winkelman, R., 358, 361
Wise, D. A., 23, 33, 36, 38, 46, 92
Woittiez, I., 238
Wolfe, B., 237, 238
Wolfers, J., 345
Woodbury, M., 180, 186
Wu, S., 32

Yen, M. F., 226
Young, J. A., 168n25, 170

Subject Index

Page numbers followed by the letter *t* refer to tables.

Activities of Daily Living (ADLs), 11, 179
Age standardization, importance of, for interpretation of results, 12
Aging. *See* Economics of aging
American Time Use Survey, 347
Asset and Health Data Among the Oldest Old (AHEAD) data, 5, 22
Asset and Health Data Among the Oldest Old (AHEAD) households: balance sheets and evolution of nonannuity wealth by family status, 23–29; evolution of wealth of, 29–38
Assets. *See* Wealth

Balance sheets, of AHEAD households, 23–29
Britain. *See* England

CAMS. *See* Consumption and Activities Mail Survey (CAMS)
Cancer in elderly: as cause of death, 203; competing risks and interpreting results for, 228–29; data for assessing expenditures and changes in survival for, 206–9; in elderly, assessing value of technology advances in treating, 204–5; lead and length-time bias of results for, 226–27; results and young patients, 229; results for age and survival trends, 209–13; results for expenditure trends for, 213–17; results for incremental cost effectiveness of progress for treating, 217–22; results for stage-specific survival trends for, 222–24; summary and interpretation of results for, 224–26; treatment of, 3, 12–13; Will Rogers phenomenon and results for, 227–28
Cantril's ladder, 347–49
Cardinal utility, 345
Causal pathways, 15
CentERpanel (Dutch), 240
CEX. *See* Consumer Expenditure Survey (CEX)
Childhood health, 16; analytical models comparing effects of, on adult health in England and the United States, 329–35; comparing, in England and the United States, 324–29; data, in HRS and ELSA surveys, 322–24; later-life health outcomes and, 3; US and English differences in, 322. *See also* Elderly health; Health
Choice utility, 345–46
Cognitive bubbles, subjective well-being and, 18
Community dwellers, evolution of health of, 196–98
Consumer Expenditure Survey (CEX), 79–80

Consumer Price Index for the Elderly (CPI-E), 9, 120, 134; criticisms of, 122; indexing to, and inflation, 122

Consumer Price Index for Urban Wage Earners and Clerical Workers (CPI-W), 8, 119–20; criticisms of, 122

Consumer price indices. *See* Cost-of-living indices

Consumption, as measure of well-being, 77–78

Consumption and Activities Mail Survey (CAMS), 79–80

Consumption paths, estimation of, 87–90

Cost-of-living indices: methodology for study of, 122–27; policy implications of study of, 135–38; results for study of, 127–35. *See also* Consumer Price Index for the Elderly (CPI-E); Consumer Price Index for Urban Wage Earners and Clerical Workers (CPI-W)

CPI-E. *See* Consumer Price Index for the Elderly (CPI-E)

CPI-W. *See* Consumer Price Index for Urban Wage Earners and Clerical Workers (CPI-W)

Day Reconstruction Method (DRM), 347

Death, finances and years leading up to, 5

Defined-benefit pension programs, 1; declining importance of, 4

DI. *See* Disability insurance (DI) benefits, people receiving

Differential mortality, 86–87

Disability, self-reported. *See* Self-reported disability

Disability insurance (DI) benefits, people receiving, 238; Dutch data for, 240–45; model of, with reference groups, 245–50; reference groups and, 238; results of model, 250–58; self-reported work disability and, 238; the United States vs. the Netherlands, 238–39; vignette questions, 259–60

DRM. *See* Day Reconstruction Method (DRM)

Easterlin paradox, 344

Economic preparation for retirement: about, 77–79; data sources, 79–80; differential mortality and, 86–87; estimation of consumption paths for, 87–90; findings for, 104–5; future earnings and, 90–91; health and, 101–2; health care spending risk and, 92–93; housing wealth and, 92; methodology for, 80–81; model for couples, 83–86; model for singles, 81–83; planning horizon and, 100–101; results of study of, 94–100; scenarios for, 102–4; serial correlation in out-of-pocket spending for health care and, 93–94; taxes and, 91–92. *See also* Retirement

Economics of aging, importance of studying, 1

Elderly health: composition change in, 192–96; data source for, 181–85; dimensions of, 185–90; evolution of, among community dwellers, 196–98; explaining improvement in, 190–92; improvements in, 179; indicators of, 179–80; over time, 10–12; as policy issue, 179. *See also* Cancer in elderly; Health

ELSA. *See* English Longitudinal Survey of Aging (ELSA)

Employee Beneficiary Survey, 21

England: analytical models comparing effects of childhood health on adult health in, 329–35; comparing childhood health in, to the United States, 324–29; health of English vs. Americans, 321–22; later-life health differences between the United States and, 16

English Longitudinal Survey of Aging (ELSA), 16, 322–24; data, in HRS and, 322–24

Experience sampling, 347

Finances, 2; analysis of, in years leading up to death, 5; single-person households and, 5–6

Financial crisis. *See* 2008 financial crisis

Financial well-being, health and, 1–2

401(k) loans, 9–10; about, 145–46; availability of, 149–52; data on, 146–49; provisions of, 152–59; utilization of, 159–71

401(k) plans, 1; affect of loan provisions on balances of, 3; use of loans and, 9–10

Gallup Healthways Well-Being Index (GHWBI), 344; effects of changes in question order in, 350–52; ladder questions in, 347–50

Grade of Membership (GOM) model of disability, 180

Granger causality framework, 268–69
Great Britain. *See* England

Health: challenges of simultaneity and
    omitted variables in studying SES and,
    273–76; effect of age and, single-person
    pathway and, 38–47; of elderly, over
    time, 10–12; evolution of, in commu-
    nity dwellers, 196–98; financial well-
    being and, 1–2; functional ability and
    dimensions of, 3; international compar-
    isons of, 321–22; potential channels
    between SES and, 269; socioeconomic
    circumstances and, 3, 14–15, 86, 267;
    wealth and, 38–47, 52. *See also* Child-
    hood health; Elderly health
Health and Retirement Study (HRS), 21, 22,
    79, 322–24; childhood data in ELSA
    and, 322–24
Health care costs, demand on financial
    resources and, 7–8
Health deterioration, with age, 11–12
Health expenditures, health outcomes and,
    12–13
Health measurement, 3
Health Survey for England, 326
Healthy, Wealthy, and Wise (HWW) study,
    268–69; approach of, 276–84; conclu-
    sions of, 295–99; future research and,
    299–300; reanalysis of, with new data,
    284–95
Hedonic well-being, vs. evaluative well-
    being, 347
Hicks, Sir John, 345
Home equity, 46–47
Household balance sheets (2008), 22, 23–29,
    24t, 58–67
HRS. *See* Health and Retirement Study
    (HRS)
Human Mortality Database, 327
HWW study. *See* Healthy, Wealthy, and
    Wise (HWW) study

Income replacement rate, 77
Inflation protection, Social Security recipi-
    ents and, 119–20. *See also* Cost-of-
    living indices
Instrumental Activities of Daily Living
    (IADLs), 11, 179

Ladder questions, in GHWBI, 347–50
Life evaluation, 347

"Living life" vs. "thinking about life," 346–47

Marital pathway groups, effects of wealth
    and age of, 49–55
Medicare Current Beneficiary Survey, 11,
    179–80, 181–85
Medicare Part B, 120–21; Social Security
    and, 8–9

National Health and Nutrition Examina-
    tion Survey (NHANES), 325–26
Netherlands: disability insurance (DI) recip-
    ients in, vs. the United States, 238–39;
    self-reported work disability in, 13

Old Age and Survivor's Insurance (OASI)
    program, 136–38
Out-of-pocket costs, 2
Out-of-pocket health care costs, financial
    resources in later life and, 4
Out-of-pocket spending for health care,
    123–26; predicted, 127–32; preparation
    for retirement and, 7–8

Private saving, growing importance of, 4

Question order effects, subjective well-being
    and, 17–18

Reference groups, 3; defined, 239; importance
    of, 14; model of people receiving DI ben-
    efits with, 245–50; questions, 260–61; re-
    ceiving disability benefits and, 238; self-
    reported disability measures and, 13–14.
    See also Self-reported disability
Reflection problem, 239
Retirement: metrics for assessing prepara-
    tion for, 77–79; preparation for, and
    out-of-pocket spending for health care,
    7–8. *See also* Economic preparation
    for retirement
Retirement saving programs, 1. *See also*
    401(k) plans
Rogers, Will, 227–28

Self-Anchoring Scale, 347
Self-reported disability: data for study
    of, 240–45; model of, with reference
    groups, 245–50; peer groups and,
    13–14; results of study of, 250–58;
    social interactions and, 13, 237–38. *See
    also* Reference groups

Self-reported disability measures, 3, 13, 238–39; investigations in, 238–39; people receiving DI benefits and, 238

Self-reported well-being (SWB): adaptation to circumstances and, 346; cross-section analysis and, 345–46; daily measures of, 16–17; determinants of, 344; measurement concerns of, 346; usefulness of temporal tracking of, 345. *See also* Well-being

SES. *See* Socioeconomic status (SES)

Single-person households, 5

Single-person pathway: effect of health and age and, 38–47; wealth and, 47–49. *See also* Marital pathway groups

Social interactions, 7, 237–38

Social norms, self-reported disability and, 13

Social Security: benefits, 126; cost-of-living indices and, 120; health care cost growth and inflation protection in, 2; inflation protection and, 119–20; Medicare Part B and, 8–9, 120–21; protection from inflation and, 8. *See also* Cost-of-living indices

Socioeconomic status (SES): causal effects from, 267–68; challenges of simultaneity and omitted variables in studying health and, 273–76; health status and, 3, 14–15, 86, 267; potential channels between health and, 269–73

Subjective well-being (SWB), 17–18; cognitive bubbles and, 18; question order effects and, 17–18. *See also* Well-being

Surveillance, Epidemiology, and End Results (SEER) Program, 207, 209

Survey of Consumer Finances, 21

Survival probabilities, 86–87

SWB. *See* Self-reported well-being (SWB)

"Thinking about life" vs. "living life," 346–47

2008 financial crisis: correlates of changes in well-being over, 358–64; life evaluation and hedonics over, 355–58; life evaluation in, 349–55; well-being and, 17–18, 343–45

United Kingdom. *See* England

United States: analytical models comparing effects of childhood health on adult health in, 329–35; comparing childhood health in, to England, 324–29; disability insurance (DI) recipients in, vs. the Netherlands, 238–39; health of Americans vs. English, 321–22; later-life health differences between England and, 16

Wealth: difficulties in judging levels of, 47–49; evolution of, of AHEAD households, 29–38; health and, 38–47, 52; in last year observed (LYO), 40–46; nonannuity, by family status, AHEAD households and, 23–29; other marital pathway groups and, 49–55; single-person pathway and, 47–49. *See also* Healthy, Wealthy, and Wise (HWW) study

Well-being: concepts and measures of, 345–49; dimensions of, 1–2; emotional, measuring, 347; hedonic vs. evaluative, 347; literature on, over business cycle, 345; measures of subjective, 3–4; 2008 financial crisis and, 17–18, 343–45. *See also* Self-reported well-being (SWB); Subjective well-being (SWB)

Will Rogers phenomenon, 227–28

Wisdom. *See* Healthy, Wealthy, and Wise (HWW) study